IRAQ

A LOST WAR

Mohamed El-Shibiny

IRAQ

Copyright © Mohamed El-Shibiny, 2010.

First published in 2010 by PALGRAVE MACMILLAN® in the United States—
a division of St. Martin's Press LLC, 175 Fifth Avenue, New York, NY 10010

Where this book is distributed in the UK, Europe and the rest of the world, this is by
Palgrave Macmillan, a division of Macmillan Publishers Limited, registered in England,
company number 785998, of Houndmills, Basingstoke, Hampshire RG21 6XS.

Palgrave Macmillan is the global academic imprint of the above companies and has
companies and representatives throughout the world.

Palgrave® and Macmillan® are registered trademarks in the United States, the United
Kingdom, Europe and other countries.

ISBN: 978-0-230-10307-8

Library of Congress Cataloging-in-Publication Data

El-Shibiny, Mohamed.
    Iraq : a lost war / Mohamed El-Shibiny.
       p. cm.
    Includes bibliographical references.
    ISBN 978-0-230-10307-8 (alk. paper)
    1. Iraq War, 2003- I. Title.

DS79.76.E42 2009
956.7044'31—dc22   2009044757

Design by Scribe Inc.

First edition: June 2010

10 9 8 7 6 5 4 3 2 1

Printed in the United States of America.

CONTENTS

Preface v

1 The Impact of 9/11 on War in Iraq 1

2 World War with Terrorism 17

3 Is the Iraq War Justified? 25

4 Coalition Forces Captured Saddam Hussein 45

5 The Global Feeling against War in Iraq 55

6 The Positions of the UN and EU toward War in Iraq 61

7 World and Islamic Condemnation of the
Abu Ghraib Detention and Abuse of Power in Iraq 67

8 Toward Accelerating Transfer of Power—from U.S.
Occupation to Iraq Government, a Historical Review 79

9 The Danger of Islamic Insurgents in Iraq 99

10 The Ignition of Civil War in Iraq 123

11 Democratization of Iraq 135

12 Is Democracy in Iraq in Flames? 169

Notes 199

Further References 227

Bibliography 229

Index 255

To Panayota, Aida, Mona, Nadia, and Shaden El-Shibiny

PREFACE

THE IRAQ OCCUPATION, IN ITS SIXTH YEAR AS OF 2009, has taken the lives of more than 3,800 American troops. An estimated 700,000 Iraqis, 2.6 percent of the population, have been killed and the cost of the war stands at over $300 billion. In addition, two million Iraqi refugees fled their homes for other parts of Iraq, and one and a half million to the neighboring countries of Syria, Jordan, and Egypt. This has created a human tragedy without precedence. Most of these refugees are women and children. Many children have lost their parents in the violence and have been forced to live on the streets. Many of them have little or no access to education or necessities of life.

Iraqis are facing the most profound cultural, political, and economic challenges ever imaginable. Iraq is at present a traumatized and suffering society. Many military commanders have described the war in Iraq as "a nightmare with no end in sight." In every conflict with too many casualties, a country becomes the loser even if it is on the winning side.

"Has Iraq posed a clear and immediate threat to world security to warrant the occupation and the suffering of its people?" For the last six years, the Islamic world has been searching for a convincing answer as to whether Iraq posed a real danger to the peace and security of the world, especially to the United States. The U.S. response to the 9/11 attacks has been primarily military; first, it was a war against Afghanistan, second, against Iraq. Many nations see no evidence for the key U.S. charges that Baghdad had possessed weapons of mass destruction or long-range missiles. They consider the war and the occupation of the country a grave error. It has not resolved, but complicated the situation of introducing democracy and security in the Middle East.

Even though Iraq was liberated from the thirty years of notorious dictatorship of Saddam Hussein, at present it is under military occupation, oppressed with sectarian violence, terrorism, and destruction. The seeds of reconciliation among the ethnic groups have vanished and been replaced with civil war among religious factions. Sectarian divisions between Shiites and Sunnis continue to escalate into a war of attrition. Consequently, Iraq at present is in an ethnic-political struggle for power. Both parties commit atrocities despite their leaders urging them to resist a sectarian civil war. Moreover, there is no formulated strategy for placing a timetable on future U.S. combat troop withdrawal and no pressure made on Iraq's leaders to reach a political settlement.

Iraq is, indeed, a traumatized society facing the most profound ethnic, cultural, political, and economic tensions. Despite all efforts for reconciliation between the two ethnic groups, Shiites and Sunnis, aggression continues and the revenge mentality worsens. Iraqis believe that the only feasible way out of this dilemma is to disband all militias in the country, including progovernment Shiite groups. "Militias" means all those who are armed other than the Iraqi army and police.

Iraq needs a lasting reconciliation between factions and a halting of attacks on each other to enhance and preserve unity among its people. Many Sunnis and Shiites have rejected the call to divide the country into separate Sunni, Shiite, and Kurdish federal regions. They oppose federalism dividing Iraq, as it would lead to further instability in the Arab region. Lately, there are renewed demands for an autonomous Shiite region in the south. This is due to an increased influence of the U.S. presence and empowerment of the Shiite majority in government and parliament.

Both parties are engaged in an ethnic and political power struggle. The constant strain between the two sects is affecting not just Iraq but the security of Arab Middle East neighboring countries. The removal of Saddam Hussein from power in 2003 by the U.S.-led invasion strengthened Iran's strategic position and increased its regional power, especially among Iraq's Shiite majority. The stability and prosperity of Iraq at large is mainly dependent on the policies and actions of Iraq's neighbors. Iraq's neighbors are perceived as not doing enough to assist Iraq to achieve peace in order to protect stability within the region.

An added complication is the presence of volunteer terrorists, suicide bombers, who are fanatic Islamists crossing the borders into Iraq from neighboring countries, using their sophisticated weaponry and intensive training against both the Iraqis and U.S. troops.

The solution toward peace lies not in excessive use of military and police force but in developing mutual political understanding, cultural awareness, and ethnic tolerance among the Iraqi people. While disarming Shiite militia and Sunni insurgents is a tactical priority, the challenge of attaining long-term peace and security is based on the promotion of cultural understanding, political conciliation, religious tolerance, and restoration of national solidarity among Iraqis.

Just after the Iraq occupation, the United States appealed to the Arab Middle Eastern countries to initiate political reform and reinforce democracy in their countries. In a free election, a new democratic parliament was established in Baghdad representing the political parties and ethnic factions. A government elected by the people. The militant Islamists express their commitment to the democratic principles and values of Islam. Democracy is homegrown and gradually earning recognition among the Iraqi masses.

As mentioned in the report of the Iraq Study Group headed by James Baker, there is no magic formula to solve the numerous problems facing Iraq and its people. However, there are actions to improve the deteriorating events and provide peace, security, and democracy. This book intends to throw light on the major problems facing Iraq and means to help promote peace and security in a devastated country.

Having touched in this preface on the various complications of the Iraqi war, we now proceed to more detailed analyses in the chapters to come; each of the twelve chapters covers a different angle of the war, thus making each one on its own a complete entity.

CHAPTER 1

THE IMPACT OF 9/11 ON WAR IN IRAQ

THE 9/11 ATTACKS ARE STILL CASTING THEIR DARK SHADOW. More than three thousand people were killed in a matter of hours in the United States when four American planes were hijacked by Islamic terrorists. The planes crashed into the World Trade Center, the Pentagon, and a field in Pennsylvania.

The final report of the congressional 9/11 Commission concluded that the United States could not protect its citizens from these attacks because it failed to appreciate the threat posed by al-Qaeda operatives, who exploited that failure and carried out the deadliest assault ever on U.S. soil. It was clear from the investigation that the fanatic, fundamentalist Islamic group al-Qaeda was responsible. Since 9/11, al-Qaeda and its militias have been implementing in Iraq acts of terror against Islamic and non-Islamic innocents. The insurgents sought support from al-Qaeda leaders to spark a religious animosity between Sunni and Shiite sects in order to promote sectarian violence and civil war. In this battle between sects, Iraq lost. In such a battle, al-Qaeda struggled for power and influence within Iraq. Today, al-Qaeda is a regional and global menace. Meanwhile, the fact remains that nowadays terrorism is a global aggressive threat without differentiating between nationalities or religions.

Innocent people killed on 9/11 were not the only victims of this tragedy. Since then, millions of victims suffered globally as well. There has been worldwide suffering and death, and an incalculable number of persons have suffered because of loss of family members, intimates, friends, and colleagues. These are the victims of international terrorism. The events of 9/11 and beyond showed the absence of universal human compassion, lack of global ethical values, unawareness of international humanitarian order, and misinterpretation of teachings of religions. Universal freedom, global peace and order, and legitimacy have suffered.

After the 9/11 events, both the Arab region and the United States remained in turmoil. The project to democratize and introduce political reform in the Middle Eastern countries ended poorly. Holding an election does not create democracy or stimulate reform. In the Arab countries such as Egypt, Jordan, Algeria, and Morocco, democratic elections brought the forces of Islamic activists and further political instability despite the fact that true Islam and democracy do not clash.

The Iraqi occupation also proved to be a disastrous venture, resulting in the United States losing its strong political influence in the Arab countries. Most of the world's oil-rich countries in the Arab region formed new alliances with other powers in both Asia and Europe. China and Russia became new economic and financial allies with the rich oil-producing countries in the Arab region. It became evident, after the Iraq occupation, that the real war is not military but political and economic.

What President Bush realized after 9/11 is that unless he could change the conditions in the Middle East, countries could give rise to terrorism, and new recruits of jihadists and fanatics would simply follow those who were eliminated. He envisaged that aggressive promotion of democracy and political reforms in these countries were the solution. Nineteen identified hijackers of 9/11 were from the Arab region: fifteen from Saudi Arabia, two from the United Arab Emirates, one from Lebanon, and the last from Egypt. These are all countries friendly to the United States.

U.S. DECLARATION OF TWO WORLD CAMPS

After the events of 9/11, and in the atmosphere of pain and shock among world citizens, President George W. Bush declared that there are two worlds: one that is pro-America and the other that is against it.[1] This statement was interpreted by the Western mass media as a division of the world into two camps: one with the United States, the Christian camp, and the other, the Arab and Islamic world. The president compared 9/11 as a clash with the Islamic world: a revival of the confrontation of the crusaders with Muslims in the twelfth century over Jerusalem and the holy places in Syria and Palestine.

The Islamic world was shocked by the president's statement. The Crusades, as known in history, were the first major clash of two civilizations between the Islamic East and Christian West, lasting for over two centuries. The crusaders had killed more than one million Muslims in their unholy mission. The crusaders were told by the church that if they died in battle, they would achieve the status of martyr. President Bush later explained that his statement should not be understood as bearing such meaning of religious confrontation between Islam and Christianity.

The clash of civilizations, in our global contemporary world, is the greatest threat to world peace and security. Religious faiths and beliefs are for individuals, not governments, to judge as an integral part of their human rights. Global religious revival and conflict among nations would take us back into the dark ages.

The anniversaries of 9/11 are remembered in Islamic worlds with empathy. The terrorists who claimed Islam as their faith committed the unforgivable crime of murdering three thousand innocent people. Muslims shared the trembling voices of parents, grandparents, and the loved ones of those killed at the World Trade Center.

MUSLIMS SUFFERING FROM 9/11

Muslims all over the world were as severely affected by 9/11 as the people of the United States. In particular, the Arab Muslims suffered the most despite their condemnation of the attack and called the tragic event un-Islamic, inhuman, and against all world ethical values and universal principles. The aftermath of 9/11 had a disastrous economic and cultural result especially on the non-oil-producing Islamic nations.

On an economic front, tourism was affected, a main source of income for some countries in the Middle East, North Africa, and even the Mediterranean region. Businesses were also affected as foreign and international investors suspended projects in Arab nations. Arab airlines also suffered enormous losses. Furthermore, prices of commodities became unstable, causing massive budget deficits in the oil-producing countries.

Islamophobic sentiments and a general misconception of Islam and Muslims increased after 9/11. America's largest Islamic civil liberties group, Council on American Islamic Relations (CAIR), recorded increasing discrimination complaints against Muslims in many states. Complaints involved attacks, unreasonable arrests, detentions, interrogations, and workplace discrimination. Complaints even involved governmental agencies.

FIGHTING TERRORISM IS NOT A WAR
BETWEEN ISLAM AND CHRISTIANITY

Due to the increasing bitterness and growing hostility of certain U.S. offices and institutions against Islam and the Islamic people after 9/11, President Bush broadcasted every year a message on the Muslim fasting month of Ramadan to the Islamic world assuring his respect for the Islamic faith. He emphasized that Islam is a religion of peace, mercy, and compassion. President Bush further emphasized that the Muslims have contributed to world civilization. America, he continued, is the country of religious freedom and respects all forms of worship. Our responsibility, he added, is to work together in order to reinforce liberty, mutual understanding, and compassion among all people.[2]

To reinforce the position of President Bush, his national security adviser insisted that the U.S. fight against terrorism was not a war declared between Christianity and Islam. The war was ultimately between the United States, with the collaboration of the free world countries, and international terrorists, regardless of their beliefs, ideologies, or nationalities. Muslims feel that they have suffered the most from this event: Afghanistan is occupied by an international force, Iraq is under an Anglo-American occupation, and the Palestinian dispute has been left unresolved. The Arab countries became associated with international terrorism as the target of Western mass media, which also spread ill-conceived information against the Arab culture and Islamic civilization.

The media has exploited the 9/11 attacks to deform the image of Islam and its civilization. They failed to distinguish between the genuine Islamic tolerance, ethical values, and compassion, and the terrorist acts practiced by some rebel groups disguised under the cloak of Islam, of which Islam itself was innocent. Such misrepresentation gradually deepened hatred among Muslims toward the United States and its policies. That is what President Bush sensed during his visit to Indonesia in October 2003. During his meeting with all groups of Muslim leaders in Jakarta, Bush was surprised by the amount of hatred these leaders expressed toward the United States. He assured them that his country bore no enmity to Muslims and the United States only abominates terrorists. Indonesia has a population of 250 million Muslims. The United States, President Bush reiterated to the Indonesians, is the country of religious freedom and embraces all beliefs. Our responsibility, he added, is to work together in order to reinforce liberty, mutual understanding, and compassion among all people.[3]

Muslims still suffer from discrimination in the United States and Europe after 9/11. Islamic countries requested their delegations abroad to respond to these claims. From a media standpoint as well, the world needed to stay aware of the true nature of Islamic civilization: that Islam had greatly contributed to world culture and that terrorism is un-Islamic.

It is the political Islamists together with Islamic fundamentalists that most threaten the established orders and security in most Islamic countries, even more than harming Western interests. Islamic fundamentalism has been the single most antimodern force over the past decades. Such fundamentalism sparked the rise of Islamic extremism that called for reverting to their ancestral cultures. Fundamentalism and terrorism are not Islam. Islamic and Western civilizations do not clash. Islam, history shows, has never been hostile to innovation, modernization, or globalization.

HAS IRAQ POSED A CLEAR AND IMMEDIATE
THREAT TO WORLD SECURITY?

The question explored is whether Iraq posed a real danger to the peace
and security of the world and especially to the United States. The U.S.
response to the 9/11 attacks had primarily military value. First, there was a
war against Afghanistan and second, against Iraq. Many nations opposed
the war in Iraq, not seeing sufficient evidence for the U.S. charges that
Baghdad possessed weapons of mass destruction.

The military response was on the pretext that the Iraqi regime of
Saddam Hussein posed a clear and immediate threat to world peace and
security. The U.S. administration insisted to the world that the key drive
for its forces was to track and destroy Iraq's purported weapons of mass
destruction. The U.S. military experts have not yet found, as of the date
of this publication, any single proof of such weapons, or even attempts
to produce such weapons after Saddam Hussein's conquest of Kuwait and
his subsequent defeat in 1991. The Islamic world saw no evidence to back
up the allegation for war.

Some politicians and economists insist that the war in Iraq was primarily and totally to control the Middle East oil. Iraq is the second largest
producer after Saudi Arabia. Iraq produces 1.8 million barrels a day that
could be increased to two million. More importantly, it has one-third of
the world's oil reserves.[4]

A few months after the U.S. troops began their occupation of Iraq, no
weapons of mass destruction were located in any part of the country. As
lack of security in Iraq intensified for its people and the Islamic world, the
U.S. and coalition forces changed the reasons for the invasion. The U.S.
administration hurriedly declared that the ultimate aim for the invasion
was fostering democracy and modernization in Iraq as well as in the Arab
Middle East countries.

Critics of the Iraq invasion claim it was highly unethical to bypass the
United Nations (UN) and infringe on the independence of a sovereign
member state, destabilizing the region. Iraq is sliding deeper into chaos
and disorder as insurgents continue to attack the U.S.-led forces and their
collaborators, government forces, and civilians.

REMOVING SADDAM HUSSEIN BY MILITARY FORCE

Islamic intellectual thinkers are still wondering about the inherent reasons for the United States to remove Saddam Hussein by military force.
The U.S. administration's reason was that Saddam Hussein was dangerous to world peace and security. As President Bush said, "A free Iraq will

make it easier for children in our own country to grow up in a safer world, because in the Middle East is where you find the hatred and violence that enables the enemy to recruit its killers."[5]

The Islamic thinkers were astonished by the U.S. administration and the mass media swiftly associating Saddam Hussein with 9/11 terrorism claiming close collaboration with al-Qaeda. There were massive arrests in the United States and Europe of Muslims from various Islamic countries and particularly from the Middle East. This was despite a lack of evidence to indicate that Saddam Hussein was involved in the terrorist attacks of 9/11. Those who accused Saddam of being a collaborator of al-Qaeda ignored the known fact that Saddam was the head of the Ba'ath Party, which is a secular political body calling for the separation of state and religion. Saddam followed the model of secular Turkey, the only secular Islamic country.

Collaboration between Saddam, a committed secularist and Ba'athist, and Bin Laden, a deep-rooted Islamic ultrafundamentalist, should have been unthinkable. After a long FBI investigation, President Bush declared that there was "no evidence to suggest that Saddam Hussein was involved in the terrorist attacks of 9/11."[6] This contradicted what many Americans had been previously led to believe.

HAS SADDAM HUSSEIN HAD ANY KIND OF RELATIONSHIP WITH AL-QAEDA?

The U.S. independent commission investigating the terrorist attacks of 9/11 released a statement in July 2004 indicating that it stands by its conclusion that al-Qaeda and Iraq had only very limited connection. The commission said it had seen no evidence to suggest that then-Iraqi leader Saddam Hussein's government was involved in the attacks.

Thinkers and politicians all over the world questioned whether a military invasion of Iraq in order to remove Saddam from power was considered lawful in the UN charter. Kofi Annan, the UN Secretary-General, in an interview with the British Broadcasting Corporation emphasized that the U.S.-led invasion of Iraq did not conform to the United Nations charter. The charter, he emphasized, allows a nation to take military action only with a Security Council resolution approving the invasion.[7]

Annan added that in February 2003 the United States dropped any attempts to get Security Council approval for the invasion of Iraq. From the UN charter point of view, the invasion was illegal. Sharing the opinion of Annan, the Arab Muslims were surprised at the insistence of the United States to invade Iraq unilaterally without the UN Security Council's approval.

REACTION OF ISLAMIC COUNTRIES TO A
UNILATERAL INVASION OF IRAQ

The French reacted to the illegal U.S. invasion of a UN member state. President Jacques Chirac shared the sentiment of Arab states by saying that the war had put the United Nations through one of the most severe crises in its history.[8]

As the military situation deteriorated and security worsened in Iraq, the Islamic nations urged an effective role for the UN in the Middle East. The Organization of the Islamic Conference (OIC) held a one-day emergency meeting in Malaysia in April 2004. The main aim of the conference was to discuss the situation in Iraq and to tackle the mounting outrage and alienation in the Islamic world over U.S. policies in the Middle East.

A declaration at the end of the conference, attended by fifty-seven delegates from the Islamic world, stated, "We recognize and stress the importance of the United Nations in playing a central role to establish peace, security and stability in Iraq."[9] The conference urged the UN Security Council to adopt a resolution restoring sovereignty and full independence to the Iraqi people and empowering the United Nations with the necessary mandate and authority to ensure the achievement of this goal. Consequently, Washington prepared a resolution asking the Security Council to give its concurrence to a new Iraqi interim government, a multinational force and a UN role in the country, after the handover of power on July 2004.

Meanwhile, Islamic nations hailed the one-day meeting under the leadership of Norway's prime minister held in New York in September 2003, in which a large number of world thinkers, from France to Afghanistan, participated. They met to seek ways to give the United Nations the lead role in fighting global terrorism. The meeting emphasized that in the same way as the UN should have the leading role in social and economic development in the world, it should also lead the fight against terrorism. The meeting stressed that military measures may not be the solution. Education and social reforms could help defuse the causes of terrorism.

The U.S. administration accuses the UN of being irrelevant to world affairs: The Islamic world was shocked when the United States argued in the General Assembly in 2003 that the United Nations needed to meet its global responsibilities toward Iraq or risk being irrelevant. Arab nations expressed through the media their shock and anger that the UN was threatened by a powerful member state and at the place where the UN headquarters is hosted.

Accusing the UN of being irrelevant to world affairs just because a rich and powerful nation disagrees with the rest of the member states

was a source of world political inconvenience to the Third World and
ethical unrest in the Islamic world. More than 190 member states have
ultimately put high hopes in the international justice, wisdom, and global
integrity of the UN.

U.S. Democratization of Iraq and Arab Nations in the Middle East

After a few months of the unilateral invasion of Iraq, the Arab Islamic
nations were surprised at the proclaimed commitment of the United States
to democratize not only Iraq but also all the Arab countries in the Middle
East. The response of the Middle East was not a welcoming one as such
democracy is envisaged to be imposed on them from a Western super-
power without previous mutual understanding, dialogue, or exchanging
of opinion as required by any democratic communication. The Islamic
intellectuals expressed their opinion that introduction of democracy to
any given society should come from within the people, their culture, their
social values, and their institutions. In the reform movement people in
the Islamic communities realize that they can be democrats and remain
faithful Muslims. In addition, Arab intellectuals had no intention to rede-
sign the Islamic culture according to Western civilization.

Overlooked in this case was the fact that Islam has its own form of
democracy that may differ from Western democracy. In his speech at
the National Endowment for Democracy, President Bush opted to make
global democracy the focus of his foreign policy with special emphasis on
the Arab Middle East nations.[10]

Bush emphasized that establishing a democratic and secular Iraq would
serve as a model for transforming the Arab Middle East into democratic
nations. In stressing introducing American-style democracy to the troubled region, he sought to send home the message that in invading Iraq the
ultimate aim was to free the Iraqi people from Saddam Hussein's tyranny
and spread liberty in the Arab countries. Today, Iraq is neither a democracy nor a safe place to live. Secretary of State Colin Powell faulted the
terrorists who have been trying to sabotage the process toward self-rule
and democracy.

The Arabs are still confused at the relationship of occupying Iraq and
spreading democracy in the rest of the region. There was no substantial
sign from the Arab countries in the Middle East to engage actively in
changing their political directions to become truly democratic in accordance with Western standards. Very few in the Muslim world see any
good reason for the U.S. administration to insist on fostering Western
democracy at gunpoint in the Middle East countries.

In the known history of humankind, there is no witness to democracy blossoming or political reform flourishing at the point of a gun. History taught us that democracy and reform must develop from within the people and their cultural values. An absolute requirement for democratic reform is to carry out dialogues with the people, to share its benefits, and to demonstrate how democracy could improve societies.

Islam and democratization do not oppose each other. A dynamic Islamic culture requires a dynamic democracy. This does not necessarily mean that democratization of Iraq and other Middle East countries leads to westernization. Democratic values are universal whether Islamic, Western, or Eastern. This is the ideological clash with the Islamic fundamentalist extremists. The Sunni al-Qaeda insurgents in Iraq emphatically reject democracy on the account that it calls for Western values. They are unaware that democracy has global ethical values, social principles, human rights standards, and cultural understanding among nations regardless of religions, beliefs, or faith. Democracy fosters peace, security, and understanding among nations and civilizations.

In Iraq, at present, the world witnesses a democratic government elected by the people. It is historically true that for the first time in half a century, a free election took place after the ousting of Saddam Hussein. Iraqi voters chose a 272-member transitional national parliament committed to putting together a permanent constitution, which was submitted to voters in a referendum in 2005. This step was ultimately a step toward democratic reform and a stable nation. Iraq is changing politically, economically, and culturally despite the al-Qaeda Sunni insurgence and Shiite militia aggression. It is hoped that a new democratic world order is emerging in the Middle East.

REQUEST FOR REDUCING RELIGIOUS ISLAMIC INSTRUCTION IN SCHOOLS

The U.S. request to a number of Muslim nations to reduce religious instruction in school curricula astounded the Islamic world. Experts in the United States believed that reducing Islamic religious instruction in schools would prevent the spread of extremists to escalate their terrorism in the name of Islamic faith.

The U.S. Deputy Assistant Secretary for Near Eastern Affairs, Liz Cheney, assured country leaders that the U.S. administration is seeking change in the school curricula in the Arab states in order to eliminate hatred and violence in the region. She added that the United States is ready to assist the countries in the Arab region to introduce such change, assuring them that such initiation has no connection with changing religious statements stated in the Quran. The United States, she continued, aims at reinforcing tolerance, goodwill, and conciliation among nations of the region and the world. In support of the U.S. direction, the U.S. and British newspapers and magazines have in fact published many essays and studies attributing Islamic fanaticism to Islamic instruction in schools and the media.[11]

WAVES OF REBEL BOMBING AND KIDNAPPING

The Nasiriyah episode in Iraq in March 2003 was the first start of a series of waves of rebellious bombing, killing thousands of Iraqis, allied troops, and personnel working in foreign companies. For the first time, a suicide bomber blew up a truck at an Italian paramilitary base, killing twenty-six people. This attack was the deadliest against an American ally and just after the occupation started. It sent a message that international troops were not safe anywhere in Iraq.[12]

Since then, a series of suicidal attacks shook all parts of Iraq. The second major blast at the UN headquarters was an indication of indignation toward the war. The attackers claimed that the UN was biased, prejudiced, and being led by the United States. The slogan carried by the rebels was "death to collaborators."

Saleem, a Shiite Muslim in his sixties, holding the rotating presidency of a twenty-five-member interim Governing Council, was the second member slain by the Arab Resistance Movement, an unknown group of insurgents. He was considered a traitor by being an active member of the interim Governing Council appointed by the U.S. administration. Abductions of foreigners and Iraqi "collaborators" were practiced daily, with a series of kidnappings taken place in a bid to drive foreign companies out of the country and to obstruct the U.S.-led reconstruction plans.

A few months after came the devastation of the Red Cross headquarters. The rebels shouted anti-occupation slogans and chanted "freedom for Iraq and death for enemy collaborators." Resistance against the U.S. forces and allies intensified, wounding and killing American and allied troops. Muqtada al-Sadr, the charismatic Iraqi Shia leader and cleric, his followers, and Sunni clerics called for a holy war, jihad, against occupying troops by all means possible, including financial and terror tactics. The occupiers have not been able to restore law and order in the country.

A UN mandate allowed U.S.-led forces to continue in Iraq: the UN Security Council agreed to continue the mandate of the U.S.-led forces in Iraq as requested by the Iraqi interim government. The government told the council that they were facing a destructive campaign of terror and violence aiming at derailing any progress toward carrying out democracy and reform in the country. Therefore, the country still required help from U.S.-led forces to maintain security as the Iraqi forces could not yet defend the country against insurgents and Islamic militia rebels. This meant that the 160,000 U.S. forces and the 20,000 from twenty-seven other nations would remain in Iraq until further notice.[13]

In the first three years of the war, over 3,500 Americans were killed. More than three-quarters of those killed died in combat. In addition, a large number of coalition troops from fifteen countries also died in the Iraqi conflict. Defense Secretary Donald Rumsfeld acknowledged the death toll of the U.S. and allied troops, laying stress on the fact that the offensive against terrorism had its cost.

ISLAM ABHORS KIDNAPPING AND STRANGULATION IN IRAQ

Muslims find it hard when they hear of the atrocities happening in Iraq in the name of Islam. An example is a group called the Jaish Ansar al-Sunna, which proudly declared that it had murdered twelve Nepalese hostages on the account that they came to Iraq to fight Islam by means of Buddha. Many other group insurgents bearing Islamic names went murdering, kidnapping, and beheading foreign civilians associated in the reconstruction of the country, regardless of their faiths, religions, or nationalities.

In the history of Islam there have never been such examples of brutal terrorism imposed on a society as what was going on in Iraq. Kidnapping, strangulation, and beheading of civilians regardless of their nationalities or faiths are indubitably not Islamic. Islam denounces such actions as they indeed defy the laws and true values of Islamic law, *Sharia*. As a result, the image of Islam in the world is suffering terribly because of such behavior from unguided Islamic rebels and militiamen.

The insurgents reason that their acts will eventually stop the rebuilding of Iraqi infrastructure by collaborators with the Americans and the Iraqi interim government. In most cases of abductions, the insurgents belong to underground groups claiming Islamic titles. There is a growing conviction that their deeds and objectives are motivated by greed rather than patriotism, as ransoms are usually claimed. In some cases, the victims are beheaded, a primitive act that cannot be justified under any circumstances.

Muslim scholars from all over the world stress the fact that such acts of aggression and destructiveness are fundamentally immoral and truly un-Islamic. They are contrary to the laws of the Quran and the genuine Islamic culture and traditions. Condemnations have poured in from Muslim scholars all over the world indicating that such acts are religiously punishable.

WHY ARABS ARE ANTI-AMERICAN

According to an opinion survey released in 2004 by the Arab-American Institute in Washington, very few Arabs think of America in positive terms: only 2 percent of Egyptians, 4 percent of Saudis, 11 percent of Moroccans, 14 percent of Emirates, 15 percent of Jordanians, and 20 percent of the Lebanese.[14]

A few days after the attack on the twin towers, the final report of the American fact-finding committee concluded that the main motive of the al-Qaeda attacks of 9/11 was American bias toward Israel in its conflict with the Palestinians and other Arabs. The deputy chairperson urged the start of a serious and sincere dialogue with the Arab and Islamic world.

In a controversial program to try to prevent potential terrorists from slipping in through its borders, the United States began fingerprinting and photographing visitors.

Federal officials said the measures ordered by Congress would tighten security without causing any undue inconvenience to travelers. However, all indications showed that such obstacles intended to restrict Muslim travelers from entering the United States regardless of their nationalities. Muslims felt that they were being discriminated against because of their faith.

An example of Muslim scholars denied U.S. visas is the case of Professor Tariq Ramadan. Acting at the request of the Department of Homeland Security, the U.S. government revoked the work visa of a Muslim scholar, Professor Tariq Ramadan, a Swiss citizen, who had been scheduled to teach at the University of Notre Dame at its invitation. He had been criticized for doubtful links to Islamic militants and branded anti-Semitic.

Caroline Fredrickson, Director of the Washington Legislative Office for the American Civil Liberties Union, cited the Immigration and Nationality Act, part of which deals with aliens who have used a "position of prominence within any country to endorse or espouse terrorist activity." She cited another section that bars aliens whose entry may have "potentially serious adverse foreign policy consequences for the United States."[15]

"We don't know a reason why either of those should apply to Tariq Ramadan," said a Notre Dame University spokesperson. "He's a distinguished scholar. He's a voice for moderation in the Muslim world."[16] Noteworthy to mention, in 2004 *Time* magazine named him one of the world's top one hundred scientists, thinkers, and innovators of the twenty-first century as he called for bridges to be built, and confidence be restored, between the West and the Muslim world.[17]

Notre Dame University appointed Ramadan to be its Henry R. Luce Professor of Religion, Conflict, and Peacebuilding at the Kroc Institute for International Peace Studies. "In many ways he has defined what it means to be a European Muslim," said Muqtada Khan, a political scientist at Adrian College in Michigan. "He has essentially tried to bridge the culture gap."[18]

In addition to such incidents, anti-U.S. sentiment had already risen in the Arab world because of prisoners' abuse at Abu Ghraib prison in Baghdad. The U.S. media uncovered sadistic, criminal abuse by U.S. soldiers of Iraqis held at a prison that was already infamous under Saddam Hussein's regime. The photographs broadcast on the CBS program showed Iraqi prisoners stripped, hooded, and tormented by their U.S. captors. Torture and abuse were part of daily routine. The images sparked anger and condemnation among Muslims around the world for the mistreatment of Iraqis.

The United States was also arresting indiscriminately Muslims in various parts of the world and shipping them away to Guantanamo Bay on the island of Cuba, under the pretext of protecting the United States from Islamic terrorists. No one knows who is who in the Cuba prison. This is in addition to the number of Iraqis in U.S. prisons in Iraq estimated at over fourteen thousand. Their families were not given reasons as to why they were detained, their whereabouts, or living conditions. Such a situation has certainly fueled anti-American feeling among Muslims and especially the Iraqi people.

The Quran desecrations at Guantanamo tarnished the image of the United States in the Islamic world after a U.S. news magazine reported that the Muslim holy book was flushed down the toilet at the prison. Muslims around the world felt that the United States had been humiliating Muslim detainees by offending their religious beliefs. In addition, the U.S. administration revealed eventually that many other Muslim prisoners were held in other countries, including European ones, on the pretext that they were Islamic terrorists.

Afghan Muslim clerics threatened to call for a holy war against the United States unless it properly investigated the incidents and punished those who desecrated the Quran. This added to the growing resentment of the U.S.-led forces in Afghanistan of eighteen thousand, most of them Americans. Sixteen were killed in Afghanistan and one hundred wounded in demonstrations against the United States for the Quran desecrations. In other Islamic countries, after Friday prayers, people carrying copies of the Quran marched in protest. In Iraq, demonstrations appeared outside mosques in Baghdad, in the holy city of Najaf, and in many other Iraqi cities.

Again, the Islamic world was surprised and angered at the worldwide publication of the pictures of Saddam in his underpants in his prison cell under U.S. custody. Other pictures showed him washing his clothes in a bucket in his cell. The pictures were a violation of the Geneva conventions, which call for respect to prisoners. Some Muslims argued that the incident meant to dehumanize the Islamic faith. The incident was further damaging the reputation of the United States.

The *New York Times* in November 2004 reported "the United States is failing in its efforts to explain the nation's diplomatic and military actions to the Moslem world."[19] Although the report did not constitute official policy, its analysis aimed to raise government awareness of the reasons why Muslims in the world are not happy with the U.S. policy toward their nations and especially in Iraq.

MUSLIMS' HUMAN RIGHTS VIOLATED

Post 9/11, Muslims have been suffering from a fierce anti-Muslim campaign. Amr Moussa, the Director General of the Arab League, requested that the Arab delegations in the UN and its international conventions respond to the campaign by stressing the Arabs' adherence to global human rights, peace, and security of all countries.[20] He emphasized that the Arabs and Muslims should prove to the whole world that they are a relevant part of the globe's human civilization, contributing greatly to its progress and achievements.

Children's games against Arabs started to be popular in some American states, such as playing "Murder the Arabs" or "Learn how to kill Iraqis." The spread of the new game among young Americans expresses hatred against the Arabs, especially the Iraqis, who are murdering American soldiers sent to "liberate" Iraq.[21] These games sparked anger among Arabs and Muslims living in the United States. They said it was provoking hatred against them, in general, and the Iraqis, in particular. Such games violate the values of justice, equality, and human rights propagated by the United States worldwide. Many Muslims think anti-Islamic sentiment— under the label "war against terror"—was always present, and merely surfaced with 9/11.

USA Today, in its issue dated March 9, 2004, published on its front page an article titled "Muslims See New Opposition to Building Mosques Since 9/11." A Muslim group proposed to turn an old building into a mosque in a suburb of Philadelphia. Building a mosque led critics to distribute fliers that warned residents that extremists "with connection to terrorists" might worship in their community. The fliers also claimed that the mosque would attract hundreds of its worshipers for prayers five times a day and would harbor terrorists.[22]

Discrimination groups in Britain have reported an increase in anti-Muslim assaults and prejudiced attitudes since 9/11. The Moslem

Council for Britain and other leading Muslim organizations in the United Kingdom made it known that Islamophobia was becoming institutionalized. The council is concerned about a generation of Muslim youth in the United Kingdom feeling they are discriminated against. The council feels that some politicians and elements of the media were also promoting Islamophobia.

Even Muslim students at American universities and science research centers suffer discrimination. Reports from universities and research centers reveal that the number of Muslim graduate students has sharply dropped since 9/11. In the *New York Times*, Joseph S. Nye, Jr., a professor at Harvard University, threw light on the sharp enrollment decline in the number of foreign students admitted.[23] He estimated the costs to the American economy are significant as educating foreign students in the United States is a $13 billion industry. Equally important, he emphasized, those foreign students return home carrying American ideas with them. Getting an American visa has been a red-tape nightmare that deterred many Muslim student applicants. Islamic human rights organizations, governments, educational institutions, and parents expressed their indignation toward such policies that discriminate against the Muslim students in the United States.[24]

ANNAN'S WARNING OF MOUNTING WEST-ISLAM TENSIONS

Former UN Secretary-General Kofi Annan warned that tensions were mounting between Westerners and Muslims and urged people to seek out common ground between their traditions. It was right to condemn attacks such as those by al-Qaeda on the United States on September 11, 2001, but people must be aware of polarizing the West and Islam.

Annan, according to the text of a lecture to University of Tübingen in southern Germany, said, "It is wrong to behave as if Islamic and Western values were incompatible . . . They are not, as millions of devout Muslims living here in Germany, and elsewhere in the West, would be the first to tell you." Annan continued, "Yet many of those Muslims now find themselves the objects of suspicions, harassment and discrimination, while in parts of the Islamic world anyone associated with the West or Western values is exposed to hostility and even violence."[25]

Following this synopsis of the events leading to the Iraqi war and its impact on the world in general, we now attempt to throw light on the extended terrorism attacks on Iraq, its reasons, and the reaction of Islam toward them.

CHAPTER 2

WORLD WAR WITH TERRORISM

ISLAM IN TOTAL WAR WITH TERRORISM

TERRORISM IS GLOBAL REGARDLESS OF NATIONALITY, RELIGION, OR CREED. It is apparent that threats from fanatic terrorists nowadays are more alarming than ever before. Militant terrorists choose their targets regardless of any national or international respect for human rights. Both non-Islamic and Islamic nations have suffered from terrorism since 9/11. The victims are the children and the people who have suffered.

These attacks sparked a series of announcements declaiming the violence committed in the name of Islam. In messages marking the Muslim feasts ending the holy month of Ramadan, leaders of Muslim nations called on all Muslims to unite against terrorism after waves of bombings hit Iraq, the Arab Gulf States, Turkey, Spain, Indonesia, Jordan, Egypt, Algeria, and the United Kingdom, killing thousands of innocent people.

King Fahd of Saudi Arabia, and the protector of the two holy Islamic shrines in Mecca and Medina, declared that bombings led by terrorists had no basis in Islam. Such actions were against Islamic faith, values, and principles. He called all Muslims to "closely work together to combat the roots of deviation."[1] Other Islamic rulers expressed a high level of concern regarding the danger of the fanatic Islamic terrorism threatening world peace and security.

Jalal Talabani, the Iraqi president, declared Iraq's need for international assistance to fight against terrorists. The perilous situation in Iraq had led, in September 2005, to a call on the General Assembly to urgently help Iraq to fight terrorists. Talabani assured the UN delegations that Iraq had declared a holy war against terrorism initiated by Islamic insurgent and militant groups. He reminded the delegates that total war on terror required "diverse" international participation. Then he stressed the "desperate need" of the Iraqi people for overseas support and international assistance. He was quoted, "Today, Iraq is facing one of the most brutal campaigns of terror at the hands of the forces of darkness. Iraq is now free. It has risen out of the ashes of Saddam's dictatorship."[2]

When the violence extended into Mecca, Islam's holy land, killing innocent pilgrims, the Islamic world wondered at how such violence could have extended into the holy land, especially in the Muslim righteous month of Ramadan. High Islamic clerics around the world exclaimed that those who kill innocent people and claim to be Muslims only deceive themselves, belonging to a criminal, not Islamic, fraternity.[3]

SAUDI ARABIA'S REACTION

The Saudi ambassador to the United States made a public announcement in April 2004 that his nation, together with other Islamic nations, was now in "total war" against Islamic terrorists after a series of bombing attacks in the Kingdom of Saudi Arabia, following a car bombing in the capital Riyadh, killing a number of people and injuring hundreds of others. This marked the third terror attack in less than a year. After meeting with the U.S. National Security Adviser at the White House, the ambassador, Prince Badr Bin Sultan, commented that "we are going to fight the terrorists hard. They are evil and consider everybody their enemy. It's a total war with them now. And there will be no compromises, and we're not going to give up on them."[4]

Since then, Saudi authorities have been fighting indigenous terrorists and Islamic militants. A series of suicide bombings at residential compounds housing Westerners in Riyadh killed a large number of people. A few months later, a car bomb exploded in a mostly Arab neighborhood near Riyadh's diplomatic quarter, killing at least twenty people. "Who else sends suicide bombers to blow up cars in the midst of urban centers? Who else has publicly said we are going after the Saudi state?" a representative of the Saudi government said.[5] He was referring to al-Qaeda.

Native terrorists continued killing foreign experts and workers in the Red Sea industrial town of Yanbu, Saudi Arabia. This was the first known attack by terrorists on industrial and petroleum establishments in the Kingdom. The U.S. embassy in Riyadh confirmed that two Americans, two British, one Australian, one Canadian, and a Pakistani were killed. Two of the attackers blew themselves up before being captured.

The Islamic judgment on the terrorist's attacks was denounced by Saudi Arabia's powerful top cleric. The Grand Mufti of Saudi Arabia Sheik Abdul-Aziz bin Abdullah al-Sheikh further said, "I tell all Moslems that this act of terrorism is a sin. It is one of the greatest sins."[6]

These Islamic *fatwas* (rulings) from highly distinguished Islamic clerics did not hinder the terrorists. The next day, in the Saudi capital, a freelance cinematographer working for the British Broadcasting Corporation, considered a leading expert on al-Qaeda, was shot. This shooting came after twenty-two people died in the Saudi oil city of Choler in a hostage standoff. It ended with Saudi troops storming the residential compound where more than two hundred hostages were taken by militant Islamists. Saudi officials blamed Islamic militants connected with al-Qaeda.

After all these attacks, the government of Saudi Arabia declared that the terrorists in the kingdom would be safe from prosecution if they surrendered themselves within a month. After that date, they would face forceful consequences. However, few terrorists showed up. Just six wanted militias took up the offer on a one-month amnesty in 2004. All six were released in November the same year. After two years, the Saudi Arabia monarch in June 2006 offered a second royal amnesty.

The monarch stated Islamist insurgents "who surrender will be pardoned." The amnesty was to invite al-Qaeda followers to turn themselves in. King Abdullah pledged to annihilate al-Qaeda-linked militants in the kingdom, vowing to "combat the ideology of those who accuse others of infidelity." Since the unrest began in May 2003 in the kingdom until the second amnesty date it was estimated that at least 90 civilians, 55 policemen, and 136 militants had died. This is in addition to four French expatriates after a terrorist ambush near Medina. They were all residents working in Riyadh and were on a desert trip.[7]

THE REACTION OF OTHER ISLAMIC COUNTRIES

War against militancy became inescapable as terrorism became eminent both for Islamic and non-Islamic countries. This prompted King Abdullah of Jordan in November 2005 to request his new prime minister to launch an all-out war against Islamic militancy in the wake of that month's triple hotel blasts that took place in Amman, Jordan, by Iraqi suicide bombers. The king stressed, "The November 9 attacks increase our determination to stick to our reform and democratization process, which is irreversible."[8] The king continued that the strategy of his new government should confront those who chose the path of destruction and sabotage to reach their goals.[9]

Meanwhile, a statement was issued by an al-Qaeda group in Iraq claiming responsibility for the suicide bomb attacks against Jordan. The group claimed that Jordan had become a target because it was "a backyard garden for the enemies of Islam and crusaders." The group further described Amman as a place for the traitors. The Jordanian king insisted in a televised address, "We will pursue those criminals and those who are behind them, and we will reach them wherever they are. We will pull them from their holes and bring them to justice."[10]

As militants became more aggressive and destructive, Muslim leaders from all over the world called for combating extremism. The fifty-seven leaders of the Organization of the Islamic Conference (OIC) declared in Mecca at the end of 2005 a "total war against terrorism." The summit repeatedly called for moderation, tolerance, and a rejection of extremist violence. Saudi King Abdullah bin Abdul Aziz said at the inauguration of the two-day summit at Islam's holiest city of Mecca, "Islamic unity would not be reached through bloodshed as claimed by the deviants. OIC should fulfill its historic role of combating extremism." He also called for a reform of educational programs in Islamic nations. He was quoted saying that "Developing the curriculum is essential to building a tolerant Muslim identity . . . and to having a society that rejects isolation." At the end of the conference, a declaration was unanimously agreed to, calling for "forgiveness . . . among peoples and for combating injustice, aggression, and corruption."[11]

Many members of the Islamic conference asked, "Did the image of Islam need to be improved after the series of terrorist attacks in various parts of the world?" The head of the Arab League and an influential Saudi prince from the Alwaleed family told journalists that Arabs should correct the misperceptions about their culture and religion in the Western press. They said Arab governments would be less open to criticism in the Western press if they implemented political reforms and countered radical interpretations of Islam.

The questions the Islamic thinkers posed were "How do we rectify the Arab Islamic image? Where do the terrorists obtain their finance, their explosives, and their weapons? Where do they go into hiding? What are the real causes of this hatred, enmity, and bitterness? What is the motivation that created so many terrorists?" The continued acts of terrorism including the holy land of Mecca made it conspicuous that the main objective was to defy the existence of the Saudi kingdom as well as the government itself. Al-Qaeda, founded in Saudi Arabia by Osama bin Laden, has generally been accused of plotting not only against the Saudi royal family but also against other regimes in various parts of the Islamic world.[12]

TERRORISTS EXTEND THEIR VIOLENCE TO IRAQ

An urgent message was sent from the Iraqi government to its neighboring countries in July 2006, three and a half years after the beginning of the "occupation," saying "Stop harboring terrorists." The government called on its Arab neighbors to turn over terrorists on the wanted list. Otherwise, they "will risk contributing to a spread of terrorism that would plunge the whole Arab region."[13]

In Iraq, gunmen shot and killed eminent Sunni and distinguished Shiite clerics and their devotees in Baghdad and other cities as they entered mosques to perform their prayers. Moreover, terrorism extended its aggression against Iraqi leaders cooperating with the U.S. occupation. A group of terrorists in a pickup truck chased a woman member of Iraq's Governing Council in her car and killed her in the first assassination targeting members of the U.S.-appointed leadership body. She was one of three women on the interim council who was a strong candidate to be appointed as Iraq's representative at the United Nations (UN). A month later, Iraqi rebels killed four U.S. workers and then set fire to their bodies and dragged the mutilated corpses through the streets of Fallujah. This barbaric incident inflamed the fierce fighting between the American troops and the people of Fallujah who, as claimed, were protecting the insurgent terrorists.

In another sad incident in Iraq, a terrorist suicide bomber killed forty worshipers at a mosque in the northern Iraqi city of Mosul. Even mosques, both for Shiites and Sunnis, where Muslims perform their prayers did not escape the brutality of the rebels. Al-Qaeda insurgents and Shiite Sadr militias staged increasingly daring attacks in their campaign to topple the U.S.-backed government. Their aim was to institute a government opposing the U.S. occupation of Iraq. It is true that many Iraqi communities were a breeding ground of insurgent and militia activists. Insurgents were responsible for many suicide bombings, abdicating foreigners, drive-by shootings, murdering the country's security services and people working with U.S.-led forces.[14]

As increasing insecurity loomed over Iraq after the occupation by U.S.-led troops, the world questioned the U.S. administration's policy concerning their role in combating terrorism in Iraq and the Middle East. A presidential address was broadcast live on television from Fort Bragg, North Carolina, in June 2005. The following are excerpts of President Bush's address as recorded by CNN.

- "Our mission in Iraq is clear: We're hunting down the terrorists. We are helping Iraqis build a free nation that is an ally in the war on terror. We are advancing freedom in the broader Middle East. We are removing a source of violence and instability and laying the foundation of peace for our children and our grandchildren."
- "Like most Americans, I see the images of violence and bloodshed. Every picture is horrifying, and the suffering is real. Amid all this

violence, I know Americans ask the question: 'Is the sacrifice worth it?' It is worth it. And it is vital to the future security of our country."

- "Our strategy can be summed up this way: As the Iraqis stand up, we will stand down."
- "We will stay in Iraq as long as we are needed and not a day longer."
- "The rise of freedom in this vital region [Middle East] will eliminate the conditions that feed radicalism and ideologies of murder and make our nation safer."
- "We fight today because Iraq now carries the hope of freedom in a vital region of the world, and the rise of democracy will be the ultimate triumph over radicalism and terror."[15]

Just a few days after the president's address that promised stability in the area, and after a new Iraqi interim government was formed, more violence erupted. An insurgent bomber struck the offices of a Kurdish party in Arbil, northern Iraq, killing at least sixty people. It was the deadliest single attack in two months, as a car bomber killed 125 people in a town south of Baghdad. The deadly attacks on offices of the Kurdish party came just a day after a new interim government was sworn in and three months after the historic elections that Iraqis had hoped would help end the acute violence spread over their country.[16]

Members of the interim Iraqi Assembly, who disputed for months before forming a cabinet, accused militant guerrillas of trying to spark a civil war with bombings aimed at deepening sectarian tensions. It was Ansar al-Sunna, a Sunni militant group, that claimed responsibility for the attack.

Since the attack in Kurdistan, Iraqi guerrillas became more daring in their assaults. They came better equipped with modern armaments and dangerous ammunitions. In April 2005, a Bulgarian commercial helicopter was shot down, killing eleven on board, including six Americans. The Russian-built Mi-8 helicopter was hit by a rocket-propelled grenade as it flew over a deserted area north of Baghdad. It was believed to be the first downing of a civilian aircraft in Iraq. The attack, in fact, came amid a series of grave Sunni violent acts aiming at overshadowing attempts by Iraq's new Shiite leaders to form a government nearly three months after elections.[17]

In 2005, the number of terrorist insurgents in Iraq was estimated roughly between thirteen thousand and seventeen thousand. It was believed that the large majority of them were devotees of the ousted Iraqi leader Saddam Hussein and his Ba'ath Party. It is important to mention that the Ba'ath Party was overthrown by the U.S.-led invasion in March

2003 and was officially considered illegal by the U.S.-led occupation. Of those, five thousand to seven thousand of the highly trained members are believed to be "committed fighters."[18]

Meanwhile, Iraqi officials estimated that there were about five hundred insurgent fighters who had come into Iraq from other countries. They were mostly young fanatic Islamists. Most were suspected to be suicide bombers from Saudi Arabia, Syria, and other surrounding countries. Another group of about one thousand was believed to be followers of al-Qaeda Jordanian-born terrorist al-Zarqawi. It should be noted, in this connection, that a difference should be made between the homegrown Iraqi insurgency and foreign groups like al-Qaeda.

There is no doubt that al-Zarqawi, as the al-Qaeda undisputed insurgent leader in Iraq, succeeded in making Iraq a vigorous battlefield between Sunni insurgents on one side and Iraqi police and U.S.-led forces on the other. In two days of mass slaughter in October 2005, 110 Iraqis were killed. The attacks aimed mostly at civilians in Shiite areas. Al-Qaeda of Mesopotamia, also known as the most radical Islamist group run by the extremist al-Zarqawi, claimed responsibility for the attacks.[19]

Arab radical fundamentalists, led by Zarqawi, continued their strategy of attacks against Shiites. The objective was to start a civil war between Iraq's two largest sects, namely, the Shiite and the Sunni. The attacks were intensified while the government was preparing to hold a national referendum on a new constitution held on October 15, 2005. The constitution was strongly opposed by most Sunni Arabs.

It became apparent that suicide attacks became the most deadly means of inflicting the greatest possible damage on crowded targeted groups. Suicide bomb attackers are mostly young fanatic Islamists who have been psychologically brainwashed to do the job. In an attack in a Baghdad market that killed a large number of people, the police found the driver's foot taped to the accelerator pedal.[20]

These terrorist activities succeeded in creating a state of psychological oppression. As a result of the intensive daily violence and sectarian tension running high between the rival two sects, namely the Arab Sunnis and Shiites, emotional tension became part of the lives of Iraqi individuals and families. Fear, as a psychological factor, can cripple the movements and thinking of human beings. Panicked by rumors of a suicide bomber, thousands of Shiite pilgrims broke into a stampede on a bridge during a religious procession. About 950 died, mostly women and children, crushing one another or plunging thirty feet into the muddy Tigris River. The tragedy was the highest single loss since the March 2003 U.S.-led invasion. The government later announced that the police found no suspects or explosives at the bridge. The tragedy took place purely because of the climate of fear built over years of killing, bloodshed, and suicide bombing.[21]

With lack of security and increase of violence, Iraq was moving from "hostage" to "lawlessness." With the constant escalation of civilians kidnapped and abducted by al-Qaeda insurgents, Arab Sunni rebels and Shiite militia squads reinforce doubts that the country will recover any time soon. Likewise, these abductions, whose victims are innocent people of different nationalities and faiths, are bound to damage the image of genuine resistance fighters to the occupation.[22]

The insurgents claim that their aggression is targeted at collaborators with the United States. Collaborators condemned by insurgents are mostly renowned contractors, distinguished skilled engineers, and technological experts invited by the Iraqi government and U.S. aides to assist in the reconstruction of the infrastructure. The aggression is motivated by power and greed. In several cases, the abductors who belong to obscure Islamic factions claimed large ransoms.

AL-QAEDA'S ROLE IN GLOBAL ATTACKS

Al-Qaeda, since the Iraq occupation, seems to have established a strong hold in Sunni territories and is directly responsible for most terrorist attacks. The Iraqi interim government reiterated that its security forces have arrested several leading figures in al-Qaeda under the command of al-Zarqawi. The government believed that he had access to a budget of more than $1 billion to wage terrorist attacks in various parts of the country.

Terrorist attacks will continue to be mentioned throughout the coming chapters as they are the major tragedy of this war, but the following chapter will concentrate on the reasons stated by the United States for launching the attack, and whether they were justified. Moreover, this chapter will depict how the Iraqi war stimulated more terrorist attacks.

CHAPTER 3

IS THE IRAQ WAR JUSTIFIED?

TO EXAMINE THE DECLARED AND HIDDEN REASONS FOR THE Anglo-American War in Iraq, we should look into the four reasons as declared by the Iraq invaders. The first of the numerous declared reasons for the Anglo-American invasion of Iraq was to "liberate" its people from the tyranny of Saddam Hussein and the despotism of his regime. The second most important reason was to destroy alleged weapons of mass destruction accumulated in Iraq by Saddam Hussein. The third reason we must consider as most important, though not declared openly by the Anglo-American invaders, is the abundance of Iraq petroleum reserve. Rated second after Saudi Arabia, Iraq is estimated to hold 115 billion barrels of proven oil reserves. Possibly much more are undiscovered in various unexplored areas in the country. Over and above, Iraq is estimated to contain at least 110 trillion cubic feet of natural gas. The fourth reason for the invasion was the alleged al-Qaeda link with Saddam. The U.S. Senate Intelligence Report of September 2006, issued to mark the fifth anniversary of 9/11, concluded that there was no link between Saddam and members of al-Qaeda. The report continued that contradicted claims were made by the U.S. government in the lead-up to its invasion of Iraq.[1]

The case for war against Iraq as orchestrated by British and U.S. officials began in the summer of 2002. The media was used to warn Americans that Iraq was disregarding international sanctions on its armament. It was in September 2002 that the U.S administration urged the Security Council to demand that Iraq allow weapon inspectors back in the country. After a month, the United States gave notice that it could not wait any more for "the smoking gun that could come in the form of a mushroom cloud." In the same month, in order to strengthen the position of the U.S. administration, Congress gave it the authority to launch military action against Iraq. This authority was carried out in March 2003.[2]

It became apparent that the U.S. National Security Council had "no patience" for waiting on the United Nations (UN) to file war against Iraq.

The UN Secretary-General declared it was illegal for a member state to attack another state by military force without previous permission from the Security Council.

The UN weapons inspectors were allowed back into Iraq in November 2002. They stayed in the country until March 17, 2003. It was then that the U.S. administration issued an ultimatum to Saddam to leave power within forty-eight hours or face war. Both leaders, President George W. Bush and British Prime Minister Tony Blair, declared that the invasion was necessary because Saddam had ignored UN sanctions requiring his government to give up its weapons programs for mass destruction. The two leaders insisted that the world was better off without Saddam Hussein in power and marched on to occupy Iraq by military force without the consent of the UN Security Council.

For thirty years before the invasion, Iraq was under the rule of Saddam Hussein, the absolute dictator and chairman of the Ba'ath Party. The party, since its creation in the 1940s, aimed to transform Iraq into a secular nation where state and religious institutions were separated. They called for pan-Arabism, a movement for unification among the Arab peoples and nations of the Middle East. During the 1980s and 1990s, Iraq was in two major wars against Iran and Kuwait. UN economic sanctions were imposed on Iraq because its Kuwait invasion and the country's educational institutions, economic system, infrastructure, health care, and all other social benefits had since deteriorated tremendously.

To develop an understanding of the basic motives for the U.S. administration to justify war in Iraq, we should go back to the remarks of the president of the United States in his address to the United Nations General Assembly in September 2002, just a few months before Iraq's invasion in March 2003.

First, Saddam Hussein has repeatedly violated UN Security Council Resolutions designed to ensure that Iraq does not pose a threat to international peace and security.

Second, evidence gathered by the U.S. and other governments leaves no doubt that the Iraqi regime possessed and concealed some of the most lethal weapons ever devised, to be used against Iraqi people and Iraq's neighbors.

Third, Iraq must unconditionally accept the destruction and removal, under international supervision, of all chemical and biological weapons.

Fourth, Saddam Hussein has repeatedly violated UN Security Council Resolutions.

Fifth, Saddam failed to destroy all his ballistic missiles with a range greater than 150 kilometers.

Sixth, Saddam supports terrorism, and terrorist organizations should be prevented from operating in Iraq.[3]

In the first four years of occupation, the U.S. military death toll reached 3,500 and war expenditure was more than $320 billion. The president prepared the nation for more casualties, saying the "defense of freedom is worth our sacrifice. We've lost some of our nation's finest men and women in the war on terror." In a speech to military spouses at Bolling Air Force Base in Washington, he stated, "Each loss of life is heartbreaking. And the best way to honor the sacrifice of our fallen troops is to complete the mission and lay the foundation of peace by spreading freedom." At the time, an estimated 26,690 to 30,051 civilians in Iraq were killed since the start of the occupation.[4]

Despite all the enormous complications in Iraq during the first four years of occupation, Bush, in a wide-ranging birthday interview with CNN's "Larry King Live" in July 2006, said that he would make the same choice again, even knowing that Saddam Hussein's regime did not have weapons of mass destruction. He insisted in the interview that the weakest approval rating of his presidency did not trouble him. "We removed a tyrant," Bush said. "He was an enemy of the United States who harbored terrorists and who had the capacity, at the very minimum, to make weapons of mass destruction. And he was a true threat."[5]

HAS IRAQ POSED A CLEAR AND IMMEDIATE THREAT TO WORLD PEACE AND SECURITY?

One of the key motivating forces of the swift U.S. military action was to "hunt for and eliminate Iraq's purported weapons of mass destruction." After years of expert investigation and highly scientific research done by specialized American researchers, not a fragment of proof was detected to back up this allegation.

Former UN arms inspector Hans Blix made his last-minute plea to British Prime Minister Tony Blair to be given more time to find weapons of mass destruction before the U.S.-led invasion of Iraq. However, Blair was convinced that all the intelligence agencies around the world agreed with the British and the Americans that such weapons existed.[6]

Wesley Clark, a 2004 Democratic presidential candidate, told a cheering college-town crowd that the invasion of Iraq was a "major blunder" and he never would have voted for war in Iraq. Clark continued that his Army career taught him the lesson: "The use of force is only a last resort."[7] That was not justified in Iraq.

A large number of economists and politicians believe that the U.S. occupation of Iraq is primarily motivated by the interests of international investors and big oil companies to guarantee the flow of its oil to the United States and other Western countries. Iraqi oil in the hands of anti-Western fundamentalist rebels could pose a clear and immediate threat to the Western economy. It has already been seen that production of oil has been sharply reduced by insurgents since the Iraqi war as occasionally they sabotage the main fuel oil tanks and pipes.[8]

Another rationale for invading Iraq, led by U.S. intelligence, was that the Saddam regime trained al-Qaeda members to use biological and chemical weapons. The *New York Times* in November 2005 revealed that "the document, an intelligence report from February 2002, said it was probable that the prisoner, Ibn al-Shaykh al-Libi, was intentionally misleading the debriefers in claiming Iraqi support for al-Qaeda's work with illicit weapons." This high al-Qaeda official in American custody was identified as a likely fabricator months before the U.S. administration began to use his statements as the foundation for its claims. At the time of his capture, Libi was the most senior al-Qaeda official in U.S. custody. He remains in custody at the detention center in Guantanamo Bay, Cuba, where he was sent in 2003, according to government officials.[9]

FALSE INTELLIGENCE ON WEAPONS OF MASS DESTRUCTION (WMD) IN IRAQ

The final verdict from the various scientific international and local sources indicated that Iraq had no WMD after 1994. The historical review of the UN inspections in Iraq was the first study to confirm the conclusion of David Kay, the former U.S. chief inspector, that Iraq had no banned weapons before the 2003 U.S.-led invasion.[10]

It became apparent that Dr. Kay's comments deeply embarrassed the United States and the United Kingdom. Charles Duelfer, a former top United Nations weapons inspector in Iraq, confirmed in a television interview on *NewsHour* on PBS, "The prospect of finding chemical weapons, biological weapons is close to nil."[11] The *Washington Post* in February 2004 highlighted the declaration of Kay in his assertion of no weapon of chemical or biological mass destruction in Iraq after the invasion of U.S. and allied troops. The fierce debate, emphasized the newspaper, was over whether the U.S. administration used intelligence information to exaggerate the Iraqi threat.

The *Post* continued, "One of the lessons here is, don't pretend to the public that the picture the intelligence services provide is clear and accurate, because it's not," said Michael Clarke, director of International Policy at King's College London. He continued, "Experts in the field of weapons and intelligence say the case illustrates the pitfalls that arise when political leaders seek to invoke intelligence findings to justify their policies."[12]

Colin Powell effectually withdrew the dramatic prewar presentation to a skeptical United Nations in 2003, during testimony before the Senate Government Affairs Committee. "There was every reason to believe there were stockpiles," Powell said. "There was a question about the size of stockpiles, but we all believed there were stockpiles. I think it is unlikely that we will find any stockpiles." The job now, he continued, was "to go back and find out why we had a different judgment."[13]

In a court outburst in December 2005, while in captivity, Saddam loudly accused the United States of lying. Speaking at the seventh hearing of his trial on charges of crimes against humanity, the former president was quoted as telling the court, "The White House is a liar. They said Iraq had chemical weapons." He continued, "They lied again when they said that what Saddam said was wrong," he added, referring to a White House dismissal of his claim during the court hearing that he was tortured. In the court, Saddam dismissed allegations that Iraq developed chemical weapons in the 1980s and used them against Iran and against Iraqi Kurds. He denied that he had destroyed its remaining stocks after the 1991 Gulf War.[14]

Furthermore, the U.S. Senate Intelligence Committee report released in July 2004 and quoted by CNN, criticized the intelligence prewar estimates of Iraq's weapons of mass destruction as overstated and unsupported. Pat Robert said, "Bush and Congress sent the country to war on flawed information provided by the intelligence community." The report by the Senate panel faulted intelligence analysts for having a "collective assumption" that Iraq already had weapons of mass destruction.[15]

Despite all these heated factors and accusations, President Bush said the United States was "right to go into Iraq. America is safer today because we did." He told a cheering crowd of supporters in Pennsylvania, "We removed a declared enemy of America, who had the capability of producing weapons of mass destruction, and could have passed that capability to terrorists bent on acquiring them."

WAS IT A MISTAKE TO LAUNCH THE WAR AGAINST IRAQ?

At a joint news conference at the White House on June 4, 2006, the two leaders, President Bush and Prime Minister Tony Blair, as reported by the *Herald Tribune*, acknowledged major misjudgments in the execution of the war. They insisted, however, that the election of a constitutional government in Baghdad justified their decision to invade Iraq. The two leaders refused to talk about a schedule for pulling troops out of Iraq. They stuck to a common formulation that they would withdraw troops only as properly trained Iraqi soldiers took control over more and more territory.[16]

Washington refuses to admit that it might not have made the right decision to invade Iraq. U.S. officials envisioned that the invasion would be praised and U.S.-led troops would be welcomed in the streets of Baghdad with flowers, olive branches, Arab songs, and oriental horse dancing. After almost five years of occupation, the situation became different. More than 3,500 American soldiers were killed and an estimated $350 billion had been spent on the war.

It is most unfortunate that the war started because of two "bulletproof" findings of intelligence released in both the United States and the United Kingdom. The first was that Iraq has been dangerously involved in producing weapons of mass destruction. The second intelligence finding was evidence of ties between al-Qaeda and Saddam, including training al-Qaeda terrorists in chemical and biological warfare. Both findings proved baseless and utterly untrue.

From Europe, voices of a number of influential heads of state faulted the war against Iraq. Chirac reiterated that the war in Iraq was unnecessary. He added that it had led to an "expansion" of terrorism in the world. He expressed his willingness to put aside France's differences with Britain and the United States. He further expressed willingness to assist in rebuilding a democratic and sovereign Iraq. Chirac said that he believed that "the judgment of history will go against the Iraq war and vindicate those who opposed it."

Chirac was certain that Saddam Hussein's departure was necessary and a positive thing. He continued, "But it also provoked reactions, such as the mobilization in the number of men and women of Islam, which has made the world more dangerous."[17]

Former CIA chief George Tenet criticized the U.S. invasion of Iraq in his recent book, *At the Center of the Storm: My Years at the CIA*, published in April 2007. He emphasized that U.S. officials who supported and encouraged the Iraq occupation did not hold a "serious debate" about whether Saddam Hussein was a threat. He added that there was never "a significant discussion" about ways to contain any threat posed by Saddam Hussein without invading. Tenet also said that he thought that the violence in Iraq was continuing to spiral out of control. He feared that sectarian violence in Iraq had taken on a life of its own. Thus, he emphasized, U.S. forces are "becoming more and more irrelevant to the management of that violence."[18]

Doug Bereuter, a retiring Republican Congressman from Nebraska, sadly confessed that he had supported launching an attack on Iraq. He bid farewell to his colleagues after long years of service in the Congress. However, before his departure in August 2004 he said, "I've reached the conclusion, retrospectively, now that the inadequate intelligence and faulty conclusions are being revealed, that all things being considered, it was a mistake to launch that military action."[19]

Iraqi victims arrive daily at the morgues with their hands and feet bound and mouths sealed shut with tape. The situation in most of Iraq became chaotic and lawless. This situation forced the government to sign into law provisions that would give the prime minister the power to declare martial law, detain suspects during antiterror sweeps, and set curfews.[20]

American casualties were constantly increasing. Take the month of September 2004, after one year of Iraq occupation as an example of rising fatalities among the U.S. and allied troops. It was one of the deadliest months for U.S. troops in the eighteen-month-old war in Iraq, and the death toll for the first time rose for four straight months. At least seventy-six U.S. troops were killed, reflecting a steady increase in American deaths since the United States transferred sovereignty to the interim Iraqi government on June 28, 2004. This was the date that the United States officially ended the occupation and an Iraqi interim government would take over. The fatalities were steadily increasing; forty-two U.S. troops were killed in June, sixty-four in July, and sixty-six in August.

In addition to the increasing military deaths, it was estimated after ten months of occupation that over twenty thousand Iraqi civilians had been killed because of military and insurgent actions. It is important to emphasize that the actual number of civilian deaths in Iraq has not been officially reported. It is expected that deaths among Iraqis since the occupation of Iraq far exceed one hundred thousand.[21]

All this raises a troubling question: is the war in Iraq, with such huge civilian and military losses, a diversion from the war on terror?

In one of his speeches, John Kerry, the Democratic presidential candidate, blamed the U.S. administration for pursuing Saddam Hussein instead of defeating Osama bin Laden. Kerry said in a speech at Temple University: "The misjudgment, miscalculation and mismanagement of the war in Iraq all make the war on terror harder to win. George Bush made Saddam Hussein the priority and not Osama bin Laden."[22]

Another ally, Australian Prime Minister John Howard, in August 2004 rejected claims by forty-three former defense chiefs and senior diplomats accusing the government of joining the war on Iraq based on false assumptions and deceptions. They emphasized that Australia's participation in the war had exposed the nation as a potential target for terrorism. The statement's signatories included former defense force chiefs and politicians. They also called on the government to end "rubber-stamping" of U.S. policies.[23]

In Italy, newly elected Prime Minister Romano Prodi declared, as soon as he took office in May 2006, that his new government believed the U.S.-led invasion of Iraq had been a "grave error." He confirmed that his government would withdraw all Italian troops stationed in Iraq. In the upper house of the Italian parliament, he said: "We consider the war in Iraq and the occupation of the country a grave error. It has not resolved, but complicated the situation of security." Italy had about three thousand troops in Iraq.[24]

In this climate of political and military pessimism after four years of the Iraq War, Harry Reid, the senior Democrat in the U.S. Senate, surprised the Arab world by saying that the war in Iraq was lost and a further build-up of U.S. troops in the country would not recover the situation. "This war is lost, and this surge is not accomplishing anything, as is shown by the extreme violence in Iraq this week," he told reporters. After holding talks with President Bush, Reid said that war in Iraq could not be won through military force. Only political, economic, and diplomatic means would bring success.[25]

WAS BRITAIN RIGHT TO ATTACK IRAQ?

The long-awaited report from a British panel headed by former top civil servant Lord Butler acquitted Mr. Blair's government and the intelligence agencies of "deliberate distortion or culpable negligence."[26] In this report, released in July 2004, blame was put on the state of prewar intelligence on Iraq's alleged weapons of mass destruction. However, the report cleared Prime Minister Tony Blair of responsibility for the failings.

After the release of this report, Mr. Blair told the House of Commons that "I have to accept, as the months have passed, it seems increasingly clear that at the time of the invasion Saddam did not have stockpiles of chemical or biological weapons ready to deploy." However, he insisted, "I cannot honestly say I believe getting rid of Saddam was a mistake at all. Iraq, the region, the wider world is a safer place without Saddam." Blair continued, "It was absolutely clear that Saddam had every intention to carry on developing these weapons, that he was procuring materials to do so. In terms of ballistic missiles, Saddam was going 'way beyond' what he was allowed to do under UN resolutions . . . However, lessons would be learned from Butler's report."[27]

As seen from Lord Butler's report, Blair was in the clear over the "flawed" UK intelligence. Indeed, the Iraqis were the ones who suffered most from the "flawed" intelligence of both the United States and Britain.

A number of former British diplomats severely criticized the prime minster. They said in their complaint that it was time for the prime minister to start influencing America's "doomed" policy in the Middle East or stop backing it. The outburst came in an unprecedented letter in April 2004 signed by fifty-two former ambassadors, high commissioners, and governors. All are the top ranks of British diplomacy. Blair was urged to sway U.S. policy in the region as a "matter of the highest urgency."

However, despite all difficulties facing the U.S.-led troops and especially the British forces occupying Basra, Blair vowed during the 2005 party election campaign to stay the course in Iraq. It was evident that Blair was weakened in his political campaign by opposition to Britain's military presence in Iraq. Despite the Iraqi protests against the British occupying forces in Basra, the deployment of British troops multiplied. In demonstration against the occupying British forces, a number of photographs showed a British soldier in flames, struggling to escape an armored vehicle that had been set on fire.[28]

To add to Mr. Blair's woes, in September 2005, a demonstration against British occupation turned bloody. The clash took place after two and a half years of British occupation of Basra. Hundreds of Iraqi civilians and police officers, some waving pistols and rifles, rallied in the southern city of Basra to denounce "British aggression" in the rescue of two British soldiers. The demonstrators put fire in two British tanks. The Iraqi governor of Basra threatened to put in jeopardy all cooperation with British forces unless the prime minister's government apologized for the fatal clash with Iraqi police. The incident put the question of the role of Britain's 8,500 troops mainly stationed in Basra in doubt.

It all started when a British armor smashed into a government jail to free, by force, two British soldiers who had been arrested by Iraqi police. After raiding the jail, the British said they rescued the soldiers who were placed in the custody of the al-Mahdi Army, the militia of radical Shiite cleric Muqtada al-Sadr. This took place while British officials were negotiating their release with Iraqi officials. Earlier that day, a crowd attacked British troops with stones and Molotov cocktails. This raised the question whether British occupation of Basra was justified amid the animosity of the Iraqi people.[29]

Animosity toward the British occupier was increasing. A few months after the Basra clash, in May 2006, a British air force helicopter was gunned down, killing four people aboard and sparking clashes between British troops and Iraqi youths chanting Shiite militia slogans and hurling petrol bombs. Two military tanks and a Land Rover were set on fire by the crowd that was seen throwing petrol bombs. The crowd was chanting, "Victory for the Mahdi army!" The Mehdi army is the Islamic militia loyal to the Shiite cleric Muqtada al-Sadr. He had demanded an end to the U.S.-led occupation of Iraq and is a key figure in the Islamist Shiite Alliance bloc.[30]

HAVE IRAQI SHIITE MILITIAS AND SUNNI
INSURGENTS BECOME OUT OF CONTROL?

It is believed that the Sunni rebels have close links to al-Qaeda and they mostly penetrated the country through Syria. It is equally suspected that a large number of Shiite militias penetrated the Iraqi frontiers from Iran. Insurgents and militias were fiercely operating in various Sunni and Shiite cities. At present, they have established a firm foothold in many northern and southern cities of Iraq.

The militant al-Qaeda insurgents, both indigenous and from abroad, are well trained and well armed. They infiltrated the northern cities and villages, where they gained strongholds. They were continuing to mount operations against the coalition troops, the police forces, and their collaborators in the area. Al-Qaeda fanatics who were previously well trained in Afghanistan led these rebels.

It is speculated that al-Qaeda insurgents also penetrate from Saudi border frontiers. They include Wahhabi Muslims, the fundamentalist sect that has been supported by bin Laden since the war to liberate Afghanistan from the Russian occupation. Bin Laden, as he repeated, has vowed a worldwide "jihad" (holy war) on the West and Islamic countries, which did not strictly follow the Sharia laws of Islam.

It is true that Iraqi rebels turned out of control. Practically every day there were a number of suicidal car bombers killing U.S. soldiers, a large number of Iraqi forces, civilians, and foreigners. Assassination, kidnapping, and abduction became everyday incidents. As the security situation deteriorated a large number of Iraqi and U.S.-led forces became involved in setting up a security cordon around Baghdad. They searched suspected vehicles and raided several houses described as "terrorist dens," killing and arresting a large number of terrorists.[31]

In another brutal incident, in October 2006, in the northern town of Hawijah, ten unidentified gunmen broke into the home of thirty-eight-year-old Halima Ahmed Hussein al-Juburi, a women's rights campaigner, and shot her dead in front of her three children. Activities of human rights women in Iraqi society have worsened dramatically since the U.S.-led invasion of March 2003. The general breakdown in law and order, the deterioration in peace and security, and the spread of ultra and conservative Islamists have added to antagonism against women's human rights in Iraq. This incident clearly meant to scare Iraqi women out of public life.

To continue the intensive sectarian violence in Iraq, Shiite militia gunmen opened fire on a convoy of Iraqi Sunni pilgrims bound for the holy city of Mecca. The pilgrims were a few miles from the city of Baquba.

Shiite gunmen showered their convoy with machine gun fire. Such killing has been part of Iraq's growing sectarian fighting between Shiite and Sunni Muslims.

Even Iraq's strategic oil pipelines, considered the most vital commodity for Iraqi people, were repeatedly hit by rebels. Undermining the government's efforts to foster economic recovery and improve the poor living conditions that feed political unrest, the insurgents continuously attacked strategic oil pipelines situated in Iraq's northern and southern fields.

ARE IRAQIS TOO FEARFUL OF AL-QAEDA MILITANTS TO SPEAK THEIR MINDS?

Because of the war against Iraq, al-Qaeda stepped up the terror war and reinforced its attacks on Saudi cities and compounds in which foreigners live. It killed and kidnapped Americans and foreign nationals. This added a new dimension to al-Qaeda's campaign to drive Westerners from Iraq and the Saudi kingdom. At the same time, bin Laden promised to oust the Saudi royal family who he considers "ungodly and submissive to America." Speaking against al-Qaeda or its insurgents or Osama bin Laden is intolerable. Al-Qaeda does not tolerate criticism.

As a start of aggression against journalists criticizing al-Qaeda, American Kenneth Scruggs was shot dead in May 2004 in front of his villa in a Riyadh suburb. Al-Qaeda claimed responsibility for the killing in a statement on an Islamist Web site. Bin Laden's al-Qaeda vowed that the years to come will be "bloody and miserable" for the Americans and the Saudi kingdom. This sent a signal that al-Qaeda followers might harm those who spoke against bin Laden or his teachings.

Meanwhile, the moderate Sunni Iraqis were fearful to speak their minds against Saddam and the dissolved Ba'ath Party. Still the Ba'ath insurgents and sympathizers were zealous, fanatic, and unyielding in their loyalty to Saddam and the party. They do not tolerate, at present, any critical comments against Saddam and the party. They radiate fear among the Iraqi Sunni citizens.

John Burns of the *New York Times* asked a sample of Iraqi citizens about the brutality of the mass graves and whether these were American fictions. He further asked whether America should see the attacks on its troops as meaning that Iraqis want the troops withdrawn quickly, with power rapidly handed over to the transitional Iraqi authority. Jasem, one of the Iraqis interviewed by Burns, said, "The truth is that we were never really with Saddam; in our hearts, we were always against him. Nevertheless, he is gone; what we are against now is America. It is different. We want the Americans to go home." Then he said, "We wanted America to get rid of Saddam, but we didn't want Americans to trespass in our land. We didn't want the soldiers to come into our villages and break down our doors and defile the honor of our women." Jasem was one of those Iraqis who spoke his mind. Other Iraqis fear criticizing Saddam, al-Qaeda, and their teachings.[32]

THE DANGER OF DIVIDING IRAQ

Let us examine the foreign and Iraqi voices that loudly suggest the division of the country into three main regions or confederates. Leslie Gelb, former editor of the *New York Times*, expressed his opinion in September 2003, just a few months after the U.S.-led troops marched on triumphantly to Baghdad. He clearly called for dividing Iraq into three sectarian areas: Sunnis, Shiites, and Kurds. He found that the only feasible strategy was to move in stages toward a three-state solution: Kurds in the north, Sunnis in the center, and Shiites in the south. He called for Washington to be very hardheaded in engineering this breakup, insisting that such partition of Iraq into three states was the only viable strategy for enhancing peace and order.

Partitioning Iraq into three states in 2003 was unthinkable. Neither the United Sates nor the Iraq government would have consented to such a concept. The Iraqi people, especially the Sunnis, were opposed to such partitioning. The Arab countries in their recent conferences reiterated their support for Iraq as a unified nation.[33]

Peter W. Galbraith, a noted diplomat and author, called for dividing Iraq in his article in *Time* magazine in November 2006, after more than three years of the occupation. He explained that "Iraq's national-unity government is not united and does not govern. Iraqi security forces, the centerpiece of the U.S.'s efforts for stability are ineffective or, even worse, combatants in the country's escalating civil war."

Galbraith continued emphasizing that the partition of Iraq has already happened. The Kurds, a non-Arab people who live in the country's north, enjoy the independence they long dreamed for. In southern Iraq, Shiite religious parties have established theocratic fiefdoms, using militias numbering in the tens of thousands. They are enforcing an Iranian-style Islamic Shiite rule.

He added that to the west, Iraq's Sunni provinces have become the breeding ground for Islamic insurgents controlling the Anbar province. This is while Ba'athists and Islamic radicals operate in Salahaddin and Nineveh provinces. "Baghdad, the heart of Iraq, is now partitioned between the Shiite east and the Sunni west," Galbraith explained. He continued, "The Mahdi Army, the most radical of the Shiite militias, controls almost all the Shiite neighborhoods and al-Qaeda has a large role in Sunni areas. Once a melting pot, Baghdad has become the front line of Iraq's Sunni-Shiite war, which is claiming at least 100 lives daily."

Despite all these calls for federalism and division, Muslim nations have insisted upon an independent and united Iraq. The fifty-seven foreign ministers (OIC) from the world's Muslim countries called for the need to preserve complete sovereignty, territorial integrity, and undivided political independence in Iraq. The conference also emphasized the need for Iraq "to be governed by its own people through a broad-based government based on full representation in line with a constitution accepted by the people."[34]

IS THE WORLD SAFER THAN BEFORE THE OCCUPATION OF IRAQ?

All indications, at present, show that the world is not safer than before the occupation. Kofi Annan, the UN Secretary-General, warned that the rule of law was at risk, pointing to Iraq, where "we see civilians massacred in cold blood, while relief workers, journalists and other noncombatants are taken hostage and put to death in the most barbarous fashion." He continued, saying, "The world has seen Iraqi prisoners disgracefully abused." He was referring to the Abu Ghraib prison scandal involving U.S. troops.[35]

In Iraq, since the occupation, Sunni and Shiite clerics have been gunned down. Sectarian tensions and bloody revenge have run high. Muslim mosques and Christian churches were bombed. Fallujah, Samarra, Tikrit, and other Sunni cities have been bombarded by U.S. warplanes to weaken the insurgency. Over 4,500 of U.S. and allied troops have been killed in the last few years since the occupation. Thousands of Iraqi police officers were blown up by timed bombs and suicide bombers. Iraqi soldiers were abducted. Journalists were butchered. Engineers, technicians, and workers assisting in the reconstruction of Iraq have been and still are massacred in a most primitive way. Most of them were butchered in front of TV cameras.

As the situation gradually deteriorated, Annan, the UN Secretary-General, in September 2004 warned that the international community now had to work hard to improve security. Annan emphasized, "We have a lot of work to do as an international community to try and make the world safer."[36]

Hans Blix, the former UN arms inspector, expressed his view[37] that the downfall of Saddam Hussein, as a treacherous and murderous dictator, was positive. However, the rest has been both a tragedy and a failure. Many political leaders, politicians, army men, and people all over the world agree with Hans Blix that the Iraqi war has been a military tragedy and human catastrophe. Over and above, it has largely stimulated terrorism, which defamed the basic message of Islam as a faith of peace, compassion, and conciliation among world religions.

It should be emphasized in our analysis that the Iraqi aggressive resistance had lost a lot of credibility and sympathizers around the world because of their action of slaughtering civilian hostages. The Western media has exploited it to discredit Arab culture. Consequently, the insurgents and militias appeared as a brutal people not differentiating between occupation forces to be resisted and civilians to be protected.

Newspaper reports avoided specific judgments about the likelihood that terrorists would strike on U.S. soil again, but concluded that the overall terror threat had increased since the 9/11 attacks. "The estimate concludes that the radical Islamic movement has expanded from a core of al-Qaeda operatives and affiliated groups to include a new class of 'self-generating' cells inspired by al-Qaeda's leadership, but without any direct connection to Osama bin Laden or his top lieutenants."[38]

Unfortunately, these operations have expanded to target subjects of friendly countries. An example of this was the kidnapping of six Egyptian engineers and technicians traveling to Iraq to provide mobile phone services to the Iraqi people. They had no connection with the American forces. The Egyptians were serving no one but the Iraqi people who had suffered the destruction of basic utilities of communication because of the war. Despite this, they were kidnapped and humiliated by insurgents.

In September 2006, for the first time, al-Qaeda announced on one of its Web sites that it had decided to establish a union with an Algerian insurgent group that has termed France as an enemy. Al-Qaeda said they would act together against French and American interests. It is clear that an al-Qaeda alliance with the Salafist (conventional) Islamic militant Algerian group was a great cause for concern. The interior minister of France, Nicolas Sarkozy (currently president), said, "We take these threats very seriously." He continued, "Absolute vigilance is required." Al-Zawahiri, al-Qaeda's second man, hailed "the joining up" with the Algerian militant group as "good news."[39]

HAS THE IRAQI WAR STIMULATED TERRORISM?

To answer this question, let us examine the views of former U.S. Defense Secretary Donald Rumsfeld. In early 2004, Rumsfeld expressed his opinion that "al-Qaeda might step up attacks in Iraq in the following months after the set-up of the interim government." His predictions were accurate. Soon after the interim government was established, the militant insurgents headed by al-Zarqawi pressed their aggression in the northern part of Iraq. Al-Zarqawi, as the third man in al-Qaeda's command, stepped up his aggression against foreigners, allied troops, police stations, workers, and engineers.[40]

As the U.S. administration has been putting all its weight since the Iraq occupation to fight terror and engage in brutal war with the insurgents, former U.S. president Bill Clinton unexpectedly expressed a diverse view other than the one adopted by the administration as its determined policy. The former president stressed the view that the United States should not disconnect itself to fight terror. In an interview with France's *Le Monde* newspaper in August 2005, Clinton insisted, "We cannot isolate ourselves from the world behind walls. We cannot kill all our enemies." Nevertheless, "We need a strategy which will create more partners and fewer terrorists. Americans' destiny is closely tied to that of other people," he continued.[41]

DID GLOBAL TERROR ATTACKS SURGE IN 2006?

According to a May 2007 State Department report, terrorist attacks worldwide shot up more than 25 percent in the previous year, killing 40 percent more people than in 2005. Iran remains the biggest supporter of terrorism, with elements of its government backing groups throughout the Middle East, notably in Iraq, giving material aid and guidance to Shiite insurgent groups that have attacked Sunni residents as well as U.S. and Iraqi forces. In its annual global survey of terrorism, the State Department revealed that 14,338 attacks took place in 2006, mainly in Iraq and Afghanistan. That represented a 28.6 percent increase. These strikes claimed 20,498 lives, 13,340 of them in Iraq—about 5,800, or 40 percent, more than the previous year.[42]

RECRUITMENT OF EUROPE-WIDE
NETWORK FIGHTERS FOR IRAQ

"Europe-Wide Network Enlists Insurgent Fighters for Iraq," the *International Herald Tribune* wrote on its front page on December 2003, after seven months of the U.S.-led occupation of Iraq. The *Tribune* said that the recruitment of insurgents from Europe had two main reasons. The first was for al-Qaeda to recruit young and Islamic terrorists to launch devilish attacks in Europe, and the second was to increase the number of insurgency in Iraq.

European intelligence and law enforcement officials made a series of arrests of al-Qaeda devotees and militants. The al-Qaeda plan became clear. Its strategy was to establish a wide network for the recruitment of Islamic insurgents to join the rebels fighting the American and coalition's troops in Iraq. It is estimated that the al-Qaeda network has successfully recruited hundreds of volunteers to join the Islamic rebels in Iraq from Italy, Germany, France, Spain, Britain, and Sweden.

It was clear from the intelligence investigations that the campaign to recruit young radical Muslims for Iraq had become highly organized and coordinated just after the U.S. invasion of Iraq. The European investigations revealed evidence that Turkey had recently become an important source for recruiting insurgents to join al-Qaeda rebels in Iraq. A series of bombings in 2003 and 2005 in Turkey, linked to al-Qaeda and affiliated groups, killed a large number of people. It is believed that Turkey had become a sanctuary for al-Qaeda insurgency.

It is therefore clear that Iraq has become the crossroads for international terrorism. The insurgents from different countries have joined al-Qaeda leader al-Zarqawi fighting against the U.S.-led troops, Iraqi police force, government officials, and collaborators with the United States in Iraq. It is widely believed that they cross undetected through the desert from neighboring countries, namely Saudi Arabia, Syria, and Iran.[43]

WAS THE WAR IN IRAQ JUSTIFIED?

The Iraqi occupation in its fifth year claimed the lives of more than 3,500 American troops and cost more than $300 billion. A new study reported by CNN in October 2006 indicated, "War has wiped out about 655,000 Iraqis or more than 500 people a day since the U.S.-led invasion. Violence including gunfire and bombs caused the majority of deaths but thousands of people died from worsening health and environmental conditions directly related to the conflict that began in 2003," U.S. and Iraqi public health researchers said. The report added, "Since March 2003, an additional 2.5 percent of Iraq's population has died above what would have occurred without conflict." The survey published online by the British medical journal *The Lancet* gave a far higher number of deaths in Iraq than other organizations.[44]

President Bush slammed the report during a news conference in the White House Rose Garden. "I don't consider it a credible report. Neither does Gen. (George) Casey," he said, referring to the top-ranking U.S. military official in Iraq, "and neither do Iraqi officials." The report further said, comparing the situation in Iraq with other wars, "In the Vietnam War, 3 million civilians died; in the Congo, armed conflict has been responsible for 3.8 million deaths; in East Timor, an estimated 200,000 out of a population of 800,000 died in conflict."[45]

Killing, kidnapping, torture, and insecurity are still going on. After all these years of occupation and a high number of deaths, the war has not been won. The country, as its Iraqi president warned, "is in front of a dangerous precipice": civil war.[46]

The late Senator Edward Kennedy, a former Massachusetts Democrat, severely criticized the Iraqi war and the involvement of U.S. troops in June 2005. In a Senate enquiry, he challenged Rumsfeld, "This war has been consistently and grossly mismanaged and we are now in a seemingly intractable quagmire. Our troops are dying. And there really is no end in sight." Kennedy added, "And the American people, I believe, deserve leadership worthy of the sacrifices that our fighting forces have made, and they deserve the real facts. And I regret to say that I don't believe that you have provided either."[47]

President Musharraf of Pakistan, a staunch ally of the United States in its war against terror, reiterated that the world has become less safe in the wake of the invasion. The Pakistani ex-president did not refer to the invasion as a mistake. He said that the war has ended up bringing more trouble to the world and it made the world a more dangerous place. In his new book, *In the Line of Fire*, Musharraf who often declares himself as being in complete agreement with President George W. Bush on the war on terror and other issues—that he never was in support of the 2003 U.S. invasion of Iraq.[48]

When asked about Iraq, the prime minister of Spain, José Zapatero, replied, "We should ask ourselves one question: were things any better in Iraq after one-and-half years of occupation? The answer was no. There was a spiral of violence and death." He continued, "We have two options: close our eyes or face that reality. Now, Iraq needs to recover its freedom, stability, and sovereignty as soon as possible." Zapatero withdrew his troops as soon as he took office in the new government. It is evident that the increasing number of casualties among the Spanish troops and the waves of kidnapping and beheading foreigners in Iraq hastened the decision made by the prime minister. This was in addition to the ten bombs exploded in trains and stations in Madrid that bore the marks of Osama bin Laden's network and his Islamic extremists.[49]

Al-Qaeda afterward claimed responsibility for the train tragedy. It warned that further attacks would be launched if Spain did not withdraw its troops from Iraq. President George W. Bush reacted promptly to the Spanish troop withdrawal. He warned Madrid against taking further actions that could give false comfort to terrorists.[50]

After three and a half years of Iraq occupation, Prime Minister Junichiro Koizumi of Japan announced the withdrawal of Japanese ground troops from southern Iraq. In a nationally televised news conference, Koizumi said the troops had accomplished their noncombat mission. In the mean-while, he pledged to continue aiding Iraqi reconstruction. Japan has about six hundred troops in the city of Samawah in southern Iraq. They helped with projects in rebuilding the infrastructure of the area. Koizumi defended the deployment by saying, "I believe we made the right deci-sion." In April 2004, three Japanese aid workers were kidnapped and threatened with death. All three were later released unharmed.[51]

Many American taxpayers also wondered whether the cost of the war is justified. This took place when the U.S. Senate's Military Forces Commit-tee recommended in May 2005 the allocation of an additional $50 billion for the American army in Iraq. This move would have increased the cost of the war to $250 billion. Many military experts forecasted this figure to rise further to $500 billion by year 2010. This huge cost of the Iraq war made Nasim el-Shawa in the *Egyptian Mail* newspaper published in Cairo wonder if "there is a surplus of the American funds, why is it not being spent on assisting poor nations instead of on acts of murder and sabotage, for enhancing people's misery." He called on the Americans to build their relations with the world for the welfare of humanity instead of warfare.[52]

According to a CNN/*USA Today* Gallup poll released in June 2005, the Americans showed dissatisfaction with the Iraq war. Nearly six in ten Americans oppose the war in Iraq and a growing number of them were dissatisfied with the war on terrorism. In an earlier Gallup poll that asked "All in all, do you think it was worth going to war in Iraq, or not?" 56 percent said it was not worth it and 42 percent said it was. Accordingly, a bipartisan congressional committee introduced a resolution that called for President Bush to submit a plan by year's end for an American pullout by the end of 2006. The president responded that announcing any sched-ule for a withdrawal would allow insurgents to wait out U.S. troops.

Time magazine on September 18, 2005, after almost two and a half years of Iraq war, said, "Despite their gloom, every one of the offices favors continuing—indeed, augmenting—the war effort. If the U.S. leaves, they say, the chaos in central Iraq could threaten the stability of the entire Middle East. And al-Qaeda operatives like al-Zarqawi could have a relatively safe base of operations in the Sunni triangle."[53]

Consequently, former U.S. Secretary of State Madeleine Albright warned of an Iraqi disaster. In May 2006, after three years of the U.S. occupation of Iraq, Albright astonished the world and especially the Arab states. She warned that the invasion of Iraq might end up as one of the worst disasters in American foreign policy. In an interview with the *New York Times*, Albright said she did not think Saddam Hussein had been an imminent threat to the United States. She explained what troubled her was that democracy is getting a bad name. This is because it is identified with imposition and occupation. "I'm for democracy, but imposing democracy is an oxymoron. People have to choose democracy and it has to come up from below," she said.[54]

Meanwhile, Kofi Annan, the UN Secretary-General, angered Washington after a fresh two-week tour in the Arab region in September 2006, three and a half years after the U.S.-led occupation. He told a news conference most of the Arab leaders he had spoken to felt the invasion of Iraq and its aftermath had been a "real disaster for them." He continued, "They believe it has destabilized the region." He further said leaders in the region were split over whether the U.S.-led force should now pull out or stay. Annan also explained the other opinion by saying, "Iran believes the presence of the U.S. is a problem and that the U.S. should leave. And if the U.S. were to decide to leave, they would help them leave." In the past, Annan had angered the U.S. administration by calling the Iraq invasion "illegal" because it was launched without the approval of the UN Security Council, and by saying that the war had "not left the world a safer place."[55]

After a short visit to Baghdad in January 2007, Hillary Clinton, a Democratic presidential contender, was pessimistic about the U.S. occupation and its strategy in Iraq. "The president's Iraq policy has been marred by incompetence and arrogance as his administration has refused to recognize the military and political reality on the ground," she said.[56]

French Prime Minister Dominique de Villepin, who opposed the 2003 invasion of Iraq, urged the United States and other foreign nations to withdraw from Iraq in 2008. He said the war in Iraq had "shattered" America's image abroad. He added, "The Iraqi conflict . . . is sapping the power of the United States to peacefully influence other players in the troubled Middle East . . . It undermined the image of the West as a whole. The war with Iraq marked a turning point. It shattered America's image."[57]

IS THE IRAQI WAR MORE SERIOUS THAN VIETNAM?

Madeleine Albright, the Secretary of State under Bill Clinton, stated, after more than three years of the U.S.-led occupation, "I hope I am wrong, but I am afraid that Iraq is going to turn out the greatest disaster in the U.S. foreign policy—worse than Vietnam."[58] The disaster was predicted after one year of the occupation and the increased pressure of insurgents. It was Ted Galen Carpenter of Cato Institute who compared Iraq to Vietnam. He asked whether the United States in Iraq was facing the rapidly expanding insurgency as Americans had encountered in Vietnam.

Ted Carpenter, however, emphasized that the U.S. military administration leaders have been facing at present a choice like the one confronted by Lyndon Johnson's administration. The first was a bold choice to withdraw

American forces from Vietnam, which would have led to damaging Washington's world credibility. The second choice was to intensify the war by sending more troops. In Iraq, Carpenter said, the U.S. military administration opted for more troops to achieve victory over the insurgents and militias.[59]

Republican Senator Chuck Hagel of Nebraska in August 2005 asserted on CNN News that the United States was getting more and more bogged down in Iraq. The longer U.S. forces remained in Iraq, he said, the more it began to resemble the Vietnam War. "The casualties we're taking, the billion dollars a week we're putting in there, the kind of commitment we've got— we're not going to be able to sustain it . . . Iraq and Vietnam still have more differences than similarities, but there is a parallel emerging."[60]

Economically, however, the Iraq war is costing the citizens of the United States far more than the Vietnam War did. A report titled "The Iraq Quagmire," issued by the Institute for Policy Studies and Foreign Policy in Focus in the United States was quoted by Al Jazeera's Web site. The Institute in September 2005 said both liberal and antiwar organizations put the cost of current operations in Iraq at about $5.6 billion per month. At present, it is estimated that the U.S. war in Iraq costs more per month than the average monthly cost of military operations in Vietnam. In 2005, Congress approved additional funds totaling $45.3 billion for spending in Iraq.[61]

After heated rhetoric criticizing President Bush's policy in Iraq, the Senate's top Democrat in February 2007 moved into a new area of criticism by declaring "the Iraq war a worse blunder than Vietnam." CNN quoted Senator Harry Reid (D-Nevada) saying, "This war is a serious situation. It involves the worst foreign policy mistake in the history of this country. We find ourselves in a very deep hole and we need to find a way to dig out of it."[62]

President Bush strongly resists the insinuation that war in Iraq is similar, largely, to the Vietnam War. Young antiwar protests have indicated that the president's rhetoric reverberated those of President Johnson in 1967, a critical year for the United States in Vietnam. They quote what Johnson said in 1967 despite the fact that the United States was losing the war. Johnson said America was committed to the defense of South Vietnam "until an honorable peace can be negotiated." President Bush, after fourteen Marines died in an attack by terrorists, said, "We will stay the course; we will complete the job in Iraq. And the job is this: We'll help the Iraqis develop a democracy."[63]

With the Iraqi Shiite militias and Sunni insurgents becoming out of control, the danger of dividing Iraq, and the Iraqi war mentioned as even more serious than Vietnam, we now come to the capture of Saddam Hussein and his trial.

CHAPTER 4

COALITION FORCES CAPTURED SADDAM HUSSEIN

INTERNATIONAL MEDIA STATIONS ALL OVER THE WORLD HAVE GIVEN full coverage the capture of Saddam Hussein by coalition forces. People were overwhelmed in various parts of the globe by the news. Paul Bremer, U.S. head of the Coalition Provisional Authority, proudly announced in a triumphant voice on a Sunday morning on December 13, 2003, in Baghdad: "The tyrant is a prisoner."[1] The audience deeply responded with cheers, joy, and elation. In celebration of the jubilant occasion, Iraqis immediately took to the Baghdad streets dancing, distributing candy and sweets, and firing rifles into the air.

By contrast, in Tikrit, Saddam's ancestral hometown in north Iraq and a base of his loyal, members of his tribe were deeply affected. The streets were quiet with no apparent signs of celebration or joy. Shops shut down, schools closed, and people remained at home.

The few, mostly from the Ba'ath political party, who had profited from his regime grieved the most. Those who suffered under his thirty-five-year iron-fisted regime welcomed the news of his capture and demanded a speedy trial.

Saddam was number one on the list of the coalition's fifty-five most wanted Iraqi former leaders. He had a $25 million bounty on his head. His deceptive disappearance had been a political blow and a source of irritation for the U.S. administration. The head of the coalition troops in Iraq victoriously announced in a press conference, "Today is a great day for the Iraqi people and the coalition."[2] He confirmed that Saddam, when captured, was uninjured, talkative, and cooperative. Thin, muddy, and hiding in the cellar of a mud hut, he willingly identified himself to interpreters.

Coalition video showed the "spider hole" six to eight feet underground where Saddam was hiding. He had graying hair and a long beard and underwent a thorough medical examination after his capture. After the video many Iraqi journalists and media stood up and shouted "death to Saddam." But this is not the whole story.

It was hard for Arabs to accept that Saddam Hussein, the deposed Iraqi dictator, would surrender without any display of resistance to the American troops surrounding the village house where he was hiding. Unlike his two sons who died fighting the allied forces that surrounded their residence, Saddam did not even fire a shot to defend himself and stand up for his honor.

Many Arabs regretted that Saddam opted not to die as a proud Arab would. Rather, he chose to stay alive as a humiliated and defeated prisoner of war under U.S. forces and allied protection.

Saddam was one of the most notorious rulers in modern Arab history. announced in a press conference, "Today is a great day to his country and the region. However, the arrest was a major triumph for the United States after seven months of increasingly violent attacks on U.S. forces and their allies following Saddam's ousting on April 9, 2003. His two sons, Uday and Qusay, were also killed by the allied troops. Their informer, an Iraqi family friend to Saddam, was paid $30 million and given refuge in the United States.[3]

IRAQIS TAKE LEGAL CUSTODY OF SADDAM

After Saddam's capture, President Bush announced that there would be a public trial and that Iraqis needed to be involved in bringing him to justice.

After some negotiation, Iraqi authorities took legal custody from the United States of Saddam Hussein and eleven high-profile members of his former regime. An Iraqi Special Tribunal was set up to try the ousted officials. "The detainees will face trial on charges of crimes against humanity, genocide and war crimes at the Iraqi Special Tribunal," the interim Iraqi Prime Minister Ayad Allawi promised the Iraqi people. "The accused will appear in front of the Iraqi court, and they will be afforded rights that were denied by the former regime. They will have access to legal counsel, and they will have the right to appoint the counsel."[4] As the interim government promised a fair trial to the deposed president of Iraq, Iraqi guerillas threatened to slay Saddam's lawyers. A group belonging to the Islamic Jihad warned all lawyers who would defend Saddam that the group "will sever their necks before arriving to court," according to a statement by a gunman on tape.[5]

The United Nations (UN) Secretary-General expressed hope that Saddam Hussein's capture would speed up the establishment of a transitional government in Iraq. The UN could not support bringing the former dictator before a tribunal that might sentence him to death. The Secretary-General added that any trial for Saddam must conform to international standards. He made clear the UN's longstanding opposition to the death penalty in any UN-sanctioned tribunal. The Iraqi government, however, disregarded the UN standard and insisted on hanging him after the court death sentence.

In a brief televised program, President Bush said he had a message for the Iraqi people: "You will not have to fear the rule of Saddam Hussein ever again. All Iraqis who take the side of freedom have taken the winning side." He continued, "Now the former dictator of Iraq will face the justice he denied to millions."[6]

EXPULSION OF SADDAM FROM COURT

Saddam Hussein was expelled from the court three consecutive times during hearings of his genocide trial in Kurdistan. Saddam and six of his former associates were accused of genocide, war crimes, and crimes against humanity during the Anfal campaign. Prosecutors said that 182,000 Kurds were killed when their villages in northern Iraq were bombed, burned, and destroyed. The accused Saddam and his codefendants pleaded innocent, claiming that the campaign was a counterinsurgency operation, code named Operation Anfal, in the late 1980s, against rebellious Kurds. Chaos in the courtroom took place following the removal of the chief judge, al-Amiri, for saying Saddam was "not a dictator."[7]

The government said that the chief judge had lost his "neutrality" after commenting in the court that the ousted leader was not a dictator. This comment angered and infuriated Saddam's opponents and today's rulers of Iraq. A Kurdish witness called Saddam a dictator after he recounted his meeting with the deposed Iraqi president to ask about the whereabouts of family members who were killed in the Anfal military campaign of 1987–1988. When questioning the Kurdish witness, Hussein said, "I wonder why this man wanted to meet with me, if I am a dictator?" Al-Amiri responded, "You were not a dictator. People around you made you look like a dictator." "Thank you," Hussein responded, bowing his head in respect.[8]

The next day, Iraq's chief prosecutor demanded al-Amiri step down, accusing him of bias toward the deposed leader and his codefendants. International legal rights groups gave a warning to the government that the sacking of the former chief judge could hurt the historic trial's credibility.

A new chief judge, Mohamed al-Ureybi, was appointed. The new judge opened the hearing with a lecture to Saddam to comply with court orders while answering questions. Although Saddam was also expelled from the courtroom during the last two hearings, it was the first time that the genocide trial proceeded without any of the defendants in court. A few days after the judge expelled Saddam from court in each of the three sessions, a brother-in-law of the judge was shot dead by gunmen while driving in western Baghdad. The criminal case was under investigation to uncover whether the crime was linked to Ba'ath Saddam loyalists for revenge.

In the following hearings, the chief judge threw Saddam Hussein and another defendant out of court after Saddam shouted during his trial. The chief judge cut off the microphone as Saddam attempted to speak. The trial scheduled was postponed for another hearing. Meanwhile, Saddam was waiting for a verdict from a first trial, for crimes against humanity in the killing of some 148 Shia men from the town of Dujail in the 1980s.[9]

Saddam Hussein's genocide trial resumed in October 2006. international legal rights groups had said the dismissal of Judge Abdullah al-Amiri, removed by the government, could hurt the trial's credibility. Saddam's lawyers boycotted the trial in protest at the appointment of a new chief judge.

DID SADDAM DESERVE A DEATH SENTENCE?

Iraqi interim president Talabani answered the question on the eve of his visit to meet President Bush: "Saddam deserves a death sentence 20 times a day because he tried to assassinate me 20 times," he said, recalling his days as a Kurdish rebel fighter. Talabani's comment appeared to be part of an orchestrated move by the Iraqi government to prepare Iraqis for Saddam's execution, expected to be carried out by hanging. This was despite the UN's long-standing opposition to the death penalty in any UN-sanctioned tribunal.[10]

The Iraqi government confirmed Saddam Hussein's trial date set for October 19, 2005. They confirmed that Saddam and several aides would go on trial on charges of killing dozens of Shia villagers at Dujail in 1982. Meanwhile, Saddam's family announced that a new international team of lawyers was recruited to defend Saddam against war crimes charges. The family legal adviser announced that Saddam's family chose a legal defense team that included high caliber lawyers from the United States, Europe, Asia, and the Arab states. They were chosen on the basis of competence and merit.[11]

Saddam's defense lawyers were under constant threat. They were in danger of kidnapping, abduction, or assassination. Just a day after the opening of the formal trial, over Saddam's massacre of Shiites, Saadoun Janabi, the Iraqi lawyer for a codefendant of Saddam Hussein, was kidnapped. A day later, he was murdered. The government condemned the killing. A few months later, the second defense lawyer, Adel al-Zubeidi, was kidnapped and killed in ambush by three masked gunmen in a speeding car in a largely Sunni Arab neighborhood of western Baghdad. The third of Saddam's lawyers was also shot to death. He was in his fifties and had six children. He was abducted from his home in Baghdad. His body was found on a street near a Shiite slum of Sadr City.[12]

Saddam Hussein repeatedly challenged the authority of the court and the Iraqi government. Saddam and seven of his associates were charged with giving orders for killing and torturing more than 140 Iraqis in Dujail in 1982. The killing took place following an attempt to assassinate Hussein when he was visiting the town. With a defiant look at the court, Saddam said, "I do not recognize the body that has authorized you and I don't recognize this aggression. I do not respond to this so-called court, with all due respect." When the judge identified him as the former president he hurriedly said, "I'm the president of the republic of Iraq. I did not say deposed." Hussein and the seven other defendants answered "innocent" when the presiding judge asked for their pleas.[13]

The prosecution of Hussein began with the Dujail case in the Sunni-Shiite town, about fifty miles north of Baghdad. Hussein and the seven other defendants were charged with ordering the killings and torture in Dujail after a Shiite group made an assassination attempt. Other charges against Saddam involved the gassing to death of thousands of Kurds in 1988 in Halabja and the slaughter of thousands of Shiites during their uprising in 1991, after the U.S.-led Persian Gulf War. The court is thought to have chosen to prosecute the Dujail case first because it was not as complex as the other charges brought against the former dictator.

Saddam, it appeared, was not content with the court. He called for a fair trial. In a letter to the court, he appealed, "I strongly refuse to be represented by lawyers appointed by the court, because they are nothing but actors ready to perform their roles in a U.S.-directed and Zionist-Iranian inspired play."[14]

During Saddam's twenty-three-year rule, human rights organizations estimated that more than three hundred thousand people, mainly Kurds and Shiite Muslims, were killed and buried in mass graves. In the Shiite holy city of Karbala, municipal workers found remains believed to be from a mass grave dating to 1991, when Saddam Hussein's regime put down a Shiite uprising in the south. At his first trial, the court accused Saddam and his codefendants of executing Shia villagers from the town of Dujail. In the court, the defense maintained that the defendants were applying a valid law at the time of the execution, and that the executed were Iraqi citizens plotting with Iran, at war with Iraq at the time, against their own country and leader's life.

However, during the trial, approximately one hundred female relatives of those who were ordered to be killed in the village of Dujail marched in

Najaf, the holy Shiite city south of Baghdad, to demand that ex-president
Saddam Hussein be put to death.

What surprised the Iraqi and Arab people, if not the Arab governments, was that the Iraq government in July 2006 unveiled a list of the
country's most wanted fugitives, including Saddam's daughter, Raghad
Saddam Hussein, and Hussein's wife, Sajidah Khairallah. The wife and
daughter were numbers 16 and 17, respectively, on the list. The accusation against Saddam's daughter was that she had taken a leading role in
organizing her father's legal defense in his trial in Baghdad for crimes
against humanity. She and her mother were believed to provide funds
for insurgents. They have been residing in neighboring Jordan since the
ousting of Saddam.

Further down the list, at number 30, was the man who Iraqi and U.S.
officials have said was the new leader of al-Qaeda in Iraq. He was identified as Abu Hamza al-Muhajir, an Egyptian terrorist who also goes by the
name Abu Ayyub al-Masri. The United States posted a $5 million reward
for his capture.[15]

SADDAM HUSSEIN'S SENTENCE TO HANG

The fact is that after being found guilty of crimes against humanity Saddam
Hussein, sixty-nine, was sentenced to death by a Baghdad court on November 4, 2006. Saddam appeared shaken after hearing the verdict. He soon
recovered and shouted, "*Allah Akbar!*" ["God is greatest!"] and "Long live
the nation." The Iraqi High Tribunal found Saddam guilty of ordering the
killing of 178 Shia civilians in the town of Dujail in 1982. Iraqi law stated
that he would be executed by hanging. However, Saddam expressed his
wish to be executed by firing squad. In his last words, Saddam urged Iraqis
to avoid civil war. He sent an open letter to Iraqis through his chief lawyer
in which he predicted "victory" against U.S. occupiers and urged Iraqis to
join forces to drive American troops from Iraq.[16]

Before the verdict was announced by the court, Iraq's government
imposed a curfew in Baghdad, the mixed Sunni-Shia province of Diyala,
and Salahaddin. The province contained Saddam's hometown of Tikrit.
However, despite the curfews, Shias had gathered in Baghdad's Sadr City
district to celebrate what they hoped would be a guilty verdict. "We
hope the sentence matched what this man deserves for what he has done
against the Iraqi people. The Iraqi people will express happiness in the
way they find appropriate," Prime Minister al-Maliki said. He added,
"We call upon the Iraqi people to be calm, to be disciplined and to express
themselves in ways that take into consideration the security challenge and
the need to protect the lives of citizens."[17]

The death sentence given to Saddam Hussein was met by varied responses from different quarters, nationally, regionally, and internationally. Nouri Maliki, prime minister of Iraq, said, "This sentence is not a sentence on one man, but a sentence against all the dark period of his rule."[18] In the opinion of Shiites, the execution of Saddam and his aides was fair and just.

Bushra al-Khalil, Saddam Hussein's defense lawyer, declared, "This is a mockery of justice and a judgment that comes from a sham and illegal court created by the U.S. occupation that cannot ever provide a fair trial."

Zalmay Khalilzad, the U.S. ambassador to Iraq, said, "The judges, prosecutors and defense attorneys in this case all showed courage in the face of intimidation. Their determination to pursue justice is a signal that the rule of law will prevail in Iraq despite the difficult situation that the country now faces."

Margaret Beckett, Britain's foreign minister, said, "I welcome that Saddam Hussein and the other defendants have faced justice and have been held to account for their crimes. Appalling crimes were committed by Saddam Hussein's regime. It is right that those accused of such crimes against the Iraqi people should face Iraqi justice."[19]

There were mixed feelings among the Iraqis after hearing the verdict. Fighting erupted in Baghdad. Clashes broke out between some Sunnis and the Iraqi army after Saddam Hussein was sentenced to death. Heavy firing took place in Adhimiyah, a mainly Sunni district of Baghdad, within half an hour of Saddam Hussein's death sentence. Some Sunnis declared the court a product of the U.S. "occupation forces" and decried the verdict. "By our souls, by our blood we sacrifice for you, Saddam," they shouted. "Saddam, your name shakes America," they roared.[20]

Thousands of Iraqis joined protests inside and outside Iraq, condemning the execution of Saddam Hussein. Iraqis in Sunni areas in the country, many of them armed, protested against the killing of the former president and blamed Shias for carrying it out.

In Samarra, a group of men marched through the town carrying a mock coffin and a photo of Saddam. In Sadr City at Basra, a Shia area of Baghdad, people danced in the streets while others fired guns in the air to celebrate the former leader's death. Kurds also welcomed the hanging. The office of the Kurdish regional president, Massud Barzani, issued a statement saying, "We hope that Saddam Hussein's execution will open a new chapter among Iraqis and the end of using violence against civilians."[21]

The Ba'athists, members of the political Ba'ath Party that ruled Iraq during the Saddam Hussein era, warned, "There will be grave consequences if former Iraqi leader Saddam Hussein is executed." The largely

Sunni-Arab Ba'athists said they would retaliate against members of the Iraqi High Tribunal. The Ba'athists had been operating as part of the Sunni insurgency against the United States and its allies since Hussein's regime fell in 2003. They also issued a warning to Iran, a key supporter of Iraq's Shiite-led government.[22]

World opinion was divided. The Associated Press (AP) on November 6, 2006, reported the range of reactions, "including a European outcry over capital punishment and doubts about the fairness of the tribunal that ordered Saddam to hang—reflected new geopolitical fault lines drawn after America's decision to invade Iraq in 2003 and depose its dictator." The AP continued, "The European Union welcomed the verdict but said Saddam should not be put to death. At the Vatican, Cardinal Renato Martino, Pope Benedict XVI's top prelate for justice issues, called the sentence a throwback to 'eye for an eye' vengeance."[23]

Fearing a spillover of sectarian violence raging in neighboring Iraq and other Arab states after the death sentence of Saddam, some monarchies and heads of Arab nations expressed their wishes not to hang him. Instead, he should be sentenced to a lifetime in prison.

The Vatican hoped for clemency for Saddam. Citing the church's opposition to the death penalty, senior Catholic clerics expressed their hopes that former Iraqi dictator Saddam Hussein would be spared execution.[24]

Under the statute of the Iraqi High Tribunal, a death sentence must be carried out within the following thirty days. Iraq's prime minister told reporters that he turned down a U.S. request to delay Saddam Hussein's hanging because he wanted to show Iraqis that no deal would let the former dictator escape punishment. "These rumors, which were started by Saddam's defense lawyers, created tension among the people, and we felt the necessity of terminating this man who was troublesome in his life and troublesome in his death." Hussein, sixty-nine, was hanged on December 30, 2006.[25]

What brought worldwide criticism of the Iraqi government was that the ousted president was televised being hanged in a Baghdad prison. Recorded on a cell phone camera, a video of Saddam's execution showed scenes of the process of hanging and taunting on the gallows shortly before his death.[26]

The *Egyptian Gazette* quoted a number of international leaders who criticized Saddam's hanging, saying, "It appeared as a sectarian lynching rather than a court-directed punishment after a guard, believed to be a Shiite, taunted the Sunni former president in his final moments." The strongest criticism came from Egyptian President Hosni Mubarak, who even said that the execution was "disgusting and barbaric." President

Bush said he wished Saddam's execution had been conducted "in a more dignified way." The remark was a response to the chaotic scene showing the process of hanging the former president of Iraq.

The Saddam execution video drew harsh criticism from British Deputy Prime Minister John Prescott. He said those who leaked the footage should be condemned. "I think the manner was quite deplorable really. I don't think one can endorse in any way that, whatever your views about capital punishment. Frankly, to get the kind of recorded messages coming out is totally unacceptable and I think whoever is involved and responsible for it should be ashamed of himself."[27]

Iraqi Prime Minister Nouri al-Maliki was unhappy with such criticism. "The Iraqi government could be obliged to review its relations with any state that fails to respect the wish of the Iraqi people," said Maliki. "We consider the execution of the dictator an internal affair that concerns only the Iraqi people," said Maliki, speaking at a ceremony on the eighty-sixth anniversary of the Iraqi army. Maliki also insisted Saddam's hanging was not a political act.[28]

POST SADDAM

After Saddam's execution, the Iraqi prime minister urged Saddam's fellow Ba'athists to reconsider their tactics and join the political process. "I urge followers of the ousted regime to reconsider their stance as the door is still open to anyone who has no innocent blood on his hands, to help in rebuilding an Iraq for all Iraqis," he said. Just after that call, at least thirty people were killed when a bomb exploded in a fish market south of Baghdad. Thus, violence continued after Saddam's death. A few days later Iraq hanged two of Saddam's aides. Barzan Ibrahim al-Tikriti, the former chief judge of the revolutionary court, was hanged at dawn. He was Saddam's half brother. Awad Ahmed al-Bandar, the former chief judge of Saddam's revolutionary court, was hanged at the same time.[29]

Taha Yassin Ramadan, Saddam's vice president, was executed in connection with the killings of 148 Shiites following a 1982 assassination attempt against the former leader in the town of Dujail. He went to the gallows on the eve of the anniversary of the start of the war in Iraq. Ramadan was nearly seventy. He was buried near Saddam as he wished. Ramadan was number 20 on the U.S. most-wanted list issued shortly after the invasion began. He was said to have presided over many court cases carried out by Saddam to eliminate rivals and strengthen his political control. Ramadan was accused of heading a court that executed forty-four officers for plotting to overthrow the regime.[30]

The judge who sentenced Saddam Hussein to death left Iraq and sought political asylum in the United Kingdom. He feared for his life and family in Iraq. Besides sending Saddam to the gallows, the judge, a Kurd, sixty-five, had also sentenced two other top Saddam aides to death in the same trial: Barzan Ibrahim al-Tikriti and Awad Hamed al-Bandar, former heads of Iraq's Revolutionary Court. The two were Saddam's half brother and former intelligence chief. They were found guilty along with Saddam of involvement in the Dujail killings in 1982.[31]

The coming chapter delineates antiwar sentiments in the United States, United Kingdom, Europe, and other countries, and the vast losses in lives and money that made demonstrations and protests break out all over the world.

CHAPTER 5

THE GLOBAL FEELING AGAINST WAR IN IRAQ

ANTIWAR SENTIMENT IN THE UNITED STATES

A SERIES OF DEMONSTRATIONS IN THE UNITED STATES PROTESTING against the war first started in New York with tens of thousands of demonstrators carrying signs and chanting "No More Bush," and "Stop War in Iraq," marching past Madison Square Garden, the site of the Republican National Convention August 29–September 2, 2004. The march was sponsored by United for Peace and Justice. Organizers said that as many as a quarter of a million demonstrators had taken part in the demonstrations.

"We are the majority," the well-known filmmaker Michael Moore told the crowd in one of the demonstrations. He continued, "A majority of this country opposes this war . . . a majority of this country never voted for this administration." Civil rights leader Rev. Jesse Jackson and Moore led the protest march as it began on Seventh Avenue. "We have an obligation to speak out until we can raise our heads above the sands of Iraq and Afghanistan," Jackson said.[1]

Three years after the invasion, the antiwar sentiment continued to worsen. Rallies were held in many cities across the United States. Demonstrators carried banners reading, "Bring the Troops Home Now," "Bush Did Not Say the Truth," "Thousands Died in Iraq." "President Bush needs to admit he made a mistake in the war and bring the troops home," said Paul Rutherford, a Republican who supported President Bush except over the war in Iraq. In the meantime, a number of polls administered in recent months revealed that national support for the Iraq war had been steadily declining in both the United States and the United Kingdom.[2]

Meanwhile, the whole world watched with sympathy as Cindy Sheehan, mother of a U.S. Army soldier killed in Iraq in April 2004, participated in an angry protest outside President Bush's ranch in Crawford, Texas. Sheehan said, "I want to ask the president, 'Why did you kill my son? What did my son die for?'"[3] Sheehan's son, Casey, was killed five days after he arrived in Iraq at age twenty-four.

Later, Sheehan met with the National Security Adviser and Deputy White House Chief of Staff, who came out and talked to her for forty-five minutes. However, the president himself did not meet her. She continued sitting on the road's pavement before the ranch's gate, clearly distressed. Sheehan vowed to remain sitting on the pavement until Bush talked to her about the war in Iraq that claimed the lives of her son and more than 2,250 other American soldiers.[4]

Sheehan began her standoff insisting that she would stay for the entire month that Bush planned to stay in Texas if he would not meet with her. Other activists joined her, including parents who had lost their sons in the Iraqi war. "I sympathize with Mrs. Sheehan," Bush said. "She feels strongly about her position. She has every right in the world to say what she believes. This is America." The president continued, "She expressed her opinion. I disagree with it. I think immediate withdrawal from Iraq would be a mistake and a policy that would weaken the United States." He further emphasized that U.S. troops in Iraq were keeping the country safe by taking the fight to the terrorists and at the same time, Iraq has been progressing toward establishing democracy.[5]

"Pulling the troops out would send a terrible signal to the enemy," he said. As for bringing the troops home, the president said he had heard the voices of those saying "Pull out now." "I have thought about their cry and their sincere desire to reduce the loss of life by pulling our troops out. I just strongly disagree." It is true that the increasing death toll made Iraq, at present, to be the most dangerous nation in the world in which to live or work. Cindy Sheehan became an activist who energized the antiwar movement in protest against war in Iraq. In a Mississippi demonstration, she insisted, "The support for this war has dwindled dramatically. The rest of America is on board with ending this war." A similar question to what Sheehan raised is the question why more than 60,000 Iraqi civilians, 65 journalists, 250 university professors, media persons, support workers, foreign contractors and labors, diplomats, and others were killed in Iraq.[6]

Sheehan believed that the Iraq war was a result of mistakes in the intelligence service. Sheehan traveled to Washington to present her case at the time of the State of the Union Address. At the Capitol, antiwar protester Sheehan in an open letter asserted, "I have lost my son. I have lost my First Amendment rights. I have lost the country that I love. Where did America go?" Sheehan was taken by Capitol police for wearing a t-shirt that said "2,245 DEAD. HOW MANY MORE?" Capitol police charged her with violating the District of Columbia's code against unlawful or disruptive conduct on the Capitol grounds. Later, the Capitol police dropped the charge against the grieving mother.[7]

In marking the third anniversary of the Iraq war, protesters took to the streets. On New York's Fifth Avenue, demonstrators carried signs, including "Resist the War—Don't enlist." At a rally in New York's Times Square marking the third anniversary of the Iraq occupation protesters denounced the war and called for complete, unconditional U.S. military withdrawal. Dustin Langley, the organizer of the march, said, "Public opinion is now overwhelmingly on our side as it became clearer every day that this occupation itself is the source of the violence in Iraq."[8]

Thousands of people gathered in the center of the U.S. capital and marched on the Pentagon protesting on the fourth anniversary of the U.S.-led war in Iraq. The group that organized the vigil, Christian Peace Witness for Iraq, held a service at Washington's National Cathedral. Four thousand people attended the service. Media stations reported that a number of celebrities, lawmakers, and protesters from distant states rallied in the capital. Marching with them was Jane Fonda. Demonstrations have shown that the Iraq war for four years has grown increasingly unpopular.[9]

ANTIWAR SENTIMENT IN THE UNITED KINGDOM

Media footage showing protesters during the visit of President Bush to the United Kingdom was an international embarrassment. In London, the British capital, war protesters gathered in Trafalgar Square expressing their anger against the war in Iraq. The demonstrators raised a big effigy of President Bush just as Saddam Hussein's statue was pulled down when U.S. forces invaded Baghdad on April 9, 2003. Both leaders were very much surprised to see the increasing number of protesters shouting slogans against the war. They both anticipated that the victory over Saddam and the strengthening of the Anglo-American relationship would be greeted positively in the United Kingdom.

Just after two and a half years of Iraq's occupation, thousands of antiwar activists marched through the streets of London requesting the British government carry out immediate withdrawal of British troops from Iraq. The Moslem Association of Britain joined the protest. Protesters from other European countries including France, Italy, and Spain held similar demonstrations.

Despite the intense pressure of demonstrators against the war in Iraq, Bush and Blair vowed to step up the war on terror. In their joint press conference in London, the American president and British prime minister pledged not to retreat from the war against terrorism. They expressed their determination to fight and defeat terrorism wherever it was found.

They further declared their belief that their mission against terrorism was "noble and necessary." The two countries vowed to stand "shoulder to shoulder" in accomplishing freedom and democracy in Iraq.[10]

ANTIWAR SENTIMENT IN EUROPE

President Bush headed for Europe to get international support for the U.S. presence in Iraq. He attended the sixtieth anniversary of the liberation of Rome by Allied forces on June 4, 1944, and the D-Day invasion two days later. This was in addition to calling for more backing for the new interim Iraqi government. He mentioned to the heads of state that more than thirty-five countries had contributed money and expertise to help rebuild Iraq's infrastructure.[11]

As President Bush began a thirty-six-hour tour of Italy, he met in the Vatican with Pope John Paul II, who remarked, "It is the evident desire of everyone that this situation now be normalized as quickly as possible with the active participation of the international community and, in particular, the United Nations organization, in order to ensure a speedy return of Iraq's sovereignty, in conditions of security for all its people."[12]

Prime Minister Berlusconi expressed his worry about the possible violence and demonstrations against the war in Iraq during the president's visit to Rome. The Italian leader called upon his fellow citizens to remember the "true bond" between Americans and Italians cemented by their liberation from Nazism and fascism during World War II. Despite his call and warm appeal to his people, anti-Bush posters and fliers spread around the city. While most of the demonstrators urged peaceful protests, others called for increased radical activity. The demonstrators accused Berlusconi of supporting the United States and committing troops to the conflict despite the opposition of a majority of Italians. Again, in defiance of the prime minister's call, Italian antiwar demonstrators marched in central Rome to protest against two issues: one was Bush's presence in Italy, and the second was Italy's participation in the Iraq war. Police estimated the number of demonstrators at half a million.[13]

ANTIWAR SENTIMENT IN OTHER COUNTRIES

Even in Turkey, the historical ally of the United States, forty thousand demonstrators protested against President Bush's visit to attend the NATO summit in June 2004. The United States is rather unpopular in Turkey as the majority of the population is Muslim, opposing the Iraqi war. The protest attracted more than one thousand foreign protesters from Greece, Britain, the Netherlands, Portugal, and Syria. This was the first in a series of protests across Europe against the U.S. Iraq invasion. Notwithstanding, President Bush told Prime Minister Tayyip Erfogan, "I appreciate very much the example your country has set on how to be a Muslim country, at the same time a country which embraces democracy and rule of law and freedom."[14]

Protests also took place in Chile. Protesters in Santiago showered police with stones as they opposed the visit by President Bush for a weekend Pacific Rim summit meeting in November 2004. The protesters said they opposed, among other things, the war in Iraq and neoliberal capitalist policies.[15] Anger at President Bush swept through many parts of India during his visit in 2005. In clashes with the police, three people were killed, and eighteen were injured. During the visit, mostly Muslim and Marxist groups held demonstrations in various Indian cities. Tens of thousands of people demonstrated during Bush's three-day visit. Muslim worshipers emerged from Friday prayers in many parts of India chanting anti-American slogans, including claims that the U.S. occupation of Iraq has only benefited American business interests.[16]

Two days ahead of President Bush's visit to Pakistan, a U.S. diplomat and his driver were among four people killed in an apparent suicide attack outside the U.S. Consulate in Karachi. Moreover, a large number of people were wounded in two explosions in a Marriott hotel parking lot next to the U.S. Consulate. Bush announced in a news conference in New Delhi that the death of the U.S. Foreign Service officer and other casualties would not deter plans for his visit.

Bush added that the bombing showed that the war on terrorism should continue. It is apparent that al-Qaeda and many political militant groups operating throughout Pakistan and the disputed region of Kashmir had not welcomed the visit. In the visit, Bush and Pakistani President Pervez Musharraf renewed their alliance in their war on terror. The two leaders emphasized in Karachi, "We will fight this war and we will win this war together." The visit served as a reminder that al-Qaeda's leader, Osama bin Laden, remained in the Pakistan-Afghanistan mountains for five years after the terrorist attacks of 9/11.[17]

With the coalition's insistence that the war must go on despite global antiwar sentiments, we now clarify the positions of the UN and the EU and how severe disagreement about the legality of the war arose between the UN and the United States.

CHAPTER 6

THE POSITIONS OF THE UN AND EU TOWARD WAR IN IRAQ

THE STANDING POSITION OF THE UN TOWARD WAR IN IRAQ

THE STANDING POSITION OF THE UNITED NATIONS (UN) TOWARD war in Iraq was clearly stated by its Secretary-General, Kofi Annan: "If the United States and others were to go outside U.N. Security Council and take unilateral action they would not be in conformity with the Charter." The Charter allows nations to take military action only with Security Council approval. The United States opted for taking military action against a UN member state without the council's approval.[1]

Allies of the United States, mainly Britain and Australia, rejected the claim by the UN Secretary-General that the war in Iraq was "illegal." The U.S. State Department hurriedly stated that the war in Iraq was legal and that that view was shared by their coalition partners.[2]

A few months after the fall of Baghdad, chaos prevailed in Iraq. The American-led troops, Iraqi police force, foreigners, and indigenous workers had suffered almost daily casualties from insurgents and Iraqi Islamic militias. The United States resorted to the Security Council for assistance. The UN had made it clear in the Security Council that its involvement in Iraq could not be maintained without ending the military occupation that was illegal from the point of view of the international organization.

The debate focused on the future role of the UN in Iraq in the restoration of the sovereignty of the country through constitutional arrangements. The United States repeatedly demanded that the multinational force should be under U.S. command. This condition was the basis of disagreement on the Security Council mandate. In addition, the United States requested that the UN should share the huge financial and security burden of rebuilding postwar Iraq. France and Germany demanded a quick surrender of U.S. authority in Iraq to the UN. This was in addition to setting a date for a transitional period to install democracy. The U.S.

delegation in the UN, however, criticized any plans to rush the transfer of power, saying it must come in "an orderly process."[3] As a result, the problem was not resolved and disagreement continued between the Security Council and the United States.

The future role of the UN in Iraq was thus unsettled at that time by the representatives of the five veto-wielding council members: Britain, China, France, Russia, and the United States. They met in Geneva to settle their disagreements. Still there were differences of opinion. They were unable to agree on the specifics of a timetable for self-rule, or on a date of a UN future role in the country. Major problems regarding the reconstruction of postwar Iraq, the writing of the new constitution, the election date for the new parliament, and the date of fully sovereign Iraqi government have all widened the split between the United States and the UN. Many nations including the Islamic ones remained opposed to continued U.S. occupation of Iraq.[4]

In May 2004, one year after the of Iraq invasion, the United States and Britain presented a draft UN resolution that called for a full transfer of sovereignty to Iraq and an initial one-year mandate for the U.S.-led multinational military force. This resolution was to be subject to the consent of the Iraqi transitional government. The United States agreed to designate the responsibility to a special UN envoy, Lakhdar Brahimi, to name Iraqi leaders for the interim government.

The draft resolution endorsed a plan for direct democratic elections by the Iraqi people to be held on December 31, 2004, if possible, and no later than January 31, 2005. The plan continued, "Transitional National Authority Assembly which will, inter alia, have responsibility for drafting a permanent constitution for Iraq under which democratic elections to a national government will be held." The text also called for lifting the arms embargo against Iraq.[5]

Consequently, in June 2004, the UN Security Council voted unanimously to approve the resolution that stipulated to endorse "first, the 30 June, 2004 to transfer of sovereignty in Iraq, and secondly to give authorization for a U.S.-led multinational force." The American-British draft resolution submitted to the council came, in fact, after weeks of intense negotiation, with many key diplomats seeking a better explanation of the multinational force's role after the June 30 handover. The compromised resolution indicated that "The U.S.-led multinational force will serve at the request of the incoming interim government of Iraq, and that the force can be requested to leave at any time." The resolution also said "the force will be able to take all necessary measures to contribute to maintenance of security and stability in Iraq and gives a 12-month deadline for the force to be reviewed." Meanwhile, the approved resolution asked member states to contribute to the force.[6]

Annan told reporters that he believed it was a genuine expression of the will of the international community, led by the Security Council, to come together again after the previous years' divisions and to help the Iraqi people take charge of their own political destiny under a sovereign government. The UN envoy Lakhdar Brahimi informed the council that Iraq would need the world's assistance for some time to come.[7]

Meanwhile, the interim Iraqi minister of foreign affairs, Hoshyar Zebari, said before the Council on Foreign Relations in New York that the significance of the resolution was to erase the concept of occupation, the cause of many Iraqi difficulties. He further said that the resolution would enhance the Iraqi interim government's legitimacy.[8]

On March 1, 2004, the front page of the *Washington Post* disclosed that the Iraqi political leaders had agreed on the terms of an interim constitution. The constitution stroked a compromise on the two most problematic issues of Kurdish autonomy and Islam's role in the government.

The U.S.-appointed Governing Council of twenty-five Iraqi members reached consensus on the interim constitution, mediated by Paul Bremer, the American administrator. A senior member of the council confirmed, "It's a historic document. It has the consensus of all 25 Iraqi members." The chairperson confirmed that every single article, and each subparagraph, had the agreement of all members. He further assured, "We drafted it in the best tradition of democracies. We are an aspiring democracy. We all compromised." The purpose of the document was to provide a legal framework for Iraq until elections were held on October 15, 2005, and a permanent constitution drafted and approved by an elected government.[9]

After intensive negotiation, the Iraq Council agreed to request UN assistance in forming an interim government to rule the country. The appeal was delayed for two main reasons. First, the Shiite members objected to the involvement of the UN in formulating an interim administration. Second, they had taken a stand against the participation of the United Nations' chief envoy to Iraq, Lakhdar Brahimi. Shiite leaders had also expressed concern that Brahimi might recommend an interim government that would increase influence of Sunnis in the Governing Council at the expense of Shiites, considering Brahimi was a Sunni, former secretary of foreign affairs of Algerian nationality.[10]

Eventually, in a written message to the UN Secretary-General, the country's top Shiite cleric, grand Ayatollah Ali Sistani, Iraq's most influential Shiite religious leader, formally assured the United Nations that he wished the organization to help guide Iraq through its transition to self-rule. It was then that Annan officially announced that the Iraqi Council asked the United Nations to provide advice to Iraq in the field of elections and the formation of a transitional government. The term of reference of the UN mission headed by Brahimi approved. Its main aim was to resolve disagreements among Iraqis over the formation of a transitional government. Iraqi members and U.S. officials agreed to the UN strategy, which was considered a breakthrough in the political stalemate of transference of power to Iraqis.[11]

As agreed by the Security Council Resolution 1637, the extension of the presence of the U.S.-led forces in Iraq should be approved annually by the council. Therefore, Hoshyar Zebari, minister of Iraq's foreign affairs, requested in October 2006 an extension, expiring on December 3, 2006. The minister's request said, "The Iraqi government is willing to take more security responsibilities from these forces to do its part." The minister, on behalf of the Iraqi government, should submit a yearly request to the Security Council to continue the presence of the U.S.-led troops in his country.[12]

Abdul Aziz al-Hakim, a powerful Shiite leader, denounced UN Secretary-General Kofi Annan's call for an international conference on Iraq to prevent a fast-approaching all-out civil war. Al-Hakim, who was holding talks with President Bush in December 2006, insisted that holding an international conference was "illegal." Al-Hakim characterized the situation in Iraq as a "political crisis" and not a "civil war." What Annan had said was "An international conference might arrest the deteriorating situation, and unless something is done drastically and urgently . . . we could be there [at civil war], and in fact we are almost there."[13] Al-Hakim replied that it was up to the people in Iraq, not a UN-spearheaded international conference, to handle Iraq's problems. "Iraqi religious figures should have a role in the crisis and should issue a *fatwa* [religious order] to stop the killing and violence in Iraq . . . We are a democratic bloc, and there are always different points of view, but we all aim to serve this country."[14]

President Jalal Talabani of Iraq rejected Kofi Annan's suggestion to have an international conference to reach a solution to Iraq's increasing sectarian war. In fact, the call of the UN Secretary included all of Iraq's major political groups and representatives from around the region. Talabani in a written statement said, "We have an ongoing political process and a Council of Representatives that is the best in the region . . . we became an independent sovereign state and we decide the issues of the country."[15]

Thus, Talabani rejected the UN call for an Iraq International Conference. The proposed conference was recommended not only by Annan, but also encouraged by a growing number of U.S. policy makers who suggested that Washington and Baghdad should hold a conference that would bring together all the countries in the region that have interests in trying to reestablish peace and stability in Iraq.[16]

Ban Ki-moon, the UN Secretary-General who took office in January 2007, made his first visit to Iraq in March the same year to discuss a five-year reconstruction plan for the country. He told reporters that he appealed for support for the International Compact, a plan outlining targets for Iraq over the next five years, including annual economic goals. Maliki, the prime minister, considered the visit of the UN Secretary-General a positive message.

While Ki-moon spoke to the reporters during a joint news conference with the prime minister, an explosion rocked in Baghdad's secure Green Zone when a suspected rocket landed outside the office of Nouri al-Maliki. Media channels recorded and showed the explosion that took place while the UN Secretary-General and the Iraqi prime minister were in conference.[17]

THE POSITION OF THE EU TOWARD WAR IN IRAQ

The UN involvement in transferring the political power from the U.S. administration to Iraqis also reconciled the political gap concerning the position of the EU toward war in Iraq.

The two world powers, the EU and the United States, agreed to work more cooperatively on the major issues concerning the future of Iraq and European defense cooperation. The softened position of the U.S. side was motivated in part by two main objectives: first, the desire of the United States for NATO countries to contribute more troops to Iraq, and second, the desire to provide financial aid to Iraq's reconstruction. The position was clear in the negotiation between the two powers. NATO members emphasized the fact that the rupture within the UN and United States because of the Iraqi war had to be restored for NATO to assist Iraq in its deteriorating situation. In fact, the United States called to NATO foreign ministers to attend meetings, mainly to consider expanding NATO's role militarily and financially in Iraq. This was, no doubt, a clear admission that the United States intended to internationalize its position in Iraq.

President Bush appealed to the world leaders who attended the June 2004 G8 summit, which was held in Georgia in the United States, for stronger NATO commitment in Iraq in order to reinforce the U.S. demand for NATO involvement. French President Jacques Chirac met the proposal with reservations. He reacted by saying, "I don't believe it is NATO's vocation to intervene in Iraq and, moreover, I don't have the feeling it would be opportune or even necessarily understood."[18]

Despite such differences in opinion between the United States and Europe concerning the legitimacy of war in Iraq, the NATO leaders at a summit in Istanbul half a year later agreed to offer training to the security forces of Iraq's new interim government on the day it was sworn. A U.S. administration official confirmed that the international community, once again, was demonstrating its support and commitment to the new Iraqi government by providing training of security forces through the NATO alliance. A statement adopted in the opening session of the two-day summit confirming in Istanbul that they were united in their support for the Iraqi people and offered full cooperation to the new sovereign interim government as it aimed to strengthen internal security and peace.[19]

Chapter 7 of this book relates examples of terrible crimes against Iraqi citizens, namely abuse and torture of prisoners at Abu Ghraib prison, and the repeated killings of Iraqi women and children "by mistake."

WORLD AND ISLAMIC CONDEMNATION OF THE ABU GHRAIB DETENTION AND ABUSE OF POWER IN IRAQ

THE ISLAMIC WORLD WAS DEEPLY APPALLED AT THE ABUSE committed by U.S. troops in Iraq. The Arabs were profoundly outraged with the news about the dehumanization of Iraqi prisoners by U.S. forces. An article published in May 2004 by the *New Yorker* magazine was the first to report that an American general found evidence of "sadistic, blatant, and wanton criminal abuse of Iraqis held at the prison west of Baghdad that was infamous under Saddam Hussein's reign."[1]

Seymour Hersh, the author of this article, wrote, "The mistreatment of prisoners was done to break down somebody before interrogation at the direction of U.S. intelligence. One Iraqi was killed during an interrogation." He reiterated that the intelligence community, the military, the Central Intelligence Agency (CIA), and private contractors were involved.[2] Photographs broadcast on the CBS program *60 Minutes II* in May 2004 showed Iraqis apparently stripped, hooded, and tormented by their American captors at Abu Ghraib prison.[3] The images triggered the fury and indignation of the Iraqi people and Muslims around the world. President Bush hurriedly condemned the mistreatment of Iraqi prisoners shown in the pictures. Other photographs showed prisoners in British custody being abused. This also drew condemnation from Prime Minister Tony Blair and Michael Jackson, the British chief of staff. Meanwhile, a spokesperson for Amnesty International reported that the human rights organization had uncovered evidence of widespread torture by coalition troops in the Abu Ghraib prison.[4]

UN Secretary-General Kofi Annan expressed his sadness and indignation at such abuse. He warned world leaders that international law was being "shamelessly disregarded" around the world and cited prisoner abuse in Iraq as an example of such violations. In Iraq, he said, civilians were massacred in cold blood, while relief workers, journalists, and others were "taken hostage and put to death in the most barbarous fashion . . . At the same time, we have Abu Ghraib prisoners outside Baghdad who were photographed being brutalized by American troops."[5]

Muslims resented such unethical treatment of prisoners. Many people in the Islamic world wondered whether some U.S. soldiers were exhibiting such inhuman behavior "just for fun" or "just for humiliation" of the Islamic Iraqi people.

A military investigator testified in a hearing court for a female soldier photographed holding a naked Iraqi on a leash. She appeared on the opening day of the military court hearing. The court determined that she had deliberately abused the Iraqi prisoners and outraged the Islamic world. When the lead prosecutor asked why the troops had abused the Iraqi prisoners, the answer was, "Basically it was just for fun . . . and to vent their frustration."[6]

What made the situation worse and increased the anger of Iraqis was the report issued by the human rights group Amnesty International in March 2006, two years after the Abu Ghraib scandal. The report condemned the detention of prisoners in Iraq, saying some fourteen thousand people were being held without charges or trials and that torture continued despite the Abu Ghraib scandal. The Amnesty International report titled "Beyond Abu Ghraib: Detention and Torture in Iraq" also said that there was mounting evidence of torture by Iraqi security forces.[7]

In the fourth anniversary of occupation, the news quoted by Al Jazeera's Arabic Web site in March 2007 that a U.S. soldier testified in court martial proceedings, "his commander ordered him to kill three Iraqi detainees, then cut them with a knife to make it look as if there had been a struggle." The crime took place during a May 9 raid on a suspected fighter's camp near Samarra. Specialist William Hunsaker told the court that the staff sergeant ordered him and another soldier to free the men, and then shoot them as they ran. Hunsaker said that he pulled down their blindfolds and looked them in the eyes and that another soldier told them in Arabic to run. "I shot him [the first detainee] where his heart should be."[8]

WAS ABU GHRAIB AN "ANIMAL HOUSE" AT NIGHT?

The world and the Islamic media wondered whether it was true that Abu Ghraib prison situated near Baghdad was intentionally made an "animal house" and "sadism shelter" at night for the Iraqi prisoners under the command of the U.S. forces. In order to put the facts on record, a four-member advisory panel appointed by the U.S. Secretary of Defense, Donald Rumsfeld, investigated abuse allegations at Abu Ghraib. The panel confirmed that the prison's activities were no secret and no rectifications were made.

The 126-page report released by the panel by its chairman, James Schlesinger, stipulated that "We believe that there is institutional and personal responsibility right up the chain of command as far as Washington is concerned . . . there was sadism on the night shift at Abu Ghraib, certainly not authorized." The chairperson continued, "It was kind of an 'Animal House' on the night shift."[9]

World newspapers and the U.S. media described more abuse of Iraqi prisoners. The *Washington Post* reported that Iraqi prisoners at Abu Ghraib were ridden like animals, groped by female soldiers, forced to curse their religion, and were required to retrieve their food from toilets. The report further said the testimony of abuse obtained from thirteen Iraqi detainees, as well as hundreds of photographs and short digital video clips, were part of the evidence gathered by U.S. Army investigators for the courts-martial of U.S. soldiers charged with abusing detainees.

In another instance, a detainee wearing an orange prison uniform was seen kneeling with his hands apparently tied behind his back as a large, black dog, restrained by a handler using both hands, snarled about three feet from his face.

The *Herald Tribune* also said the *Wall Street Journal* reported that a translator employed by the U.S. Army at Abu Ghraib had been accused of sexually humiliating prisoners there. The man helped hold down three detainees who were "nude, handcuffed to each other and placed in sexual positions."[10]

DID U.S. SOLDIERS ABUSE IRAQIS FOR FUN?

Republican Representative Christopher Shays said at a debate in October 2006 concerning Abu Ghraib prison abuse, "They were more about pornography than torture. Now I have seen what happened in Abu Ghraib and it was not torture. It was outrageous; outrageous involvement of National Guard troops from [Maryland] who were involved in a sex ring and they took pictures of soldiers who were naked." Added Shays, "And they did other things that were just outrageous. But it was not torture." Abuse of prisoners by U.S. soldiers at Abu Ghraib prison led to an international controversy. At least eleven U.S. soldiers were convicted in the scandal.

One of the U.S. soldiers accused of prisoner abuse was quoted as saying her job was to "make it hell" for Iraqi prisoners so they would talk. The *Washington Post* reported that the U.S. military police reservist told in e-mail interviews that detainees were handed over to her military police unit at the Abu Ghraib prison by military intelligence officers, or by civilian contractors who conducted interrogations. Her assignment was to break the detainees down for interrogation.[11]

Al Jazeera in May 2006 wrote that a U.S. Army sergeant was tried in a military court on charges of abusing Iraqi inmates with his dog at Abu Ghraib prison. He was accused of maltreatment of prisoners, dereliction of duty, and assault while allowing his dog to intimidate detainees in 2003 and 2004. Another dog-handler was convicted on similar charges. Both were sentenced to 179 days in prison, after they allegedly tried to scare prisoners so badly they urinated and defecated on themselves. Both used the technique, they confessed, on the theory that Arabs, in general, have a dislike of dogs.[12]

A former prisoner of the U.S. forces, Hashim Muhsin, told Arabic television Al Jazeera and the *Egyptian Gazette* in May 2004, "They wanted to degrade us." He continued, "They hit us on the back with spiked implements. They took off our clothes, put us up against a wall and did immoral things to us that simply we cannot speak about." The pictures were shown by the American television channel CBS, sparking worldwide indignation.

It became clear from the confessions of Abu Ghraib prisoners mentioned in the *Gazette* that torture, agony, and distress were part of the daily routine practiced in the prison. Political prisoners were mixed in with murderers and rapists. Prisoners were shot dead at random to make "space" for newcomers. To top it, there were soldiers who were sexually humiliated and coerced as shown in the photographs. Families were seldom informed of the imprisonment even if prisoners were detained for days or months at Abu Ghraib or other detention facilities in Iraq.

More and more Iraqis were victimized in U.S. detention camps. This was based on suspicion of involvement in guerrilla assaults or insurgents' attacks on U.S.-led coalition troops. Violent raids and break-ins by U.S. troops on local houses where elderly men, women, and children lived continued to fuel anti-American feeling among Iraqis.[13]

Regarding the issue of whether U.S. officials covered up abuse at Abu Ghraib, the reports of the international advocacy group Human Rights Watch (HRW) said, as reported by CNN in June 2004, that the U.S. administration "circumvents" the Geneva Convention with the abuse of Iraqi prisoners at Abu Ghraib prison. Its thirty-eight-page report, "The Road to Abu Ghraib," told that the U.S. administration deliberately allowed illegal interrogation techniques to be practiced in the prison. It further claimed that it covered up or ignored reports of torture and abuse taking place in the prison. In reply to these accusations, the U.S.

administration claimed that the Geneva Convention did not apply to al-Qaeda detainees. Donald Rumsfeld reiterated, "They did not have those rights." Reed Brody, the attorney for HRW, stated, "But even when they are not prisoners of war, they are entitled to some protection."[14]

The HRW report said, "First, the U.S. Administration adopted the position that the war on terror allowed circumvention of international law, meaning laws prohibiting torture were no longer binding. Secondly, the U.S. military used 'coercive methods' to cause pain and humiliation for detainees to prepare them for interrogation. Thirdly, before the publication of photographs of the abuses, the U.S. Administration ignored reports of mistreatment of detainees in both Afghanistan and Iraq."

Intelligence records cited Quran abuse allegation in the prison. Some of the guards claimed that the abuse of prisoners was meant to be as a weapon to break their will to confess their alleged crimes.[15]

AMERICA FREES ABU GHRAIB PRISONERS

A day after U.S. Defense Secretary Donald Rumsfeld visited the Abu Ghraib jail outside Baghdad, the U.S. forces immediately freed dozens of Iraqis from the infamous prison. Several buses filled with detainees pulled out of the compound, past families of other detainees. The number of the inmates was estimated at 3,800. Between 1,500 and 2,000 were released by the end of April 2004.[16]

Meanwhile, as reported in August 2005, Sunni Iraqis requested the government to intervene with the U.S. administration to release an estimated number of ten thousand detainees in U.S.-run facilities in Iraq. Most detainees were Sunnis. Voices were heard from both Shias and Sunnis to release prisoners before the October 15, 2005, referendum so they could participate in the vote.

There was no evidence that the soldiers involved in the abuse were acting under orders from above. It was a relief for both the U.S. military command and the Iraqi people that the abuse of prisoners at Abu Ghraib was not a policy directed from the military headquarters at Washington against an Islamic nation.[17]

Shocking photos of U.S. soldiers abusing Iraqi prisoners at Abu Ghraib, as reported by the *Egyptian Gazette* of mid-September 2004, have made their way into two American museums, creating controversy over the propriety of exhibiting the damaging pictures. The International Center of Photography (ICP) in New York and the Andy Warhol Museum in Pittsburgh, Pennsylvania, cooperated to present an exhibit dubbed "Inconvenient Evidence: Iraqi Prison Photographs from Abu Ghraib."

The exhibition offered a look at the extraordinary impact that amateur digital photographs have had on the public's view of the Iraq War, and the human rights issues that this technology exposed at Abu Ghraib prison and elsewhere as the Warhol Museum of Pittsburgh said on its Web site. The ICP in New York said that few photographs in recent years have had the explosive impact of the grainy images of Iraqi detainees being tortured by U.S. troops at Abu Ghraib prison in Iraq. "As photographs of war, they offer a quite different view from the studied heroics of the twentieth century war photography," said the New York Center, which was founded by photographer Cornell Capa.[18]

ABU GHRAIB ABUSERS GET JAIL SENTENCE

A military court convicted army personnel who pleaded guilty to charges of Abu Ghraib abuses. A female reservist was convicted on six of seven counts. She appeared in the most notorious photographs, including one that showed a pyramid of naked Iraqi detainees. She also appeared in photos posing with Iraqi prisoners in humiliating positions, including a photograph showing her holding a leash tied around a prisoner's neck. In another photo she was shown making fun of a row of naked detainees. She faced charges of conspiracy, dereliction of duty, and maltreatment of prisoners.

Other military staff were sentenced as they confessed to their involvement in the abuse of prisoners, particularly the abuse of a hooded Iraqi prisoner in rags standing on a box with electrical wires attached to parts of his body. Some U.S. staff admitted to handcuffing the Iraqi prisoners and forcing them to crawl on the ground. They stripped them naked and mocked them sexually.

It was clear that the court martial was aware of the fact that the publications of those appalling photographs caused widespread condemnation of the U.S. presence in Iraq. This was while the U.S.-led forces were trying to improve their image after the occupation of Iraq and damaging America's reputation as the most democratic country in the world. In the meantime, the Army announced it demoted a U.S. brigadier general as his unit was in charge of the Abu Ghraib compound during the period of abuse. Some in Congress sharply criticized the Pentagon for failing to hold more senior officers accountable for the Abu Ghraib tragedy.[19]

The *Herald Tribune* in September 2005 reported that lenient sentences for Abu Ghraib prison abuse angered many Iraqis. They expressed fury over the three-year prison sentence for the female U.S. soldier for holding naked inmates by a leash in Abu Ghraib prison. They suspected the sentence would have been more severe had she been convicted of abusing

Americans. Many Iraqis expressed their opinion that such a mild sentence was the best evidence of double standards.[20]

What also angered the Iraqis was the female army officer who announced to the jury of five army officers that she was only trying to please her soldier boyfriend when she took part in Iraqi detainee abuse. What further infuriated the Iraqis was that she appeared on NBC's *Dateline* program saying the pictures did not convey the full extent of Abu Ghraib that took place in the cellblock. She said, "I know worse things were happening over there."[21]

To make it worse, the *New Yorker* published a photograph of a dead Iraqi prisoner on its Web site, saying the man had died during an interrogation by U.S. officials. He had never been registered as prisoner there and his body was removed from the building and dumped. They packed him in ice until it was the appropriate time. They put the corpse on a hospital trolley, walked it out to an ambulance, drove off, and dumped the body.[22]

The *Herald Tribune* reported that a federal judge in September 2005 rejected the U.S. government appeal not to release dozens of horrifying pictures of the Iraqi detainees. The judge was not convinced and ordered the release of the pictures.[23] He said that terrorists "do not need pretexts for their barbarism and that suppressing the pictures would amount to submitting to blackmail."[24]

BUSH: "I HAVE NEVER ORDERED TORTURE."

The scandal of the abuse by U.S. soldiers of Iraqi prisoners in Abu Ghraib had widely taken regional and international dimensions; demonstrations in large numbers were held in many Islamic countries. President Bush found it necessary to address the world and Arab nations. He wanted to let them know that the images seen were shameful and unacceptable.[25]

The president was interviewed by United Arab Emirates-based Al-Arabia and Al-Hurrah (the latter being a U.S. government-funded satellite station broadcasting from United States to the Arab world). In June 2004, from his Oval Office, the president of the United States addressed the Islamic nations and the world saying, "Look, let me make very clear the position of my government and our country." He continued emphasizing that the U.S. administration had never sanctioned any torture techniques: "We do not condone torture. I have never ordered torture. I will never order torture. The values of this country are such that torture is not a part of our soul and our being."[26]

After the abuse scandal, Iraq's government formally took over the Abu Ghraib prison. Coalition forces transferred operations of Abu Ghraib to the Iraqi authorities. "There's not a single prisoner left there," Deputy Justice Minister Busho Ibrahim told the Associated Press. They were moved in 2006, after three years of occupation, to a new $60 million detention facility that had been built as part of Camp Cropper, near Baghdad International Airport. At that point the multinational force authorities still had about thirteen thousand Iraqi detainees in their custody.[27]

BLAIR APOLOGIZES FOR PRISON ABUSE

In an interview with a French television network, British Prime Minster Tony Blair expressed his apology for British soldiers' treatment of some Iraqi prisoners, emphasizing three major commitments. First, "We have already made it absolutely clear we apologize deeply to anyone who has been mistreated by any of our soldiers." Second, "We went to Iraq to end those types of abuses, not to engage in them." Third, "Any abuse of prisoners is totally and completely unacceptable. We must make sure that anyone responsible for that is properly disciplined and we will do so." The *Sunday Times* reported that military police recommended the prosecution of three soldiers following a year-long investigation of photos appearing to show Iraqi prisoners in British custody being forced to engage in unethical acts.[28]

PENTAGON DETAILS ABUSE OF IRAQI DETAINEES

In June 2006, the Pentagon released a report detailing abuse of Iraq detainees on incidents dating 2003 and 2004. The investigation was conducted by Brigadier General Richard Formica who examined the treatment of Iraqi prisoners following the Abu Ghraib prison scandal in 2004. The report stated that U.S. special operations forces fed some Iraqi detainees only bread and water for up to seventeen days. The forces kept prisoners in a room on a chain about a meter long. They used unapproved interrogation practices such as sleep deprivation, and loud music to stop them from sleeping, with their eyes taped shut for up to seven days at a time.

The heavily censored report of one thousand pages of documents was given to the American Civil Liberties Union under court order as part of a Freedom of Information Act lawsuit." What surprised the Islamic world was that the report concluded that some detainees' treatment was wrong but not illegal and reflected inadequate resources and lack of oversight and proper guidance rather than deliberate abuse. No military personnel were punished because of the investigation. The report added that while the treatment of the prisoners was wrong the special operations facilities were inadequate to accommodate detainees. At the end, the report called for providing the U.S. forces abroad with more understanding, education, and training in the principles of the UN Geneva Conventions in treating prisoners of war.[29]

IRAQI CIVILIANS' DEATHS BY U.S. TROOPS WERE UNJUSTIFIED

Iraq's government stated that many Iraqi civilians' deaths were unjustified. In June 2006, the U.S. military announced it charged two soldiers for the death of an Iraqi in Ramadi. They were both members of the Pennsylvania National Guard's First Battalion, and were charged with one count of voluntary manslaughter for allegedly shooting the man on February 15 near Ramadi. They were accused of conspiring with another soldier who allegedly placed an AK-47 rifle and a shovel by his body to make it look as if he were an insurgent caught planting a bomb.[30]

In June 2006 it was reported that the U.S. Army charged three soldiers in connection with the murders of three Iraqi men who were in military custody in Iraq in early May. "A non-commissioned officer and two soldiers each have been charged with violating several articles of the uniform code of military justice including murder, attempted murder, conspiracy, communicating a threat, and obstructing justice," a military announcement said.[31]

The story started with the Marine Corps initially reporting fifteen deaths caused by a roadside bomb and an ensuing firefight with insurgents. A separate military investigation took place to determine whether the Marines reported the truth, as it included the deaths of innocent women and children. It was clear that this episode was not the result of a usual combat situation. If confirmed as unjustified killings, the episode could be the most serious case of criminal misconduct by U.S. troops during three years of combat in Iraq.[32]

HADITHA: A TERRIBLE CRIME AGAINST IRAQI CITIZENS

The tension arising from the repeated killings of Iraqi civilians by U.S. troops continued drawing condemnation from Iraqi people and their government. President Bush promised that there would be no interference from the military in an investigation.

Nouri al-Maliki, the newly appointed prime minister, expressed his high concern for the deaths of twenty-four Iraqis in the western town of Haditha in November 2005 apparently at the hand of U.S. Marines. "The crime and misery of Haditha . . . is a terrible crime where women and children were eliminated," Prime Minister al-Maliki said. He further expressed that his patience was wearing thin with excuses that U.S. troops kill civilians "by mistake." He requested an investigation into Haditha and other similar cases. Al-Maliki then expressed his outrage by saying, "There is a limit to the acceptable excuses. It is not justifiable that a family is killed because someone is fighting terrorists. We have to be more specific and more careful." According to government agreements, Iraqi courts have no power to arrest or prosecute the U.S.-led troops, their missions, or their consultants.[33]

A videotape aired by an Arab television station showed images purportedly taken in the aftermath of the encounter. The images showed a bloody bedroom floor, walls with bullet holes, and bodies of women and children. An Iraqi human rights group called for an investigation of what it described as a deadly mistake that had harmed civilians. Forensic evidence from the military showed that the Haditha victims had bullet wounds. This contradicted earlier statements from Marines that the victims had been killed by roadside bombs. The Iraqis called for an independent investigation, as there was inconsistency in the evidence.

A military investigation into the deaths of two dozen Iraqis in November 2005 found that a small number of Marines in western Iraq carried out extensive, unprovoked killings of civilians. The inquiry revealed that the civilians killed at Haditha, a lawless, insurgent-plagued city deep in Sunni-dominated Anbar province, did not die from a makeshift bomb, as the military first reported, or in cross-fire between Marines and attackers, as was later announced. A separate inquiry was begun to determine whether the events were deliberately covered up. Evidence indicated that the civilians were killed during a sustained sweep by a small group of Marines that lasted three to five hours and included shootings of five men standing near a taxi at a checkpoint, and killings inside at least two homes that included women and children.[34]

The killings were first reported by *Time* magazine in March 2006, based on accounts from survivors and human rights groups, and members of Congress have spoken publicly about the episode. Nevertheless, the new accounts from congressional, military, and Pentagon officials added significant new details to the picture. Women and children were among those killed. If the accusations proved to be true, the human rights activists said the incident would rank the worst deliberate killing of Iraqis since the U.S.-led invasion in 2003.[35]

The Haditha incident and other similar cases have undoubtedly indicated the enormous pressure on U.S. troops in Iraq. Psychologically speaking, away from their families and folks at home for months if not years, they are also isolated from Iraqi culture by language and custom barriers.

Over and above, they are fighting insurgents and militias that are described among the troops as a "phantom enemy." The troops may receive little sympathy or assistance from Iraqi civilians. This is in addition to the fact that many Iraqis conceive the Americans and other foreign troops as occupiers. They believe that the Americans mainly occupy their country for the oil wealth and not for deposing Saddam, their despotic leader.

The spokesperson for the U.S.-led multinational forces in Iraq said that allegations about U.S. troops using undue force were a blow to the credibility of the coalition. "The behavior of our forces is a key component in the overall success of our mission," he told Arab journalists. "The credibility of our coalition forces is too valuable a commodity to squander needlessly. Every incident and allegation, no matter how small, strikes a blow against that credibility." It was true that allegations of rape and murder have bolstered Iraqi accusations of misconduct by American soldiers, including illegal killings, beatings, and inhuman treatment. Consequently, the allegations increased the mistrust and resentment among Iraqis of the American military and increased calls for their withdrawal.[36]

Four U.S. soldiers were court-martialed on charges of murder and the rape of a fourteen-year-old Iraqi girl. A prosecutor told a U.S. military court that the four soldiers involved should be court-martialed on charges of murder and rape. The actions of the soldiers could not be justified by the strains of war, a prosecutor told the court.[37]

The soldiers had abandoned their checkpoint, changed clothes to avoid detection and headed to the victims' house, about two hundred yards from a U.S. military checkpoint in the so-called Triangle of Death, a Sunni Arab area south of Baghdad known for its violence, the affidavit said. One of the soldiers was accused of raping the girl and killing her and three relatives: an adult male and female and a girl estimated to be five years old. An official familiar with the investigation said he set fire to the rape victim's body in an apparent cover-up attempt. One of the soldiers was charged with failing to report the attack but was not believed to have participated in it directly. The case outraged Iraqis and led Nouri al-Maliki, the Iraqi prime minister, to continue to call for a review of the immunity of foreign troops from prosecution under Iraqi law.[38]

The U.S. administration was concerned, as the case strained relations with Iraq's new government. Iraqis perceived the soldiers receiving lenient treatment. The case had already increased demands from the Iraqi people and government for changes in an agreement that exempts U.S. soldiers from prosecution in Iraqi courts.

Justice prevailed against the U.S. soldiers in the Iraq rape case. In November 2006, a civilian grand jury gave its verdict charging Steven Green, twenty-one, and four other soldiers. Among the charges brought against Green were murder, murder in perpetration of aggravated sexual abuse, conspiracy charges, sexual abuse of a minor, and obstruction of justice.

Robert Pennington, a U.S. Marine radio operator, was sentenced to fourteen years' confinement, reduced to eight years. He pleaded guilty to conspiracy regarding the death of an Iraqi, Hashim Awd, in the same town of Mahmudiya. Investigators said that Pennington was part of an eight-member squad accused of kidnapping and killing the fifty-two-year-old Awad. They dragged him from his home before shooting him ten times in the head.

Revenge was taken by an al-Qaeda-linked group that claimed killing three U.S. soldiers to avenge the rape and murder of the young Iraqi girl by U.S. troops of the same unit. Al Jazeera's Web site reported that the al-Qaeda Mujahedeen Shura Council claimed in a video showing on the Internet the mutilated bodies of two of the soldiers attacked on June 16, 2006, near Youssifiyah, southwest of Baghdad. Pictures from the video released also showed that the two soldiers had been decapitated.[39]

Further tensions increased between the Sunni Arabs and the U.S. forces when the sudden detention of Sheik Jamal Abd al-Karim al-Dabaan, the mufti (the highest religious authority for Iraq's Sunnis). He was detained in the northern Iraqi city of Tikrit, 130 kilometers north of the Iraqi capital, Baghdad, in June 2006. This outraged four million Iraqi Arab Sunnis. The U.S. forces released him after a few hours.

The Sunni Association of Muslim Scholars said that Sheik Jamal was taken into custody, along with at least two of his sons, in the early morning hours following a raid by U.S. forces. The U.S. military said it had been acting on intelligence gathered following the killing of Abu Musab al-Zarqawi, the leader of al-Qaeda in Iraq. The *mufti* was released following protests of Sunni people, responding to calls broadcast over mosque loudspeakers to gather in front of the governor's office to protest against the detention.

The military had overlooked the fact that the Arab Sunni *mufti* represents the highest Islamic and national symbol to the sect in Iraq. His detention by U.S. forces could have caused a further deterioration of the security situation in Iraq. The U.S. military said it had not known beforehand that it was the mufti's home.[40]

All the previous tragedies and world condemnation of these events made it necessary to accelerate transfer of power to an Iraqi government. Chapter 8 provides a historical review of the establishment of a new Iraqi interim government and the attempts to accelerate reconstruction.

TOWARD ACCELERATING TRANSFER OF POWER—FROM U.S. OCCUPATION TO IRAQ GOVERNMENT, A HISTORICAL REVIEW

OUR CONCERN IN THIS CHAPTER IS TO CLOSELY EXAMINE the stages of acceleration of power transfer from the U.S. administration to Iraqis. We shall also assess how effective this transfer was.

Critics of the American policy who openly condemned the U.S.-led invasion of Iraq believed that it was only under the pressure of increasing American casualties and the high cost of occupation that the U.S. administration was moved to accelerate the establishment of an Iraqi interim government.

Other critics assumed that the U.S. administration was faced by internal policies in the United States and a president running for reelection who intended to inform the American people that more improvement had been taking place in Iraq. The White House emphasized that the United States had no desire to be in Iraq, or to be involved in Iraqi political affairs more than it was necessary.

Furthermore, the spokesperson stressed that their presence would be only for the progress of defeating insurgents and militias and making Iraq a country safe and secure, and not for any political reasons. Iraq can expect an expedient transfer of power. The president repeatedly said that the U.S. forces would not leave until they defeated the insurgents and militias.

U.S. LEGISLATORS PRESSURE
U.S. ADMINISTRATION TO EXPEDITE THE IRAQI VOTE

The U.S. administration was under immense pressure politically and militarily from legislators, as the June 30, 2004, deadline neared to transfer more responsibilities to an Iraqi interim government. The pressure was increased with the scandal of the Iraqi prison abuse at Abu Ghraib and the assassination of the president of the Iraqi Governing Council, Izzedin Salim.

Senator Richard Lugar of Indiana, who headed the Foreign Relations Committee in the Congress, repeatedly urged the administration, with the support of other senators, to do its utmost to accelerate the political transition and to speed up the election. Delays in action, he emphasized, undercut U.S. credibility and increased suspicion among Iraqis. Meanwhile, he strongly advocated that control of military prisons should be given to the Iraqi administration as rapidly as possible.[1]

Under such pressure from within the United States and abroad, the U.S. administration outlined steps for the Iraq transition. In May 2004, just one year after occupation, President Bush in his speech at the U.S. Army War College in Pennsylvania stated that intended to make the Americans aware of difficult days ahead in Iraq that might sometimes appear chaotic. However, he strongly stated that no power of the enemy would stop Iraq's progress. In his speech, he extended his goodwill to world leaders who had expressed their position against his policy in invading Iraq. He further asserted to seek international cooperation, after the June 30, 2004, handover of power to an interim Iraqi government to provide peace, security, and reconstruction. The president emphasized the fact that despite past disagreements, most nations had indicated strong support for the success of a free Iraq. He continued that he was confident they would share in the responsibility of assuring that success.[2]

He further made it clear that the Americans' task in Iraq was not only to defeat an enemy, but also to give strength to a friend—a free, representative government that serves its people and fights on their behalf. In his speech, the president laid down five broad steps to restore Iraqi sovereignty and get the country back on its feet:

- Handing over authority to a sovereign Iraqi government
- Establishing security
- Continuing to rebuild Iraq's infrastructure
- Encouraging more international support
- Moving toward a national election in Iraq that "will bring forward new leaders empowered by the Iraqi people"[3]

With regard to the ill-famed Abu Ghraib prison and the atrocities per-petrated there by some U.S. military personnel, Bush reiterated that the United States would build a modern maximum-security prison to replace that prison, and that Abu Ghraib would be demolished if the new Iraqi government agreed. The president went on to disclose the fact that the U.S. commanders had estimated a troop level below 115,000 to be suf-ficient at this point in the conflict. He added that because of the recent increase in violence, the United States would maintain its troop level at the current 138,000 as long as it was necessary. The president then fur-ther emphasized that the U.S. actions were guided by a vision. The U.S. administration believed that freedom could advance and change lives in the greater Middle East.[4]

ESTABLISHMENT OF A NEW IRAQI INTERIM GOVERNMENT

A new Iraqi interim government was formed on June 30, 2004. The U.S.-appointed Iraqi Governing Council dissolved itself after the announce-ment of an Iraqi interim president and other new government positions. The interim government was in charge after the political handover until national elections were to be held in January 2005. The U.S. occupation authorities in Iraq set up the governing council in order to lay the ground for a future Iraqi political regime. The twenty-five-member governing council was composed on sectarian and ethnic grounds:

- Thirteen Shia Arab Muslims
- Five Sunni Arab Muslims
- Five Kurds
- One Turkoman
- One Assyrian

The selected members held various professional backgrounds and political affiliations. Most of them were living in exile. They were opposing the deposed president Saddam Hussein. The council enjoyed the power to nominate and dismiss ministers, and direct policy, and was expected to help draw up a new constitution, which would pave the way for free elections.[5]

Soon after the United States returned the nation's sovereignty, mem-bers of Iraq's interim government took an oath of office. Headed by Iraq's interim Prime Minister Ayad Allawi, each member of the new interim government promised to serve the country with utmost sincerity and impartiality. Iraq flags covered the wall behind them. On this occasion, Bush said, "After decades of brutal rule by a terror regime, the Iraqi people have their country back. The handover begins a new phase in Iraq's progress toward full democracy."[6]

Three main steps were outlined. First, the National Assembly should draft the permanent constitution. Second, after the draft was completed, it should be submitted to the public in a referendum by October 15, 2005. Third, if the draft constitution was adopted, an election for new government under the constitution should be held, and the new government would take office no later than December 15, 2005.[7]

Some Iraqis dismissed the event as meaningless as long as U.S. troops occupy the nation. Others said the handover was a step in the right direction. "This is a historic and happy day for us in Iraq," al-Yawar, the interim president, said. "It is a day that all Iraqis have been looking forward to. This is the day that we take our country back into the international community. We want a free and democratic Iraq, and we want a country that is a source of peace and stability for the whole world," he affirmed.[8]

It was indeed noticeable that Iraqis had been expressing hope for better peace, permanent security, and enhanced justice in their country. When the U.S. formal transfer of sovereignty to an interim Iraqi government was televised, some Iraqis on crowded streets in downtown Baghdad dismissed the occasion as a cosmetic change in a country destabilized by the U.S.-led occupation.[9]

ELECTION UNCERTAINTY AS INSURGENTS AND MILITIAS ACCELERATE THEIR ATTACKS

Despite all political efforts and military arrangements, there was uncertainty about the election. Since the occupation of Iraq, there were daily suicide car bombings, continuous shootings, and constant kidnappings of foreign and indigenous helpers. These incidents had been seriously affecting peace and order in the country. Several cities and towns in the Sunni triangle had been effectively under insurgent control. Because of the deteriorating peace in the Sunni areas, there were concerns that Iraq might not be ready to hold a vote as previously agreed.[10]

However, the Shiite majority, who make up about 60 percent of Iraq's 25 million people, were eager to hold elections as they expected to dominate whatever government was formed. Iraq's top Shiite Muslim cleric, Grand Ayatollah Ali al-Sistani, insisted that elections promised for January 2005 should be held on time. The leaders of Iraq's dominant Shiite Muslim political parties reiterated that no delay should take place in postponing the confirmed election date.

Insurgents accelerated terrorism before the handover of power to the Iraqi new government to disrupt the handover. It was clearly the case as they used suicide car bombers to kill U.S.-led troops, police officers, work-ing foreigners, journalists, foreign service representatives, and Iraqis. This was in addition to senior Iraqi civil servants and clerics who were gunned by Islamic rebels. The U.S.-led administration announced that it had informa-tion that guerrillas would step up attacks before and after the U.S. adminis-trative occupation formally assumed to end on June 30, 2004.[11]

These heavy attacks led many Iraqis all over the country to call for the delay of the January 2005 election. However, both the interim gov-ernment and the United States were determined not to change the date of vote. The call to postpone the date of the vote became louder after the Baghdad Governor Ali al-Haidri was assassinated in Baghdad. On the same day, a suicide truck bomb killed ten people and wounded sixty others near Baghdad's Green Zone, where the Iraq government and U.S. embassy were based.[12]

Al-Qaeda insurgents warned people in Ramadi and other Sunni areas not to vote. They threatened to kill those who would participate in the election. Outside Iraq, voting was gearing up at more than five hundred polling stations in fifteen countries where exiles had concentrated. The start of voting coincided with the second anniversary of the capture of Saddam near his home town of Tikrit where insurgents threatened the Sunni Iraqis not to vote. However, the main overseas voting took place in Jordan, Australia, Austria, Britain, Canada, Denmark, Germany, Iran, Lebanon, the Netherlands, Sweden, Syria, Turkey, the United Arab Emir-ates, and the United States. The turnout was highly satisfactory, and the majority vote was for a transitional parliament.[13]

THE IRAQI NATIONAL CONFERENCE CONVENES IN BAGHDAD

The Iraqi National Conference convened in Baghdad in August 2004 was interfered with by protesters who demanded an end to violence in Najaf, the Shiite holy place. After the interference, a series of mortars touched down less than a mile from the conference site in Baghdad. There were casualties among the people. The attack happened despite a daytime curfew for central Baghdad in order to avoid violence during the conference.

The conference also faced a difficult start. More than one hundred delegates walked out of the conference to protest against fighting in the holy city of Najaf.

The three-day conference, attended by delegates from various parts of Iraq, was not affected. Speaking at the conference in Baghdad, interim Prime Minister Allawi said that Iraq needed to push on trying to cre-ate democracy after decades of brutal rule under former dictator Saddam Hussein. He continued, "Your presence here today is the biggest challenge to the forces of darkness that want to tear this country apart. This is not the end of the road; it is the first step on the way to democracy."[14]

The delegates represented the country's political parties, nongovernmental groups, and religious and tribal bodies. At the conference, the Iraqi leaders chose a one-hundred-person interim body to advise and oversee the newly installed interim government.

UN IRAQI COUNCIL AGREES ON TERMS OF INTERIM CONSTITUTION

As stipulated in United Nations (UN) Security Council Resolution 1546, the Coalition Provisional Authority ceased to exist on June 28, 2004. On this date, the occupation ended and the Iraqi interim government assumed and exercised full sovereign authority on behalf of the Iraqi people. L. Paul Bremer, ex-administrator of the Coalition Provisional Authority, assured the Iraqi people that the United States welcomed Iraq to take its rightful place of equality and sovereignty among the free nations of the world. Al-Yawar, the president of the interim government, said that it was a historic and happy day for all Iraqis.

The interim constitution reached by the Iraqi political leaders agreed to make a compromise on the argumentative issues of Kurdish autonomy and Islam's role in the government. These two critical issues had been a source of heated discussion. At last the country's twenty-five-member, U.S.-appointed governing council reached consensus on the final articles of the document.[15]

The leading Iraqi drafters and senior advisors in the council considered the interim constitution a historic document. They confirmed to the Iraqi people that every single article, and each subparagraph, had the consensus of all twenty-five members in the best tradition of democracy. The document provided a legal framework for Iraqi elections to be held on January 30, 2005, and a permanent constitution to be drafted. It granted broad protections for individual rights, guaranteeing freedom of speech, assembly, and religion, and other liberties long denied by the government of former president Saddam Hussein. For providing gender equality, the document set aside 25 percent of the seats in the provisional legislature for women.

It was the Shiite conservative Muslim leaders who demanded that the document should stipulate "Islam as the principal foundation for legislation."[16] This position was opposed by Sunni Muslims, liberal Shiites, and the council's sole Christian. Kurdish leaders demanded the right to maintain their 150,000 militiamen in northern Iraq and receive a proportional share of the country's oil revenue. The final draft, however, called for Islam as the official religion and to be "a source of legislation." This was in an apparent effort to conciliate conservative Shiites while providing protections against religious domination. The Kurds won the right to retain their militia as a National Guard force under the northern Iraqi administration and the Kurdish regional government. In the future, the militia would be integrated into the country's new army or other security services.[17]

DO IRAQI PEOPLE HAVE THEIR COUNTRY BACK?

President Bush, addressed reporters at the NATO Summit in Istanbul on June 2004, "A day of great hope for Iraqis and a day that terrorist enemies hoped never to see." He continued that after decades of brutal rule by a terror regime, the Iraqi people had their country back.

At the same time, Prime Minister Tony Blair of the United Kingdom called the day "an important staging post on the journey of the people of Iraq toward a new future, one in which democracy replaces dictatorship, and in which freedom replaces repression." He emphasized that the terrorists were doing all they could to stop the rise of a free Iraq, but their bombs and attacks had not prevented Iraqi sovereignty or democracy.[18]

On this occasion UN Secretary-General Kofi Annan commented, "I think this is a new beginning. It is not an end. There's lots of hard work ahead." Russia called for world cooperation on Iraq. After meeting with President Jacques Chirac of France and German Chancellor Gerhard Schroeder near the Baltic Sea in July 2005, Vladimir Putin stressed that the past disputes of Europe on Iraq occupation should not prevent future cooperation. He said all nations should cooperate and join hands in efforts to give the country back to the Iraqis in order to stabilize the nation.[19]

Millions of Iraqis who had fled Saddam Hussein's rule turned up to vote for the interim government at centers in the countries where they lived. Countries with the largest number of Iraqis are Syria with an estimated 250,000 voters, the United States with 200,000, and Britain with 150,000. This is in addition to those living in Europe and Jordan and other Middle East countries.

Nations hosting overseas polling were the United States, Australia, Britain, Canada, Denmark, France, Germany, Iran, Jordan, the Netherlands, Sweden, Syria, the United Arab Emirates, and Turkey.[20]

Despite all these historic efforts, the alarming question arises, "Did Iraqis fear the rise of an 'Iraqi Hitler' especially after the absence of peace and security in the country?" Pressures of terrorists, militiamen, and rebels, in addition to the spread of violence and anarchy all over Iraq, have made life in the country rather unbearable. Iraqi people criticized the U.S. and British forces for dismantling Iraqi security forces that were highly trained during Saddam's regime. Ghazi al-Yawer, the Iraqi interim president, agreed with his people that the decision to dismantle Saddam Hussein's defense and interior ministries contributed to the violence and disorder seen since the Iraqi dictator was captured. Al-Yawer continued, saying to BBC radio that long-term instability in Iraq could give rise to an "Iraqi-Hitler."[21]

ACCELERATION OF RECONSTRUCTION OF IRAQ

The aggressive violence in Iraq had been threatening the plans for rebuilding the country as it moved toward a new phase of democracy. The rampant bloodshed continued to take place while the interim national assembly was engaged in drafting its post-Saddam constitution. Meanwhile, on the banks of the Dead Sea in Jordan, officials from Iraq and international donor countries began two days of closed-door meetings to review the pace of reconstruction in the violence-ravaged country.

The problem of reconstruction in Iraq became serious. It affected accelerating the departure of the U.S.-led groups and hindered expediting the steps for Iraqis to achieve full sovereignty. During the years of occupation, Iraq's infrastructure was vastly devastated. Violence including kidnappings, and beheading and torturing foreign contractors, engineers, and assistants was a key factor in delaying the reconstruction plan in Iraq. Consequently, basic infrastructure such as electricity, pure water, sewage systems, and telephone communication was greatly affected.

As violence increased in Iraq and the need for reconstruction required immediate action, World Bank President James Wolfensohn stated in July 2003 that the bank's assistance for Iraq's reconstruction could come after "a constitution and an elected government" were in place. The World Bank estimated that a total, long-term reconstruction cost could reach $100 billion or higher. The bank, furthermore, estimated costs of reconstruction would reach $55 billion over the following four years.[22]

In October 2003, a donors' conference was held in Madrid. It resulted in pledges of $33 billion for the International Reconstruction Facility Fund for Iraq (IRFFI).[23] In February 2004, the donor countries pledged $1 billion to be injected into trust funds run by both the UN and the World Bank for Iraq's infrastructure in the year 2004. This was while the Iraqi government stated that Iraq would need $4 billion for 2004. In addition, the U.S. Congress in November 2003 authorized $18.7 billion for Iraq in a "supplemental allocation." The sum was for boosting Iraqi reconstruction of the deteriorating infrastructure and economic development.[24]

After one year, in October 2004, a meeting of international donors and Iraqi officials was held in Tokyo. They ended a two-day conference with assurance on taking immediate steps toward helping to rebuild Iraq. The main aim of the conference was to gain new pledges to the reconstruction of Iraq's deteriorating infrastructure. The European Union (EU) pledged $200 million more and Iran pledged $10 million. Iraqi officials repeatedly urged delegates to speed up promised funding. It was noticeable from the deliberations that took place in the conference that donor countries were cautious about sending the funds pledged for reconstruction until they noticed concrete actions in improving peace and security in the country.[25]

Iraq appealed to donors to come up with innovative ways to reconstruct Iraq's infrastructure and to encourage their national nongovernmental organization to help with some of the work. Forty countries and international lending institutions attending the conference promised $13.6 billion in grants and loans.[26]

To expedite the reconstruction of Iraq, the EU leaders, in their summit meeting in November 2004, urged the Bush administration to find a way out of the violence in Iraq and adopt a more multilateral approach that would involve Europe in consultations over the Iraq crisis. The EU expressed its willingness to deepen its role in Iraq's reconstruction efforts despite reluctance, particularly from France and Germany, to get involved on the ground. Ayad Allawi, Iraq's interim prime minister, participated in the summit. He called on EU countries that had been acting as "spectators" of the war in Iraq to become involved in rebuilding his country. EU leaders offered Iraq a trade deal as part of the efforts to help rebuild the country. So far, the EU had already committed 305 million Euro in humanitarian and reconstruction aid for Iraq.[27]

In another development, the United States and the twenty-five-nation EU cohosted a conference in Brussels in June 2005, at the foreign ministers' level, that gave Iraq a forum to present its plans for the transition period leading to a next round of elections toward the end of the year. At the conference were representatives of over eighty countries and international organizations. The conference was an opportunity to mobilize international support for the Iraqi transitional government and its institutions. Iraq's al-Qaeda group, led by Abu Musab al-Zarqawi, denounced the conference saying, "The enemies of God gather at the conference in Brussels to destroy Iraq, not to build it."[28]

Despite Zarqawi's threatening statement, Iraqi leaders continued the meeting in Brussels. Iraqis requested assistance to boost security and reconstruction and to reinforce the rule of law in their country. The new transitional government was given strong support from the world community. Prime Minister Ibrahim al-Jaafari wanted actions from the countries attending the conference on two fronts. The first action was to speed up delivery of promised aid and the second was to forgive Iraq's huge financial debt. The minister of Iraq's foreign affairs added, "Iraq interim government calls on the world community to expedite providing expertise and more financial help to assist in the reconstruction of the country . . . We need assistance for the political process, for the constitution, for conducting a referendum, and for holding elections from the United Nations and other member states . . . in order to enhance civil society."[29]

American and Iraqi people questioned if funds allocated to Iraqi construction went to security purposes. The *Washington Times* of February 9, 2006, reported that the State Department had spent nearly half the U.S. money allocated for Iraqi reconstruction on security, not on the projects themselves, according to testimony at a Senate hearing. The testimony showed that the Iraqi government faced difficulties in providing basic water and electrical services, hospitals, and schools. Terrorists had been so destructive at knocking out electric power and water that huge sums of money ought to be diverted to protect reconstruction projects.[30]

In the testimony, it was revealed that the European nations and Japan had sent the money they pledged at a conference in Madrid in October 2003, but commitments from Iraq's Middle East neighbors were not coming through. Senior State Advisor on Iraq James Jeffrey said, "We're pushing real hard on the Kuwaitis and the Saudis, for example, who between them pledged $1 billion, and we haven't seen very much of that yet." He further confirmed that only $3.2 of $13 billion promised by foreign countries for rebuilding had reached Iraq.[31]

In the plan, constructing new clinics in Iraq became a priority because of the large number of casualties in the country. The plan has been scaled back to 142 clinics due to the current unsafe situation and continuous fighting among clerical factions in the country. The senior U.S. consultant for health care construction said only a little more than half of the projects were finished. The work was slower than they anticipated and they were behind schedule.

It was apparent that reconstructing the infrastructure in Iraq had been a major part of the overall U.S. strategy to win public support of the Iraqi people and undermine backing for the insurgency at the same time. *USA Today* revealed in January 2006 that the delays reflected a broader problem facing U.S.-funded reconstruction in Iraq. It further disclosed that Congress approved $18.4 billion for Iraq reconstruction in November 2003, but by the following year nearly one-third of the money had been diverted to help train and equip Iraq's security forces as the insurgency and militias gained steam.[32]

While major financial difficulties have been confronting the reconstruction of Iraq, the Iraqi people were surprised to know that three U.S.

reserve officers were to stand trial by the U.S. judicial system for allegedly taking part in a "bid-rigging scam that steered millions of dollars for Iraq reconstruction projects to a contractor in exchange for cash, luxury cars and jewelry." The accused were said to have used the $26 billion Iraqi rebuilding fund "as their own personal ATM machines."[33]

The insurgents' mission was to convince the Iraqi people of the failure of the existing Shiite government to enforce peace and security in the country. They planned to make it more difficult and dangerous for the U.S. occupation force to continue in Iraq. Hiring workers and engineers for repairing the infrastructure became more difficult. Attacks on workers, engineers, and security men became a daily event in most parts of the country. The aggression had been intensified, killing scores of workers and security men in reconstruction projects. In one case, in 2006, after three years of U.S. occupation, gunmen pulled workers off buses northeast of Baghdad and killed forty-seven of them. The insurgents immediately revealed the motive for the killing.

Just two weeks after this incident, armed men in camouflage uniforms stormed an office of a private Iraqi security company and kidnapped fifty employees. The company was located in Zayouna, an explosive Sunni-Shia neighborhood in east Baghdad. The company is one of many providing protection for businesspersons, contractors, engineers, workers, and other clients.[34]

THE NEW INTERIM GOVERNMENT CALLED ON THE UN TO GIVE IRAQ FULL SOVEREIGNTY

The good news for the Iraqi people was when their interim President Ghazi Yawar, an influential tribal chief appointed to succeed Saddam Hussein, called for the United Nations to give Iraq "full sovereignty" when the U.S.-led occupation authority was to cease on June 30, 2004.

The interim government named a team responsible for organizing its first free elections in January 2005. This was the next step in establishing its independence from the U.S. military administration. The formal selection of the electoral commission came three days after the appointment of an interim government in a process overseen by Washington with UN participation.[35]

The new government informed the United Nations it wished to have the right to decide on the future presence of U.S.-led forces and other security issues. This was granted. The United States, in fact, had tried to persuade other major powers, including France and Russia, to support a UN mandate to keep U.S.-led troops in Iraq until the country had a fully legitimate, constitutionally elected government scheduled for January 30, 2005.[36]

The United States returned sovereignty to Iraq as agreed with the UN as soon as members of Iraq's interim government took an oath of office. Each member of the new government placed a hand on the holy Quran and promised to serve the Iraqi people with sincerity and impartiality. Iraq flags could be seen everywhere in the capital.[37]

The United States, by returning sovereignty to Iraq, made its people express mixed opinions. On the one hand, there were Iraqi pessimists who utterly dismissed the event as not only meaningless, but also worthless as long as U.S. troops remained present in Iraq. On the other hand, there were Iraqi optimists who considered the handover as a step forward in the right direction of the United States returning full sovereignty to Iraq's independence. In a request to the Security Council from Ibrahim al-Jaafari in September 2005, the Iraqi prime minister expressed the need of his country for continued support of the multinational force because its own forces were not yet ready to take on the responsibility of establishing "lasting peace and security." Thus, the Security Council unanimously adopted a one-year renewal of the United Nations mandate for the U.S.-led multinational force in Iraq. As agreed, this renewal of the UN mandate for U.S.-led force in Iraq is reviewed yearly at the request of the Iraqi government.[38]

IRAQ LOOKED FORWARD FOR BETTER SECURITY AND PEACE

The most unfortunate event was that peace and security continued to deteriorate after the transfer of sovereignty to the new government. This was not expected. In his meeting with President Bush in Washington in June 2005, Iraqi Prime Minister Ibrahim al-Jaafari informed the president of the acute problem of peace and order in Iraq. Iraqis and U.S. troops were dying in car suicide bombings and lawmakers were pressing for a timeline for U.S. withdrawal. Al-Jaafari assured the president that a draft constitution to lead his country toward democracy and peace would be concluded by August 15, 2005, and then ratified on October 15 in a popular referendum as agreed.

Just a few months after the handover of sovereignty there were a large number of car bombs in Iraq. At least 2,174 people were killed and 5,520 wounded. The Iraqi Sunni insurgency and Shiite militias had not weakened as expected since the interim government was established.[39]

Nevertheless, the general masses of Iraqi people, especially in the Shiite and Kurdish parts of the country, representing 80 percent of the population, welcomed the U.S.-led troops on the account that they would support the interim government to help stabilize peace and order in the country.[40]

Whether the United States had given the Iraqi people complete power and sovereignty was a debatable political and military issue. Commenting on the importance of giving full power to the Iraq interim government, William Pfaff of the *Herald Tribune* in May 2004, after more than one year of occupation, called for the U.S. administration to give Iraqis complete sovereignty. He emphasized that any American effort to hand over less than complete sovereign control would provoke comprehensive resistance that would include confrontation with the mainstream Shiite community, led by the Grand Ayatollah Ali Al-Sistani.

Pfaff highlighted that if, on the other hand, "the United States offers complete sovereignty and a genuine American military withdrawal, then effort to make the political and security transition work can be expected from the United Nations and its agencies, and from the European allies." Thus, new possibilities would be opened such as a national consultation of tribal, religious, and other established community and professional leaders in Iraq.

He continued to emphasize that "the White House also must give up the ideas that American corporate investors are going to have a big role in Iraq's economy in the near future, and that the United States will be able to influence oil prices through its leverage over a new Iraqi government . . . If Washington has economic influence in Iraq in the future, or enjoys its military cooperation; this will have to be earned from a sovereign Iraqi government."[41]

Pfaff rightly stressed two important and necessary points. First was to set a deadline for U.S. military and political withdrawal, and begin that withdrawal. He further suggested the end of 2004 would be a suitable date for its completion. Second, was to request the United Nations assume complete responsibility for the formation of a sovereign Iraqi government, and to assure the United Nations and the other members of the Security Council of disinterested American financial and political support for this undertaking.[42]

To reinforce the sovereignty of Iraq, NATO leaders at the summit in Istanbul in June 2004 agreed to offer training to the security forces of Iraq's new interim government on the day it was sworn in.[43]

HAS IRAQ GIVEN VETO POWER OVER MILITARY U.S.-LED OPERATIONS?

Prime Minister Blair's statement was indeed the strongest explanation and clear commitment to date by a coalition leader assuring that Iraq's sovereign interim government was able to restrict the use of coalition combat power in civilian areas where active insurgents and militias were still present. His statement emphatically made it clear at a news conference at No. 10 Downing Street. He confirmed what the transfer of sovereignty meant. It appeared that Blair's strong statement was directed to the U.S. administration to send a message to the American military commanders in Iraq who relied on excessive force.[44]

To clarify the position of the Iraqi government, Allawi, the interim prime minister, in June 2004, repeated his call for U.S.-led troops of 138,000 in Iraq to remain beyond the formal handover of sovereignty to help struggling Iraqi security forces combat the guerrillas and militias. This request was submitted to the UN Secretary-General. The Iraqi prime minister expressed the desire of his interim government for the multinational forces to stay in Iraq for some time until Iraq would be capable of handling its own security problems. International divisions over how long foreign troops should stay in Iraq and how much control the new government should have over them were agreed on in the new UN Security Council resolution. It was for the Iraqi interim government to decide on the issue.[45]

ARAB STATES CALLED FOR RECONCILIATION OF AN INDEPENDENT IRAQ

As peace and security were deteriorating, it became apparent that Iraq needed Arab presence and support, especially with regard to easing tensions and conflicts with Arab Sunnis. Amr Moussa, the Secretary-General of the Arab League, confirmed that the "League is giving a hand in rebuilding what had been destroyed over the past year out of its commitment to the UNSC [UN Security Council] resolutions and its interest in the destiny of Iraq and its people. Moussa noted that he informed Iraq of the League's intention to open a representation office there to aid Iraqis closely follow up conditions, help restore stability in cooperation with the United Nations" and enforce peace and order among all sects, including all and excluding none.[46]

As peace among the three ethnic groups in Iraq was deteriorating and tension steadily increasing between the Sunnis on one hand, and the Shiites supported by Kurds on the other, the Ministerial Arab Committee on Iraq met in Jeddah, Saudi Arabia, in October 2005. The committee comprised ministers of foreign affairs of Egypt, Iraq, Saudi Arabia, Bahrain, Kuwait, Syria, Jordan, Algeria, and the Secretary-General of the Arab League Council. This committee was entrusted with the task of formulating a strategic vision to assist the country "to promote peace among the sectarian groups in order to preserve Iraq's territorial integrity and at the same time its Arab identity."[47]

To lay the groundwork for an Iraqi "reconciliation conference" in Cairo, a delegation from the Arab League arrived in Iraq in early October 2005. The Arab states were eager to be supportive of all efforts to stabilize and reconstruct Iraq. The Arab League met with government officials, heads of parties, and eminent clerics in order to reach conciliation among the various factions. As a first step for reconciliation, the delegation called on all Iraqi political and religious leaders to engage in national dialogue and communication in order to resolve outstanding disputes. The Arab League ministers of foreign affairs reiterated the need to secure an appropriate climate to achieve a national reconciliation. This could only be achieved through opening paths of discussions and dialogues among all Iraqi national powers.

It was the first time the pan-Arab organization had taken a direct role in Iraq since the 2003 U.S.-led invasion. The delegation found that the political situation in Iraq was tense. Indeed, the delegation felt, there was a threat of possible civil war. Consequently, the Arab League warned of such disaster in an interview with the British Broadcasting Corporation. The insurgents expressed their hostility by killing three police escorts as the convoy of eight vehicles was under attack on its way for the delegation to meet representatives of the Muslim Clerics Association. Gunmen opened fire as the Arab League convoy passed the Um al-Qora mosque in the west of Baghdad where the Sunni Clerics Association is located.[48]

In November 2005, political and ethnic Iraqi leaders met in Cairo at the invitation of the Arab league. In their meetings, Iraqi leaders put aside their perpetual differences and agreed on a statement that called for the importance of laying down a timetable for the withdrawal of foreign troops from the country. Shia, Sunni, Kurdish, and Christian leaders also requested the release of prisoners and laying down a comprehensive program for rebuilding Iraq's armed forces. The leaders stressed the urgent need for ending conflicts between their communities and achieving national reconciliation.[49]

The most acrimonious part of the deliberations was on the definition and implications of "resistance," seen by some Iraqis as a just struggle against invaders. Other members considered "resistance" as futile fanaticism and rebellion. "The compromise formula said: 'Although resistance is a legitimate right of all peoples, terrorism does not represent legitimate resistance, so we condemn terrorism as acts of violence, murder and kidnapping.'"[50]

In the meetings, the Arab League expressed that Iraq was sliding toward chaos and civil war unless urgent and sincere conciliation took place in the country among the ethnic groups. The position of the Iraqi government was clear. It refused to deal with anyone who attacked the U.S.-led troops, civilians, or whomever they suspected of seeking to restore Saddam's Ba'athist rule. It welcomed to the conference those Iraqis who believed in the political process. They also planned a security ring for Baghdad.[51]

There were heated discussions and bitter deliberations regarding the debatable issue of preservation of the country's Arab identity. Iraq's Arab identity was subject to fierce argument among members of the assembly. Some think that Iraq is not all Arabs. Only the Sunnis, who represent 20 percent of the population, are Arabs. They argued that the majority of the Iraqi population is non-Arabs. They have their own languages as in the case of the Kurds, the Turkomans, and the Assyrians.

In February 2006, the country underwent an ethnic civil war between Sunnis and Shiites. The Arab League negotiated with Iraqi ethnic and political leaders to assist in the promotion of national reconciliation. The league members met the prime minister and held talks with the president, the Shiite cleric Ayatollah Ali al-Sistani, and leaders of the ethnic groups. The Grand Ayatollah Ali al-Sistani expressed his support to the conference in Cairo. Eighty Iraqi leaders from all political and ethnic factions were invited to Cairo for preliminary reconciliation talks.[52]

In a landmark visit to the Kurdish parliament in the northern part of Iraq, aiming at calling for national reconciliation, the Arab League Secretary-General expressed the hope of all Arab states for "stability and security to reign in Iraq, and that fraternity and cooperation will prevail between its different communities."[53] Amr Mousa, the head of the twenty-two Arab member league, told journalists that his aim to visit Iraq was to assist in laying down a framework for national dialogue and national reconciliation to be the basis for Iraq's future. The Secretary-General warned again that civil war might erupt at any moment unless immediate action was taken to reconcile various ethnic factions.

Meanwhile, a number of Iraqi leaders blamed the Arab League for neglecting their country and for overlooking assistance in solving its political and ethnic problems since the war started. The Shiite and Kurdish approval of the October 15 constitution had further worsened the political and ethnic situation in Iraq. It was the strong opposition of Sunni militants to the constitution that caused the intensifying of suicide bombings and insurgent attacks.

Iraqi Sunnis made threats to withdraw from a tentative agreement reached in reconciliation talks in Cairo. They complained of continued violence against Sunnis. The situation became unacceptable, they added. A spokesperson for the Association of Muslim Scholars (AMS), the highest Sunni authority in Iraq, informed a news conference that the association found itself forced to "reconsider the decisions" reached at the Cairo conference. "What is happening on the ground differs completely from what was promised."[54] At talks in Cairo, Iraqi leaders reached a tentative agreement that violence should stop, some detainees should be freed, and U.S. forces should gradually withdraw.

Regardless of the bitter criticism from some factions in Iraq against the Arab League, a head of the Arab League mission in Iraq arrived in Baghdad, signaling the resuming of diplomatic ties between the pan-Arab body and post-Saddam Hussein Iraq. The appointment of a Moroccan diplomat as head of the league's Iraq mission in Baghdad aimed at paving the way for a more active Arab involvement in the country. The mission's responsibilities included consulting with various Iraqi factions: Shiites, Kurds, and Sunni Arabs. The aim of the consultation was to provide Arab support for the political process and complete preparations for an Iraqi reconciliation gathering.[55]

The Sunni neighboring Arab countries wondered whether Iraq's conflict was fueling a bitter Middle East split. The traditional power balancing between Sunnis and Shiites in the neighboring Gulf countries is rapidly shifting in favor of Shiite Islam. Shiites have a majority of followers in three Middle Eastern countries: Iraq, Bahrain, and Iran. Their leadership is asserted by Iran. This has deeply disturbed the regional Arab states, especially Saudi Arabia, which leads the cause of Sunni Islam that is spread in most Muslim countries.

It is a concern that the ethnic conflict in Iraq could cause wider sectarian animosity and ethnic antipathy across the Muslim world. It was clear from the polls conducted in the various countries in the Middle East that people in Arab nations believe that the Iraq war had caused more terrorism and instability and less peace. This is contrary to political claims that the Iraqi war brought more democracy to the Arab region.[56]

Shiite-Sunni tension had been increasing in the Arab neighbors since the Iraq war and ousting of Saddam. It is expected that when Shiite Iraq came to power, neighboring Shiites living in Bahrain, Saudi Arabia, and Kuwait would feel stronger. This, in the long term, may lead them to demand political and economic privileges. It is worth mentioning, historically, that the present Shiite government in Iraq is considered the first Shiite government assuming power in more than eight hundred years.[57]

Saudi reformist Mansour Nogaidan said that the most dangerous phenomenon is not the war between Sunni insurgents and American forces in Iraq, but the Sunni-Shiite sectarian strife. He added, "For them, the biggest danger is loosing the influence of Sunni Islam to Shiite Islam."[58] Though Iran repeatedly denied any meddling in Iraq's internal affairs, it has strong relations with the new Iraqi Shiite leadership in power. Among these leaders are the prime minister, the majority of ministers, and parliament members. In fact, most of them found refuge in Iran during Saddam's rule. Neighboring Arab leaders had been enduring Saddam's authoritarian policies for years simply because they saw him as an assurance for continuous Sunni power and stability in Iraq.

Prime Minister Blair, in October 2005, clearly accused Tehran of help-ing the Shiite militias. He asserted that evidence pointed to Iran and its Lebanese Hezbollah guerrilla allies as the source of armaments and explosives used in the powerful roadside bombs in Iraq. Meanwhile, U.S. commanders were voicing increasing concern at the power and sophisti-cation of roadside bombs, which killed seven U.S. troops in three road-side bombings in one day near Baghdad. The side-bomb is the biggest killer of the U.S.-led troops. It is a device capable of penetrating armored vehicles, based on up-to-date technology, American and British officials said. They claimed that the dangerous bomb had been introduced from Iran. Tehran denied helping militants in Iraq.[59]

In addition to such claims, in May 2006, Iraq accused Iran of border violence. The Iraqi Defense Ministry appointed in the new government said Iran had violated Iraq's borders twice in April. The Iranian army crossed the Iraqi borders on April 21 and April 26. In the second viola-tion, there was bombing against the positions of Kurdistan Workers Party (PKK). The ministry said, "The Iranian troops reached five kilometers into Iraqi territories before they withdrew," though Iran denied it.[60]

Iraq's foreign minister requested that the Arabs should forgive the country's debts. They also should open diplomatic missions. He con-cluded that the Arabs left a void for Iran to fill.

As Arab foreign ministers met in March 2006 in the Sudanese capital of Khartoum to prepare for a summit of Arab leaders, Hoshyar Zebari, the Iraqi minister of foreign affairs, unexpectedly said, "We in Iraq have complaints about the Arab role in Iraq. There is nothing tangible and there are no concrete measures to help the Iraqi people . . . The Arab role is absent in Iraq while there are regional and international initiatives."[61]

In another development, in October 2006, Saudi Arabia's king met prominent Iraqi Sunni and Shia clerics in Makka. He urged them to seek an end to the violence. It was apparent that Saudi Arabia, along with many other countries in the region, was worried about the prospect of civil war in Iraq.[62]

Furthermore, King Abdullah called for unity in the Arab League sum-mit meeting held in Saudi Arabia in March 2007. The king stressed that Sunni-Shia violence in Iraq threatened the stability of the entire oil-producing Gulf region. "In beloved Iraq, blood flows between broth-ers in the shadow of illegitimate foreign occupation and hateful sectari-anism, threatening a civil war," he said, in an unusually strong criticism of the U.S. presence in Iraq from a strong ally. One of several world fig-ures invited to the summit's opening session was the Pakistani president,

Pervez Musharraf. In his speech, he warned that rising tensions in the Gulf region would affect the security and peace of the region and the world.[63]

Having clarified the worry of the constant threat of civil war in Iraq, it is appropriate that the next chapter be dedicated to throwing light on the severity of the damage caused by Islamic insurgents, assassinating clerics and abducting foreigners, and basically making Iraq become out of control."

CHAPTER 9

THE DANGER OF ISLAMIC INSURGENTS IN IRAQ

IT WAS APPARENT THAT THE DANGER OF ISLAMIC INSURGENTS and militias in Iraq became imminent after a few months of the U.S.-led occupation. Insurgents became more destructive and brutal. In marking the first anniversary of the occupation of Iraq, in March 2004, a powerful car bomb exploded at night outside a downtown hotel, killing or injuring at least sixty-seven people. The explosion collapsed part of the fortified building and threw bodies into the street. It was clear that the attack was a protest message to the occupation of Iraq. The bombing came just two days before the first anniversary of the start of the U.S.-led war in Iraq. On this occasion, the coalition officials had warned the people that insurgents might step up their attacks, especially on Baghdad. Their aim was to mark the date of occupation and at the same time to disrupt U.S. plans to transfer power to Iraqis on June 30, 2004.

After a few days, another attack on a hotel took place at night, throwing downtown Baghdad into chaos. Military officials estimated that the car bomb was packed with one thousand pounds of explosives. These two incidents showed that the insurgents shifted their tactics from attacks against U.S.-led troops to attacks on nonmilitary targets and toward Iraqi policemen and civilians who were cooperating with the U.S. coalition troops. The main aim was to intimidate and terrorize them in order to cease their services, assistance, and cooperation with the occupier.[1]

The U.S. military and many Iraqi officials described the insurgency as a mix of former Saddam Hussein loyalists to the outlawed Ba'ath Party, foreign militants, and disenfranchised Sunni Arabs. The estimated number of insurgents by 2006, according to the U.S. military, ranged from 8,000 to 20,000; however, Iraqi intelligence officials have estimates as high as 40,000 fighters plus another 160,000 supporters, of which about 10 percent are foreign.[2] U.S. officials said since August 2006, Saudis were among the top five nationalities among foreign fighters captured by coalition forces in Iraq. Around 41 percent were Saudis, followed by 18 percent from Libya, then Yemen, Algeria, Morocco, Tunisia, Jordan, Turkey, and Egypt.[3]

Let us examine this pressing question: was the Iraqi insurgents' ferocity expected to intensify during the first year of the occupation? In other words, was it true that the U.S.-led occupation troops expected that the Iraqi terrorists planned to increase their aggression and ruthlessness?

Prime Minister Tony Blair clearly admitted that he had not expected such a degree of ferocity from the insurgents. Nevertheless, he insisted in front of a Labor Party gathering that he had not set a deadline for withdrawing the British soldiers from Iraq.[4]

ESTIMATED NUMBER OF ISLAMIC INSURGENTS IN IRAQ AND THEIR AFFILIATIONS

With the intensive attacks of terrorists, especially in the Sunni triangle, there were many rumors about the strength of the Islamic insurgents. The interim government reports said in October 2004 that there was a maximum number of about twelve thousand insurgents across the country. This included a number of foreign fighters from Arab and Islamic countries.[5] The majority were Islamic rebels and al-Qaeda sympathizers, and the minority were former members of the Ba'ath Party. Insurgents in Iraq belong to many Islamic factions. The most active faction has been the Unification and Jihad." It has claimed responsibility for a large number of attacks and kidnappings since the fall of Saddam Hussein's regime.

Al-Zarqawi, the right hand man of al-Qaeda's leader Osama bin Laden and head of that group, said in an audiotape posted on a Web site that he was behind the bombing of the United Nations (UN) headquarters in Baghdad. The bombing resulted in the bombing of the United Nations (UN) headquarters in Baghdad including the chief envoy to Iraq, Sergio Vieira de Mello. Furthermore, the group announced that it has killed numerous Westerners in Iraq, including two Americans and a Briton kidnapped and later beheaded. A statement from the Unification and Jihad group posted on an Islamist Web site said two Iraqi "martyrs" from the group blew themselves up in attacks on a base and in an Iraqi police station. Since then, October 2004, the suicide bombings became the most terrifying tool in terrorism.[6]

The other major Islamist militant group, Ansar al-Sunna, claimed responsibility for the killing of a police chief in the northern city of Erbil. Ansar al-Sunna called the Kurdish leaders traitors for cooperating with U.S. forces in the invasion of Iraq. The group also claimed responsibility for the killings of three Kurdish political party members and twelve Nepalese contractors on the ground that they were cooperating with the U.S. occupiers.[7]

Al-Zarqawi Insurgent Group Designated by U.S. Administration as Terrorist Organization

Owing to the increasing attacks of terrorism under the command of al-Zarqawi in the northern part of Iraq against the U.S.-led collision troops, high-ranking employees in the interim government, policemen, and Iraqi civilians, the U.S. State Department designated Abu Musab al-Zarqawi's Unification and Jihad group a "foreign terrorist organization." This meant that he was wanted by the U.S. government for crimes committed against its troops and citizens.

The State Department spokesperson declared that the organization run by al-Zarqawi's group carried out many terrorist attacks in Iraq and elsewhere, trying to foment civil war and holding back the progress of the Iraqi people. Therefore, al-Zarqawi and his group were considered a terrorist organization. The designation published in the Federal Register included "a travel ban and a freeze on any assets of members of the group and their supporters in U.S. banks." In addition, the U.S. designation made it illegal under its law for persons in the United States or subject to its jurisdiction to knowingly provide material support to the group.[8]

It is believed that the highly planned and executed terrorist attacks taking place in Iraq since the occupation were arranged and carried out by al-Zarqawi and his group. He has been considered the most capable and cunning terrorist working in Iraq, trying to set up a foothold for al-Qaeda in the Sunni triangle. His list of attacks includes the bombings of the UN headquarters and the Imam of Ali mosque in Najaf, and killing American military personnel and Iraqi forces at checkpoints at the U.S. occupation headquarters in Baghdad and other towns.

In addition, a group said to be linked to al-Qaeda and headed by al-Zarqawi claimed that it was holding the senior Egyptian diplomat abducted in Iraq. "The Foundation of Holy War in Mesopotamia group" made the announcement in an Internet statement saying, "We, the al-Qaeda in Iraq, inform that the Egyptian ambassador has been kidnapped by our mujahidin and is under their control."[9] A few days later, the al-Qaeda group announced that it had killed the Egyptian ambassador. That was the start of a series of attacks on diplomats in Iraq. After a few days, the group announced the slaughtering of two high officials in the Algerian embassy.

In addition, the al-Zarqawi militant group was blamed for church bombings in Baghdad and Mosul. Muslim leaders in all Iraq condemned the car bombings that were timed for Sunday evening church services in Baghdad and the northern city of Mosul in mid-August 2004. In a statement, the Shiite Sistani, the eminent cleric, condemned the blast as a great crime and insisted that Iraqi minorities had to be protected. Pope

John Paul called the bombings an unjust aggression. Christians make up no more than 3 percent of the Iraqi population and generally had good ties with the Muslim community.[10]

Nevertheless, let us tackle the question, "Who is Musab al-Zarqawi?" Not much is known about Zarqawi's history. What we know is that he was born Ahmad Fadeel Khalayl in 1966 in Jordan. He is from the town of Zarqa, a poor industrial town thirty minutes northwest of Amman. He is wanted by the government of Jordan for killing an American diplomat working in the U.S. embassy in Amman. Many Arab and Islamic countries consider him an international terrorist. He is believed by many intelligence sources to be a senior associate of Osama bin Laden in al-Qaeda and head of the Iraq-based Ansar al-Islam group (The Supporters of Islam) in Iraq.

Some intelligence sources believe that Zarqawi's operation is a rival to al-Qaeda with similar goals. Others describe him as a fanatic "jihadist." In any case, he has been accused of participating in violent actions against the U.S.-led coalition troops, foreigners, and Iraqis. The United States offered a $25 million reward leading to his capture. This is the same sum offered for information leading to the capture of Ayman al-Zawahri and Osama bin Laden. U.S. and Iraqi officials believed that the al-Zarqawi network was based in Fallujah but left it with his group ahead of an anti-insurgency offensive launched on the city. Al-Zarqawi, as al-Qaeda's leader in Iraq, has declared war against democracy and Iraqis who support it. He vowed, on many occasions, to kill any "infidel" who voted in the January 30, 2005, general election.[11]

In April 2006, a Web site posted a video of Abu Musab al-Zarqawi in which he vowed that the United States "will be defeated in Iraq." The video shown in April 2006 was Zarqawi's first public appearance since he emerged as one of the most wanted militants in the world. The video was titled "Communiqué to the Iraqi people." It said, "Your mujahedeen sons were able to confront the most ferocious of crusader campaigns on a Muslim state." He continued by saying, "They have stood in the face of this onslaught for three years. When the crusader enemy entered Iraq, he intended to control the Islamic nation and support the Zionist state." At one point in the video, Zarqawi said, "By God, America will be defeated in Iraq."[12]

It was very true that al-Zarqawi assumed extensive power among Sunni Islamic rebels and insurgents in Iraq. In September 2005, al-Zarqawi surprised the Islamic world by declaring "all-out war" on Shiite Muslims in Iraq in retaliation to a U.S.-Iraqi military offensive on the town of Tal Afar at the Syrian border. Tal Afar was known as the sanctuary for foreign insurgents and Sunni rebels. For a Sunni Muslim to declare war against a

Muslim country was highly condemned by the Arab and Islamic governments as well as the mass media. In September 2005, an audio clip posted on the Internet said, "The al-Qaeda Organisation in the Land of Two Rivers [Iraq] is declaring all-out war on the Rafidha [a pejorative term for Shia], wherever they are in Iraq," said the voice, which was verified as al-Zarqawi. He continued by saying, "Any religious group that wants to be safe from the blows of the mujahidin must [disavow] the government of al-Jaafari and its crimes. Otherwise it will suffer the same fate as that of the crusaders."[13]

Just a few days after Zarqawi's declaration of all-out war on Shiite Muslims in Iraq, a Sunni suicide car bomber blew himself up outside Shiite's Great Prophet mosque, Tuz Khurmatu, in a mixed Sunni and Shiite town north of Baghdad. The attack killed at least ten and wounded more than twenty worshipers as they were emerging from Friday's prayers.[14]

Shiites gathered in large numbers in defiance of Zarqawi's threats for a holy war against them and despite intimidations of his group of insurgents. Hundreds of thousands of Shiites gathered in the holy city of Karbala. They celebrated a religious occasion in September 2005.

Meanwhile, the U.S. and Iraqi troops continued the offensive against the insurgents. The U.S. and Iraqi troops moved through cities, battling guerrillas hidden inside houses, mosques, and schools. The U.S. and Iraqi military troops revealed that their soldiers killed a large number of insurgents. Some insurgents, disguised as women, were foreign fighters. They were trying to hide among women and children to carry out their attacks. The offensive, in part, aimed at curbing the flow of foreign fighters into Iraq through neighboring countries.[15]

"What are the whereabouts of Zarqawi? In which part of Iraq does he live and direct his attacks? Where does he give training to his insurgents?" American military spokesperson Major General Rick Lynch in May 2006 said Zarqawi's whereabouts had been traced to the area of Baghdad and a town south of it called Yusufiyah. "Zarqawi is zooming in on Baghdad and we are zooming in on him. His center of activity is Baghdad, but it's only a matter of time that we take him down." Lynch added that Zarqawi's forces were believed to be responsible for 90 percent of the suicide bombings that regularly rock Baghdad. While the American forces had been working to cut off the flow of foreign fighters he recruited for such missions.[16]

TERRORISM EXPANDS ITS RUTHLESS OPERATIONS IN IRAQ

Since September 2004, terrorism against foreigners living in Iraq has taken a ruthless turn. Arab and Islamic nations raised their deep feeling of indignation against terrorists who were killing, kidnapping, and slaughtering people in the name of Islam. It is true that no one should deny the people's right to resist occupation. However, killing and slaughtering innocent people in the name of occupation resistance are crimes, not rights as universally agreed.

But kidnapping foreign and indigenous civilians to be slaughtered like sheep in front of cameras is a mostly inhuman and principally savage practice. Such a merciless act distorts the Arab nation's image. It also defames the standing principles of Islam that urge the protection of civilians—regardless of their religions or creeds—visiting or working in Islamic countries.

After three years of occupation, insurgents became more ruthless and brutal. They captured and killed four Russian diplomats in Baghdad in June 2006. The Mujahedeen Shura Council, an umbrella organization linking seven insurgent groups including al-Qaeda in Iraq, announced in a statement that all four Russian diplomats had been killed. "God's verdict has been carried out on the Russian diplomats . . . in revenge for the killing and expulsion of our brothers and sisters by the infidel Russian government," the statement said.[17] Four Russian workers had been killed in Iraq in 2004. This aggression on the part of the Iraqi insurgents astonished many foreign diplomats serving in Iraq as Moscow emphatically opposed the U.S.-led military occupation and continued to dissociate itself from Washington on the issue of Iraq.

Such killing has made the Iraqi resistance movement lose a great deal of sympathy and respect. It is evident that the Western media has widely exploited such actions to defame Islam. They made Islamic nations appear as crude people not differentiating between occupation forces and civilians. To make it worse, such unlawful and inhuman operations expanded to target subjects of friendly countries.

Even Arabs, including Egyptians, Sudanese, and Algerians, became targets of terrorism. Six Egyptian engineers working in Iraq to provide mobile phone service to the Iraqi people were kidnapped. Their work had no connection with the occupation forces. The Egyptian engineers were actually serving no one but the Iraqi people who had suffered the destruction of basic wired and wireless communication infrastructure because of the war.

In Basra, an American journalist was found shot dead a few days after he wrote an opinion piece in the *New York Times*. Steven Vincent's crime was that he criticized Shiite Islamist fundamentalism in the city. Witnesses said gunmen kidnapped the journalist and his translator shortly after they left a hotel. His body was found hours later. This was a deliberate act against human rights and the freedom of expression.[18]

As peace and security deteriorated, U.S. and Iraqi forces carried out a full inspection in Baghdad, street by street. The objective was to take back control of the capital. Thousands of troops surrounded Baghdad's notorious neighborhoods. They disarmed residents through house-to-house inspections. However, political observers reiterated that success in maintaining peace and security depended upon the ability of the Iraqi government to build a dialogue with both the Shiite militias and the Sunni fighters inspired by fundamental Islamism or loyal Ba'athists to Saddam Hussein. Undoubtedly, if the government of Maliki would not make such progress in political reconciliation it would lose its credibility.[19]

After the U.S.-led security sweep, terrorists became more aggressive than ever before. Four U.S. civilians were attacked, and townsmen mutilated the bodies of at least two of the men, dragged them through the streets, suspended them from a bridge, and burned them while crowds danced and cheered. Earlier, twelve miles away, near the town of Habbaniya, five U.S. soldiers were killed when their armored vehicle ran over a roadside bomb. It was the deadliest roadside bombing against U.S. forces since the invasion of Iraq. The new attacks signaled a new level of violence and brutality against the U.S.-led occupation. The violence took place after a gun battle between the insurgents and U.S. Marines in the streets of Fallujah, twenty-five miles west of Baghdad.[20]

The attacks of the insurgents against U.S. subjects stunned U.S. officials. There was a notable increase of violence and unexpected brutality in these attacks. Videotapes in 2004 showed the beheading of American hostages by fanatic militant groups. The captors issued a statement addressed to President Bush: "Your worst days are coming, with the help of God . . . You and your soldiers will regret the day when your feet touched the land of Iraq." [21]

In a video, a man identified himself as Nicholas Berg, twenty-six, of Pennsylvania. He was shown sitting in an orange jumpsuit in front of five armed, hooded men. The hooded men standing behind the American read in Arabic from a paper a message addressed to mothers and wives of American soldiers serving in Iraq: "We tell you that we offered the U.S. administration to exchange this hostage for some of the detainees in Abu-Ghraib and they refused."[22] The Web site claimed that the killing had been carried out by Abu Musab al-Zarqawi, the leader of the Islamist terrorist group that had claimed responsibility for a number of attacks on U.S.-led coalition forces in Iraq.

Iraqi Human Rights Minister Bakhtiar Amin promised that the government would do its utmost to bring Berg's killers to justice. He called the terrorists who committed the immoral crimes psychopaths. However, it is unfortunate that at the time of this writing, the killers have not been brought to justice and are still at large.

In the same period, one and a half years since the occupation began, insurgent gunmen grabbed two Americans and a Briton from a house in a rich section of central Baghdad. The kidnapping evoked a sense of insecurity and instability. It gave rise to doubt in the UN Security Council whether elections could be held as planned by Iraq's interim government and its U.S. supporters. As of September 2004, more than 130 foreigners had been kidnapped. A number of them have been killed but most have been freed. At least five Europeans were being held: two French journalists, two female aid workers from Italy, and one Iraqi woman working in a nongovernmental organization (NGO) providing humanitarian services to the Iraqis since the start of U.S.-led occupation. The two Italian women were later freed, after the Italian prime minister repeatedly called for their release. The Iraqi-British woman, Margaret Hassan, was slaughtered despite the strong plea of the British prime minister to free her. With such kidnapping and butchery, the terrorists entered a new stage of horror.[23]

Has al-Qaeda declared "all-out war on Iraqi Shiites"? The insurgents in Iraq had tremendously increased their ruthlessness and ferocity to include their fellow citizens, the Shiites. Just before the date of the voting for the new draft constitution held in October 2005, more than a dozen highly coordinated bombings ripped through Baghdad, killing at least 160 people. Many of the victims were day laborers. Al-Qaeda insurgents claimed responsibility for the attacks. Violence continued to terrorize the capital as deadly car explosions hit the predominantly Shiite neighborhood of Kazimiyah.

Up to the present, the question that remains unanswered is "Is Tal Afar's U.S.-Iraqi military heavy expedition the real cause for al-Zarqawi to proclaim all-out war against Americans and Shiites?" To answer this question one must look into the Tal Afar's military drive, whether it meant targeting al-Zarqawi himself, his insurgents, or the peaceful Sunni inhabitants of the town.

The Tal Afar military drive in September 2005, as officially announced, targeted in the first place insurgents and not Iraqi inhabitants. It aimed primarily either to catch Zarqawi or to kill him. Thousands of Iraqi and U.S. troops launched severe bombing on the Sunni city. The aim was to completely eliminate suspected guerrillas and al-Qaeda sympathizers in the town. U.S. and Iraqi soldiers have inspected by force mosques, houses, and stores to search for foreign and native insurgents as well as militant rebels. Within two weeks of continuous fighting, the troops freed the town from the terrorists, both indigenous and foreign. Prime Minister

Ibrahim al-Jaafari said at a news conference that he ordered the offensive "to remove all remaining terrorist elements from the city of Tel Afar."[24]

The heavy destruction in the town and massive casualties among men, women, and children made the government reveal that it had wasted no efforts to advise the town in advance to rid itself of the insurgents and place them in a peaceful manner in the custody of the American-Iraqi troops. However, fighting persisted and the terrorists refused to give up. During the first few days, over 140 insurgents were killed and more than 190 detained. A large number of modern weapons caches were discovered.[25] The town was being used, claimed the U.S. and Iraqi militaries, as a center for providing military equipment and foreign fighters possibly smuggled in from Syria to fight Kurds in the north and Shiites in the south.

In the same month when the U.S. and Iraqi troops heavily attacked Tal Afar, al-Zarqawi declared an all-out war against the Shiite government. In a show of power, al-Zarqawi sent his insurgents to a Shiite Muslim mosque in Hilla, blasting themselves and twenty-five people and wounding eighty-seven others. Tragically, the explosion that happened at noon, at the Ibn al-Nima mosque in central Hilla, occurred while funeral services were being held for a Shiite Muslim who was killed in a separate suicide attack.[26]

Just one month after the Tal Afar U.S.-Iraqi military expedition, a man wearing a suicide bomb belt walked into a crowded restaurant in the heart of Baghdad and blew himself up. He killed at least twenty-nine people and wounded thirty, many of them police officers. It was the deadliest such assault to date and occurred just one day after three suicide bombings in Amman, the capital of Jordan, killed fifty-seven people in a coordinated attack also claimed by al-Qaeda. The bombing, as stated by the al-Qaeda insurgents' Web site, was in retaliation for a military operation in the western Iraqi city of Husayba. That was where U.S. and Iraqi forces had been battling insurgents for six days.[27]

Retaliation continued. Insurgents' suicide attacks continued to affect Shia pilgrims. After three days of attacks on pilgrims that killed more than 150 people, 2.5 million Shia pilgrims arrived at the Iraqi holy city of Karbala. Rituals and religious festival mark the end of a forty-day mourning period commemorating the death of Imam Hussein, Prophet Muhammad's grandson, more than 1,300 years ago. Muqtada al-Sadr, head of the strong militia Shiite movement, issued a statement urging pilgrims to join in chants and denounce the attackers. He loudly said to his devout pilgrims, "I ask almighty God to protect you from the sectarian sedition."[28]

It was after three years of occupation that al-Zarqawi decisively stepped up his attacks on Iraqi civilians, aiming at inciting violence between Sunnis and Shiites in Baghdad. Daily attacks against civilians steadily enhanced in sectarian violence. The attacks continued to increase, especially after the February 22 attack on a Shiite shrine in Samarra. Slain bodies were found almost daily in the capital. Many showed signs of being cruelly tortured. It was apparent that the mosque attack on the holy shrine inflamed tensions between Sunni and Shiite Muslims.

Consequently, Baghdad's morgue reported that 1,091 people were killed in the city's daily violence. President Jalal Talabani said about the violence, "These killings are no less dangerous to Iraqis than terror strikes."[29] He further demanded all Iraqi security forces and political leaders to take immediate and forceful action to end the bloodshed. Talabani again urged factions to end the feud by issuing another statement saying, "What is asked of the political parties is that they strenuously and clearly condemn these crimes, regardless of who the perpetrators are."[30] Figures from the ministries of health and interior showed that during April 2006 alone, the Medico Legal Institute in Baghdad issued 1,294 death certificates in March and 1,155 in April. Most of those bodies died as a result of gunshot wounds, from politically and sectarian-motivated violence.[31]

As security in the country was deteriorating, insurgents and militias targeted university professors, schoolteachers, and children. Nouri al-Maliki, the Iraqi prime minister, said "terrorists and Saddamists" were behind the bombing at Al-Mustansiriya University and schools in Baghdad. Sixty-five people were killed when a car and a suicide bomber exploded outside the university. More than one hundred people were injured in the blast, mostly students and staff leaving the university.[32]

Students of the university were shocked and angered. While mourning the dead students, they staged a protest demanding more protection for students and professors. Some students held banners protesting the deadliest violent attack in the war-torn country.

Just a few days after the bombing at Mustansiriyah University, early one morning in February 2007, a female suicide bomber killed forty-one people at Baghdad College, mostly attended by Shiite women. Witnesses said a woman carried out the attack at the business school annexed to the university. Interior Ministry officials said they were still investigating those reports. The college is located in a mostly Shiite district of northeast Baghdad. Suicide bombings by women were not unusual in Iraq at the time. The U.S. ambassador to Iraq, Zalmay Khalilzad, said, "This cowardly act of violence underscores that the terrorists are the enemies of all Iraqis, regardless of sect. They want Iraq to fail. Now is the time for the Iraqis to come together against these terrorists."[33]

After the U.S. and Iraqi troops swiftly invaded Tal Afar, killing and arresting a large number of insurgents, rebel gunmen added teachers to their target lists. This was revenge against Shiites. They assembled five teachers, brought them to an empty classroom, and executed all of them. All those killed were Shiites. As many as ten terrorist gunmen dressed in police uniforms broke into the school building and shot the teachers. As the insurgents fled the building, they also shot and killed the teachers' driver.[34]

The insurgents continued their aggression against school teachers. Four teachers were slain northeast of Baghdad. Gunmen killed them near Balad Ruz, fifty miles northeast of Baghdad. The teachers were traveling to their school in a minibus when gunmen stopped their vehicle and forced seven teachers and the driver from the vehicle. The gunmen shot four of them. The other teachers and the driver were allowed to leave. The attack took place as the trial of former Iraqi President Saddam Hussein and seven codefendants resumed after a three-week delay.[35]

In another incident, a homemade bomb killed four children on their way to school in central Baghdad, three girls and a boy. They were ten to fourteen years old and included two daughters and a son of an Iraqi vendor working in a nearby public market. Brokenhearted, he said, "We are poor people who have nothing to do with politics. We only wanted to live a decent life. What is the guilt of my dead children? They were only heading to school."[36]

Meanwhile, children continued to be targeted by insurgents. A bomb exploded outside a family home hosting a wedding reception in north Baghdad just as the bridegroom's party was arriving in a convoy of cars. Twenty-three people were killed in the blast, including nineteen infants, and another nineteen were wounded, many of them seriously. In another attack on schoolchildren, two mortars slammed into a girls' school in a mainly Sunni neighborhood in western Baghdad, killing at least one girl and wounding nearly two dozen others. Several bombs exploded in the courtyard of the al-Khulood school.[37]

As shown above, after four years of U.S.-led occupation, the security situation in the country had tremendously deteriorated. Bloodbaths, butchery, and holocaust became worse than ever before. Insurgent Sunni groups, led by Abu Musab al-Zarqawi, increased their revenge by killing 150 Iraqis in Baghdad. The attack, the insurgents announced, was in revenge for a U.S.-Iraqi offensive in the northern town of Tal Afar. A statement on an Islamist Web site often used by the Sunni Muslim group led by Zarqawi said, "We would like to congratulate the Muslim nation and inform it that the battle to avenge the Sunnis of Tal Afar has begun."[38]

Fears of civil war grew ahead of an October 15, 2005, referendum on a new constitution for Iraq. The government accused Sunni rebels of attacking the Shiite majority, in a bid to spark a civil war. Most of the victims of rebel attacks were Shiites. Divisions between Iraq's two main

Islamic sects deepened considerably when Shiite religious parties were elected to head the government and hold majority in the interim assembly, leaving Sunnis with a minor role. Moreover, deep tensions increased as the government held a national referendum in October on the draft constitution that was largely opposed by Sunni Arabs.

September 28, 2005, marked the witness of the first female suicide bomber. For the first time in the history of insurgency, the Iraqi rebels started to use female suicide bombers. It was a woman disguised in a man's robe and headdress. She rushed into a group of Iraqi army recruits and detonated explosives strapped to her body. She killed at least eight and wounded up to thirty. A female suicide bomber might have been chosen because she could get through checkpoints, at which women are rarely searched, then dress in her disguise to join the line of men. Iraq's most blatant insurgent group, al-Qaeda, claimed responsibility for the attack saying a "blessed sister" carried it out. Iraqi military officials suggested that using women suicide bombers could be a sign that the insurgency was getting greater support among the population of both men and women. They were getting more militant and willing to take on a greater role. It could also be a sign that the insurgents were having trouble finding male recruits.[39]

The insurgents are mostly Sunnis. The militias are highly trained and militarily equipped Shiites. Both Sunni insurgents and Shiite militias attacked each other, including policemen, people praying in mosques, participants in religious celebrations and funerals. The attacks undoubtedly had sectarian overtones. Authorities believe the insurgents are mainly Sunni Arabs intensifying their attacks largely after the Shiite transitional government came to power. The authorities also believe that Muqtada al-Sadr Shiite militias have been trained, equipped, and supported by neighboring Iran. For revenge, the militias killed Sunni inhabitants by firing squads of Shiite militias of al-Sadr. Many Sunni victims arrive at the morgues with their hands and feet bound and mouths sealed shut with tape. The blood baths overflowed in Baghdad. Iraq seemed to be verging on an all-out civil war.[40]

The Sunni insurgents and Shiite militias consequently became more brutal and heartless. In a grave incident, ten workers were seized from a bakery in a mostly Shiite-populated neighborhood of Kazimiyah in Baghdad. The gunmen arrived in two trucks. They broke into the bakery and abducted the workers. The kidnapping came a day after a mortar shell hit a well-known market in the area, killing four people. On the same day, police found the bullet-riddled bodies of ten men who apparently had been tortured. Sectarian revenge had taken a serious bend toward civil war. It became apparent that both sectarian parties were engaged in a power struggle.[41]

In March 2007, four years after the occupation began, terrorism continued its ruthless operation in Iraq. The bodies of fourteen policemen were found northeast of Baghdad. The Islamic State of Iraq, an al-Qaeda-affiliated Sunni group, said it abducted and killed fourteen policemen in retaliation for the rape of a Sunni woman by members of the Shiite-dominated police force. The Islamic State of Iraq had threatened to kill the hostages within twenty-four hours if the Iraqi government did not hand over officers accused in the rape case and release all Sunni women held in Iraqi prisons.[42]

While al-Qaeda suicide attacks intensified, Shiite pilgrims defied the attacks. In March 2007, around 2.5 million Shia pilgrims arrived at the Iraqi holy city of Karbala after three days of attacks that killed more than 150 people. At least ten thousand police officers were on around-the-clock patrol in an unprecedented security operation. It was estimated that 120 Shia pilgrims were killed in twin suicide blasts. Muqtada al-Sadr, head of the Sadrist Shiite movement in Iraq, denounced the attackers, saying, "I ask almighty God to protect you from the sectarian sedition."[43]

INSURGENTS ASSASSINATE IRAQI ISLAMIC CLERICS

It would be a great mistake for the West to refer to Islamic insurgents in Iraq as enemies of Christians, Buddhists, or those from other faiths who were kidnapped and killed for religious reasons. As is evident above, it became clear that the war in Iraq is not between Muslims and non-Muslims. In fact, it is a war declared by Islamic fundamentalist rebels, both Sunnis and al-Sadr Shiite militias, against the U.S.-led coalition and those cooperating with their forces regardless of their nationalities, religions, creeds, or faiths.

It is evident that the neofundamentalist Islamist rebels were fighting against occupation. At the same time, they were fighting to gain religious as well as political power. They kidnapped and killed a large number of Iraqi Muslim clerics, civil servants, policemen, and civilians. They also kidnapped and killed Muslim Turks, Egyptians, Saudis, Pakistanis, Indonesians, and those of other Islamic nationalities.

Furthermore, insurgents assassinated a number of members of influential religious groups in Iraq itself. Gunmen shot and killed Sheik Mohamed al-Janabi as he entered a mosque to perform noon prayers. Gunmen also kidnapped Sheik al-Zeidi and two of his bodyguards as they left a mosque after prayers in a largely Shiite neighborhood. Sheik Faidh Amin al-Faidh met the same fate. Gunmen shot him at his home in northern Mosul. The three clerics belonged to the Association of Muslim

Scholars, a group of conservative clerics who opposed the occupation of Iraq and the elections on January 30, 2005.

In another ethnic attack in September 2005, two suicide bombers blew themselves up, killing at least seventy and wounding eighty people. The bomb destroyed two Shia mosques in northeastern Iraq. The attack aimed, in the first place, at fueling sectarian tension before the elections. The bombers walked into the Shiite mosques in Khanaqin when they were full for Friday noon prayers. While inside, the bombers detonated explosive belts strapped to their waists. Many children died, as a considerable number of fathers had taken their sons for prayer.[44]

The slaying further broke off Iraq's Sunni Arab minority before the time of the elections. The Sunni Association of Muslim Scholars had already called for a boycott of the vote. However, interim Prime Minister Ayad Allawi affirmed that his government was determined to hold the election as scheduled. He described those calling for a boycott as a small minority. The vote for the 275-member National Assembly was the first election since Saddam Hussein was deposed. Government saw the election as a major step toward building democracy in Iraq.

The fierce fighting against the insurgents escalated with the U.S.-led offensive against Fallujah, Mussel, and other northern cities. To a large number of Iraqis, the election scheduled for end of January 2005 might be practically impossible in the torn northern regions. However, the interim government insisted that ballots should be cast even in unstable areas in the Sunni triangle. The election was carried out on the scheduled time with only a small percentage of Sunnis going to the poll stations.

It was apparent that the Sunni-led insurgency intended to deepen the sectarian rift, ahead of elections. Tensions were already high following the Iraqi government's admission that a number of Sunni detainees had been tortured in an Iraqi Interior Ministry prison. The UN Assistance Mission for Iraq issued a Human Rights Report that called for an international inquiry into the Iraqi government jails in the wake of the scandal. This happened while the U.S. administration was hoping that October elections would help bring greater stability to the country and would facilitate significant troop withdrawals in 2006. However, these attacks demonstrated that the insurgency and militias still threatened to drive the country into civil war.

INSURGENTS ACCELERATE ABDUCTIONS OF FOREIGNERS AND IRAQIS

Just before the election of January 30, 2005, Judge Qais Shameri was killed along with his son in an ambush as they left their home in eastern

Baghdad. The attack took place during morning rush hour. The attack clearly showed the ability of insurgents to strike before the national election. Ansar al-Sunna claimed responsibility for the assassination.[45]

As we have seen, after the abductions of foreigners, the pattern of terrorism changed to the abduction of indigenous Iraqis. In a videotape aired on an Arabic television station, pictures of several Arab men surrounded by gun-toting masked men were shown. They were purportedly kidnapped Iraqi soldiers. The announcer said they were threatened with death unless an arrested Shiite leader was freed within forty-eight hours. The video was from a group calling itself the "Brigades of Mohammed bin Abdullah" and claimed to have eighteen captive members of the Iraqi National Guard.

The Islamic Unification and Jihad group led by Musab al-Zarqawi claimed responsibility for the massacre of forty-four Iraqi soldiers after they were ambushed near the Iraq-Iran border. They were killed along with their four drivers. The killings occurred about eighty miles east of Baghdad. In another incident, two car bombs killed sixteen Iraqis and wounded thirty-eight others when they exploded at an entrance to Baghdad's fortified Green Zone. Five Iraqi police officers were among the dead. Iraq's interim government is based in the Green Zone, which is also the home to the U.S. embassy. An embassy official said the area's security was not breached during the attack.[46]

The Iraq Resistance Movement claimed the killing of Izzadine Saleem, also known as Abdel-Zahraa Othman, head of Iraq's Governing Council, as he was waiting at the U.S. checkpoint along a tree-lined street, preparing to enter the Green Zone in Baghdad. Saleem, a Shiite Muslim in his sixties, held the rotating presidency of a twenty-five-member Governing Council for May 2004. He was the second council member murdered since their appointment in the council. The mentioned "movement" claimed responsibility. Saleem was a highly devoted Iraqi in the service of his country in its chaotic situation. A short time later, gunmen opened fire on a car carrying Nashe Hassan, an imminent Iraqi National Guard general, killing him and his driver on his way to work. The attack took place in Baquba, about thirty-five miles north of Baghdad.[47]

News of kidnapping, abducting, and killing of officials in embassies discouraged Arab and Muslim governments from sending their diplomats to strengthen ties with Iraq. Just before the killing of the Egyptian ambassador, the Iraqi foreign minister had announced that Egypt would be the first Arab country to upgrade its diplomatic representation by appointing a full-fledged ambassador. After the killing of its high-ranking official, the government of Egypt withdrew its diplomatic mission from Iraq for safety reasons.

The most intriguing question asked by Iraqis at this time became "Was there any money given to Iraqi kidnappers to release their foreign hostages abducted and kidnapped by the insurgents?" Money paid as ransom was totally denied by governments. However, according to a report issued in May 2006 by Al Jazeera, the Arabic broadcaster well known for its accuracy, it was reported that France, Germany, and Italy paid about $45 million to obtain the release of hostages kidnapped in Iraq, despite denying it in public. Al Jazeera quoted British newspaper reports based on "documents seen by *The Times*," which said, "Britain has not handed out any money to kidnap gangs . . . The list of payments has been seen by Western diplomats, who were angered at the behavior of the above-mentioned governments and said that it encouraged organized crime gangs to grab more foreign captives." Britain never paid to free its citizens, but it was understood to have paid intermediaries "expenses" for their efforts to make contact with the kidnappers. France, Italy, and Germany all publicly denied paying any ransom money. "But according to the documents, held by security officials in Baghdad who played a crucial role in hostage negotiations, sums from $2.5 million to $10 million per person have been paid over the past 21 months," the paper said.

According to the unofficial report, France paid out a combined $25 million for the release of Georges Malbrunot in December 2004 and Florence Aubenas in June 2005, while Italy handed over $11 million for the freedom of Simona Pari, Simona Torretta, and Giuliani Sgrena in 2004 and again in 2005. Also, Germany was said to have given kidnappers $8 million to secure the release of three hostages, including Rene Braeunlich and Thomas Nitzschke, who were freed earlier. The Italian daily *Repubblica* cited an official report according to which Rome handed over several million dollars in ransom for Iraqi hostages. Germany's national broadcaster, ARD, earlier reported that a $10 million ransom had been paid out for Braeunlich and Nitzschke, a claim the government in Berlin denied.[48]

IRAQI REBELS OUT OF CONTROL

It became evident that Iraqi rebels had become out of control in the northern regions as foreign insurgents kept supporting them. The interim government and the U.S.-led coalition force suspected that foreign insurgents were closely linked to al-Qaeda network. They were operating in the Sunni city of Fallujah, thirty miles west of Baghdad. It was believed that Fallujah was the home of Iraq's most rebellious and aggressive Sunni Muslim fighters.

It was also believed that the insurgent groups in Fallujah were led by two rebel leaders: al-Zarqawi, the Jordanian rebel who bore a fierce hatred for the Shiites and occupation troops, and Abu-Abdullah, a young Saudi Wahhabi fanatic. Both were closely associated with al-Qaeda. They declared responsibility for many of the kidnappings.

The insurgents' logic that their acts of aggression were aiming at ousting collaborators of the U.S.-led troops from Iraq was obscure, ambiguous, and morally wrong. In fact, there was a growing conviction that their deeds were motivated by fanaticism, conservatism, and political ambitions. The abductors, mostly affiliated with vague, little-known Islamic groups, claimed substantial ransoms or requested unrealistic demands to secure their captives' release. In other instances, they beheaded their victims without mercy, an act that cannot be justified under any condition. These irresponsible resistance fighters had the boldness to record their inhuman performances on videotapes, to be shown to the world.

Condemnations have strongly been declared by eminent Islamic thinkers, institutions, and clerics in different parts of the world. All denounced such acts as utterly un-Islamic as well as inhuman. Despite such condemnation, the perpetrators showed no sign of discontinuing their kidnapping.

Regardless of such strong pleas, more foreigners and Iraqis were held hostage, facing the threat of slaughter. They were Americans, French, British, Egyptians, Indians, Kenyans, Turks, and people of other nationalities. They were persecuted despite the fact that the countries of some of these captives had not contributed military personnel to the U.S.-led multinational troops in Iraq. Even a senior Egyptian diplomat was seized as he left a mosque in Baghdad after Friday prayers. These and other incidents clearly indicated that Islamic insurgents in troubled Iraq did not differentiate between nationalities, religious convictions, faiths, or beliefs. To these insurgents, we conceive, political power is the aim.[49]

The situation gradually deteriorated. In his article "Can you tell a Sunni from a Shiite?" Jeff Stein of the *New York Times* said, "For the past several months, I've been wrapping up lengthy interviews with U.S. counterterrorism officials with a fundamental question: 'Do you know the difference between a Sunni and a Shiite?' If knowing your enemy is the most basic rule of war, I do not think it is out of bounds. And as I quickly explain to my subjects, I'm not looking for theological explanations, simply the basics: Who's on what side today, and what does each want?" The question remains unanswered after the sectarian confusion and political frustration in which Iraqis live.[50]

FALLUJAH EPISODE AND AL-ZARQAWI TERRORIST REBELS

The U.S. military intelligence indicated that Fallujah had become a haven for the Iraqi rebels and sanctuary for the Zarqawi group, which was blamed for much of Iraq's bloodiest violence. Zarqawi's followers started to move to outlying areas of Fallujah. They hid amid the civilian population of the town. Allawi, Iraq's interim prime minister, warned in October 2004 the people of Fallujah to hand over foreign fighters or face a major operation to root them out. The people of Fallujah did not respond favorably to the plea, as they feared Zarqawi and his followers. In the end, the U.S. troops and Iraqi military invaded the city.[51]

The massive Fallujah invasion, involving some ten thousand U.S. and Iraqi troops, launched raids and arrested suspected rebels. The aim was to destroy the al-Qaeda insurgent hotbeds. It took ten consecutive days for U.S. combat forces to capture this Iraqi city and root out guerrillas entrenched in its buildings. It was the most sustained period of street-to-street fighting, similar, as many witnessed, to what the American forces encountered in the Vietnam War. This left the former guerrilla strongholds mostly in the hands of the U.S. forces. More than fifty U.S. military members were killed and 425 wounded in the operations.

As a result, the formidable Sunni city of Fallujah came under siege after the invasion and fierce military intervention. The insurgents ceased to fight after a long resistance. "We have got Fallujah under siege," proudly declared Lieutenant General Ricardo Sanchez in a news conference held in April 2004.[52] He refuted the claim that the U.S. forces deprived its inhabitants of humanitarian supplies. The hospital director in Fallujah confirmed that up to three hundred Iraqi citizens had been killed and at least four hundred hurt in the Sunni town in the four days since U.S. Marines began a series of air strikes and artillery fire on guerrillas. A third of the city's three hundred thousand residents had fled their homes earlier to other areas.

U.S. warplanes pounded Fallujah with five-hundred-pound laser-guided bombs, tanks, and artillery. Some struck targeted buildings where militants were meeting and mounting attacks on Marine positions. There were pockets of resistance and the U.S. military, along with Iraqi forces, determined to make sure that Fallujah was a secure city. However, many Iraqi citizens were killed as some air raids and artillery bombarding failed to hit the insurgent sanctuaries in the city. Building destruction was enormous.

Meanwhile, thousands of angry Sunni and Shiite protesters gathered outside Baghdad's Um al-Aura mosque, chanting mottos in support of the people of Fallujah. Similar heated rallies took place in Mosul and Baquba, north of the capital.[53]

Huge caches of arms were discovered in Fallujah. U.S. Marines and Iraqi soldiers found the residences of Zarqawi and his followers. Some of their residences were packed with a large supply of weapons and loaded with explosives. American and Iraqi officials believed that it became evident that Zarqawi and some of his followers had not been living in the city for some time.[54]

In searching the city of Fallujah, Iraqi troops found hostage "slaughter houses" where people were held captive and beheaded. In addition, they found CDs labeled "beheaded on . . ." and showing the decapitations of hostages. Black clothing and masks worn by the kidnappers when they made the videos were found, along with black banners hoisted in the background on which names of the Islamic groups were written.[55]

AGGRESSION OF SUNNI INSURGENTS IN MOSUL AND SAMARRA

When the U.S. military and Iraqi forces launched a major offensive on Fallujah, it became evident that there were large numbers of insurgents that fled to Mosul. The insurgents' plan was to launch attacks from there. The military conducted an offensive against insurgents in Mosul, but the violence and kidnappings continued. With about 1.7 million people, Mosul is the third-largest city in Iraq. It is located in the northern region of Iraq with its rich oil fields.

The insurgents in Mosul, six times the size of Fallujah, exhibited deadly aggression toward U.S.-led troops and Iraqi collaborators. As a result, thousands of Iraqi police fled their posts, and more murdered bodies of Iraqi National Guardsmen were seen every day. In December 2004, a large number of Iraqis and U.S. troops were killed. In a dining hall at a U.S. base near Mosul, a suicide bomber killed more than twenty-two U.S. troops and wounded another seventy-two, including members of the Iraqi National Guard, U.S. military, and civilian officials. The casualties included seven U.S. military contractors. "It's a sad day in Mosul," said the commander of the Army's Task Force Olympia, which included about 8,500 U.S. troops in the Mosul area.[56]

Jaish Ansar al-Sunnah (the Army of Islamic Sunna Supporters), the Iraqi militant group, promptly claimed responsibility for the attack in a posting on Islamist Web sites. The group also claimed responsibility for a series of previous attacks on U.S. military bases and Iraqi police stations. The attack took place shortly after the visit of the British prime minister to UK troops in Iraq. It was considered by the military one of the deadliest incidents for the U.S. forces since the invasion in March 2003. Owing to the pressure of the insurgents in the Sunni Triangle and in order to improve security for scheduled January 15 elections, it became necessary for the U.S. military to boost its troops in Iraq to 150,000. This was the highest level of U.S. combat since the war began.[57]

After Mosul, Iraqi forces and U.S. Marines in October 2004 tightened their hold on the insurgents' stronghold in Samarra, some sixty miles north of Baghdad. The offensive forces killed 125 guerrillas and captured 88. It was considered the largest offensive since the fall of Saddam Hussein. About five thousand Iraqi and U.S. troops, backed by artillery and fighter jets, launched the operation. Forces backed by tanks pushed through the streets as guerrillas unleashed mortar attacks and fired rocket-propelled grenades and rifles from the rooftops. The Samarra offensive took place after a day of bloodshed in Baghdad, where car bombs were detonated near a U.S. military envoy, killing a large number of Iraqis.

It was true that Iraqi officials and U.S. advisors conceived that violence in the Sunni Triangle would likely frustrate the arrangement made by the interim government as the date of the election approached. Increasing attacks in the northern regions raised new questions about the security of the voting. In Washington, a White House spokesperson said fifteen out of eighteen Iraqi provinces had peace and security. Other areas were ongoing security challenges.[58]

WILL INSURGENTS BE GONE IN A YEAR'S TIME?

Iraq's interim president, Ghazi al-Yawar, wishfully vowed that insurgency would be gone in a year's time. In a CNN interview, al-Yawar said, "Iraq is not fighting the Viet Cong, which had principles and popular support. We have been fighting Saddam loyalists . . . They knew they were fighting a losing battle. The whole Iraqi population was against them." He continued, saying, "I'm sick and tired of them. I think one year from now, exactly, we'll be very busy preparing for our free democratic election after we have a constitution." In the interview, al-Yawar added that he believed the United States was wrong when it eliminated the Iraqi army. It was a mistake to disband the Iraqi military. Then he continued, saying that he foresaw U.S. forces remaining in Iraq until enough Iraqi forces had been recruited and trained to replace them. Three years have passed since his remarks. Iraq acquired a draft constitution, democratically voted on December 15, 2005. However, the Sunni insurgents and Shiite militia fighters continued to be active, powerful, and dangerous.[59]

The good news was, despite increasing aggression of terrorists, Iraqi voters chose a 275-member transitional national assembly. The assembly was able to put together a draft constitution that was presented to voters in a referendum. The constitution was approved.[60]

As a result of the election, the U.S. administration and the Iraqi government repeatedly declared, "No Concessions to Terrorists." However, Iraqi voices became louder, indicating that dialogue with insurgents may help bring back security and peace to the country. During his visit to Cairo in June 2005, former Iraqi Prime Minister Ayad Allawi stressed that stability in Iraq could be realized through dialogue with all factions. Military force alone, he added, cannot defuse the tensions. Meanwhile, U.S. Defense Secretary Rumsfeld said American forces might take as long as twelve years to beat the insurgents. He expected that more difficulties lay ahead as terrorist attacks had been growing more frequent. Rumsfeld affirmed that only the Iraqis, not foreign forces, could defeat the insurgents.[61]

Condoleezza Rice arrived on an unexpected visit in Iraq in May 2005 for talks with Iraqi government leaders and U.S. military commanders. She discussed ways and means to move the political process forward in Iraq to reduce violence that had killed many Iraqis and U.S.-led troops. She emphasized that "the insurgency is very violent, but you defeat insurgencies not just militarily—in fact not especially militarily—you defeat them by having a political alternative that is strong." She continued telling the reporters, "The Iraqis are now going to have to intensify their efforts to demonstrate that in fact the political process is the answer for the Iraqi people."[62]

"Could Iraqi insurgency last for years to come?" To answer this question, Rumsfeld in his several visits to Iraq reinforced the policy of the U.S. administration that insurgencies in Iraq could continue for years. "Coalition forces, foreign forces are not going to repress that insurgency. We're going to create an environment that the Iraqi people and the Iraqi security forces can win against that insurgency," he declared.[63]

In June 2005, the *Sunday Times* reported that U.S. officials met secretly with Iraqi insurgent commanders north of Baghdad to try to negotiate an end to the bloodshed. U.S. and Iraqi officials, as reported, were looking for the right people in the Sunni community to talk to. Iraqi sources said that U.S. officials met purported guerrilla leaders. U.S. and Iraqi officials had repeated continual consultations with Sunni tribal leaders, clerics, and others who profess to represent elements of the resistance. However, the U.S. officials explained that these were not negotiations and any talks have not involved the most violent groups such as Ansar al-Sunna or Zarqawi's group.[64]

THE UNITED STATES DECLARES NO
CONCESSION TO TERRORISM

It became evident that the administration appeared to be shifting its strategy, subtly, focusing more on political solutions with the Sunnis. Defense Secretary Rumsfeld confirmed that talks had taken place with some insurgent leaders. Meanwhile, the U.S. commander of the multinational coalition in Iraq said, "The conflict will ultimately be resolved in a political process." President Bush used the first anniversary of Iraq's sovereignty to try to ease Americans' doubts about the mission. He outlined a winning strategy for a violent conflict that had cost, in the first two years of the occupation, the lives of more than 2,500 Americans.

President Bush, in his address in June 2005 at Fort Bragg, North Carolina, home of the Army's elite 82nd Airborne Division, argued that there was no need to change course in Iraq despite the upsetting images produced by daily insurgent attacks. He said, "The key to success in Iraq is for the Iraqis to be able and capable of defending their democracy against terrorists." Bush continued, "Parallel with the security track is a political track. Obviously, the political track has made progress this year when eight million people went to the polls and voted."[65]

Fighting terrorism become an extremely important issue in the U.S. poll for the election of the president for a second term, carried out in December 2004, just before the new year. The situation in Iraq was at the top of a list of eighteen issues that concern Americans, with 90 percent of respondents to a national poll describing it as "extremely important" or "very important," up from 81 percent a year before.

Results of the CNN/USA Today Gallup poll suggested that terrorism was among four other issues that ranked nearly as high, with 87 percent of respondents saying it is "extremely important" or "very important," down only slightly from the highly charged weeks after the terrorist attacks of September 11, 2001.[66]

Several U.S. troops backed by helicopter gunships, artilleries, and tanks attacked towns in the far west of Iraq to hunt down al-Qaeda rebels hiding in towns and villages near the Syrian border. Operation "Iron Fist" was launched against what the U.S. military called a "known terrorist sanctuary" near the borders. Previous operations appeared not to have much success, as insurgents had quickly returned to reoccupy the towns and resume guerrilla activities. The main objective of "Iron Fist" was to root out al-Qaeda terrorists in Iraq operating within the area and to disrupt insurgent support systems.

The offensive increased a few weeks before a referendum on the draft constitution. This took place when the Iraqi government and U.S. commanders expected a surge in violence across the country similar to that experienced in the first post-Saddam Hussein elections in January 2004. The offensive came two weeks before a referendum on a new constitution, when U.S. commanders and the government expected a big rise in violence across the country.

The Iraqi National Assembly speaker denounced the U.S. military operations: "In this respect, I have called before these attacks for halting the military operations so that people will not believe the attacks are aimed at preventing them from participating in the referendum."[67]

After three years and two months of U.S.-led occupation, insurgents were still powerful and dangerous. Insurgents shot down a U.S. helicopter south of Baghdad and killed two U.S. soldiers, bringing the weekend death toll of American service members to seven. The helicopter attack took place during fighting insurgents in Youssifiyah, twelve miles south of Baghdad. It was the second helicopter shot down in six weeks over that area commonly known as the "Triangle of Death." An Apache helicopter was downed there a few months prior. The fatalities rose to 2,443, the number of U.S. military personnel who have died since the war began until May 2006.[68]

An Iraqi farmer reported to the police that he had witnessed an attack on a U.S. military checkpoint. Insurgents swarmed the scene, killing the driver of a military car before taking two of his U.S. comrades captive. U.S. troops, supported by helicopters and warplanes, flew over the "Triangle of Death" south of Baghdad searching for the missing service members. The captives were not found. The representative for U.S. forces in Baghdad said, "Coalition and Iraqi forces will continue to search everywhere possible, uncovering every stone, until our soldiers are found, and we will continue to use every resource available in our search." After a few days, their bodies were discovered.[69]

ARAB NATIONS FIGHT TERRORISM FUNDING IN IRAQ

Arab nations teamed up to fight terrorist funding in Iraq. They formed a governmental group to bolster the fight against illegal cash flows to insurgents in Iraq. The Financial Action Task Force (FATF), an intergovernmental body, issued directions that set global standards in the fight against the global financial system followed by al-Qaeda and its affiliates. The UN member states were advised to implement the UN and FATF rules on preventing money-supported terrorism.[70]

Arab thinkers and enlightened politicians warned their countries not to be conventional in confronting terrorism. They emphasized that their countries should adopt an advancing unified Arab vision and mechanism to effectively combat terrorism in cooperation with regional and international organizations. Combating terrorism requires tremendous human, technological, and financial resources that might not be readily available in each country today. Many different terrorist groups are able to easily communicate and coordinate over vast distances. They have made ample use of the tremendous resources made available to them by modern telecommunication systems and the Internet. This fact should induce the

Arab countries into confronting terrorism in a more coordinated manner; this is needed to abort new, technologically driven terrorist plots.[71]

A Department of Homeland Security (DHS) advisory, in November 2006, cautioned that al-Qaeda might be planning cyber attacks on banking and financial institution Web sites. A DHS spokesperson told CNN that the threat apparently was posted on a jihadist Web site and translated into English. The Department of Homeland Security put financial institutions in New York City and Washington, DC, including the headquarters of Citigroup and Prudential Financial on high alert, saying it had specific intelligence of possible terror attacks.[72]

An examination of the ignition of civil war in Iraq is continued in the following chapter, with the bombing of Holy Shiite shrines by Sunnis, and the Shiites' explosive reaction. This chapter will also show how the intense sectarian violence and deterioration of peace was not hindered by the death of Zarqawi, the notorious civil war advocate, although this was a long-sought victory.

CHAPTER 10

THE IGNITION OF
CIVIL WAR IN IRAQ

PRESIDENT BUSH SAID IN THE FIRST OF A SERIES of speeches marking the third anniversary of the start of the U.S.-led war, "I wish I could tell you that the violence is waning and that the road ahead will be smooth. It will not. There will be tougher fighting and more days of struggle, and we will see more images of chaos and carnage in the days and months to come."[1]

Three years into the occupation and Iraq was slipping closer to all-out sectarian war, the U.S. administration seeing that as being the ultimate aim of the Sunni insurgence and Shiite militias. Civil war would delay the hope of the American people to withdraw their troops from Iraq as soon as possible.

On this occasion, former interim Prime Minister Ayad Allawi told British Broadcasting Corporation (BBC), "It is unfortunate that we are in civil war. We are losing each day as an average 50 to 60 people throughout the country, if not more." He continued, "If this is not civil war, then God knows what civil war is."[2]

BOMBING THE HOLY SHIITE SHRINES
IN THE TOWN OF SAMARRA

The sectarian nervousness reached its highest level in February 2006 when a dozen men, apparently Sunni militants, dressed in paramilitary uniforms, entered the holiest shrine in Samarra, sixty miles north of Baghdad. They handcuffed four guards who were sleeping in a back room. The attack was at early morning after the *Al-fagr* (dawn) prayers. The attackers quickly placed a bomb in the dome of the holy shrine and detonated it. The bomb caused severe damage to the shrine. The force of the blasts caused the dome to collapse and scattered its 72,000 pieces of gold on the ground. A Tunisian terrorist was held accountable in the

Samarra mosque bombing. He was accused of playing an active role in the bombing that triggered a wave of sectarian violence in all Iraq. The Tunisian, Abu Qudama, as a foreign insurgent, was suspected to operate under a terrorist cell of al-Qaeda in Iraq.

What profoundly angered the Shiites was that the shrine is considered one of four major Shiite holy shrines in Iraq. The site in Samarra has a deep religious meaning as two of the twelve imams revered by mainstream Shiites are buried there. Moreover, according to Shiite belief, the twelfth Imam, Muhammad al-Mahdi, was at the site of the shrine before he disappeared. This incident attacking the most holy Shiite sites was a severe blow to peace and security in Iraq. Such an attack on an important and holy religious shrine constituted a grave aggression toward Shiite Islamists at a time of rising sectarian tensions between Shiites and Arab Sunnis. Samarra is a predominantly Sunni city and the Askary Shrine falls under the Sunni government endowment.[3]

There was a growing fear that the incident would increase the possibility of civil war in the country. Thus, President Bush issued a statement extending his sympathy to Iraqis. "The United States condemns this cowardly act in the strongest possible terms. I ask all Iraqis to exercise restraint in the wake of this tragedy and to pursue justice in accordance with the laws and Constitution of Iraq," he said. The U.S. ambassador in Iraq, Zalmay Khalzad, commented that the attack was carried out in a critical moment for Iraq with deliberate attempt to create sectarian tension.[4]

To put an end to the Shia-Sunni violence, the Shia highest cleric, al-Sistani, issued his strongest call yet for an end to Shia-Sunni violence. He urged Iraqis against "falling into the trap of sectarian and ethnic strife." He continued saying that such tension between Shiites and Sunnis would only delay the departure of American and other foreign troops.[5]

What made the situation worsen between the two sects was that just seven months after bombing the holiest Shiite shrines in the town of Samarra, a terrorist pulled his minivan into a busy market in the sacred Shiite city of Kufa. He blew himself up, killing 59 people and wounding 132 people in one of the bloodiest attacks in Iraq in 2006. The explosion was fifty meters from the gold-domed Shiite shrine of Kufa. The blast sparked clashes between police and angry Shiite protesters calling for revenge. This incident dealt a fresh blow to the new Prime Minister Nouri al-Maliki's efforts to promote national reconciliation and avoid a slide toward civil war. The Shiites blamed the Kufa attack on the "criminal Baathists and terrorists of Mahmudiya."[6] A total of 5,818 civilians were reportedly killed and at least 5,762 wounded during May and June 2006, according to a report prepared by UN Assistance Mission for Iraq.[7]

SHIITE ANGER EXPLODES IN IRAQ

Following that bombing attack on one of the country's most sacred Shiite shrines located in Samarra, Shiite anger exploded in various parts of Iraq. Across Iraq, thousands of Shiites demonstrated against the attack in Samarra, which destroyed the dome of Al Askariya, also known as the Golden Mosque because of its color.

Shiite protesters demanded retaliation. In the chaotic twenty-four hours following the bombing, 140 Iraqis, most of them Sunni Arabs including a number of eminent clerics, were killed in central Iraq in the turmoil of sectarian violence for revenge. At least forty more Sunni bodies were found south of Baghdad, and more were being discovered throughout the day across Iraq. Dozens of Sunni mosques were attacked and several burned to the ground. As a result, the situation became tenser between the Shiites and Sunni Arabs. Sunni politicians broke off talks with Shiite leaders over the formation of a new government. The Sunnis accused the Shiite employees in the government of encouraging reprisals against Sunnis.

Shiite and Kurdish political and religious leaders continued their call for restraint. They warned that Iraq could slip into full-fledged civil war as ethnic tension rose across the country. They also warned the militant Shiites not to make retaliatory attacks on Sunni mosques. It was apparent that the attack on the Askariya Shrine had strengthened the position of hard-line and prejudiced Shiites. They manipulated the attack as grounds for using the strong and aggressive Shiite militias that the U.S. forces had been instructed to disband.[8]

In a series of acts of political revenge, gunmen from Shiite militias assassinated a Sunni community leader, Sheik Nazal, in the stronghold of Fallujah. He was a Sunni preacher and chairperson of the Fallujah City Council.[9] In addition, a top commander in Iraq's army was shot to death on a western Baghdad road. This took place in a series of attacks that killed at least ten. Major General Mubdar Hatim was the commander of the Iraqi army's sixth division, which was given the responsibility for security in Baghdad. He was shot while visiting troops in the Baghdad district of Khadamiya.[10]

As security in Baghdad deteriorated and violence intensified, lawyers representing Saddam announced that they would boycott the special tribunal trying of the ousted president until they were provided with better security. One of the lawyers was kidnapped and killed just before the first hearings in the court. Hence, a statement issued by the team of lawyers: "In view of the dangerous security conditions in Iraq and their impact on Iraqi members of the defense team, along with the never-ending threats against them and their families, a decision has been taken to fully boycott the Iraqi Special Tribunal unless they are fully protected."[11]

IS IRAQ SLIPPING CLOSER TO ALL-OUT SECTARIAN WAR?

International sociologists would say, "Iraq meets the definition of civil war." This was despite the fact that the U.S. administration continued to insist that it was not. A growing number of Arab and political science professors in different parts of the world say, "the fighting in Iraq, in every way, apparently meets the standard definition of civil war." Let us again examine the definition of "civil war." The universally accepted definition of civil war in social science requires two main criteria. First, national fighting groups are indigenous. Each group fights against another group to achieve victory. Their fight is mostly for controlling another group or groups, politically, ethnically, or economically. The second criterion generally says that at least one thousand people must have been killed, with at least one hundred from each side. In general, American professors who specialize in the study of civil wars suggest that the conflict in Iraq is a civil war. In Iraq, sectarian violence and revenge killing have become common between Sunni Arabs and Shiites. The sectarian cycles of violence are ignited by Sunni insurgents and Shiite militia leaders who each have their political goals.[12]

As time passes, sectarian violence is increasing. More than 2,660 Iraqi civilians were killed in the capital in September 2006, amid a wave of killings by insurgent and militia attacks, an increase of four hundred over the month before. The increase took place despite the fact that in mid-August an intensified U.S.-Iraqi sweep of Baghdad was launched, aimed at putting down the wave of violence that had swept over the capital. The violence had been a result of bombings and shootings by Sunni insurgents and Shiite death squads. This brought the number to 655,000 Iraqis who have died in the four-year-old conflict in Iraq. Those deaths mostly included bodies found dumped around Baghdad. They were victims of explosions, shootings, and other attacks. All wore civilian clothes of men between the ages of twenty and forty-five and were bound at the wrists and ankles. The bodies showed signs of having been tortured before death.[13]

Former Secretary of State Colin Powell in November 2006 told CNN, "Iraq's violence meets the standard of civil war" and that if he were heading the State Department now, he might recommend that the administration use that term. Many media organizations had already been calling the Sunni-Shiite sectarian warfare "a civil war." Powell's comments were made in the United Arab Emirates at the Leaders in Dubai Business Forum. His statements were significant because he had originally backed the war. Powell was secretary of state when the United States invaded Iraq in March 2003.[14]

On November 23, 2006, a deadly sectarian explosion from three powerful car bombs killed at least 144 people and wounded 206. The attacks

against targets with strong Shiite identities seemed intended to build sectarian anger and to accelerate the cycle of secular retributive killings. In
revenge, Shiite militias killed hundreds of Sunnis with sectarian death
squads on the same day.[15]

In an article titled "Baghdad oasis 'falling to terrorists'" that appeared
in the *New York Times* and *Herald Tribune* in June 2006, Sabrina Tavernise wrote how the Iraqis felt that their country was falling to the insurgents. The writer cited examples of what had happened in the past two
months. "It [Baghdad] is falling to terrorists. They are coming nearer to
us now. No one is stopping them."

Tavernise continued, "For most of the past six months, Iraq has drifted
without a government and its security forces have largely stood by and
watched at most crucial moments, like the one in February, when Shiite
militias killed Sunnis after the bombing of a sacred shrine." Tavernise
continued explaining how peace and order were deteriorating: "Neighborhood after neighborhood in western Baghdad has fallen to insurgents,
with some areas bordering on anarchy: Bodies lie on the streets for hours.
Trash is no longer collected. Children are schooled at home."[16]

Declaring that he believed the situation in Iraq had devolved into a civil
war, Senate Minority Leader Harry Reid reported to CNN in July 2006
that he planned to try to bring the war issue into debate on the Senate floor.
"There is a civil war going on in Iraq. In the last two months, more than
6,000 Iraqis have been killed. That's averaging more than 100 a day being
killed in Iraq and we need to make sure there is a debate on this."[17]

Senator Lindsey Graham, a Republican who has been a frequent critic
of the administration policies in Iraq, said in an Associated Press interview in October 2006, "We're on the verge of chaos, and the current plan
is not working . . . U.S. and Iraqi officials should be held accountable for
the lack of progress."[18]

It was very true that the security situation had been steadily deteriorating. In the month of October 2006, the U.S. military announced the
death of the one-hundredth service member killed in combat.[19] Meanwhile, statistics showed that at least 156 Iraqi university professors had
been killed since the occupation began. It is believed that hundreds,
possibly thousands, more university professors fled Iraq to neighboring
countries. This is while Sadr City, a stronghold of the Mahdi Shiite Militia Army loyal to radical Shiite cleric Muqtada al-Sadr, was the scene of
repeated bomb attacks by suspected al-Qaeda fighters. The purpose of
such attacks had been to incite Shiite revenge attacks and drag the country into full-blown civil war. An official in the government commented,
"If current conditions continue, Iraq will be destroyed."[20]

TALABANI WARNS OF CIVIL WAR

As peace deteriorated and the situation worsened among the Shiite and Sunni groups in Baghdad and surrounding regions, the president of Iraq, Jalal Talabani, called for all Iraqis to help stop the country from sliding into civil war after a series of bomb blasts continued in Baghdad, killing large numbers of both groups. This was a clear message to the newly elected parliament of October 25, 2005, which failed for six months to agree on a new government and who should lead it. To avoid slipping into civil war, Iraq's president further pressed political parties to accelerate efforts to form a broad government of national unity encompassing Kurds, Shiites, and Sunnis. This was widely seen as the only way to avoid civil war and bring stability to the country.[21]

Despite the call of President Talabani on March 13, 2006, to Iraqi people to avert civil warfare, it was on March 14, just one day after his call, Iraqi authorities discovered at least eighty-seven corpses—men shot to death execution-style. Twenty-nine of the bodies, dressed only in underwear, were dug out of a single grave in a Shiite neighborhood of Baghdad. Some of the bloodshed appeared to be retaliation for a bomb and mortar attack in the Sadr City slum that killed at least fifty-eight people and wounded more than two hundred two days earlier. Meanwhile, frightened Shiite and Sunni families fled their homes, some at gunpoint, to other places where they could find peace.

In new violence, a large number of Iraqis died, including a car bombing that killed twenty-five people in an attack on a police lockup. A suicide car bomber detonated his explosives at the entrance to the Interior Ministry Major Crimes unit in Baghdad, killing ten civilians and fifteen policemen. Roadside bombs targeting policemen and U.S. troops were increasing. In the fourth week after the attack on the shrine, police discovered hundreds of corpses who were victims of religious militants on a rampage of revenge killing including Sunnis and Shiite pilgrims. The call of Talabani for peace was ignored as the situation was worsening in most parts of the country.[22]

Despite the discouraging results of calls of the president for peace, a number of armed groups in Iraq responded to his call for talks and contacted his office. Talabani announced, "We want to convince every sincere Iraqi who is carrying arms to come and participate in the political process." Talabani, however, did not name the groups that contacted his office. It became known that residents of al-Anbar province said that four Sunni armed groups that were active in that area were conferring among themselves to choose a representative to meet government officials.[23]

Amid intense sectarian violence and deterioration of peace, Talabani in December 2006 requested U.S. troops to stay for up to three more years in Iraq to allow local authorities to build up their own security forces. He rebuffed assertions that his country was in a civil war. He further accused the media of focusing only on negative stories. Speaking at a conference, Talabani said, "We need time; not twenty years, but time. I personally can say that two to three years will be enough to build up our forces and say to our American friends 'bye bye with thanks.'" He further said international terrorists were still concentrating all their efforts on Iraq, which meant the country needed outside help to defeat them.[24]

AL-ZARQAWI, THE NOTORIOUS CIVIL WAR ADVOCATE, KILLED

Al-Zarqawi, the notorious civil war advocate, was killed by an F-16 warplane that fired two five-hundred-pound bombs on the house, once U.S. forces located him with the help of intelligence from cell phone technology. He was the most-wanted terrorist in Iraq, waging a bloody campaign of beheadings and suicide bombings, killed on June 7, 2006. Two F-16 warplanes dropped five-hundred-pound bombs on his isolated safe house near Bawuba, reducing it to rubble and killing Iraq's most-wanted insurgent and five other people. Intelligence from cell phone technology and other terrorist network sources helped U.S. forces find and kill Zarqawi.

His death was a long-sought victory in the war in Iraq. He and several aides, including spiritual adviser Sheik Abdul Rahman, were killed in a remote area thirty miles from Baghdad in the explosive province of Diyala, east of the provincial capital of Baquba. Two years before, the United States had put a $25 million bounty on Zarqawi's head. The Jordanian-born head of terrorists was Iraq's most-wanted al-Qaeda militant.

At the White House, President Bush hailed the killing as "a severe blow to al-Qaeda and it is a significant victory in the war on terror." However, he cautioned, "We have tough days ahead of us in Iraq that will require the continuing patience of the American people." In London, British Prime Minister Tony Blair said al-Zarqawi's death "was very good news because a blow against al-Qaeda in Iraq was a blow against al-Qaeda everywhere." He continued, "If it's true Al-Zarqawi was killed, that will be a big happiness for all the Iraqis. He was behind all the killings of Sunnis and Shiites. Iraqis should now move toward reconciliation."[25]

Meanwhile, al-Qaeda in Iraq confirmed al-Zarqawi's death, vowing to continue its "holy war." Iraqis around the country expressed mixed feelings toward the killing of al-Zarqawi. They mostly reacted along sectarian lines to news of his death. He was deeply mourned in Anbar province, the heart of the Sunni-led insurgency. They saw the killing of al-Zarqawi as a great loss for the Iraqi Sunnis. Nevertheless, in the Shiite cities, many Iraqis welcomed the news of his death.

While intellectual Iraqis welcomed the news of his death, they expressed fear that sectarian and militia violence would intensify. They hoped the death of al-Zarqawi would be a turning point in bringing peace and terminating violence in the country. This is while a large number of Iraqi citizens expressed hope that the government would hit with an iron fist the Sunni insurgents and Shiite militias.[26]

Al-Qaeda insurgents claimed they were still powerful after the death of their leader. They pledged "to prepare major attacks that will shake the enemy like an earthquake and rattle them out of sleep." The statement further said al-Qaeda in Iraq's leadership met after al-Zarqawi's death. They "agreed to continue jihad [holy war] and not be affected by his martyrdom."[27]

It did not take long for al-Qaeda's deputy leader, Ayman al-Zawahiri, to pay tribute to the slain leader of al-Qaeda in Iraq, Abu Musab al-Zarqawi. He called him a brave soldier, an Islamic cleric, and a prince of martyrs. The videotaped statement, broadcast by Al Jazeera, was the first acknowledgment by al-Qaeda's central leadership of the death of al-Zarqawi. Meanwhile, al-Zawahiri attacked al-Maliki, the Iraqi prime minister, and Zalmay Khalilzad, the U.S. ambassador to Iraq. He said, "Al-Maliki trades with Islam for power." He also described Khalilzad as "the Afghan apostate."[28]

It became evident that the death of Zarqawi did not halt the aggression of al-Qaeda. In a show of power, an al-Qaeda suicide bomber struck Iraq's parliament building in the heavily fortified Green Zone of Baghdad. The blast, which killed and wounded at least thirteen people, took place in a cafeteria while several ministers were eating lunch. A member of parliament from the Sunni National Dialogue Front was killed in the blast and three Shiite female MPs from Muqtada al-Sadr's parliamentary list were wounded in the explosion.[29]

IN THE AFTERMATH OF ZARQAWI'S DEATH

A week after the death of Zarqawi, the Jihadi Web site Al Hesba announced the name of a new leader in Mesopotamia. Abu Hamza al-Muhajir to replace Zarqawi. Muhajir was something of a mystery to the public. His name had not appeared on any of the previous statements by al-Qaeda in Iraq posted on the Web. Furthermore, his name had not appeared on any of the charts of wanted leaders of al-Qaeda previously issued by the American Command.

"Sheik Abu Hamza Al-Muhajir, 'May God Preserve Him', a good brother, has previous jihadi experience and a deep foot in the pool of knowledge," the statement on the Web said. "We ask God to guide him and to continue what Sheik Abu Musab started by his hands." Even senior Iraqi officials said they were unfamiliar with anyone by that name.[30]

Zarqawi's successor did not waste time in vowing revenge and immediate vengeance. "The day of vengeance is near and your strong towers in the Green Zone will not protect you," said the statement posted on the Islamic Web site often used by al-Qaeda militants. The new leader, Abu Hamza al-Muhajir, signed the statement. He further vowed to avenge the killing of his predecessor, Abu Musab al-Zarqawi, saying Americans and their Iraqi allies would not be safe in their strongholds. He meant the Green Zone in Baghdad that houses the headquarters of the Iraqi government, foreign embassies, and a U.S. military base that have always been threatened by suicide insurgents.

"Coming battles will reveal the falseness of your power and the cowardliness of your soldiers," Al-Muhajir said. "Do not rejoice that you killed him [al-Zarqawi], he has left behind lions that . . . trained under him." In the Web statement, al-Muhajir also addressed al-Qaeda leader Osama bin Laden saying, "We await your signal and follow your orders, and we give you the good tidings that morale is high among your soldiers." In Arabic, al-Muhajir means "the immigrant." Nevertheless, what the two men, al-Zarqawi and al-Muhajir, have in common is their pledge of allegiance to al-Qaeda leader Osama bin Laden. In addition, the new al-Qaeda leader called on Muslims to support the Iraqi uprising, according to an audiotape received by Al Jazeera in September 2006. The speaker on the tape was identified as Abu Hamza al-Muhajir. He was quoted saying, "Place your hand on our hands . . . our enemy has unified his ranks, now is the time to unite." The speaker urged Islamists to kill U.S.-led troops occupying Iraq.[31]

What puzzled the Iraqis and the Arabs in general was the claim of an Egyptian lawyer that Abu Hamza al-Muhajir, the purported successor of al-Qaeda in Iraq, is still in an Egyptian prison and not living in Iraq. The Egyptian newspaper *Al-Masri Al-Yawm* has quoted the lawyer as saying he met al-Muhajir, also known as Sharif Hamzaa, or Abu Ayub al-Masri, in Cairo's Tura prison, where he had been held for the past seven years. Al-Muhajir is on the "most-wanted" list issued by the Iraqi government. The U.S. military in Iraq has put a $5 million price on his head. The U.S. Army media center in Iraq said, "We cannot comment on the news that . . . Al-Masri is in an Egyptian prison and not in Iraq, we have to clarify that from the Egyptian government." What is known at present is that al-Masri was born and brought up in Egypt, and he then went to

Afghanistan, where he was trained in the making of bombs before going to Iraq in 2002.[32]

Nevertheless, what was not understood was a posting on a Web site often used by Islamist insurgents saying that the newly named leader of al-Qaeda in Iraq, Abu Hamza al-Muhajir, vowed to target Sunni ministers and officials appointed in the new government of Maliki. This is despite the fact that al-Qaeda is a deep-rooted devout Sunni group. It opposed participation in the newly elected government headed by Maliki, who is a conservative Shiite. The threat, it seemed, was meant to discourage Sunni leaders from joining the new elected government led by a conservative Shiite.

The Web site also said the death of al-Zarqawi had done nothing to discourage the al-Qaeda insurgency. It continued, "Don't let the joy of killing our Sheikh Abu Musab, May God bless his soul, fool you, for he left behind lions. He raised them by himself and they were trained in his den."[33]

Meanwhile, what amazed the Iraqis was al-Muhajir's message calling Sunni Arabs who participated in Iraq's new government traitors. The fundamentalist Sunni accused them of having "sold their soul to the crusaders," and threatened, "Our swords are ready for your necks." The Web message continued, "Your punishment is near, and your vain towers in the Green Zone won't protect you."[34]

The most controversial question was, "Has bin laden instigated Muslim Sunnis to fight Muslim Shiites in Iraq?" It is true that just after the death of Zarqawi, Osama bin Laden, in a tape posted on the Web, incited Sunnis in Iraq to retaliate against Shiites after the killing of Zarqawi. This incitement was indeed a deviation from al-Qaeda's stand of not promoting Islamic sectarian violence. Bin Laden assured that Iraqi Sunnis were experiencing annihilation and the only way for them to win freedom is by "holding on to their jihad and ousting the occupying power from Iraq." On the tape, bin Laden mourns the death of former al-Qaeda in Iraq leader al-Zarqawi. He further referred to Shiites as "projectionists," "traitors," and "agents of the Americans." He continued, "Our brothers, the mujahedeen in the al-Qaeda organization, have chosen the dear brother Abu Hamza Al-Muhajir as their leader to succeed the Emir Abu Musab Al-Zarqawi. I advised him to focus his fighting on the Americans and everyone who supports them and allies himself with them in their war on the people of Islam and Iraq."[35]

The question that aroused the curiosity of Iraqis was "Has the death of Zarqawi finally brought peace to Iraq?" Let us examine this question in the light of the opinion of the Iraqis in the Baghdad streets. The general feeling was that "Al-Zarqawi's killing certainly is a victory, but insurgency is not dead." Four years had passed since the United States invaded Iraq and peace in Iraq still was a hope. Until present, it is hard to predict how much good would become from disposing of Zarqawi. The U.S. administration avoided any predictions concerning how much benefit would come from the elimination of al-Qaeda's leader in Iraq. U.S. military officials warned that the death of al-Zarqawi might not do much to bring down the insurgency's vigor in the near future. An al-Qaeda commander in Iraq claimed that the militant Islamic organization had a strong succession to take the place of al-Zarqawi.

After all, statistics showed that Zarqawi's death did not decrease the casualties among U.S. troops. On the contrary, the U.S. deaths in Iraq were increasing. A few months after Zarqawi's death, the number of American troops killed in October 2006 increased, reaching 104 troops, the highest monthly total in a year. This has resulted in the majority of Americans polled indicating their opposition and calling for troop withdrawals. "I know many Americans are not satisfied with the situation," President Bush said. "I'm not satisfied either." Meanwhile, Mahdi Shiite militiamen rushed into the north of Baghdad, forcing large numbers of residents belonging to the Sunni Arab minority to flee their homes. The Shiite militiamen killed scores of Sunnis in massacres in the nearby city of Balad, forcing U.S. troops to return to the area after Iraqi forces were unable to stem the bloodshed.[36]

The crucial and most debatable question asked was, "Did Zarqawi help train Sunni fighters before his death?" No official answer was given. However, let us seek the answer in a report published in the *New York Times*. In June 2006, the newspaper reported that Abu Musab al-Zarqawi, before his death, had recruited hundreds of insurgents. They received training in Iraq and then returned to their home countries to await orders. The *Times* further said that in addition to recruiting volunteers and suicide bombers to fight in Iraq, Zarqawi had recruited some three hundred people who received training in Iraq before returning home to await orders to carry out strikes.[37]

A few months after Zarqawi's death, Iraqi and coalition forces arrested the second most senior figure in al-Qaeda in Iraq. Iraq's national security adviser announced this news, saying the al-Qaeda group now suffered from a "serious leadership crisis." The name of the second al-Qaeda leader arrested was Hamed Jumaa Farid al-Saeedi, known as Abu Humam or Abu Rana. He was captured north of Baghdad with another group of his aides and followers. It was known that he was the second most important al-Qaeda leader in Iraq after Abu Ayyub al-Masri. "We believe that al-Qaeda in Iraq suffers from a serious leadership crisis. Our troops have dealt fatal and painful blows to this organization," the government security adviser reassured.[38]

After the death of al-Zarqawi, the controversial question asked by Iraqis was, "Is it true that sectarian violence increased and al-Qaeda weakened?" To answer this question, we refer to what Zalmay Khalilzad, the U.S. envoy to Iraq, said to CNN four months after Zarqawi's death. He said that al-Qaeda was no longer the main threat to stability in Iraq: "The importance of the sectarian violence has increased while . . . the al-Qaeda terrorists have weakened." However, with the U.S. Republican administration under pressure in congressional elections in November 2006, the president warned against a hasty withdrawal of the 140,000 U.S. troops as that, he said, could afford al-Qaeda a new base from which to operate.[39]

Christopher Allbritton, Web blogger and journalist, quoted Zalmay Khalilzad, the U.S. ambassador to Iraq, saying, "Zarqawi's death will not end the violence in Iraq. But it is an important step in the right direction." Khalilzad continued, "Zarqawi was the godfather of sectarian killing in Iraq. He led a civil war within Islam and a global war on civilizations."[40]

The political alternative to this violence was reiterated to be in the democratization of Iraq. The following chapter will shed light on the various steps taken toward the attempts to defeat insurgency by putting Iraq on the road to democracy and forming an Iraqi National Assembly, while the United States still refused to set a timetable for withdrawal of U.S. troops from Iraq.

CHAPTER 11

DEMOCRATIZATION OF IRAQ

COMMENTING UPON THE FIRST SESSION OF THE IRAQ NATIONAL Assembly held in March 2005, as a step toward democracy in Iraq, President Bush proudly said it was a "bright moment" for Iraq. Nevertheless, he added there was no timetable for withdrawing U.S. troops. "We've always said this is a process, and today was a step in that process. It's a hopeful moment," he said in Washington.[1] The meeting of the first Iraq National Assembly was almost the result of Bush's insistence that the election in Iraq should go ahead as scheduled on January 30, 2005, despite the increasing insurgents' attacks in the Sunni zone. The Sunnis, 20 percent of Iraq's population, declared their boycott of the election.

As a result, Iraqi voters chose a 275-member transitional national parliament. The National Assembly was committed to putting together a permanent constitution submitted to voters in a referendum by the end of 2005.

The elections were to allow the Iraqi people to elect a transitional parliament to draft a new constitution. This ultimately allowed for a step toward a democratic reform and stable nation. In order to bolster security before the election, the Pentagon dispatched more troops to the troubled areas in Iraq. That brought the number of U.S. forces in Iraq from nearly 140,000 to more than 150,000. Meanwhile, Defense Secretary Donald Rumsfeld vowed to do everything possible to safeguard more than 5,500 designated polling centers.

It was estimated that more than a hundred political parties and movements registered to contest the election. A coalition was formed, United Iraq Alliance, backed by the Shiite Ayatollah Sistani. The coalition included eighteen parties and movements as well as independent individuals who won the majority of the assembly's seats. Prominent Sunni leaders from the north joined the Alliance, including a number of Turkmen and Kurds.

The law stipulated that the first phase 275-seat National Assembly should draft a new Iraqi constitution no later than December 2005. The following phase should be a new government elected by the people of Iraq in accordance with the new constitution. As emphasized by the interim government, the elections should be a first step toward achieving national reconciliation among the three ethnic populations.

IS IRAQ ON THE ROAD TO DEMOCRACY?

The Associated Press reported on the White House news conference on May 25, 2006, where Tony Blair and George Bush acknowledged difficulties in the Iraq war, but vowed to keep troops there until the new government establishes control. Both admitted making mistakes. "Despite setbacks and missteps, I strongly believe we did and are doing the right thing . . . Not everything has turned out the way we hoped," Bush said.[2]

For his part, Blair informed the audience that he had met with Iraq's new prime minister in Baghdad. "The challenge is still immense, but I also came away thinking more certain than ever that we should rise to it," he assured. Blair also said allies seriously underestimated the strength and determination of the insurgency. "It should have been very obvious to us from the beginning," Blair said. Bush mentioned the mistreatment of Iraqi prisoners at the U.S.-run Abu Ghraib prison near Baghdad. "We've been paying for that for a long time," he said. "We're going to work with our partners in Iraq, the new government, to determine the way forward," Bush continued. "The goal remains: an Iraq that can govern itself and sustain itself and defend itself. They want us to stay until the job is done," referring to the new democratically elected Iraqi government.[3]

In the annual State of the Union address for 2006, President Bush forcefully defended his Iraq policy for democratization and freedom. He told Congress that "even those who oppose the war have no choice now but to support efforts toward victory . . . However we feel about the decisions and debates of the past, our nation has only one option. We must . . . defeat our enemies and stand behind the American military." He warned against "isolationism" and "defeatism" in the war against terror. He further rebuked his critics by saying, "Hindsight alone is not wisdom, and second guessing is not a strategy."[4] Just six months before the president's State of the Union address, Vice President Cheney confidently assured the American people, "We will succeed in Iraq, just like we did in Afghanistan. We will stand up a new government under an Iraq-drafted constitution. We will defeat that insurgency, and, in fact, it will be an enormous success story." Cheney furthermore reassured the American people that Iraq, with the assistance of the U.S.-led coalition, would be soon on the road to victory and democracy.[5]

In order to enhance democracy in Iraq, the U.S. administration appointed in November 2005 a new U.S. envoy, Zalmay Khalilzad, the U.S. ambassador to Afghanistan. In starting his position, he vowed, "I will work with all Iraqis, all sects, all ethnic groups, men and women, to accelerate success in Iraq." The U.S. administration, in addition, was keen to expedite the introduction of democracy in Iraq through free elections.[6]

Some liberal Iraqis questioned if democracy would be achieved with purely free elections. Fareed Zakaria surprised the liberals in his article titled "Elections Are Not Democracy" in *Newsweek* magazine in February 2005. He quoted Larry Diamond, one of the leading experts on democratization in the United States, saying, "The one precondition for democracy to work is a consensus among major ethnic, regional, or religious groups." This has not happened as of this writing, despite the fact that two consecutive Iraqi interim governments were in power after the U.S.-led occupation.[7]

It is true, at present, that with all the political and military efforts since the occupation of the country in March 2003 and the collapse of Saddam's regime, Iraq has not become the expected model of democracy for the Middle East Arab countries as desired by the U.S. administration. Rather, the country became a breeding ground for dissensions, rebels, fanatics, insurgents, and militias. Since the occupation of Iraq, terrorism expanded to the neighboring countries of Jordan, Egypt, and Saudi Arabia. Meanwhile, al-Qaeda-trained terrorists in Iraq have been spreading their suicide bombers in many Muslim countries such as Pakistan, Indonesia, and Afghanistan.

To assure the Iraqi people that the country is on the road to democracy, Barham Salih, the Iraqi deputy prime minister, who was a Kurd in the outgoing interim government, declared in April 2005 that "Iraq is at present embarking on a democratic process in the heart of the Middle East. The outside world should recognize the amazing achievement we have come to here in Iraq."[8] However, after April 2005, Iraq has been sliding into civil war among ethnic groups, mainly Shiites and Sunnis. Democracy became only a dream of the Iraqi people.

Nevertheless, the Arab people in the Middle East wondered if it was possible to transform Iraq from absolute dictatorship of more than thirty years to a democratic country. Many of them watched the difficult case of the Kurds, who physically and politically suffered immensely for years under Saddam's tyranny. However, the constructive spirit of the Kurdish leaders helped to integrate the Kurdish region in the election as one united Iraqi nation. This was achieved while the Sunnis boycotted it.

The election, as announced by all its political Kurdish parties, meant providing democracy to the Kurdish people. They believed that the election and the introduction of democracy would make it possible to transform Iraq from a country of tyranny and racial discrimination to a country of equal human rights. The Taliban's Patriotic Union for Kurdistan party assured the Kurdish people that it was possible at present for the Kurds to feel they belong and fit as an integral part of the Iraqi nation with equal rights.

POLLS OPEN IN THE COUNTRY

Introducing democracy has its casualties. As Iraqis were voting in the first free election in half a century, suicide attacks and several car bombs targeted polling booths, killing and wounding a large number of people in Baghdad and other major cities in the North and South. This is despite the fact that thirty thousand polling booths operated under the watchful eye of U.S. troops and Iraqi police forces.

In Tikrit, Saddam Hussein's hometown, polling centers were mostly empty as the Sunnis boycotted the election. However, in other parts of the country, especially in Kurdish and Shiite areas, booths were packed with people casting their ballots. Many of them, especially the elders, were voting for the first time in their lifetime, as fair voting in Saddam's era of thirty years was inconceivable. In the Kurdish and Shiite towns and villages, long lines of Iraqi voters chanted and happily clapped their hands in front of media cameras.

The voting was heavily covered by the media, including CNN, which reported that former interim President Ghazi al-Yawer, a Sunni, was among the first to vote, and expressed hope that the voting would be the first step toward establishing a democracy that Iraqis would be proud of. "Deep in my heart, I feel that Iraqis deserve free elections." Iraqi people were concerned how many of the 14.2 million Iraqis registered to vote would actually cast ballots despite threats from the insurgents who vowed to "wash" the streets with voters' "blood." A spokesperson for the interim prime minister announced, "Your participation will foil the terrorists. The elections are a great success for the people—it will represent the rule of law, not the rule of violence."⁹

In order to secure peaceful balloting, in Baghdad alone there were fifteen thousand U.S. soldiers on patrol amid travel and weapons bans. Airspace and borders were sealed. However, the guerrillas still focused their deadly attacks on voters on their way to these election centers and on Iraq's national security forces whom they branded as collaborators with foreign occupiers.

Just before the election date, on a visit to Baghdad, British Prime Minister Tony Blair praised Iraqi election officials as "heroes" and vowed that their efforts brought democracy to the country. He explained they were heroes of the new Iraq because they were people who were risking their lives every day in order to make sure that the people of Iraq got a chance to decide their own destiny. He called the violent insurgency a battle between democracy and terror. Ayad Allawi, the Iraqi interim prime minister at the time, assured the British prime minister that Iraq, for the first time in history, had witnessed democracy in action.[10]

TIGHT SECURITY MEASURES FOR THE ELECTION

Security measures for the election were very tight as guerillas told Iraqis not to vote. Al-Qaeda's leader in Iraq, Abu Musab al-Zarqawi, the nation's most feared terrorist group leader, announced his followers' determination to launch attacks on polling stations. He condemned Iraq's Shiites and Kurds, most of whom were backing the polls. He further accused the United States and the interim government of taking the risk of worsening the political situation in Iraq by alienating the minority Sunni Arabs while favoring the Kurds and Shiites. He claimed that the ballot was a U.S. plan to transform Iraq from dictatorship to Western sectarian state. Such a plan, Zarqawi said, risked reinforcing the resistance by further alienating minority Sunni Arabs.[11]

Despite the threat of Zarqawi and his insurgents, an alliance of candidates formed under the guidance of Iraq's top Shiite cleric, Ayatollah Ali al-Sistani, and the Kurdish Talabani won the most votes as the Sunnis boycotted the election. The election was for a 275-member National Assembly that would oversee the drafting of a permanent constitution for Iraq.

Osama bin Laden himself urged Iraqis to boycott the elections. The audiotape broadcast on the Arabic-language Al Jazeera television network. Al-Zarqawi had recently renamed his insurgent group to al-Qaeda in Iraq instead of Unification and Jihad Group. This confirmed the news that Zarqawi and bin Laden had indeed been communicating with each other. On the audiotape, it was clear that bin Laden was aligned with the attacks of the insurgents against the U.S.-led forces and those cooperating with them.[12]

In an Internet recording, Zarqawi vowed a merciless war against the principle of democracy and all those who seek to enact it. He condemned democracy as "the big American lie."

Zarqawi rebels targeted politicians and escalated beheading foreign hostages just before the election. Iraqi interim Prime Minister Ayad Allawi told the BBC's *Breakfast with Frost* program that they will do their best to end the escalation of violence in response, as a warning to Zarqawi threats.[13]

Despite waves of violence committed by al-Zarqawi suicide attackers, Iraq's interim government insisted the ballot should go ahead as planned. It added that it would not allow the terrorists to stop the political process in Iraq. Regardless of the increasing death toll from insurgent attacks, which reached over ninety in the four days since the start of the election, the government insisted that the election process was to continue.[14]

Despite the threats, millions of Iraqis cast ballots in the nation's first free election in half a century. All indications were that the voting process was a success despite sporadic violence that killed many people.

It was estimated that 98.8 percent of the polling centers were actually opened. Of about 8.46 million votes cast in the election, the United Iraqi Alliance received 4.08 million. The combined Kurdish parties cast 2.17 million and the Iraqi list of interim Prime Minister Ayad Allawi, 1.17 million. The Sunni Arabs looked upon the results of voting as illegitimate.

President Bush said the balloting was a "resounding success" and praised Iraqis who "have taken rightful control of their country's destiny." Prime Minister Tony Blair urged Britain to "embrace the bright future of Iraq's new democracy." Embracing a bright future and installing democracy in Iraq had its price, as the insurgents determined to be more aggressive against high officials in the elected government.[15] General "Jihad Luaibi," a highly respected police anticorruption inspector-general, was killed after armed rebels in two cars opened fire outside his home in Baghdad.

After the election and formation of the Iraqi government, guerrillas increased their aggression by shooting down a Bulgarian commercial plane, killing all eleven on board including six Americans. The rebels' attack came amid waves of violence across the country, which threatened to delay the forming of a democratic government after elections.

The good news was that Iraqi expatriates were keen to vote. Despite the threats of insurgents against relatives of Iraqi expatriates, about 66 percent of those expatriates who were registered to vote, 186,619 people, cast ballots in the first two days of their three-day voting period. This voting was under the United Nations "Iraq out-of-country voting program." More than 280,000 expatriates registered for the election and most of them cast their votes.[16]

VOTING AS A RELIGIOUS DUTY IN IRAQ'S HOLY CITIES

A few days before the election, the Grand Ayatollah, Ali al-Sistani, the most eminent and powerful Shiite cleric in Iraq, declared voting as a religious obligation. During Friday sermons in Najaf just before the election date, one of his senior aides declared voting more important than fasting and praying. This was a strong statement, as these two duties, fasting and praying, are among the five pillars of Islam. Holy Shiite cities, such as Najaf and Karbala, were covered with banners and posters urging people to vote. The most noticeable were posters of Sistani reminding people that voting was to be considered a "religious duty." Some posters showed a list of 169 candidates who were the Sistani-backed United Iraqi Alliance. The list, indeed, fared best in the elections.[17]

The elections transformed the once maltreated Shiites and Kurds under Saddam's regime into the new holders of power. The attempt was to include Sunni Arabs in the political process in a bid to defuse the Sunni-led violence and crack down on insurgents.[18]

IRAQI SUNNI CLERICS: "ELECTION LACKED LEGITIMACY"

It was evident that the minority Sunni Arabs who formed the backbone of Saddam's Ba'athist ruling party were determined to pose a major challenge to Iraq's new leadership ruled by members of the Shiite majority. As expected, the election results favoring Shiites and Kurds fueled the Sunni-led insurgency and incited sectarian strife. Iraq's Muslim Clerics Association railed against the country's first multiparty voting since the start of Saddam's regime a half century before. The association declared together with Sunni clerics that any government emerging from Iraq's present election would lack legitimacy and authenticity. It called Sunni Arabs to boycott the election as it was influenced by the U.S.-led occupation. Al-Qaeda's leader in Iraq, Abu Musab al-Zarqawi, vowed to pursue "holy war" against the new government and U.S. troops.[19]

The *Egyptian Gazette* reported in January 2005 that just three weeks before the election date, an influential group of Iraqi Sunni Muslim clerics met a senior U.S. embassy official over poll boycott by Sunnis. They informed the official that the election boycott could be reversed in return for a U.S. timetable to withdraw its troops from Iraq. The American diplomat informed the Sunni clerics that the United States had no plan to schedule the withdrawal of roughly 150,000 U.S. troops.[20]

The statement issued by the influential Sunni Muslim Clerics Association (SMCA) that called to boycott the Iraqi election was signed by sixty independent political groups, religious authorities, tribal leaders, and other public figures. The statement advocated an "absolute boycott" of the elections. However, a large number of Sunnis accused the Association of Muslim Scholars, claiming it did not present the case correctly. They predicted that if the Sunnis had participated in the political process and the election of parliament, terrorism and insurgency would not have intensified their violence. The moderate Sunni disagreed with the boycott of the elections.

Ghazi al-Yawar, the interim president and a Sunni Arab, was actively running under the slogan "Dignity, Security, Justice." Al-Yawar admitted that he comprehended the argument of the Sunni Arabs for postponing the elections. He admitted, however, that the interim government did not wish to give the insurgents the satisfaction of having their own way. Al-Yawar, though his campaign was low profile, called for a permanent nonsectarian constitution, true democracy, justice, and equality for all Iraqis.[21]

IRAQI NATIONAL ASSEMBLY FORMED

After a long period of tension, Iraqis elected a 275-member transitional National Assembly, which drew up a draft for a new constitution, chose a prime minister, and picked the country's president and two vice presidents. Voters also elected members of eighteen provincial councils. In addition, residents of the semiautonomous Kurdish region elected a Kurdish parliament. The results of the country's January 30, 2005, elections allocated 140 National Assembly seats to the United Iraqi Alliance, giving the Shiite-dominated party a majority in the new parliament. The Kurdish alliance received 26 percent of the vote, giving it seventy-five seats. Ninety-nine parties did not win enough support to get parliament seats. A draft of the new constitution was finalized in August 2005. It consequently went before Iraqi voters on the October 15 referendum. As stated in the constitution, "If it is approved, a new government would be elected in December 2005. The new government will assume power by year's end. The transitional government would take into consideration the competing interests and aspirations of all Iraqi groups." This eventually became the most critical test for the future of Iraq.[22]

Records showed that in starting drafting the constitution there were fierce arguments over two crucial principles: first, the extent to which Islamic Sharia law should form the basis of Iraqi law, and second, the degree of autonomy the treaty should grant to Iraq's diverse ethnic groups—most notably the Kurds in the North. Until the approval of the new constitution by the people, Iraq had been governed according to the Transitional Administrative Law (TAL), an interim constitution laid down by Iraqi authorities with a strong backing from the United States. It was ratified in March 2004. The new constitution was supposed to replace it, providing Iraq with a more permanent legal framework agreed to by the Iraqi people in a referendum.[23]

In May 2005, Iraqi Prime Minister Ibrahim al-Jaafari unveiled before parliament his new government's political program aimed at building a federal system in the country. He emphasized the necessity of building a federal, pluralist Iraq while respecting human rights and public freedoms.

His foreign policy would be based on reinforcing the unity of Iraq, on integrity of its territory, and on mutual honor for the affairs of its neighbors. He further insisted on accelerating a return to stability in Iraq. He stressed security as a vital issue for the new government in Iraq.[24]

The Iraqi transitional assembly elected Kurdish leader Jalal Talabani as the nation's president. The selection of a Kurdish president was indeed a symbolic and emotional moment for a country where Saddam's regime was prosecuting the Kurds. Talabani had been the longtime leader of the Patriotic Union of Kurdistan Party. Along with the appointment of Talabani and drafting the constitution, the transitional government took into consideration the competing interests and aspirations of all Iraqi groups. This eventually became the most critical test for the future of Iraq. The assembly chose two deputy presidents: Shiite Arab Adel Mahdi, a member of the United Iraqi Alliance who served as interim finance minister, and Sunni Arab Sheik Ghazi al-Yawar, who had served as the previous interim president. Talabani offered his new government's top post of premiership to Ibrahim Jaafari, a former Shiite opposition figure.

Talabani stressed in his inaugural address in the new parliament the enforcement of democracy and national unity among the country's different ethnicities and religions. In drafting the constitution, he favored laws with a secular underpinning by the respected Iraq's Islamic identity.

Many people in the Arab countries questioned why a Kurd was elected to the presidency of Iraq." Some saw it as a direct and fair result of democracy. Others thought it reflected U.S. control and manipulation that tried to create a model of Iraq for the rest of the regional countries to follow.

Regardless of the motives behind selecting a Kurd as president, the action showed a high level of political maturity in Iraq. Democracy should neither underestimate the minority in any nation nor undermine the high caliber political leaders in the society. Talabani, as the Arabs knew, had a long history of patriotism during Saddam's regime, a deeper commitment to the unity of Iraq, and above all, a genuine drive for reconciliation among Kurds, Sunnis, and Shiites. Extended negotiations focused on persuading the minority Sunni Muslims into the government since the majority of the proposed government members were Shiites and Kurds. The true intention, as seen, was to compose a government of national unity, with all the main parties participating, not just a Shiite-Kurdish government.[25]

POLITICAL IMPASSE TO FORM A GOVERNMENT

The political agreement to have a first democratically elected government in Iraq was finally on its way in April 2005. The formation of a national government represented a landmark after months of political stalemate. The politicians elected were finally able to name a government after three months of laborious negotiations among different parties.[26]

After heated and prolonged negotiation, it was possible for the main Shiite alliance to form a government with the Kurds and minority Sunni Muslims. The *New York Times* in April 2005 reported that U.S. Secretary of State Condoleezza Rice and Vice President Dick Cheney urged top Kurdish and Shiite politicians to move more quickly and avert a political deadlock. With about thirty cabinet seats to decide, Shiite and Kurd politicians disputed for the most influential ministries. The assembly was also trying to ensure that Sunni Arabs were not left out.

More than twelve weeks after the country held parliamentary elections, the assembly designated Prime Minister Ibrahim al-Jaafari in mid-April 2005. This announcement came shortly after armed men shot and killed a female member of Iraq's parliament. The victim, identified as Lamia Abid Khadawi, was a member of Prime Minister Ayad Allawi's political party. Khadawi was the first person in the 275-member National Assembly to be killed.[27] Iraqi interim Prime Minister Ayad Allawi also escaped an assassination attempt when a car bomb exploded at a checkpoint. Hundreds of Iraqi soldiers and citizens were killed. Nearly four hundred Iraqis were killed in the two weeks after the new government was formed. An Iraqi guerrilla Sunni group opposing the government, called Army of Ansar al-Sunni, claimed responsibility.

Ministers of foreign affairs from the Arab neighboring countries met to express support for the new Iraqi government. They stressed the political integrity and sovereignty of Iraq and called for international support for reconstructing the infrastructure of the country. The ministers further expressed their full backing to stabilize the country and assist the Iraqi government to overcome its numerous problems. Meanwhile, Sunni-dominated neighbors, including Egypt, Jordan, and the Gulf countries, expressed concern that Sunni underrepresentation in Iraq would bypass the once powerful minority and influential Islamic sect. They expressed their concerns regarding the troubled peace and order of their oil-rich neighbor, and that the Shiite-dominated government would treat Iraqi Sunnis fairly.[28]

IS THERE A POLITICAL ALTERNATIVE TO DEFEAT THE INSURGENCY?

Bloodshed came as one thousand U.S. forces, supported by aircraft battle fighters, attacked Tikrit and other Sunni towns situated in northern

Baghdad. A large number of Iraqi citizens were killed in a series of U.S. military actions. This prompted a surprise visit from U.S. Secretary of State Condoleezza Rice, who arrived in Iraq in May 2005 for talks with Iraqi government leaders and U.S. military commanders. The purpose of her mission was to discuss ways to move the political process forward in Iraq, and to help quell the violence that had killed more than four hundred people in just over two weeks since the new government was named on April 28, 2005. The casualties of U.S. troops had been increasing, reaching a total of 1,629. It was estimated, by that time, between twenty-one thousand and twenty-four thousand Iraqi civilians had been killed since the start of the war.

Rice told the reporters that the insurgency was very violent, but "you defeat insurgencies not just militarily—in fact not especially militarily—you defeat them by having a political alternative that was strong."[29]

She urged them to increase inclusion of Sunnis in the political process. She assured them that Iraq is emerging from a long national nightmare of tyranny into freedom. She called for the participation of Sunnis in drafting the constitution that would be the basis for the December 2005 election. Al-Jaafari, the prime minister, assured Rice that the government was determined to involve Sunnis Arabs in drafting the constitution.[30]

Before Rice's departure, Prime Minister Ibrahim al-Jaafari conveyed to her that Sunni Arab legislators had already reached a deal to appoint Sunni Arab figures chosen by them as ministers in the interim government. It was true that Sunni Arabs were underrepresented in the cabinet. Shiite and Kurdish politicians spared no efforts to draw Sunni Arabs into the political process. They saw inclusion of Sunnis in political Iraqi affairs as the appropriate way to defuse the Sunni-supported insurgency in the North.

The new Iraqi cabinet included almost all secular, ethnic, and religious groups. It consisted of thirty-three ministers and four deputy prime ministers. Most of the posts went to Shiite Muslims. They took the opportunity of election to be politically represented after decades of Sunni-led rule under Saddam. Kurds were also active participants. For reference, Shiites make up 60 percent of Iraq's 26 million people; Kurds make up 20 percent; and Sunni Arabs, who largely boycotted the elections, are roughly 20 percent.

It was agreed that the cabinet would have seventeen Shiite ministers including a prime minister, eight Kurds including the president of Iraq and minister of foreign affairs, six Sunni Arabs including a defense minister, and one Christian. It was also agreed that seven ministers would be women. This agreement fulfilled promises by leaders of the Shiite majority to share power with religious minorities.[31]

WAS THERE AMERICAN FEAR REGARDING AL-JAAFARI?

Concerns arose regarding al-Jaafari's inclinations, as a devoted Shiite, to follow directions of the strong Shiite spiritual cleric al-Sistani. The fear was to push Iraq toward an Islamic state siding with Iran and team up with its political ambitions in the Greater Middle East Region. Al-Jaafari had been all his life a devout Shiite from Negev, Iraq. It is known that Shiites of Negev, however, do not favor the clerics' interference with the running of their government. The other concern of the United States was that al-Jaafari might force his Islamic Shiite vision on the draft constitution as he expressed his opposition to reducing the role of Sharia (Islamic law) in Iraq's legal system.

The U.S. administration was aware that the majority of Shiites wished the new constitution to be based solely on the Sharia and not a main source of legislation. This was while most of the Kurds and Sunnis desired a constitution based on the Sharia as a source but not the only source of law. The Kurds and Sunnis envisaged that the constitution should take into consideration the needs of contemporary societies and demands of living in a sectarian global world.[32]

To throw light on Ibrahim al-Jaafari's political background, the fifty-eight-year-old had led the Daawa Party for many years. Members of the party find him more a secularly oriented Shiite than other Shiite devotees. In fact, it was the Alliance of Shiite parties holding 140 of the 275 seats in the transitional assembly that selected Jaafari as their choice to succeed Ayad Allawi as prime minister.

The United States originally feared that al-Jaafari might impose his strong Islamic vision on the country. However, he had particularly presented his opposition to reducing the role of Sharia in Iraq's legal system. He opposed one of the articles in the draft interim constitution that stated Islam was a source of legislation and not the main source of legislation, as most Shiites called for. The Daawa Party headed by al-Jaafari had been conducting a campaign to increase, in depth, the Islamic flavor of the draft constitution.

In forming the new government after the December 15, 2005, election, the Shiite Alliance requested al-Jaafari to continue holding the post of prime minister in the new government for a second term. The alliance became the majority in the new parliament. Both Sunni and Kurdish members of the parliament rejected his nomination as prime minister for the new government for being sectarian. The United States gave him a warning, which further angered him.

The source of such sensitivity occurred when the U.S. ambassador to Iraq, Zalmaly Khalilzad, said that the United States, which led the 2003 invasion to oust Saddam Hussein, was investing billions of dollars in Iraq and did not want to see that money go to support sectarian politics. The British minister of foreign affairs said, "This is a crucial moment today for the people of Iraq. We had the elections on December 15. We have now the final accredited results. What they show is that no party, no ethnic or religious grouping can dominate government in Iraq."[33]

In forming the new cabinet in the government headed by al-Jaafari, the question raised was why Iraqi Shiites resented Allawi, the capable former prime minister ad-interim in the last cabinet, despite his high popularity among the Iraqis, competency, and full support by the United States. The answer was that many Shiites had long resented Allawi's devotion to secularization that calls for separation of religion and state. They also accused his outgoing administration for including former members of Saddam's Ba'ath Party, which had brutally repressed Shiites and Kurds.[34]

THE UNITED STATES CALLS FOR SPEEDING UP POLITICAL PROCESS

The loss of American troops, Iraqi citizens, and police force continued to increase. Destruction of infrastructure and car bombing worsened the lives of the Iraqis. This situation spurred the U.S. military leadership to call for speeding up the political process in Iraq. It has been evident that military force, however mighty, cannot win peace and maintain security in Iraq.

In April 2005, Air Force General Richard Myers, chairperson of the U.S. Joint Chiefs of Staff, said speeding up the political process would be the best way to weaken insurgency and militias. He continued that Iraq must form a cabinet quickly. Despite nearly 140,000 troops and similar number of Iraqi forces, the insurgents had been continuously attacking. They staged fifty to sixty attacks a day, Myers added.[35]

On a quick visit to Iraq in April 2005, Donald Rumsfeld pressured the country's new leaders to avoid delays in developing a constitutional government and defeating the insurgency and militias. "Anything that would delay that or disrupt that as a result of turbulence or incompetence or corruption in government would be unfortunate," Rumsfeld said before he began a round of talks with Iraqi leaders. He insisted that the new Iraqi leadership should avoid delays on either the political or the security front. He reminded them that U.S. troops were still being killed and billions of dollars had been invested in the reconstruction of the country.[36]

HAS IRAQ BECOME A MODEL FOR DEMOCRACY?

The U.S. Secretary of State, after two years of U.S.-led occupation, was optimistic. Rice was confident that Iraq would become, in the future, a citadel of democracy in the Middle East after the election and formation of the first democratic government in its history. She renewed her call for a new Middle East based on a good relationship between Islam and democracy. Democratic Iraq, as envisaged by Rice, will become a model for Arab Middle East countries to follow.[37]

Despite this state of optimism of the U.S. administration, on the second anniversary of American occupation, Iraqi protesters in April 2005 roamed the streets of major cities chanting, "No, No to America." Several thousand demonstrators gathered in Baghdad to urge the withdrawal of American troops from Iraq as well as to call for national unity and denounce terrorism. The protest marchers denounced President Bush, Prime Minister Blair, and ex-dictator Saddam Hussein. Followers of a Shiite radical cleric, Muqtada al-Sadr, also marched in Baghdad denouncing the U.S. presence in Iraq. They demanded a speedy trial of Saddam Hussein on the second anniversary of his overthrow. Many protesters chanted "No America! No Saddam! Yes to Islam." At the Grand Mosque in Kufa, south of Baghdad, they demanded all political forces in the country take part in the demonstration. On the other hand, many Iraqi intellectuals believe that guns will not solve the chronic problem of peace and security in the country. They call for political approaches and dialogues with the Sunni insurgents and Shiite militias.[38]

In arguing the issue of whether Iraq had been on the road to democracy after almost three years of U.S.-led occupation, we may recall what Ayad Allawi, the former Iraqi prime minister, said. Allawi told *The Observer* newspaper, published in the United Kingdom, that human rights abuses in Iraq were as bad as they were under Saddam Hussein, if not worse. Allawi's comments came as Saddam's trial was set to resume in Baghdad at the end of September 2005. "It is an appropriate comparison. People are remembering the days of Saddam. These were the precise reasons that we fought Saddam and now we are seeing the same things." The remarks followed the discovery of an Iraqi government facility holding 170 prisoners, including some showing signs of torture. "We are hearing about secret police, secret bunkers where people are being interrogated. A lot of Iraqis are being tortured or killed in the course of interrogations," Allawi said. He continued, "We are even witnessing Sharia courts based on Islamic law that are trying people and executing them." Allawi was Iraq's first prime minister of the post-Saddam Hussein era who was also known as a Shiite with secular beliefs.[39]

Allawi's message was disturbing, as after years of Iraqi occupation, democracy had not found its way to the government. The drama staged in Abu Ghraib detention center of Iraqi prisoners was repeated after one year in a main prison under the custody of the Ministry of Interior's administration. U.S. and Iraqi forces discovered 173 malnourished Iraqi detainees in the main prison. Some of them showed signs of torture. Many of the inmates were believed to be Sunni Arabs. Hundreds of Sunnis were found dead with gunshot wounds indicating signs of torture and heavy affliction. The Shiite militias incorporated into the Ministry of Interior were suspected to be responsible for the crimes against Sunni Arabs. It is believed that the Shiite militias formed death squads to carry out abductions and executions against Sunnis. The Sunni Arabs believed that the Shiite government was hiding the truth behind the torture. A U.S. general was so concerned with what he found that he took immediate control of the jail.[40]

Those who watched the interview with Al Jazeera Arabic television, including the writer of this book, were extremely surprised as a senior U.S. diplomat said, "The United States had shown 'arrogance' and 'stupidity' in Iraq but was now ready to talk with any group except al-Qaeda in Iraq to facilitate national reconciliation." In the interview, Alberto Fernandez, Director of Public Diplomacy in the Bureau of Near Eastern Affairs at the State Department, offered an outspoken and blunt assessment of America's war in Iraq. He was speaking in Arabic. "We tried to do our best but I think there is much room for criticism because, undoubtedly, there was arrogance and there was stupidity from the United States in Iraq," he continued. He added, "We are open to dialogue because we all know that, at the end of the day, the solution to the hell and the killings in Iraq is linked to an effective Iraqi national reconciliation . . . The Iraqi government is convinced of this." This interview was quoted by the Associated Press in October 2006.[41]

No Timetable for U.S. Troops to Leave Iraq

President Bush repeatedly warned he would not accept "surrender" dates for the war in Iraq. This sentiment was reiterated by the U.S. administration that the president would not set a timetable for the withdrawal of American troops until Iraqis are capable of defending themselves.[42]

Though President Bush acknowledged painful losses in Iraq, he insisted that the United States was winning and should not think about withdrawing. James Baker's final report indicated that the Iraqi war in its fourth year became a top issue as the majority of Americans were opposed to the administration's handling of it.[43]

In order to clarify the position of the U.S. administration, Bush held two days of urgent talks with al-Maliki in Amman, Jordan, before attending a NATO summit held in the Baltic Capital. The president assured al-Maliki, "We'll continue to be flexible, and we'll make the changes necessary to succeed." Al-Maliki was trying to rally moderates in Sunni, Shiite, and Kurd communities into the government to face the radical insurgents and militiamen who refused to become part of the political process. Al-Maliki expressed his request "to be given time to his newly formed government before withdrawing the U.S. troops." Meanwhile Iraqi officials said the United States wanted other Sunni governments in the area, such as Saudi Arabia, Jordan, and Egypt, to persuade moderate Sunnis in Iraq to line up with Maliki. That would give him the political strength needed to challenge Sadr's Shiite militias.[44]

With the Iraqi Sunnis and the Shiite al-Sadr militant factions pressing for withdrawal of foreign troops, the United States reduced the number of troops to 139,000 from 160,000. Bush insisted in April 2005, "I know there's temptation to try to get me to lay out a timetable for withdrawal. I do not think it is wise for me to set out a timetable. All that will do is cause an enemy to adjust." He continued assuring that U.S. troops would be pulled out of Iraq as soon as possible, depending upon the Iraqis being able to fight and do the job. He added that he believed that the United States had been making really good progress in Iraq by forming a new democratic government and training the Iraqi force.[45]

In his State of the Union address in January 2006 regarding withdrawal of U.S. troops, President Bush said, "The road of victory in Iraq will bring U.S. troops home, but only when military commanders determine it's safe. Meanwhile, allied forces are defeating terrorism, and a new democracy is spreading hope." So far, statistics revealed by the U.S. military indicated that violent attacks continued. It reported that insurgents launched more than thirty-four thousand attacks against American and Iraqi government forces and civilians in 2005. That was more than ninety per day, and a 19 percent increase over the previous year. Meanwhile, the Pentagon said it had trained more than two hundred thousand Iraqi troops, which allowed them to replace U.S. units in parts of Baghdad and other cities. Although U.S. deaths dropped slightly, from 714 killed in 2004 to 673 in 2005, polls showed that support among Americans for the U.S. plan to keep troops in Iraq indefinitely had fallen sharply.[46]

Iraqi intellectuals and politicians questioned if President Bush actually believed that his strategy in the Iraq war was working. On many occasions, the president reiterated not giving up on the mission. Such withdrawal of troops would only prompt the insurgents to "wait us out . . . You know, if you give a timetable you're conceding too much to the enemy," he insisted.[47]

Secretary of State Condoleezza Rice, supporting the president, said, "It would be a mistake for Congress to micromanage the Iraq war." She encouraged lawmakers to support President Bush's troop increase. "I would hope that Congress would recognize that it's very important for them to have the oversight role," Rice said. "But when it comes to the execution of policy in the field, there has to be a clear relationship between the commander in chief and the commanders in the field." It was apparent that Democrats, now the majority party on Capitol Hill, were unhappy with Bush's plan to send more U.S. soldiers. Rice emphasized it would be a major mistake to disrupt the chain of command. "I think it's best to leave the flexibility of what to do on the ground to commanders on the ground who understand the intricacies and the relationship among these various tasks that the American armed forces have to do."[48]

When the new U.S. military commander in Iraq, General David Petraeus, took over his post in February 2007, he joined Condoleezza Rice in supporting the increase of U.S. military presence. He warned that Iraq was "doomed to continuing sectarian strife" if the new joint military operation under way in Baghdad failed to hit sectarian violence. He had been appointed to carry out the U.S. administration's new strategy in Iraq, including sending 21,500 extra troops, most of them to Baghdad. The troops' mission was to help the government secure the capital and the western province of Anbar.[49]

A bipartisan group of lawmakers in the Congress submitted a resolution calling on the Bush administration to develop a plan by the end of 2006 to pull out all U.S. troops from Iraq. They proposed to begin the withdrawal by October 1, 2006. Rumsfeld testified that it would be a grave mistake to set a date for withdrawal from Iraq before preparing the Iraqi forces to be able to continue defeating the insurgents and militias.[50]

Many senior U.S. politicians raised an intense argument over the U.S. military presence in Iraq. Senator Carl Levin, a senior Democrat, voiced to CNN in rather simple and decisive words, "I believe our message to Iraqis has got to be the following, 'You folks have got to solve your political issues, not duck them. Unless you come together in a comprehensive way, reach an agreement through this draft constitution, we are going to have to consider setting a timetable for departure.'"[51]

As the violence in Iraq was on the increase and pressure from the Democrats in Congress had intensified, Iraqi Prime Minister M. Maliki came under pressure from the U.S. administration to step up efforts to control the Shiite militia sectarian killing. Maliki said at a news conference broadcast on national television in October 2006, "This is an elected government and only the people who elected the government have the right to make time limitations or amendments," he added. Apparently that remark pointed to a widening gap between the policy of Shiite-led Iraqi government and the Americans who support it.[52]

To make the situation worse, Turkey expressed fears of "endless war" in Iraq. Turkey told the United States not to leave a power vacuum by abruptly withdrawing its forces without careful planning or allowing Iraq to split when the forces leave. Abdullah Gül, Turkey's foreign minister, said in January 2007 at the World Economic Forum in Davos, Switzerland, "If Iraq is divided, there will be a real civil war and all the neighbors will be involved in this." He continued, "If that happens, there will be another dark era in Iraqi history, there will be endless war, civil war. We [Turkey and its neighbors] are all having the same target: to keep Iraq as one . . . If there is a division, we will not recognize any new government in the region."[53]

So would strategizing the exit from Iraq be the solution? Nicolas Kristof's conceptual strategy for exit from Iraq was published in the *Herald Tribune* in November 2005. He asked, "What would happen if we pulled out right now?" and visualized the following scenario: southern Iraq might devolve into quasi-theocratic city states under a heavy Iranian influence, with neighborhoods controlled by militias like the Badr Organization and the Mahdi Army. Anbar province could become a Taliban-style terrorist training ground that would destabilize Jordan and Saudi Arabia. Baghdad would be a war zone, with Sunni and Shiite militias slaughtering each other. In Kirkuk, Kurds and Arabs would fight for control of oil wells and for the city itself. Kurdistan would drift toward independence, leading to skirmishes with Turkey and conceivably even to a Turkish invasion of Kurdistan. To exit Iraq without strategy, as envisaged by Kristof, means chaos and civil war all over the country.[54]

There remain controversial political and military opinions regarding the time for withdrawal of foreign troops from Iraq. The last surprise was in a declaration of withdrawal of South Korean troops while President George W. Bush was attending a summit in the port of Pusan. Seoul's defense ministry released a plan for the withdrawal of a third of the country's 3,200 Korean troops in Iraq in the first half of 2006. The new prime minister of Italy in his first address to the Italian Parliament in May 2006 promised to withdraw all three thousand Italian troops from Iraq by the end of 2006.[55]

Britain's leading commander in Iraq said that most British troops would be pulled out by the middle of 2008 under a phased withdrawal plan expected to begin within months. British forces currently number eight thousand were stationed in southern Iraq. Britain believed this would give time for Iraq's newly trained 225,000-strong security forces to prepare to assume full control.[56] The British commander, Lieutenant General Nick

Houghton, was quoted saying to the *Daily Telegraph*, "There is a fine line between staying too long and leaving too soon."[57]

Tony Blair in February 2007 announced that the government decided to reduce the number of the British troops in Iraq by 1,600 within the coming months. He further said that UK forces would maintain a presence into 2008. Blair made the announcement to the British parliament saying, "The actual reduction in forces will be from the present 7,100—itself down from over 9,000 two years ago and 40,000 at the time of the conflict—to roughly 5,500." Consequently, the Danish prime minister also announced the withdrawal of 450 Danish troops stationed in southern Iraq under British command. The newly appointed prime minister, Gordon Brown, made a reduction of 2,500 British troops stationed mostly in al-Basra, southern Iraq. He said he could not guarantee that any British troops would remain in Iraq by end of 2008. Since the U.S.-led invasion in March 2004, an estimated 170 British soldiers had died in Iraq.[58]

Many Shiite armed militia demonstrations in the southern port city of Basra shouted slogans calling for the British troops to leave. The city was the scene of persistent killings between Sunni insurgent bombings and Shiite-on-Shiite slayings amid a competition for political control. Despite the disputes between the two rival factions they declared that the British presence only provided a target for attackers, seeking to end the "occupation."[59]

Many countries started to withdraw troops from Iraq. Poland and Italy announced the impending withdrawal of their remaining troops. Polish President Lech Kaczynski said his country, a U.S. ally in Iraq and Afghanistan, would pull its remaining nine hundred soldiers out of Iraq by the end of 2007. In addition, Italian Prime Minister Romano Prodi said the last of Italy's soldiers in Iraq, between sixty and seventy troops, had returned home, ending the Italian contingent's presence in the south of the country of more than three years.[60]

It was true that in the third year of the Iraq occupation, the U.S. military dismissed media reports that America and Britain planned to pull all troops out of Iraq by spring 2007. "This is an ongoing assessment and not linked to any timeframe."[61]

As mentioned before, the United Nations Security Council had agreed to continue the mandate of the U.S.-led forces in Iraq after a request submitted by the Iraqi government. The U.S. forces consisted of 145,000 Americans and 20,000 from twenty-seven other nations. In his letter to the council, Iraq's foreign minister stated that his country "still requires help from U.S.-led forces to maintain peace and security."[62]

To appease the Iraqi protesters, the newly elected president, Jalal Talabani, said to the media in April 2005 that U.S. troops would eventually leave his country within the following two years.[63] He further assured that the Iraqi government would remain in full consultation and cooperation with the American friends. Talabani made it clear that the number one priority of the newly established government was to uproot terrorism and spread the atmosphere of democracy and freedom that would eventually lead to economic prosperity.[64] On many occasions, Talabani distinguished between Iraqi insurgents and foreign fighters. He expressed no tolerance toward the "criminal terrorism that is imported from abroad."[65]

Talabani called for reconciliation among all those who believed in democracy and were opposed to terrorism. He pointed out that Iraqis had been suffering from a lack of security and all efforts ought to be directed toward rectifying that before negotiating the issue of U.S. troops leaving the country.

In this light, a U.S. general warned against pulling out from Iraq. It was General Richard Myers, ending his years of service as the top U.S. military officer, who warned that pulling out of Iraq would only make the United States more vulnerable. He admitted in October 2005 that there had been great progress in Iraq. However, his optimistic statement was indeed at odds with the growing anxiety among Americans over the war.[66]

As a major policy address after two and a half years of U.S.-led occupation of Iraq, President Bush said the fight against terrorism must continue there because it was the center of a terrorist movement to "intimidate the whole world." He further asserted that if U.S. forces withdrew from Iraq, insurgents would "use the vacuum created by an American retreat to gain control of the country, a base from which to launch attacks and conduct their war against non radical Muslim governments."[67]

However, the president's address had not satisfied the majority of Americans. This was clearly shown in the polls in which his popularity with regard to war in Iraq was dwindling. Among those who were dissatisfied by the president's speech and showed deep concern about the presence of U.S. forces in Iraq was the Senate Minority Whip, Dick Durbin (D-Illinois). He insisted that the speech left too many questions about the Iraq war unanswered. "He owes it to the American people—and the Democrats are calling on him to tell the American people—how will this end? How can we measure success? How can we get beyond the generalities of the speech that we heard today?" Responding to increasing congressional calls for U.S. withdrawal, Vice President Cheney assured that the move would hand victory to Islamic terrorists. The warning was in a speech Mr. Cheney made to the American Enterprise Institute, a neocon-servative think tank.[68]

The White House in September 2005 made it clear that President Bush insisted he would not withdraw U.S. forces "without having achieved vic-tory." The president further clarified, "That's what's important for the American people to understand; one, we are not going to cut and run; two, we'll achieve our objective; and three, the president is going to listen to those who are on the ground who can make the best assessment."[69] About 159,000 American troops were in Iraq, up from about 138,000 in the summer of 2005.

As American critics of the Iraq war became more hostile, President Bush forcefully attacked those critics. In his Veterans Day speech in November 2005, the president said, "The stakes in the global war on ter-ror are too high and the national interest is too important for politicians to throw out false charges." He continued, "While it's perfectly legitimate to criticize my decision or the conduct of the war, it is deeply irrespon-sible to rewrite the history of how that war began."[70]

The question constantly raised by many U.S. politicians was, "Could the U.S. start pullout from Iraq after the people in a referendum approved the October 15, 2005, Iraq constitution?" General George Casey, the top U.S. military commander in Iraq, said, "I do believe we'll still be able to take some very substantial reductions after these elections in the spring and summer of next year."[71]

Talabani, speaking at a conference during his visit to France in Novem-ber 2006, said, "We need time . . . not 20 years, but time. I personally can say that two to three years will be enough to build up our forces and say to our American friends 'bye bye with thanks.'" He accused the media on focusing only on negative stories. The president of Iraq continued, "However, international terrorists and militias were still concentrating all their efforts on Iraq which meant the country needed outside help to defeat them."[72]

The consequent question was, "Were there any U.S. military plans to cut troops in Iraq after three years of occupation?" Defense officials said that the Pentagon plans intended to shrink the U.S. troop presence in Iraq to about 138,000 from 155,000 after the December 15, 2005, Iraqi elections. If security conditions improved in the country, U.S. military planners said that the United States might consider dropping the number to about 100,000 in summer 2006. However, until 2008, that plan had not materialized as sectarian violence had intensified.[73]

Representative John Murtha in 2004 warned that "premature with-drawal" of U.S. troops could lead to a civil war in Iraq. He continued that hasty withdrawal from Iraq would leave American foreign policy in "disarray." It was known that Murtha had been a staunch Pentagon supporter in occupying Iraq and removing Saddam Hussein from the presidency. However, after his visits in 2005 to Iraq, after two and a half years of U.S. occupation, he came home as "an antiwar symbol." He called for immediate withdrawal of the American troops from Iraq within six months. This short time surprised the U.S. administration and many of his constituents. He explained his change of opinion was the result of the pain he felt to see wounded and handicapped American soldiers at Walter Reed Medical Center outside Washington and by his steady disillusionment with the U.S. administration in managing the war. "I just came to the conclusion finally that I had to speak out. I had to focus this administration on an exit strategy," he said.[74]

However, it is apparent that an exit strategy without full preparation of competent Iraqi police and army forces could ultimately lead to increasing chaos. Withdrawal of U.S. troops, as expressed on repeated occasions by both the Iraqi military and the United States, should be gradual and unhurried. In mid-December 2005, the U.S. military handed over full order and security responsibility to Iraqi forces in a number of towns and regions. The transfer took place before the elections of the new parliament held on December 15, 2005. This handover of full security to Iraqi forces incited Zalmay Khalilzad, the U.S. ambassador to Iraq, to say that America could start to pull out some of its 158,000 troops "beginning the following year."

Were there U.S. talks about reducing its troops from Iraq on Iran's agenda? It has been true that Iran had not expressed any plans or hints for direct talks with the United States on Iraqi disputes. This is despite the fact that the United States and Iran were encouraged by influential Iraqi Shiite politicians to negotiate on enforcing peace in Iraq as sectarian tension had run high in the country. The leader of the Supreme Council for the Islamic Revolution in Iraq (SCIRI), a key Shiite Muslim party connected to Iran, said, "Talks between Iran and the United States are in Iraq's interests and could be in Iran's interests as well because the United States is present in Iraq and in the region."[75]

After four years of occupying Iraq, White House spokesman Tony Snow said, "General G. Casey is assigned the business of making a lot of plans and . . . this [cutting troops] is one of the plans that is under consideration." President George Bush discussed the plan with Casey but insisted that any decision would depend on the conditions on the ground in Iraq. The president emphasized that any recommendation by Casey would be aimed toward achieving victory. The U.S. troops serving in Iraq were close to 145,000. It was apparent that President Bush had been under pressure to bring home at least some U.S. soldiers before the coming congressional elections in 2006 as the U.S. deployment in Iraq became increasingly unpopular.[76]

During the U.S. election, the war was the top campaign issue. A poll indicated that a majority of Americans were opposed to Bush's handling of Iraq. Meanwhile, an increasing number of Republican candidates had expressed impatience with the U.S. policies as deaths among American troops in Iraq had climbed above three thousand and the total cost of the war exceeded $300 billion. However, President Bush asserted, "Absolutely we're winning." He rejected Democratic calls for a timetable for U.S. troop withdrawals.[77]

President Bush also admitted concern over Iraq strategy. At a press conference in the White House, he insisted that victory in Iraq was vital. The president remarked in October 2006 as follows:

"The events of the past month have been a serious concern to me," he said. "I know many Americans are not satisfied with the situation in Iraq. I am not satisfied either."

Americans have no intention of taking sides in a sectarian struggle or standing in the crossfire between rival factions.

The consequences in Iraq will have a decisive impact on the security of our country.

"The outcome will determine the destiny of millions across the world." He warned that turning Iraq over to America's enemies would destabilize the Middle East and provide a "safe-haven for terrorism and hijack world oil production."

They [terrorists] will launch new attacks on America from this new safe haven. They will pursue their goal of a radical Islamic empire that stretches from Spain to Indonesia.[78]

However, in February 2007, a U.S. House of Representatives resolution condemning the plan of President Bush to send an additional 21,500 troops to Iraq passed by a vote of 246 to 182. Nancy Pelosi, the House Speaker and a California Democrat, said, "The stakes in Iraq are too high to recycle proposals that have little prospect for success." Bush dismissed the rebuke, stressing that it was "non-binding." The congressional resolution added, "Congress and the American people will continue to support and protect the members of the United States armed forces who are serving or who have served bravely and honorably in Iraq." Democratic leaders announced they would not cut money for troops abroad but would try to attach conditions on war funding that could force Bush to stop the buildup.

Finally, in March 2007, the U.S. Congress voted to impose a "September 2008 deadline for withdrawing all American combat troops from Iraq." The House voted 218–212 in favor of imposing a September 1, 2008, end date, attaching it to a bill that authorizes more than $124 billion in emergency funds, mostly for the wars in Iraq and Afghanistan. Before the vote, Pelosi said the bill would address the problems in Iraq by "rebuilding our military, honoring our promises to our veterans, holding the Iraqi government accountable and enabling us to bring our troops home." She continued, saying, "The American people have lost faith in the president's conduct of this war." She added, "The American people see the reality of this war—the president does not."[79]

Immediately, President Bush said he would veto the deal. At a White House press conference he remarked, "A narrow majority in the House of Representatives abdicated its responsibility by passing a war spending bill that has no chance of becoming law and brings us no closer to getting the troops the resources they need to do their job." The president had earlier insisted that no time limit was to be imposed on withdrawal of U.S. troops from Iraq. In addition, he requested approval for sending an additional thirty thousand American troops into Iraq.[80]

However, Carl Levin, the leading Democrat on the Senate Armed Services Committee, said in the U.S. Senate, "Nothing else has been successful in convincing the Iraqis that they have to take responsibility for their own country, and that they must make the political compromises that are necessary to end the sectarian violence and defeat the insurgency in Iraq." The senator continued, "Only when the Iraqis realize that the mission of U.S. forces in Iraq is changing and that we are going to reduce the number of U.S. forces in Iraq, will they realize that we cannot save them from themselves. Iraqis need to act to meet the commitments they made to us and to themselves."[81]

Under such pressure from Democratic leaders in Congress President Bush reiterated in May 2007 that he knew the nation was weary of war and questioning if the United States could win. Still, he said, any strategy to pull troops home from Iraq only makes the United States more vulnerable to attack from an enemy that is "pure evil." "The enemy does not measure the conflict in Iraq in terms of timetables," Bush said to U.S. soldiers, a reference to congressional Democrats' plans to start phasing in troop withdrawals. "A strategy that encourages this enemy to wait us out is dangerous—dangerous for our troops, dangerous for our security," Bush said. "And it is not going to become law."[82]

SUNNI ARABS AND SHIITE AL-SADR FACTION DEMAND A TIMETABLE FOR WITHDRAWAL OF FOREIGN TROOPS IN IRAQ

The Sunni Arabs and the influential cleric Shiite al-Sadr were not satisfied with President Bush's explanation. They demanded setting a timetable for withdrawal of all foreign troops. They asserted that such a timetable reflected a growing popular demand of the Iraqi people. Shiite leader al-Sadr decided to ally his strong group with the Sunnis due to "first, the difficult situation facing the country, secondly to prevent the occupier and 'enemies of Iraq' from attaining their goals, and thirdly to consolidate national identity and to reaffirm its unity." The influential Sadr and his followers had been ardently opposing the U.S.-led occupation of Iraq. He had aligned with Sunni Arabs who formed the backbone of the tirelessly persistent opposition in Iraq. However, fixing a timetable for the withdrawal of foreign troops was not, in principle, among the new Iraqi government's immediate priorities. It was evident that improving the security situation in the country was the main concern of the new cabinet.[83]

There were growing fears that the latest continuous violence and outburst of Sunni insurgency would plunge Iraq into civil war. The Sunnis felt that both Shiites and Kurds apparently marginalized them in the formation of government and reshaping Iraq's future. The Sunnis, who long directed the political destiny and shaped the fate of Iraq, felt deeply that they had lost their glory days. Psychologically, they felt neglected and not given their due status in the formation of the government.

In order to strengthen ties with the Sunnis and quell violence, the prime minister appointed a Sunni Arab former military officer with tribal ties to Iraq's western Anbar province as the defense minister. The Association of Muslim Scholars and al-Sadr Shiite militia faction had conditioned their participation in the political process with a clear-cut timetable for withdrawal position. "We are not saying that they should leave Iraq immediately," said al-Dhari, spokesperson of the Muslim scholars' association. "We are asking them to set a timetable to withdraw in stages, but we need, at least, to see some progress on this front. This is a very legitimate right."[84]

However, it was previously envisioned that foreign troops in Iraq would have probably started leaving the country in large numbers by mid-2006. It was further agreed by the Iraqi government and U.S. military that numbers expected to leave would have depended upon how quickly Iraqi troops could be trained and armed in order to take over the responsibility of maintaining peace and order in the country. Two years after the invasion of Iraq, the United States had over 140,000 troops in the country battling fierce fights against Sunni insurgents and Shiite militias.

What surprised the Iraqis was that Iraq's parliament speaker, Mahmoud Mashhadani, a Sunni, bitterly criticized U.S. forces in Iraq, accusing them of "butchery" and demanding that they pull out of the country. He was speaking at a United Nations (UN)-sponsored conference on transitional justice and reconciliation in Baghdad in July 2006. His strongly worded attack appeared to embarrass the Iraqi government. "Just get your hands off Iraq and the Iraqi people and Muslim countries, and everything will be all right," the conservative Sunni Islamist said. "What has been done in Iraq is a kind of butchery of the Iraqi people," he added. Mashhadani was a member of the main Sunni Arab parliamentary bloc, the National Concord Front, which was a member of Maliki's national unity government.[85]

As the violence in Iraq increased and midterm elections in the United States neared, the *Herald Tribune* in October 2006 said that Maliki had come under pressure from the Bush administration to step up efforts to control the killing. The paper conveyed the U.S. administration's view "that the very forces that elevated him to power and whose support he must retain—religious Shiite parties with their own militias—are complicit in the killing." Maliki, a Shiite himself, apparently was not pleased with that view. He promptly tailored his remarks on the U.S. view for his own domestic audience. "I want to stress that this is a government of the people's will and no one has the right to set a timetable for it," Maliki said at a news conference broadcast on national television. The remarks pointed to a widening gap between the Shiite-led Iraqi government and the Americans who support it.[86]

As peace and security had been deteriorating in Iraq and Iran was accused of training, providing armaments, and above all financially assisting Shiite militias, Saudi Arabia warned it would provide financial support to Iraqi Sunnis if the United States pulled its troops out of Iraq. The *New York Times* reported in December 2006 that King Abdullah of Saudi Arabia sent the warning to Vice President Dick Cheney during his visit to Riyadh. The message also emphasized the kingdom's displeasure with proposed talks between the U.S. government and Iran. The Saudi warning reflected fears of Iran's rising nuclear influence in Iraq.

The recently released Iraq study group report said that the Bush administration engaged Iran and neighboring Syria in talks aimed at applying pressure on Iraqi Shiites to keep what some analysts are calling a civil war from spiraling into a regional conflict. "Saudi Arabia has expressed concern that once U.S. troops leave Iraq, the controlling Shiite majority could massacre the Sunni minority, believed to comprise a large faction of the deadly insurgency that has claimed thousands of Iraqi civilian and U.S. military lives."[87]

Muqtada al-Sadr, the hard line Shiite cleric, threatened that the six Shiite members of the party would leave the Iraqi government in protest at the prime minister's failure to back calls for a timetable for U.S. military pullout from the country. Prime Minister al-Maliki's response was that he saw no need to set a timetable but his government was working to build up Iraq's security forces as quickly as possible so U.S.-led forces could leave.[88]

IRAQI TROOPS FORM SHIELD IN BAGHDAD AGAINST INSURGENTS

In order to enforce peace and security, the government announced it had deployed forty thousand Iraqi police and soldiers in the capital and rings of the city with hundreds of checkpoints. In Baghdad, the new Prime Minister al-Maliki said that the Iraqi troops would restore the dignity of the government and enforce peace in Iraq.[89]

With the continuous aggression of Sunni insurgents and Shiite militias, the government feared violence would deepen sectarian division. A string of attacks that hit southern and northern Iraqi cities killed many Iraqi citizens. The main attack took place in the mostly Shiite town of Suwayra, which is near Iraq's so-called Triangle of Death south of Baghdad. This is where Sunni guerrillas launched many deadly attacks and carried out kidnappings. Iraqi leaders feared the extreme violence would increasingly deepen sectarian hostility among Iraqis. Sunni Arabs who were most powerful under Saddam had been greatly marginalized and politically neglected. This was while Shiites and Kurds that Saddam oppressed became the new powers in Iraq.[90]

In Baghdad, after one year of occupation, in April 2004, a senior official confirmed that guerrillas in cars carrying rocket-propelled grenades entering Madaen and seized up to 150 hostages, including women and children. A large number of Iraqi forces, supported by U.S. troops, took up positions around Madaen, a small town near Baghdad. Insurgents threatened to kill the hostages unless all Shiites left the town. This raised deep fears that such an incident could lead to a wider sectarian conflict and consequently contribute to the start of a civil war.[91]

As seen, the situation became worse in Madaen and villages nearby. The police officers counted sixty corpses floating over the surface of the Tigris River. The police distributed the photographs of the bodies for identification. Shiite politicians accused the insurgents of ethnic cleansing. They demanded that the government should act firmly.

Meanwhile, violence continued in another town, Haditha, near Baghdad, with the kidnapping of nineteen Shiite fishermen and National Guardsmen. The insurgents lined them up against a wall in a sports stadium and shot them dead. During Friday prayers, a suicide car bomber in east Baghdad hit the Shiite Al Subeih mosque, killing nine and wounding twenty.[92]

In Baghdad, an aide to Iraq's most powerful Shiite cleric was shot to death. This was the second of his aides to be assassinated in the same week. The attack was designed as part of an upsurge in violence since the largely Shiite transitional government came to power. Most of the attacks targeted Shiites and Kurds. Authorities believe those responsible were mainly Sunni Arabs. It became evident that the insurgents used mosques to stage attacks and to hide guns and explosives. Meanwhile, antigovernment fighters assassinated three clerics in Baghdad.[93]

The terrorist wing warned the country's Sunni Arabs to take no part in drafting a new constitution. Not only were the insurgents attacking Shiite clerics and Sunnis serving the government, but also killing many peaceful Kurds walking in a Kurdish funeral procession.

As security continued deteriorating in Baghdad, U.S. troops began placing six-ton sections of wall around Adhamiyah in east Baghdad. It is a mainly Sunni Arab area surrounded by Shiite residential areas. The construction drew sharp criticism from Sunni leaders who expressed their opposition to the wall. They complained that the concrete wall would isolate their community.

With the worsening of peace and security in Iraq, polls showed nearly six in ten Americans wanted to see U.S. troops leave Iraq either immediately or within a year, and more would rather have Congress running U.S. policy in the conflict than President Bush. A CNN poll in March 2007 found most Americans supported a withdrawal from Iraq.[94]

In May 2007, President George W. Bush's approval rating fell to 28 percent in a *Newsweek* poll, an all-time low for Bush in that survey. Nearly two out of three Americans—62 percent—believed Bush's recent actions in Iraq showed he was "stubborn and unwilling to admit his mistakes," *Newsweek* reported. Just 30 percent thought Bush's execution of the Iraq war demonstrated he was "willing to take political risks" to do what was right. Bush's unpopularity cast a dark shadow over Republican chances for keeping the White House in 2008.[95]

SISTANI CALLS NOT TO USE FORCE AGAINST SUNNIS

Sistani, the eminent Shiite Cleric in Najaf, Iraq, decided neither to use force nor to retaliate against Sunnis. The Iranian-born al-Sistani is Islam's

Shiiah cleric and commands deep respect in both Iraq and Iran. It was declared among Shiite followers that "Sistani and the religious authorities in Najaf decided not to use force, so the Shiites couldn't retaliate." To Shiites of Iraq, Grand Ayatollah Ali Sistani's word is law and his faithful must obey.[96] It was apparent that there was no single verifiable incident of a counterattack from the Shiites of Iraq against the Sunni at that time. One of Sistani's fellow ayatollahs issued a warning to the Shiite faithful: "Beware of sectarian war." Indeed, it was very true that if it were not for the influence of the clerics and leaders there would have been a civil war in the country long before.[97]

Unfortunately, this peaceful coexistence on the part of the Shiites did not last long despite the continuous call of ayatollahs for no retaliation against the Sunni insurgents. In May 2005, the head of the Association of Muslim Scholars made fiery accusations against Shiites. He directed his anger at a group that once was considered a militia for a powerful Shiite organization called "Badr," which was accused of assassinating Sunni clerics and preachers. The Badr Brigade was formerly the militia of the Supreme Council for Islamic Revolution in Iraq. The Sunni Association stated that Badr had members in the government. The Badr Brigades spent many years in exile in Iran during Saddam's regime. They returned to Iraq after Saddam was overthrown. Despite these facts, the Sunni Association still promoted that Iraqis, including both Sunnis and Shiites, should all stand against terrorism and sectarian battle.

The Sunnis were concerned that the Shiite government might have allowed groups like the Shiite Badr Organization to act like death squad militias. The government denied the accusation.

Bitter tensions between Shiite and Sunni Muslims dominated sermons in Iraqi mosques. If their clerics and preachers were further attacked, Sunni leaders threatened to close their mosques durations to protest anti-Sunni assassinations. Because of the escalating sectarian tension, animosity flared up between rival Shiite and Sunni districts in Baghdad after a car bomb killed two people in the Shiite district of Kazimiya. However, the real source of that acute ethnic tension in Iraq was that four prominent Sunni imams were assassinated and a number of Sunni clerics were arrested at the same time, prompting a three-day Sunni mosque strike.[98]

The Sunni Arab Coalition, which comprised Iraqi tribal leaders, clerics, and Islamic thinkers, is the highest Sunni authority in Iraq. The official name is the Association of Muslim Scholars, established after the fall of Saddam Hussein. The association declared that it could not be silent "toward the criminal and inhumane actions in which both ministries of interior and

defense and other collaborating Shiite parties are involved." The association held the transitional Shiite government responsible for the results of
these actions. However, it should also be noted that the Shiite-dominated
government had been making all efforts possible to bring Sunni Arabs into
the political process and the all-important writing of a constitution.[99]

In order to bring the tensions to a halt, Shiite cleric Muqtada al-Sadr
mediated between the influential Iraqi Association of Muslim Scholars
(AMS) and the Badr Organization. Al-Sadr, together with other Shiite
and Sunni Muslim representatives, held together several meetings to
explore a way to put an end to the most alarming sectarian violence in
Iraq. He also met with the Supreme Council for the Islamic Revolution
in Iraq in order to pacify the two ethnic parties.

The strategic call of al-Sistani, the eminent Shiite cleric, for maintaining peace and security between Shiites and Sunnis, asking neither to use
force nor to retaliate against each other, was a step forward to initiate
dialogue between the two sectarian factions. In his speeches, al-Sistani
emphasized to religious Sunni and Shiite radicals the importance of
reaching peace in the country.

To end Iraq's sectarian fighting among Sunnis, Shiites, and Kurds, leaders of the three sects called for an end to conflict and vowed to track down
those responsible for bloody attacks on citizens in Iraq. The three Iraqi
chiefs spoke on national television in an effort to keep the country from
sliding into civil war. Furthermore, the Political Council for National Security in Baghdad met there to discuss the violence. The Shiite prime minister, Nouri Kamal al-Maliki; the Sunni speaker of Parliament, Mahmoud
al-Mashhadani; and the Kurd president, Jalal Talabani, made their joint
statement on television. They assured, "We promise the great martyrs that
we will chase the killers and criminals, the terrorists, Saddamists and Takfiri
[Islamic extremists] for viciously trying to divide you."[100]

THE BAKER U.S./IRAQ STUDY GROUP
FOR GRADUAL EXIT FROM IRAQ

The Iraq bipartisan Study Group was an advisory panel of Democrats
and Republicans examining alternatives to U.S. policy toward Iraq. James
Baker, the former U.S. Secretary of State, and former Indiana Congressman Lee Hamilton chaired the group. In December 2006, the U.S. group
handed President George W. Bush its report.

In the report, the group advised the president for a gradual pullback of
U.S. combat troops. However, it did not recommend setting a firm timetable for withdrawal. The group warned of dwindling chances to change
course before crisis turned to chaos. The group also said the United States

should establish communication with Iran and Syria over the Iraqi conflict as the U.S. administration previously ruled out talks with Iran unless Tehran suspended its uranium-enrichment activities. This was despite the fact that Talabani, the Iraqi president, had repeatedly emphasized that securing Iraqi and Iranian cooperation should be linked to secure border areas rather than political issues. Meanwhile, the group stressed the issue of oil revenues. It recommended that oil revenues in the north and south of the country should be under central control of the government in Baghdad.

In addition, the group exerted pressure for the U.S. administration to end the unpopular Iraqi war that cost in four years nearly $400 billion and killed 2,900 Americans and 150,000 Iraqis. It advised the U.S. president that troops in Iraq should evolve "to one of supporting the Iraqi army," and that Iraqi troops should take over primary responsibility for combat operations.

The report also drew attention to the fact that Iraqi leaders had failed to enforce peace and reconciliation in the country. The military force had not achieved security for the Iraqi communities. Therefore, the group recommended, "Military priorities must change," toward a goal of training, equipping, and advising Iraqi forces.

Among the seventy-nine recommendations, the report indicated that unless the Iraqi government in Baghdad made "substantial progress," the United States should reduce its political, military, and economic support. "Because none of the operations conducted by U.S. and Iraqi military forces are fundamentally changing the conditions of sectarian violence, U.S. forces seem to be caught in a mission that has no foreseeable end," the report emphasized.[101]

While James Baker handed over the Group Report to President Bush in December 2006, new research obtained by Aljazeera.net, the Arab Web site, showed that, "More than 90 per cent of Iraqis believe the country is worse off now than before the war in 2003." The findings followed a poll by NBC News and the *Wall Street Journal* that established that fewer than one in four Americans approved of the U.S. administration's handling of the conflict in Iraq. The Iraqi survey, revealed by Al Jazeera on December 14, 2006, further indicated that nearly 66 percent of respondents thought violence would decrease if U.S. forces were to leave. Thirty-eight percent were "not confident" that Nouri al-Maliki, the Iraqi Shiite prime minister, would be able to improve the situation in Iraq and nearly 90 percent described the government's implementation of its commitments and promises as very poor.[102]

A day after the critical Baker Iraq Study Group called for a change in U.S. strategy, President Bush called for a "new way forward" in Iraq.

"I believe we need a new approach," he said, following talks with Tony Blair, the British prime minister and his closest ally on the Iraq war. Blair said he welcomed the recommendations of the Iraq Study Group despite its criticism of past policies. He further added, "I think it is important now we concentrate on the elements that are necessary to make sure that we succeed—because the consequences of failure are severe." The two leaders acknowledged that, "It's bad in Iraq." The group advised Bush to begin to withdraw U.S. combat forces from Iraq by early 2008 to avoid "a slide toward chaos." Meanwhile, the report called for a diplomatic push that would include Iran and Syria. Bush made it clear that he would only welcome Iran and Syria to group talks on Iraq if they agree to end support for extremists and to help Baghdad's government to maintain peace and security.[103]

It is very true that the Baker group's Iraq Report for gradual withdrawal of U.S. troops had raised many questions. Prime Minister Nouri al-Maliki, however, expressed the willingness of his government to speed turnover of security responsibility to Iraqi forces to release the U.S. troops of this burden. However, the question of timing the withdrawal was a bothersome issue of concern to the Iraqi government. The president thus acknowledged the pressure at home for the beginning of U.S. troop withdrawals. However, he assured the prime minister that "We shall be in Iraq until the job is complete, at the request of the sovereign government elected by the people."[104]

John Abizaid, a senior U.S. commander in the Middle East, rejected calls to withdraw American troops in Iraq. He expressed his views on the question of troop withdrawal to a congressional panel in Washington, DC, in December 2006. He said, "Under the current circumstances, I would not recommend troop withdrawals or to send more." He added, "More American forces prevent the Iraqis from doing more, taking more responsibility for their future. Troop levels need to stay where they are." Pressure was mounting on the U.S. administration for a change of direction in Iraq after the Baker Report. The poll released by the Pew Research Center said that 61 percent of U.S. citizens opposed Bush's plan, while 31 percent were in favor.[105]

To build support for the commitment by President Bush to send twenty thousand extra U.S. troops to Iraq, which the Baker Report and Democrat Senators opposed, Condoleezza Rice, U.S. Secretary of State, flew to Kuwait. She met foreign ministers from six Gulf Arab states, as well as from Egypt and Jordan. At a joint news conference with Rice, Sheik Mohammad al-Salem al-Sabah, the Kuwaiti foreign minister, said that the United States had already won Saudi Arabia's and other Gulf States backing for the plan.

The joint communiqué said, "All countries in the region are concerned about interference in Iraqi internal affairs . . . We'd like neighboring countries to work together for peace and stability in Iraq." The joint communiqué did not mention Iran by name. It said, however, that relations among countries should be based on the principle of noninterference in the internal affairs of other countries.[106]

What raised eyebrows was the accusation of al-Qaeda deputy leader Ayman al-Zawahiri in an audiotape posted on the Internet criticizing the U.S. plan to send 21,500 more troops to Iraq as a gamble that was bound to fail. He assured that the Mujahedeen (the Islamic fighters) would continue carrying on war against the U.S. troops in Iraq.[107]

Although the report of the study group chaired by James Baker was received with understanding in the Iraqi government, it faced a strong rebuke from the leader of the northern Kurdish region of the country. Massoud Barzani, the president of the northern Iraqi Kurdistan region, accused Baker's team of trying to impose the "wrong solutions" on the Iraqi people. Barzani was very critical of the report's recommendation that the Iraqi central government should have control over the natural resources of the country. In his opinion, the natural wealth distribution in the constitution was sufficient. Barzani further criticized the panel that its members had not even bothered to visit the Kurdish region before publishing their report. "We are in no way abiding by this report," he said. Barzani was known as a key ally of the United States in Iraq.[108]

The forthcoming chapter, the last one in this book, sums up the situation up to the time of this publication. It portrays the conflicting positions of Sunnis, Kurds, and Shiites regarding many aspects of the constitution, and shows how they finally came to agree in order to form a new Iraqi government.

CHAPTER 12

IS DEMOCRACY IN IRAQ
IN FLAMES?

AFTER MORE THAN FOUR YEARS OF MILITARY OCCUPATION, THE U.S. military commander in Iraq admitted that military might alone could not solve the ongoing violence in the country. General David Petraeus, in his first news conference in March 2007 in Baghdad since he took command a month before, rightly said, "There is no military solution to a problem like that in Iraq, to the insurgency of Iraq. Military action is necessary to help improve security . . . but it is not sufficient." He added that political progress would require talking to, and reconciling with, some of the militant groups in Iraq, describing them as "some of those who have felt the new Iraq did not have a place for them." His position was that a two-way strategy is required: military action is necessary for enforcing security, and political dialogue is essential for reconciliation and peace.[1]

Facing threat of civil war, relentless suicide bombings, assassinations, and kidnappings, Iraqi leaders and the U.S. administration had hoped the Iraq Interim Assembly would produce a draft constitution presented for elections planned for December 2005 in order to stabilize the country and restore its threatening peace and order. Nevertheless, sectarian tensions were fracturing politics and delayed agreement on the draft constitution.

It became clear to the Iraqi Assembly representatives that in writing the draft constitution there appeared major obstacles including the role of Islamic religion, Iraq's official languages, and women's rights. This was in addition to division among the members of the Interim Assembly concerning crucial issues of federalism and the formation of federal units, and sharing of power and oil resources in areas such as the mainly Kurdish north and the Shiite south, where local leaders want autonomy from Baghdad and control of oil wealth.

Other major debatable political subjects for discussion were the mentioning of the Ba'ath Party in the constitution and the division of powers between the president, the parliament, and the cabinet. Obviously, the Kurds demanded federalism in order to protect their self-rule in their three northern provinces. Sunni Arabs opposed federalism, as they feared that Kurds wanted to declare independence in the future. It was thus understood that Sunnis, who once enjoyed dominance under Saddam Hussein's regime, wanted a central government with tight control over oil resources near Kurdish areas in the north and in the Shiite south.

The Shiite communities were apparently divided. A large number of them supported federalism to build a Shiite region in the south. The Shiite Daawa party, a major part of the ruling coalition, found that differences emerging among Shiites regarding federalism would further complicate efforts to strike a deal in the draft constitution. Many Shiites, however, were of the opinion that a federal system is the only insurance policy for the unity of Iraq.[2]

After making final minute changes to meet the requirement of Sunnis, the Iraq's interim parliament approved a final draft of a new constitution and submitted it to the United Nations, which printed five million copies and distributed it around the country. It was considered the official absolute final draft of the constitution before being put to the last referendum. For weeks, the document was delayed repeatedly by several last-minute amendments. That was mainly due to objections raised by the country's Sunni Arabs. At last, the draft was submitted to the Iraqi people.

The final draft made some further minor concessions to Iraq's Sunni Arab minority. The concessions included that Iraq was a founding member of the Arab League. However, it is true that the draft constitution largely reflected the views of the Shiite majority and the Kurds who controlled the interim parliament as they won elections in January 2005. The Sunnis largely boycotted the elections. Therefore, they marginalized themselves politically. The constitution was approved in the referendum, as was ultimately expected, and elections for a new parliament were held in December 2005.[3]

The possibility of the constitution being defeated in the referendum was low. First, the majority Shiite community and minority Kurds represent 80 percent of the Iraqi population. They overwhelmingly supported the document, while the 20 percent minority Sunnis, who were believed to form the backbone of the country's raging insurgency, opposed it. The constitution would be defeated only if two-thirds of voters in three of Iraq's eighteen provinces voted against it. There is a majority Sunni population in three provinces, al-Anbar, Salaheddin, and Nineveh, and all three locations reported a strong voter turnout. In the end, the constitution was approved as only two provinces rejected it. Salaheddin and Nineveh provinces said no to the constitution, while in al-Anbar the majority of voters agreed to it.[4]

THE SUNNI POSITION

The Shiites and Kurds who had the majority in parliament were able to approve the draft constitution in the National Assembly without the consent of the minority Sunnis who objected to the draft. As scheduled, the approved text was put to a referendum. Sunnis were already rallying their supporters to vote "NO."[5]

Sunnis hoped followers of Shiite cleric al-Sadr, who had a strong wealth of support among poor Shiites in Baghdad and the south, would vote "NO." If the document was defeated, then a new election would be held. To the disappointment of the Sunnis, the referendum indicated victory for the draft constitution.

Sunnis boycotted the January 30, 2005, vote, which went overwhelmingly to Shiites. Sunni-led insurgency convinced many Arab Sunnis that they would be marginalized in the new Iraq if they participated in the election. On the other hand, political efforts to encourage Sunni extremists to join in the building of a new Iraq were encouraged in the General Conference for Sunnis in Iraq. The conference called on Sunnis "to organize themselves to take part in the coming elections and to register their names at the offices of the electoral commissions."[6]

In another step to increase the Sunni involvement in the government, fifteen Sunnis were approved to join the committee for drafting the new constitution. The incorporation of Sunnis on the drafting committee was delayed because majority Shiites and Kurds had accused nominees of links to Saddam's Ba'ath Party. What made the participation of Sunni members in the committee seem vulnerable was that three of them were shot dead as they left a Baghdad restaurant. Other Sunni members on the committee suspended their participation, apparently because of security reasons.

Let us elaborate on this controversial question, "Is federalism really needed in Iraq?" It was the issue of "federalism," the formation of autonomous regions, that remained one of the basic issues of dissention. The Sunnis strongly objected to federalism in Iraq altogether, while Shiites and Kurds agreed to include it in the draft constitution. Abdul-Aziz al-Hakim, leader of the country's biggest Shiite party, called for a Shiite federal state, saying it was needed "to keep a political balance in the country after decades of dictatorship under Saddam Hussein."[7] Kurds in the north and Shiites in the south favored language in the draft constitution permitting such federalism. Sunni Arabs, noting that Iraq's oil wealth was centered in those areas, said that such federalism would benefit those groups in the long term. Geographically, the oil wealth is largely concentrated in the Kurdish north, about 20 percent, and Shiite south, about 80 percent. Most Sunnis living in central and western Iraq believed that the draft constitution would create two powerful and wealthy oil-producing regions in the north and south. In the long term, the power and wealth may be excluded from the center and west.

It is evident that federalism and petroleum appear to be the most controversial issues, drawing opposition between Sunni Arabs and the other two factions, namely the Kurds and Shiites. It is feared that such a disputed issue might lead, in future, to the breakup of the country.[8]

Problems stirred by Sunnis in their participation in writing the Iraq draft constitution aggravated both the government and the assembly, which both had Shiite majorities. Such outstanding problems as federation, employment of professional former Ba'ath Party members in government, renaming of the country, source of laws in the constitution whether Islamic or secular, and distribution of oil wealth among regions were main debatable issues. Such issues had delayed finalizing the draft constitution.

The Iraqi foreign minister said during his visit to Jordan that Iraq would finish writing the constitution and hold elections at the end of 2005, even if the once-dominant Sunni minority continued to boycott the process. He continued, "It is in the interest of the Sunnis to participate without making excuses." However, the spokesperson for the Sunni National Dialogue Council hurriedly replied, "My message to brother Zebari, Minister of Foreign Affairs, is that we are not Sunni members, we are sons of Iraq. We represent a wide proportion of the Iraqi people."[9]

The new constitution also affected the position of top-level Sunnis. The Sunnis saw the "de-Ba'athification" as an excuse to deprive members of their community of government jobs.

It was no surprise that in Takrit, Saddam Hussein's hometown, politicians called for Sunni Arabs to vote "no" in the referendum for the draft constitution. The Iraqi Islamic Party said that the constitution was threatening "national unity and the identity of Iraqi people." The party brought copies of the draft constitution from Baghdad so that the members could see it and know the reasons that the party was calling on Sunnis to vote "no." In Mosul, three Sunnis promoting votes of "yes" were killed by masked gunmen outside a mosque. The gunmen grabbed them as they hung posters appealing to fellow Sunnis to vote "yes" in the October 15 referendum on the new constitution. Meanwhile, preachers at Sunni mosques warned their congregations not to accept any constitution "that would rip away the unity of the nation."

A last-minute deal was made. It aimed at obtaining the consent of the Sunni Arabs. Lawmakers introduced a paragraph that allowed the next parliament of December 15, 2005, referendum to amend the draft constitution. The main Sunni Arab political groups announced, "Some of our demands were met so the Arab political groups have endorsed the constitution and is urging people to vote yes." This meant that the Shiites and Kurds agreed to a key demand from minority Sunni Arabs that parliament should review possible amendments to the constitution four months after December's election. It provided the Sunnis with an assurance that the constitution would not be rigid, but flexible. It was subject to amendments.

Despite the fact that the newly elected Iraqi parliament had approved postponing the thorny subject of federalism for a few months, a law backed by some Shiite leaders was presented in a session of parliament. These leaders aimed to set up a big, autonomous federal state in their oil-rich south. The Shiite majority and Sunni Arab minority in the parliament boycotted the vote. The action was in defiance of an agreement between Shiite and Sunni leaders. They had agreed to put off discussion on the disputable "federalism law" for at least eighteen months in order to delay the creation of any autonomous regions until 2008. It is indeed true that Sunni Arabs believe that federalism would hand northern and southern oilfields over to Kurds and Shiites who were both loyal to Iran.[10]

What disturbed Arabs living in Kirkuk in northern Iraq was that they faced forced relocation. An Iraqi government committee had recommended moving tens of thousands of Arabs currently living in the oil-rich northern city of Kirkuk. Al Jazeera's Web site in February 2007 quoted the Iraqi Higher Committee for the Normalization of Kirkuk: "Arabs descended from those who moved to the city after 1957 would be returned to their original home towns and given compensation." The committee said that decision would only apply to Arabs who arrived in Kirkuk during the "Arabization" campaign of Saddam Hussein's government, a move that seemed certain to anger the Arab settlers. During the rule of Saddam Hussein, thousands of Arabs were moved to the city and thousands of Kurds were made to leave. Al Jazeera further quoted a Kurdish official saying, "The committee will allot them land and pay 25,000 dollars [per household] as compensation." However, the Arab Sunnis were not happy with such reallocation.[11]

THE KURDISH POSITION

Northern Iraq elected veteran leader Masoud Barzani as president of the region, thus giving the Kurds greater autonomy after decades of oppression under Saddam Hussein. Barzani is the head of the Kurdistan Democratic Party (KDP). He took the oath of office before the 111-member Kurdish parliament as president of Iraqi Kurdistan. In addition to his parliamentarian position, Barzani also led the 100,000-member Kurdish Peshmerga militia. Iraqi Kurdistan has been an autonomous region including three northern provinces of Sulaimaniya, Irbil, and Dohuk.

In writing the constitution, Iraq's Kurds declared their insistence on federation. They expressed unwillingness to compromise on their demands for autonomy. They rejected suggestions that the country should be proclaimed an Islamic state in the new constitution. They also refused to compromise on the incorporation of oil-rich Kirkuk into their autonomous northern region. Massoud Barzani, the president of Iraq's autonomous Kurdistan, assured Kurdish people that he would insist on full federalism and keeping the Kurdish Peshmerga militia when discussing the draft constitution in Baghdad.

According to Article 2, Iraq's Kurdish region consists of the three current provinces of Dohuk, Arbil, and Sulaimaniyah and also Kirkuk province and parts of Diyalay, Nineveh, and Wasit provinces. The constitution goes on to state that the Kurds have "chosen a liberal federation with Iraq as long as it respects the federal constitution, its federal, democratic and multiparty parliament."[12]

In the Kurdish parliament, Barzani rejected suggestions that Iraq be termed "an Arab nation" saying, "Let Arab Iraq be part of the Arab nation—we are not." He added decisively, "We will not accept that Iraq's identity is Islamic." He insisted, "This is a golden chance for Kurds and Kurdistan—if we don't do what is important for Kurdistan, there will be no second chance. We will not make our final decision in Baghdad, the Kurdish parliament will decide." It is evident that Iraqi Kurds, who number about 4.5 million, want a constitution that will guarantee federalism and preserve their region's autonomy. One major problem facing the new parliament is the question of the future role of Kurdish regular militias (the Peshmerga) estimated at one hundred thousand highly trained fighters. The prospect of their integration within the Iraqi army is under further negotiations in the parliament.

To reinforce unity between the two main factions in the north, the Kurdistan parliament in May 2006 unified the administration of the Kurdish region of Iraq. This action helped end the previous system of two separate local governments. In fact, there were two regional governments in Kurdistan, one headed by Kurdistan Democratic Party (PDK), the other by the Patriotic Union of Kurdistan (PUK). Unification of the two regional governments was unanimously approved by the 105-member parliament in Arbil, in the north, in May 2006. The new government of Kurdistan is not only for the Kurds, but also for the other sects and ethnic groups such as the Christians and Turcomans.[13]

The crises between the central government in Baghdad and Kurdistan's regional government started when, in September 2006, Iraq's prime minister issued a stern rebuke to ethnic Kurds after the autonomous Kurdistan region ordered the national Iraqi flag to be replaced by the Kurdish tricolor on government buildings in northern Iraq. The prime minister issued a statement defending the national flag. The statement also implied that the Kurds' own banner was illegitimate. Moreover, the statement made it clear that "The present Iraqi flag should be hoisted on every inch of Iraqi soil until the parliament takes a decision about it."[14]

Barzani, the president of the Kurdish region, said, "According to the Kurdistan Administration of Iraq's decree number 60, we decide to hoist the flag of Iraqi Kurdistan officially on all offices and government institutions in the Kurdistan region." It is evident that the Kurdish region had gradually been gaining more autonomy since the 2003 U.S.-led invasion. Many leaders in Baghdad feared they were pushing for independence.[15]

Iraqis ask this crucial question: "Has Kirkuk become the potential spark for declaration of independence of Kurdistan?" It is known that Kirkuk, Iraq's oil-rich northern city, is considered the most critical city for the future unity of Iraq. Historically speaking, Kirkuk has been sheltering people from the three major ethnic groups, namely Turkmen, Arabs, and Kurds. These groups have been in a continuous quarrel, each group claiming ownership of the very old city. Arab Sunni insurgents have continuously attacked Kirkuk, as a vital oil industry in northern Iraq, since the U.S.-led invasion of Iraq in 2003. As an important center of Iraq's northern oil industry, the Kurds see the Kirkuk region as vital for their long-awaited "independent state of Kurdistan."

The major obstacle confronting the Iraqi government was the distribution of the oil wealth among Shiite, Sunni, and Kurdish regions. Kurdish authorities agreed at last to back a draft law to manage and share the country's oil wealth between its ethnic and sectarian communities. The agreement would also set out terms regulating how foreign firms would operate in Iraq.

At a joint news conference in Baghdad with Iraqi President Jalal Talabani and Massoud Barzani, president of the Kurdish government in the north, the agreement of a new draft Iraq oil law was announced. The U.S. ambassador attended the conference. Maliki's government required a new law to encourage international companies to invest in Iraq to repair pipelines, upgrade wells, and develop new fields in order to exploit the country's vast petroleum reserves estimated at about 115 billion barrels. It is believed that the country's proven oil reserves lie in the Kurdish north and the Shiite-dominated south. Arab Sunnis, however, were assured of a share of the oil wealth. After the agreement al-Maliki said, "The benefit of this wealth will form a firm pillar for the unity of Iraqis and consolidate their social structure."[16]

THE SHIITE POSITION

It became apparent that major gaps remained among the Shiite, Kurdish, and Sunni members of the draft constitution on major issues, including first, Iraq's identity as an Arab nation; second, the role of Islam; and third, federalism. As was expected, the Shiites insisted on a greater role for Islam in civil law. They conceive Islamic Sharia (law) as the principal foundation for legislation, while Kurds and Sunnis are opting for Islamic Sharia as the principal source for legislation. It is worth mentioning that Iraq, under Saddam's rule, had been operating under a secular civil status law.

The majority of Iraqi Shiite leaders called for a federal state of their own in the south. Al-Hakim, head of the Supreme Council for the Islamic Revolution in Iraq (SCIRI), clearly called for an autonomous Arab Shiite region in central and southern Iraq. This is where the Shiite population is strongest in Iraq. Al-Hakim in September 2005 openly stated, "Regarding federalism, we think that it is necessary to form one entire region in the south." He was speaking in the Shiite holy city of Najaf, 130 kilometers south of Baghdad. Other Shiite leaders also favored federalism. "They are trying to prevent the Shiite from enjoying their own federalism. We have to persist in forming one region in the south or else we will regret it," a top Shiite leader told his people.[17]

Muqtada al-Sadr, the powerful Shiite leader, said, "I reject this constitution which calls for sectarianism and there is nothing good in this constitution at all." He criticized federalism in the draft constitution, which was, at the same time, rejected by Iraq's Sunni Arabs, who feared it would give Kurds and Shiites too much power and control over Iraq's oil resources. Al-Sadr further criticized federalism in the constitution. He said, "If there is a democratic government in Iraq, nobody has the right to call for the establishment of federalism anywhere in Iraq whether it is the south, north, middle or any other part of Iraq." His remarks, as a Shiite powerful leader, raised eyebrows and surprised members of the Shiite Alliance. Many saw it as an explosive issue.[18]

One of the major problems to enforce peace and stability faced by the newly elected El-Maliki Shiite in the country was the Shiite militia insurgents and specifically the Mahdi Army. These militias were well trained, mostly in Iran. They were also equipped with modern armaments. These Shiite militias had been responsible for attacking Sunni Muslims and exercising power in the country. The U.S. and Iraqi forces fought Shiite militiamen in Diwaniyah, a southern city under the growing influence of the Mahdi Army loyal to radical Shiite cleric Muqtada al-Sadr. Diwaniyah, eighty miles south of Baghdad, was the scene of a fierce fight in August 2006 between the Mahdi Shiite Army and Iraqi forces that left twenty-three Iraqi troops and fifty militiamen dead as well as scores wounded. The government decided to ban all Shiite militias.[19]

AMERICA'S INTEREST IN THE FINALIZATION OF THE CONSTITUTION

The U.S. administration and Iraqi government hoped that the constitution would put Iraq on a solid political path to root out the violence in the country and allow Washington to bring many, if not all, of its troops home. It was clear that under intense pressure from the United States, Iraqi politicians had been focusing on resolving problems that cross sectarian and ethnic lines. This was despite the fact that the insurgents and Islamic hard-line rebels defied any settlement while Iraq was under military occupation.

With all the differing opinions among Shiites, Sunnis, and Kurds in laying down a draft constitution suitable to all factions, the U.S. administration felt uncomfortable with the delay in finalizing it and the increase of insurgent and militia attacks at the same time. President George W. Bush cited the constitution in his weekly radio address in August 2005, describing it as a "critical step on the path to Iraqi self-reliance." He assured that violence in Iraq would not cause U.S. troops to withdraw prematurely. The Iraqi government and U.S. administration hoped the constitution would set Iraq on a political path to bring to a halt the violence in the country.[20]

It was clear that Iraqi politicians, under excessive pressure from the U.S. administration, were charged with tackling critical political, sectarian, and ethnic issues of difference among the three factions. U.S. officials demanded they reach an agreement for the interim National Assembly to present a draft acceptable to its members. The interim constitution stated that amendments could be made only with the approval of three-fourths of the 275-member parliament and the unanimous approval of the president and his two deputies. The draft was presented to Iraqi voters in an October 15, 2005, referendum. The U.S. administration and the Iraqi officials described the completion of the draft charter on time as a "victory for democracy."[21]

However, top Sunni Arabs in Iraq's government criticized the draft constitution. Sunni negotiators submitted counterproposals on the document. Despite the repeated Sunni requests for revisions, the Shiite-Kurdish majority discarded further changes to take place in the constitution. However, a Shiite leader said only minor editing would be accepted, as the draft was ready to be presented to voters in an October 15 referendum.[22]

The U.S. envoy in Iraq pursued talks with Iraqi rebels after the October 15, 2005, referendum without the knowledge of the Iraqi government. Al Jazeera, the Qatar-based Arabic media, referred in November 2005 to a news conference in which the U.S. ambassador to Iraq had said, "Washington was seeking talks with some rebels and would reach out to Iran for help in quelling the uprising that has raged since the fall of Saddam Hussein." Al Jazeera quoted the ambassador further saying, "We are reaching out to everyone but two groups: the Zarqawi group and associated forces who are jihadists . . . and the Saddamists, those who want Saddam Hussein to return."[23]

Khalilzad, the U.S. ambassador, added that if the United States wanted a properly functioning Iraq, Sunnis must be given the opportunity to take part in the political process. In strong insinuations to Shiites and Kurds that Washington wanted more efforts to accommodate the Sunnis, Khalilzad said to journalists, "A final, final draft has not yet been presented yet." He continued, "That is something that Iraqis will have to talk to each other about and decide for themselves." The U.S. administration desired a draft constitution acceptable to all Iraqi factions in the hope of quelling the Sunni-dominated insurgency so that the United States and other foreign troops could begin to go home.

In order to solve the problem of federalism in the draft constitution, the Americans suggested that federalism be included in the constitution but discussed by the parliament that would be elected in December 2005. However, the Shiites and Kurds rejected that. They wanted decentralization to be clearly mentioned in the draft. Then, they asserted, "Let the Iraqi people decide in the new parliament whether or not they accept federalism." Iraq's constitutional committee approved a final draft of the constitution and put it before the National Assembly despite the rejection of Sunni Arab leaders. At a press conference, Sunni Arab negotiators called the document "illegal." They vigorously called on the United Nations and the Arab League to intervene and prevent its passage.[24]

THE DRAFT CONSTITUTION SIGNED

President Jalal Talabani insisted that the August 15, 2005, deadline for the interim parliament to approve the draft charter ought to be met. He refused to extend the date of submission of the draft constitution to the assembly. Consequently, the parliament ratified the charter and submitted to a referendum on October 15, 2005. Iraq's constitutional committee approved a final draft of the Iraqi constitution and put it before the National Assembly, despite the rejection of Sunni Arab leaders.

However, if voters approved the constitution, a new election would have to be held in mid-December 2005. This would then lead the United States and its coalition partners to begin withdrawing forces by summer 2006 in consultation with the first democratic Iraqi government established in fifty years. The Americans and their Iraqi allies insisted that evolving a constitution would help develop Iraq's democracy and serve to reinforce the fight against the insurgency.

An alliance including the Sunnis' Association of Muslim Scholars and the movement of Shiite cleric Muqtada al-Sadr condemned the draft as a "politically incentive process which has been led by occupiers and their collaborators." The group further declared that this draft did not represent the genuine will of the Iraqi people. Thus, it was evident that the main fear of the Sunnis was the imposition of federalism in the draft constitution strongly supported by Shiites and Kurds. The Sunnis insisted that federalism could be implemented in the future when there is a parliament that represents all Iraqis. The Interim Assembly only has seventeen Sunni Arab members of the 275 legislators. Sunnis also resented attempts from the Shiite and Kurd delegations to ban former Ba'ath Party members from government posts. The Sunnis believe that would deprive them of a livelihood and prevent Iraq from using the talents of thousands of professors in Iraqi universities, senior executives, and others who joined the organization to advance their careers.[25]

In addition, the Sunnis insisted the constitution identify Iraq as an Arab nation. This subject was under discussion as Kurds and Shiite members in the draft constitution were of the opinion that Iraq should have its own identity, Islam as the state religion without specifying it as an Arab nation.[26]

The other major obstacle was that the Shiites wanted the new constitution to be based on strict Sharia (Islamic law), while most of the Kurds and the secular powers in Iraq wanted a constitution based on certain principles, while respecting the Islamic identity of the majority of Iraqis. Top aides said al-Sistani (who remained secluded at his home in the holy city of Najaf during the opening session of the Iraqi parliament) had no desire to push for a constitution that turned Iraq into an Islamic republic by force. Nevertheless, the seventy-five-year-old al-Sistani, it was said, would not sign off on a document that "disregards the Islam's basic tenets," including, for example, women's place in public life and the laws governing divorce. Many Iraqis believe he might eventually be chosen for the country's ultimate position of power, the way Ayatollah Ruhollah Khomeini once was in Iran. However, experts on political Islam at Cairo's Center for Political and Strategic Studies said al-Sistani and Khomeini, in essence, may be two sides of the same coin. That means the Islamization of Iraq remains a strong possibility even with a secular-oriented constitution.[27]

An alliance of influential Sunni Muslims in Iraq announced it would not participate in drafting a constitution unless its community was given a fair number of seats on the committee working on the project. The participants of the Sunni people agreed at a conference that twenty-five Sunni Arabs be named to the committee, on which fifty-five members of parliament sit. The Shiite-led government said it could expand the committee to accommodate more Sunnis—at that time there were only two seats on the body. Under Iraq's political timetable, once a constitution was written, it must be approved by a referendum. If it was approved, a new general election would be held by the end of 2005.[28]

A Sunni Arab group called on Sunnis to take part in future elections. Because of Sunnis boycotting the January 30, 2005, vote, the interim parliament seats went overwhelmingly to Shiites and Kurds. It was believed that the outcome of the election boosted the Sunni-led insurgency by assuring many Sunnis they would be marginalized in the new Iraq.

There were tremendous political efforts to encourage Sunni extremists to join in the building of a new Iraq. The General Conference for Sunnis in Iraq not only called on Sunnis to vote, but further asked Sunni clerics to issue a religious decree repeating the call. Clerics were at the forefront of boycott calls before the January election. The head of the committee to draft a new constitution said fifteen Sunnis were approved to join the committee and draft the constitution.[29]

The draft constitution was presented in a referendum for the Iraqi people to give their judgment on the first democratically elected parliament in the past fifty years.

THE REFERENDUM ON THE CONSTITUTION

As President Bush was eager to show progress in initiating democracy and introducing political reform, he told the U.S. troops, "I am going to assure you of this: that so long as I'm the president, we're never going to back down, we're never going to give in, we'll never accept anything less than total victory." Meanwhile, Iraq's Kurdish President Jalal Talabani said, "Today is a day for national consensus."[30]

Arab leaders called on Iraqi factions to avoid violence in order to contribute to the success of the December 15 referendum. In a statement announced by the Secretary-General of the Arab League, Amr Mousa, called for "All detention operations, assassinations and bombardment of Iraqi towns must be suspended before the polls to provide calm and stability for the balloting process for the sake of the fairness and transparency of the polls."[31]

The militant Sunnis and al-Qaeda insurgents declared on an Islamist Web site, "This so-called political process—and those who take part in these apostate elections—is forbidden by God's laws. They go against our Muslim constitution, the Quran." The statement continued, "We declare that we will carry on our jihad in the name of God until an Islamic state ruled by the Quran is established." It became apparent that there was a strong Sunni opposition to the draft constitution. What was important was that a large number of Sunni parties and associations had endorsed the draft constitution after amendment for referendum.[32]

Iraq announced in October 2005 security measures for the voting. The government imposed a curfew, weapons ban, border closings, and other security measures to prevent insurgent attacks. A nationwide nighttime curfew was enforced and nobody was able to carry weapons in public. On the eve of the referendum, travel was banned between provinces, international borders, airports, and other ports.[33]

Despite all security precautions, insurgents attacked five of Baghdad's 1,200 polling stations with shootings and bombs, wounding seven voters. However, there were no other major attacks reported as U.S. and Iraqi forces clamped down with major security measures around balloting sites.

At Iraq's approximately 6,100 polling stations, voters marked their paper ballot "yes" or "no" under one question, written in Arabic and Kurdish: "Do you agree on the permanent constitution project?" The country's Shiite majority—some 60 percent of its 27 million people—and the Kurds another 20 percent—supported the approximately 140-article charter, which provided them with autonomy in the regions where they were concentrated in the north and south. It is worth noting that Shiites and Kurds can easily gain a simple majority in favor of the constitution in the vote. However, that was not enough to ensure passage. If two-thirds of voters in any three of Iraq's eighteen provinces voted "no," the charter would have been defeated.[34]

At the end of the December 15, 2005, referendum election, the final tally revealed the following results. The Shiite United Iraqi Alliance won 128 seats, the Kurdish alliance got 53 seats, and the Sunni Iraqi Accord Front won 44 seats. The secular list headed by former Prime Minister

Ayad Allawi won 25 seats, the Sunni Iraqi Front for National Dialogue won 11 seats, the Kurdistan Islamic Union got 5 seats, and a number of smaller parties won 9 seats. The vote elected 275 members of a national parliament. Some nine million Iraqis cast ballots with a turnout of 61 percent. About 250 of the country's 6,100 polling stations, mostly in the north and west, did not open due to technical or security problems.[35]

Despite major difficulties in security during the referendum, the UN envoy to Iraq called the approval of Iraq's constitution a "major advance." He highlighted the ethnic divisions reflected in the vote. The UN statement said, "The result of the referendum has indicated the degree of political polarization in Iraq. This poses an ongoing challenge for all Iraqis and underscores the importance of an inclusive national dialogue."

The Shiite Alliance at the beginning announced al-Jaafari to continue office. According to Iraq's constitution, President Jalal Talabani must convene the new 275-seat parliament within two weeks of election certification. In the ninety days following the election, parliament should elect a three-person presidency council, which in turn appoints a prime minister. The prime minister then names a cabinet, which must be confirmed by parliament. However, a delay in approving the candidacy of a prime minister and the cabinet in naming the prime minister and ministers took place for more than six months after the date of the referendum. Power struggles among the various political factions started to emerge.

As a result of the delay, the country faced a profound political confrontation among leaders. They failed to resolve a bitter dispute over who should be the prime minister." The country was without a government more than six months after the December 15 referendum as the Iraqi leaders disputed the premiership and other key posts. This was while the Shiites opposed the Sunni candidate for the post of parliament speaker.[36]

While members of the Parliament were in disagreement in forming a new government, Iraq's situation worsened. U.S. Secretary of State Rice and Britain's minister of foreign affairs, Jack Straw, flew in secret into Iraq in April 2006, in a dramatic mission to form a united government that could halt a slide to civil war. They made it clear that "We [the United States and United Kingdom] are entitled to say that whilst it is up to you, the Iraqis, to say who will fill these positions, someone must fill these positions, and fill them quickly."[37]

Rice said the troubles in Iraq called for a strong leader who could help unify the war-ravaged land. She added, "It's not our job to say who that person ought to be." She continued, "The quick formation of a new government is something that the international community has a right to expect. You cannot have a circumstance in which there is a political vacuum in a community who faces so much threat of violence."[38]

Pressure on Prime Minister Jaafari mounted. Leaders of the biggest party, Shiite Alliance, joined the call for him to step aside in the name of national consensus and stability. Meanwhile, the minority Sunni and Kurdish leaders insisted they would not join a cabinet under Jaafari and wanted a different Shiite nominee. The United States made clear that the "Iraqi people have one enemy; it is terrorism. There were no Sunnis against Shiites.[39]

Jaafari condemned American and British "interference" in Iraq's new democracy. An aide said he was ready to fight "to the end." Jaafari continued, "We do not need anybody to remind us, thank you." Jaafari, it seemed, was referring to the comments of the U.S. ambassador to Iraq, Zalmay Khalilzad, who said that the United States was investing billions of dollars in Iraq and did not want to see that money go to support sectarian politics.

In this political dilemma and national embarrassment, it was April 2006, after almost seven months of debates in the parliament, that Iraqi Sunni and Kurdish leaders officially rejected the possibility of Ibrahim al-Jaafari continuing his position as prime minister in the next government. Sunni and Kurdish leaders accused the prime minister of monopolizing power and failing to lead the country adequately. They insisted they would not join a cabinet under Jaafari. They reiterated their desire for appointing a different Shiite nominee. At the same time, the United States and Britain advised al-Jaafari to step aside to break the deadlock over the formation of a government. They both believed that the political vacuum in Iraq was fueling ongoing violence. The United States and Britain, in fact, urged Shiite leaders to agree to a broad-based governmental coalition. This, they believed, was of great significance to win the support of the Sunni to fight against insurgents.[40]

Iraq's interim Prime Minister al-Jaafari rebuffed and brushed off all calls to quit. He rejected growing pressure on him to resign, saying Iraqis must be left alone to choose their leader democratically. He expressed no intention to step aside and give up his nomination for a second term. This was despite public calls for him to do so within his own Shiite bloc. Senior officials in Jaafari's Daawa Party assured he was definitely not going to step down. After six months of deadlock over setting up an Iraqi government, a large number of Shiite Alliance leaders in the parliament called for al-Jaafari to step down. This took place after a declaration of Sunni and Kurds saying, "Our position regarding Jaafari is clear and has not changed."[41]

Because of such political chaos, peace and security in Iraq was gradually diminishing. The rate of suicide bombers detonating explosives increased at police stations, in crowded areas, and where U.S.-led forces were present. Fears for the future of Iraq were complicated by the continuing struggle among Iraqi politicians to form a new government.[42]

As portrayed by the *Herald Tribune* in April 2006, the delay in forming the new Iraqi government for a long time further damaged the country's crippled oil sector. The absence of a minister-designate for the oil ministry affected the oil industry. Iraq has the world's third-largest oil reserves. Sabotage, political instability, mismanagement, and lack of foreign investment seriously affected the sector. Exporting of oil was the country's economic lifeline and important for needed reconstruction capital. The delay in forming the government and insurgents' sabotages have been main causes of hindering oil exports as required. Iraq, at present, exports less than 1.5 million barrels a day, compared with 1.7 million before the U.S.-led invasion in 2003. The oil sector was waiting for a new government to raise exports to 1.8 million barrels a day as planned. Meanwhile, the majority of Iraqis complained that these companies use Iraq's current political instability to push for higher gains. Iraq's oil should be for the benefit of the Iraqi people, not foreign multinational companies. The Iraqi public opinion is favoring the government to handle control of the country's oil.[43]

However, after a year of such deliberation on the oil debate, the new Iraqi government adopted through parliament a controversial new oil bill. The bill required placing control of its oil wealth in the hands of foreign companies. This is despite the fact that the general policy adopted by oil-producing countries normally seeks to nationalize their oil wealth in order for governments to exercise control of their oil production. In addition, as most of the country's reserve oil is located in the Shiite and Kurdish-dominated areas, the minority Sunnis would have a minority share. Many Iraqis claim American oil companies stand to benefit from this new law.[44]

THE FORMATION OF A NEW DEMOCRATIC GOVERNMENT

The long-awaited first session of the parliament lasted just over thirty minutes and was adjourned because there still was no agreement on a permanent speaker for the legislature or on his deputies. However, members stood together and pledged to "preserve the independence and the sovereignty of Iraq and to take care of the interests of its people." After long controversial deliberations and political maneuvering, parliament approved the appointments of the members of the government in a voting session. The new government was the first full-term, sovereign Iraqi administration since the U.S. invasion of 2003.[45]

The parliament agreed on Nouri al-Maliki for the post of prime minister designate. He read out names and positions of his ministers. In May 2006, after eight months of hot deliberations, the 275 members of the parliament approved, in a show of hands, the new cabinet.

Al-Maliki further said that he would run the country's interior ministry and the deputy prime minister designate would be temporary defense minister. That compromise was made after tensions between Iraq's factions over the posts of interior and defense that threatened to delay the parliament sessions further. Sunni Arabs wanted the post of defense ministry that runs the army, while the Shiites wanted the interior ministry that controls the police. After two weeks of deliberations and debates, the parliament backed the appointment of two ministers submitted by the prime minister. Jawad al-Bulani, a Shiite, was chosen to lead the ministry of interior. He was a member of parliament in 2005. General Abd al-Qadir, a Sunni, was also approved as defense minister. He served in the Army under Saddam Hussein. He was demoted when he opposed the invasion of Kuwait in 1990.[46]

The approval of parliament of the two candidates for interior and defense ministries ended acrimonious disputes that had threatened to plunge the new government into crisis. The vote took place shortly after Maliki promised the parliament that his government vowed to heal sectarian wounds and crush a Sunni Arab insurgency. The minister of the interior added, "I promise the Iraqi people that the interior ministry will be neutral, independent and will not be under the influence of anyone." That declaration of neutrality of the interior ministry was welcomed by the Sunnis. The ministry was previously accused of accommodating the Shiite militias who infiltrated the security and police service and were responsible for killing a large number of Sunnis.

The Sunni community in Iraq was satisfied with the appointment of Tarek al-Hashmi as vice prime minister. However, al-Qaeda criticized al-Hashmi in a released recording for participating in the Shiite government. The statement from the Iraq al-Qaeda leadership was considered a warning to Sunnis not to join the political process under a Shiite-led government and its U.S. backers. However, Prime Minister al-Maliki, supported by U.S. forces, continued fighting Sunni insurgents, al-Qaeda, and Shiite militants. He vowed to end sectarian rifts. He announced a plan to put an end to the critical divisions between Shiite and Sunni parties in his government. The four-point plan, which emerged after talks between both sides, the Sunni and Shiite, is to "resolve disputes by giving every party a voice in how security forces operate against violence on a neighborhood by neighborhood level." In this connection, Iraq's prime minister said, "We have taken the decision to end sectarian hatred once and for all. We have vowed before Almighty God to stop the bloodshed." Local committees were formed in each Baghdad district, made up of representatives of every party, religious and tribal leaders, and security officials, to consult on security efforts. A central committee, also made up of all the parties, would coordinate with the armed forces. For example, a Sunni representative could raise a complaint if he feels police are not pursuing Shiite fighters after an attack.[47]

Al-Maliki further explained that disarming Shiite militias, whose members were believed to have infiltrated the security services, would be a priority. This should take place alongside the promotion of national reconciliation, the improvement of the country's collapsing infrastructure, and the setting up of a special protection force for Baghdad.

In a wise step toward unification of the various factions, Iraq's prime minister made an important peace offer to unite the Iraqi people in support of his government. He offered an olive branch to former supporters of Saddam Hussein, including the army. It was known that a large number of Saddam's supporters joined the insurgents after the previous governments expelled them from the army, police, and government offices. Al-Maliki made the offer at a national reconciliation conference designed to halt increasing sectarian violence. He urged former soldiers from Saddam's former army to join the country's new security forces to fight the armed factions threatening peace and security of the country. Al-Maliki urged the parliament delegates to review the law that banned tens of thousands of Saddam's Ba'ath Party activists from working in the civil service. He added that pensions for those not brought back would be paid. He further called parliament to review the de-Ba'athification process that made many Sunnis lose their jobs under the previous government.[48]

The good news regarding the Iraqi Sunnis was when the government announced, "The Iraqi political parties have agreed to delay the formation of any new autonomous federal regions for at least 18 months." As a result, discussion in the parliament about the volatile issue of federalism would be delayed among the political parties. The delay took place because the Kurds started to debate their own constitution.[49]

WORLD LEADERS WELCOME NEW IRAQI GOVERNMENT

President Bush vowed that Washington would stand by Baghdad as it joined world leaders in welcoming Iraq's new government. "Iraqis now have a fully constitutional government, marking the end of a democratic transitional process in Iraq that has been both difficult and inspiring."[50]

In a surprise face-to-face visit to Baghdad, which lasted five hours in June 2006, Bush met with the new Prime Minister Nouri al-Maliki, assuring al-Maliki that the fate of his war-scarred country was in Iraq's own hands. Al-Maliki requested the delay of U.S. troop withdrawal. As Bush flew back to the United States, he said, "There's a worry . . . that we will leave before they [Iraqis] are capable of defending themselves." He continued, "When America gives its word, it keeps its word." Al-Maliki thanked Bush for the U.S. protection and expressed a general hope for the day when American troops would be gone. "God willing, all of the suffering will be over, and all of the soldiers will be able to return to their countries with our gratitude for what they have offered."[51]

British Prime Minister Tony Blair hailed the new Iraqi government, considering it a crucial step forward for Iraqis who struggled to form a government despite sectarian wrangling between main Sunni, Shiite, and Kurdish groups. In a surprise visit to Iraq in December 2006, Blair pledged his support to the government. At a joint news conference with al-Maliki, Blair reiterated, "We stand ready to support you in every way." He said that preparations to hand over Basra to the Iraqi army were going well. "The British troops would not leave before Iraqis could handle security on their own," he asserted.[52]

In April 2006, just after the formation of the Iraqi government, Rice and Rumsfeld stood "united" in Iraq. The secretary of state and defense secretary paid an unannounced visit to Iraq. The aim of the visit was to advise the new prime minister to take immediate steps to reestablish confidence among Iraqis, and rid the country's security forces of influence by sectarian militias. They both vowed to support the Iraqi government, which was being put together by the newly designated prime minister. The two cabinet secretaries both praised Maliki, a relatively untested leader nominated by Iraq's Shiite voting bloc. Al-Maliki had made an impression as a committed leader devoted to ending sectarian strife in the country.[53]

To reiterate his full support of the new Iraqi leadership Tony Blair flew into Baghdad in May 2006 to personally support the new government in carrying out its duties in restoring security and curbing the tide of violence. After meeting with the leaders of Iraq's new government, Prime Minister Blair called its inauguration a true "new beginning." He emphasized that with setting up of the new government representing the Iraqi people there should be no excuse for insurgents and ethnic militias to commit violence. However, Blair refused to set a timetable for the withdrawal of British troops. He said their return home was governed by conditions on the ground. A timetable for withdrawal would be dependent on the security situation. "Peace will allow us to go," he insisted.[54]

Just one month after the visit, the chief of the British Army called for a pullout of British troops from Iraq "sometime soon." He said that postinvasion planning for that war was "poor, probably based more on optimism than sound planning." Gen. Richard Dennett told London's *Daily Mail* newspaper in an interview in October 2006 that he had "more optimism" that "we can get it right in Afghanistan." He added, "Britain's continued presence in Iraq had made the country less secure. Britain should get us out sometime soon because our presence in Iraq exacerbates security problems round the world."[55]

He continued that the U.S.-led coalition's plan to establish a democracy in Iraq that would be "exemplary for the region" was unlikely to happen, "That was the hope, and whether that was a sensible or naïve hope, history will judge . . . I don't think we are going to do that. I think we should aim for a lower ambition."[56] Undoubtedly, Dennett's views directly contradicted the position of Prime Minister Blair, who had been a strong supporter of the war and President Bush's closest ally in the fight. Blair and Bush both reiterated that troops must stay in Iraq until Iraqi security forces are able to stand up on their own. Later on, Dennett softened the views expressed in the interview.

Tony Blair, the outgoing British prime minister, who became unpopular by his decision to join the Iraq war, arrived in Baghdad on a farewell visit in April 2007. While Blair was meeting the Iraqi prime minister and leaders, three mortar shells slammed into the compound. Although he believed security would be improving in Iraq, mortar and terrorist attacks were still daily occurrences.

Blair assured al-Maliki and Talabani that Britain would continue to support them after he left office in June 2007. Meanwhile, he urged them to expedite reconciliation between Iraq's divided communities. He also called for new provincial elections and, at the same time, to increase efforts to bring tribal leaders linked to violence into the political process.

On the local front, the new Iraqi government was trying to win the confidence of the Iraqi people by releasing about six hundred detainees. These were the first of 2,500—nearly 10 percent of those held in Iraqi and U.S. detention centers—freed: the largest group since the U.S.-led invasion. Iraqi and American officials had agreed upon this decision in a joint review. The Iraqi prime minister emphasized that those freed would not include any deemed "guilty of serious crimes such as bombings, torture, kidnapping and murder." He further said that Iraq would adopt a "national reconciliation" plan to reintegrate former members of Saddam Hussein's ruling Ba'ath Party into society. A spokesperson for the U.S. military command said there were about 14,500 detainees in the detention centers run by the U.S.-led coalition, including several thousand at Abu Ghraib prison outside Baghdad.[57]

IRAQ MOVES TO BAN ALL MILITIAS

The new Iraqi government vowed to disband all militias in the country including progovernment groups. Al-Maliki, the prime minister, made it very clear that "every militia which is loyal to a party is a militia." He affirmed, "We must have one decision: When we say militia we mean all those who are armed other than the army and police." He further confirmed that even the biggest militias run by governing parties would have to go, specifically naming the Kurdish Peshmerga, the al-Mahdi Army of Shiite cleric Muqtada al-Sadr, and the Shiite Badr movement as being among those that would have to be disbanded.[58]

The prime minister ordered at least 75,000 Iraqi police officers and multinational forces deployed throughout the capital of six million people to search cars and secure roads leading into and out of Baghdad. Maliki called on Iraqis to be patient with the security measures and promised Iraqi forces would respect human rights and would not single out any ethnic or sectarian group. He assured the Iraqi citizens, "We are only going to attack areas that are dens for terrorists." They established checkpoints, launched raids against insurgent hideouts, and called in air strikes as necessary.

Many asked, "What was the reconciliation plan offered to the Iraqi people?" In fact, the PM presented to parliament a twenty-four-point national reconciliation plan that included an amnesty for insurgents and opposition figures who had not been involved in terrorist activities. He stressed, however, that insurgent killers would not escape justice. "The launch of this national reconciliation initiative should not be read as a reward for the killers and criminals or acceptance of their actions," he said. The Iraqi leader, who had been in power just over a month, said he was realistic about the difficult road that lay ahead. The plan also called for a reconsideration of policies against former President Saddam Hussein's outlawed Ba'ath Party. The plan emphasized a dialogue should be opened with all organizations willing to participate in political process except al-Qaeda members and hard-line supporters of Saddam.[59]

However, the plan endorsed by al-Maliki to stop sectarian killings in the country offered a "ray of hope" for peace and security. It was an optimistic plan as many Iraqis voiced concerns that the plan lacked means and

ways to disband the Shiite militias and quell Sunni insurgents that were
blamed for most of the ethnic and sectarian violence in the country.

As a response to al-Maliki's reconciliation plan, Iraqi tribal leaders met
in October 2006 in Babylon governorate, south of Baghdad. They signed
a pact of honor to end the violence and the forced removal of people from
their homes. About seventy tribal leaders held their meeting in the capital
of Babylon. They agreed to form committees to work on locating those
displaced and bring them back home. A senior Iraqi official said at the end
of the meeting, "They were full of determination and hope, but at the same
time they knew they did not have the ability to work independently to
achieve what they agreed on. They need a lot of cash and equipment." The
twenty-four-point National Conciliation Plan to heal the nation's severe
political and ethnic wounds took the form of a solemn pledge signed by
leaders of tribes and political factions. One Sunni leader said the cost of
the plan's failure would be "the end of Iraq." The signed statement said,
"We pledge to God, his Prophet and the Iraqi people to address the crisis
and we pledge to stop this bleeding of Iraqis." The reconciliation plan, as
conceived by the government, was a crackdown on the activities of illegal
armed groups of the army of Shiite cleric Muqtada al-Sadr and Sunni insurgents that held sway in many cities in the country.[60]

In order to carry out his government plan for reconciliation among the
various factions al-Maliki, Iraq's Shiite prime minister, made a surprising
visit to Ramadi, the Sunni insurgent stronghold situated west of Baghdad.
The Shiite al-Maliki and the Sunni governor vowed to work together in
order to combat al-Qaeda insurgents who had been fighting the U.S.-led
troops since the invasion started in March 2003. Many observers saw the
trip as a concrete sign that the Shiite government was determined to carry
out the reconciliation plan among the Shiite and Sunni factions. The
prime minister held meetings with Sunni leaders and tribal sheikhs.[61]

In response to the meetings of the prime minister with Sunni tribe
leaders for reconciling against al-Qaeda militants in Iraq, the militants
killed twenty-one people in bomb attacks targeting Sunni Arab tribes
who had formed an alliance against the hard-line Islamist group. There
had been a growing struggle in Anbar between the al-Qaeda militant
group and Sunni tribes.[62]

Al Jazeera's Web site revealed in March 2007 the result of the poll
commissioned by the BBC and ABC News. The poll disclosed, "Only
26 percent of 2,000 people questioned across all 18 Iraqi provinces said
they felt safe in their own neighborhoods." The poll further indicated,
"Forty percent said they thought the general situation in the country will
improve. About 78 percent of Iraqis opposed the presence of coalition
forces, and 69 percent said their presence worsened the security situation.

Necessities were lacking, with 88 percent of respondents saying the availability of electricity was either 'quite bad' or 'very bad.' About 69 percent
gave similar responses for the availability of clean water, and 88 percent
said so for the availability of driving or cooking fuel."[63]

Iraqi Prime Minister Nouri al-Maliki in a speech in parliament
urged politicians and all heads of factions on all sides to support his
Baghdad security plan, backed by some seventeen thousand U.S. rein-
forcements, seen by many as a last chance to quell sectarian violence
in the capital.

Maliki, himself a Shiite, was criticized for not doing enough against
Shiite militia groups linked to some of his allies. He vowed to take on
armed groups regardless of sect or political affiliation. "We have worked
hard to get professional officers to lead this plan, with no political affiliations. So let's all help these officers," he said, answering criticism that
the Iraqi army and police are infiltrated by sectarian armed groups. Shiite
militia commanders confirmed that Prime Minister Nouri al-Maliki had
stopped protecting radical cleric Muqtada al-Sadr's Shiite Mahdi Army,
under pressure from Washington. Shiite militias described themselves as
under siege in their Sadr City stronghold in the town of Basra, southern
Iraq. During much of his nearly eight months in office, al-Maliki, who
relied on al-Sadr's political backing, had previously ordered an end to
many U.S.-led operations against the Mahdi Army.[64]

After one week on the new government reconciliation plan the office
of the prime minister confirmed that several Sunni-led insurgent groups
had approached the government to try to start serious negotiations in its
efforts to foster national reconciliation and restore law and order. They
offered to stop attacks on U.S.-led forces in Iraq if a two-year timetable
for the withdrawal of U.S. soldiers was set. The groups did not include
the powerful Islamic Army in Iraq, Muhammad Army, and the Mujahidin Shura Council or the umbrella for eight groups including al-Qaeda in
Iraq. Meanwhile, many Sunni organizations expressed the view that they
were alarmed at the close ties between the most powerful Shiite organizations in Iraq and Iran.[65]

HAVE IRAN AND SYRIA BECOME AN OBSTACLE TO
ACHIEVING PEACE AND SECURITY IN IRAQ?

On his first official visit to the Islamic Republic of Iran, Iraqi Prime Minister Nouri al-Maliki held talks with the government in Tehran, which
offered to help the prime minister establish security and stability in Iraq.
Iranian President Ahmadinejad said at a joint news conference after his
meeting with the Iraqi leader, "We will give our full assistance to the Iraqi

government to establish security in Iraq. Strengthening security in Iraq means strengthening security and stability in the region."[66]

The Iraqi cabinet issued a statement indicating the objective of the visit of the prime minister to Iran. "The trip is to confirm the establishment of friendly and balanced relations based on common interest and respect of the sovereignty of the two countries without any interference in internal affairs." It is worth mentioning that Iraq's new Shiite leaders have close ties to Iran. However, Maliki's visit to Iran deeply concerned Sunnis. Analysts pointed out that Iran's increasing influence in postwar Iraq became obvious since the fall of Saddam, who was a Sunni. This influence was particularly felt in the mainly Shiite south, where Shiite leaders expressed renewed demands for an autonomous Shiite federal state. It is true that Iran generally views Iraq as its own backyard. Political Islam experts believed the removal of Saddam Hussein from power by U.S.-led troops in March 2003 had strengthened Iran's influence especially among Iraq's Shiite majority and increased its regional popularity among Shiites in the Arab Gulf states, namely Bahrain, Saudi Arabia, and Kuwait.

Intelligence sources believed that Maliki had delivered a clear message to Ahmadinejad, requesting Iran not to interfere in Iraq's affairs. An Iraqi official, Ali al-Dabbagh, was reported saying, "We want to pass a message to the Iranian leaders that Iraq needs good relations with neighboring countries, without interference in our internal affairs."[67] U.S. and British officials claim high-powered explosives used against their soldiers in the past years had been supplied through Iran. It is not necessarily, though, with Iranian government approval.

During his visit to Tehran, al-Maliki met Iran's Supreme Shiite leader Ali Khamenei. Shiite Islamist leaders expressed their support and security for Iraq. The United States suspected that the Shiite leaders had been funding militia fighters in Iraq. Khamenei called on the U.S.-led troops to leave Iraq. "Most problems in Iraq will be removed with the departure of occupiers. So we wish for their immediate evacuation," stated Khamenei. Maliki said he wanted the Americans gone, "but not until Iraqi forces were capable of handling the violence they face."[68]

All indications were that Iran had offered to expand its economic and military ties with Iraq, including offering training to Iraqi forces and opening an Iranian bank branch in Baghdad. In January 2007, Iran's ambassador to Iraq, Hassan Kazemi, told the *New York Times* in an interview that his country was prepared to offer training equipment and advisers to Iraqi government forces for "the security fight."[69]

Khalilzad added he identified Iran and Syria as backers of extremist forces "that are spilling blood and preventing the stabilization of the country." General George Casey, the leading U.S. commander in Iraq, also said Iran and Syria had been "decidedly unhelpful" over America's attempts to stabilize Iraq. Furthermore, U.S. military commander William Fallon accused Iraq's neighbor, Iran, of fomenting violence beyond its borders and called its behavior "destabilizing and troubling." The two countries denied the allegation.[70]

In response to these allegations, in December 2006, Mahmoud Ahmadinejad, the Iranian president, again called on the United States to get out of Iraq. In an exclusive interview with Al Jazeera's Darren Jordon, Ahmadinejad said that Iraqis should govern themselves without any interference and blamed the United States for stirring up divisions between Iraq's Shiites, Sunnis, and Kurds. His comments came after President Bush met with Nouri al-Maliki, the Iraqi prime minister, urging him to crack down on Shiite militias blamed for sectarian violence.[71]

Iran had been trying to display its influence on Iraq and bolster its position in the Middle East. It invited Syrian President Bashar al-Assad and Iraqi President Talabani for an official visit to Tehran, the Iranian capital. Talabani visited Iran for talks to engage Tehran to help stop Iraq from sliding into civil war. Meanwhile, the U.S. administration reiterated that there was no intention to negotiate with Iran and Syria to assist in controlling the sectarian violence in Iraq.[72]

President al-Assad told Rome's *La Republic* newspaper Damascus was ready to cooperate with Washington to resolve regional issues. In 2007, the U.S. administration, under political pressure of Democrats, authorized the U.S. embassy in Syria to talk to Damascus about Iraqi refugees. Secretary of State Condoleezza Rice further downplayed expectations about a wider dialogue with the Syrian government.[73]

In November 2006, Walid Moallem, the foreign minister of Syria, on the first visit of a senior Syrian official to Baghdad since the ouster of Saddam Hussein in 2003, assured that his government was prepared to help end the violence in Iraq and repair the country.

The two leaders of Iran and Syria repeatedly accused the United States of destabilizing the region. They warned against the dangers of disunity between Sunni and Shiite Muslims in Lebanon and Iraq. The Syrian president, furthermore, told Rafsanjani, the eminent Iranian cleric, "Creating conflict between Shiite and Sunni in Iraq and Lebanon is the final card that America and its allies have . . . they try to cover their failure with false propaganda."[74]

In November 2006, there was a *New York Times* enquiry of indications of training of Iraqi Shiite militias by Iranian-backed Hezbollah. A senior U.S. intelligence official was quoted as saying that Syrian- and

Iranian-backed Hezbollah provide training for the Mahdi Army, the Iraqi militia led by an anti-American cleric. According to sources, Hezbollah in Lebanon had trained one thousand to two thousand Shiite fighters.[75]

The Iraqi commission headed by James Baker, a former Democratic Party lawmaker, called for direct talk with Tehran and Damascus in order not to interfere with the troubled internal affairs of Iraq. This was in addition to Saudi Arabia's warning to Iran not to interfere in Iraq's affairs. Saudi Arabia's king remarked that Iran was putting the Gulf region in danger and advised Tehran leaders to know "their limits." He would provide financial support to Iraqi Sunnis if the United States pulled its troops out of Iraq. He expressed concern that once U.S. troops leave Iraq the controlling Shiite majority could massacre the Sunni minority.[76]

The U.S. administration had frequently accused Iran of "supplying terrorists and insurgents in Iraq with improvised explosive devices that have become the most lethal threat to U.S. forces." The administration said it decided to take a "tougher line with Tehran after months of evidence showing Iran was assisting anti-U.S. forces." He added, "It makes common sense for the commander in chief to say to our troops and the Iraqi people and the Iraqi government that we will help you defend yourself from people that want to sow discord and harm. And so we will do what it takes to protect our troops."[77]

At the end of December 2007, President Bush made a decisive message to Iran that the United States "will respond firmly" if Iran escalates military action in Iraq and endangers American forces.[78]

It was becoming evident that the militias had been acquiring most sophisticated war weapons from Iran to increase the sectarian war in Iraq.

The forty-page report commissioned by the Saudi Arabian government indicated that Iran had indeed created a Shiite "state within a state." It had been providing support to armed militia with weapons and providing funds for social programs. According to the *Washington Times*, the report stated, "Where the Americans have failed, the Iranians have stepped in."[79]

The newly appointed U.S. Defense Secretary Robert Gates announced in January 2007, after thorough technological investigationsand on evidence the military had collected, that "Iran has been supplying Iraqi militants with highly sophisticated and lethal improvised explosive devices and other weaponry. Among the weapons is a roadside bomb known as an explosively formed penetrator, which can pierce the armor of Abrams tanks with nearly molten-hot charges." An intelligence official source added that the United States was "fairly comfortable" that it knew where the explosives came from. The Iran dossier also laid out alleged Iranian efforts to use these weapons and train Iraqis in military techniques.[80]

The situation became tenser when the U.S. military said in a statement in January 2007 that it had arrested five Iranians in the Iraqi city of Arbil in northern Iraq. The military stated that they were connected to an Iranian Revolutionary Guard group that had been providing weapons to Iraqi fighters. This was the second such operation in a month. U.S. military officials believed that the Iranian government ordered the weapons smuggled into Iraq. They based their claim on the belief that the weapons were moving into Iraq through Iran's Revolutionary Guards.[81]

"We're going after their networks in Iraq," Zalmay Khalilzad, the U.S. ambassador to Iraq, and General George Cascy, the outgoing U.S. military commander, told in a joint news conference. Khalilzad added, "We will target these networks in the expectation of changing the behavior of these states." The U.S. general stressed that "militias will not be allowed to be an alternative to the state or to provide and to take on local security around the country."[82]

Despite the political strain and ethnic bickering between Shiite Iran and Sunni Saudi Arabia, the two leaders, Saudi Arabia's King Abdullah and Iran's Ahmadinejad, met in March 2007, pursuing dialogue and pledging cooperation between their countries. They agreed to fight the spread of sectarian strife between Sunnis and Shiites in Iraq and elsewhere in the Middle East. They also discussed the war in Iraq in their first face-to-face meeting. "The two parties have agreed to stop any attempt aimed at spreading sectarian strife in the region," Saudi foreign minister Prince Saud al-Faisal told reporters without elaborating. Saudi Arabia, Iran, and Syria accepted Iraq's invitation to a March 2007 regional conference on easing tensions in Iraq, held in Egypt. However, no definite progress came out of the conference.[83]

Syria also declared to stabilize Iraq as mentioned by Tariq al-Hashemi, Iraq's vice president, after concluding a four-day visit to Damascus. Syria will "support any solution that leads to bringing security to Iraq and leads to a new Arab Iraq with very good relations with its neighbors," said Farouk al-Sharaa, Syria's vice president.[84] American and Iraqi officials had repeatedly accused Damascus and Iran of not doing enough to stop insurgents and militias from crossing the border into Iraq to fight U.S. and Iraqi troops, a charge Syria and Iran continue to deny.[85]

TOWARD REGIONAL AND INTERNATIONAL COOPERATION FOR ENFORCING LAW AND ORDER IN IRAQ

It was apparent that Nouri al-Maliki, the Iraqi prime minister, had been under pressure from his Washington backers to control the sectarian violence that was pushing Iraq to the brink of civil war. In December 2006, al-Maliki told reporters, "We will send envoys to neighboring countries to exchange opinions on matters and to ask the governments of these countries to help reinforce security and stability in Iraq." He continued, "After settling the political climate, we will call for a convening of only those countries that want to ensure the security and stability of Iraq."[86]

The Iraqi prime minister announced that his government "will hold a conference in Baghdad that could lead to talks between the U.S., Iran, and Syria and hopes the meeting between neighboring countries and world powers on March 10, 2007 will help bring reconciliation and support for his government." The U.S. State Department agreed to attend, but would not be holding bilateral talks with Iran or Syria. However, the department did not rule out the possibility that U.S. officials might hold talks with Iranians on the conference sidelines. The invitation was sent to neighboring Arab countries; Egypt; the five permanent members of the Security Council, the United States, Russia, China, Britain, and France; as well as the Arab League and the Organization of the Islamic Conference. In a statement the prime minister said, "We hope the meeting will bring political backing for the national unity government in providing security and stability that will help national reconciliation in Iraq." Al-Maliki said, "We will ask all neighboring countries to stop interfering in the Iraqi affairs and put pressure on the armed groups with whom they have links to end the violence."[87]

Iraq's neighboring countries welcomed the regional conference as they feared the conflict would spill over into the region. The United States welcomed the conference. Iraq and Syria also welcomed joining such a regional conference though they had been accused by the United States of supporting militant Islamic militias and insurgents. The conference focused on ways and means to end sectarian violence.

In the opening speech of the regional conference in Baghdad, Iraqi Prime Minister Nouri al-Maliki urged regional powers not to use the country as a political battleground. He made the plea with an aim at ending sectarian violence in Iraq. He demanded that regional or international states refrain from interfering or influencing Iraq's state of affairs through supporting a certain sect, ethnic group, or party. [88] Al-Maliki stressed the following points:

- Iraq needs support in this battle that not only threatens Iraq but also will spill over to all countries in the region.
- Iraq requests help in stopping financial support, weapon pipelines, and "religious cover" for the relentless attacks of car bombings, killings, and other attacks that have pitted Iraq's Sunnis against majority Shiites.

- Iraq does not accept that its territories and cities become a field where regional and international disputes are settled.
- A clear warning is given to Syria and Iran, to stay away from using Iraq as a proxy battleground for fights against the United States.
- Claims were made that Syria had been allowing foreign jihadist and Sunni insurgents to cross its border into Iraq, and that weapon shipments from Iran reached Shiite militias. (Both nations deny the allegations.)
- Iraq has become a front-line battlefield.
- Terrorism that kills innocents in Iraq came from the same root as terrorists' attacks around the world since September 11, 2001. (This was in reference to groups inspired by al-Qaeda.)

The conference provided a rare opportunity for delegations from the United States, Iran, and Syria to meet together and exchange their views regarding peace and order in Iraq. Hoshyar Zebari, the Iraqi foreign minister, said, "Confronting terrorism means halting any form of financial support and media or religious backing, as well as logistical support and the flow of arms and men who transform themselves into bombs that kill our children, women and elders, and destroy our mosques and churches."[89]

In a media meeting, the Iraqi minister described the conference as "constructive and positive." He said Iraq and its neighbors had decided to hold another midlevel conference in Turkey (later held in Egypt instead of Turkey). Khalilzad, the U.S. ambassador, urged Iraq's neighbors to do more to stop the flow of fighters, weapons, and sectarian media contributing to the violence. He concluded saying, "The future of Iraq and the Middle East is the defining issue of our time."[90]

It is apparent the United States and Iran have shared interests in Iraq since its occupation in March 2003. On one hand, Iran is keen for the United States to crack down on Sunni attacks made on Iraq's Shiite population. On the other, the United States requires Iranian help to control Iraq's Iranian-aligned Shiite militias.

In the International Conference for Security and reconstruction of Iraq held in April 2007 in Sharm El-Sheikh, Egypt, the United Nations Secretary-General, Ban Ki-moon, appealed to Iraq's neighbors to open their doors to tens of thousands of people fleeing the violence in Iraq. He also called on other countries to share the burden of the growing number of displaced Iraqis. More than 450 officials from sixty countries, along with aid groups, met in the conference to explore ways to aid Iraq and to help Iraqi refugees in other countries. About fifty thousand people are still leaving Iraq every month, according to the UN's refugee agency, United Nations High Commissioner for Refugees (UNHCR). Ki-moon continued, "For neighboring countries this means keeping borders open, for other countries it means continuing to provide asylum or other forms of protection." Amnesty International, the London-based human rights group, said that the refugee problem threatens to spread across the whole of the Middle East unless immediate action is taken. The United States said it would allow about seven thousand Iraqis into the United States this year (up from only 202 in 2006) and will contribute more to help Iraq's neighbors cope with the situation. The Human Rights Watch, a New York-based group, said in a statement read at the conference that the United States and Britain generated the conflict in Iraq and must now help the fleeing Iraqis.[91]

Delegations at the International Conference expressed disappointment that Iran and the United States had failed to hold widely anticipated talks on the sidelines of the conference held in Egypt to discuss ways to stabilize Iraq. Iranian Foreign Minister Manouchehr Mottaki said the United States should issue a clear troop-withdrawal plan to return stability to Iraq. "The continuation of, and increase in, terrorist acts in Iraq originates from the flawed approaches adopted by the foreign troops," he stated. "The United States must accept the responsibilities arising from the occupation of Iraq, and should not finger point or put the blame on others."[92]

PRESIDENT OBAMA SETS FIRM DATE TO END IRAQ WAR

After winning the American election in 2008, Obama promised the American people "by August 2010, our combat mission in Iraq will end." He continued his speech saying after the U.S. combat forces withdraw, thirty-five thousand to fifty thousand will stay behind for an additional year for support and counter-terrorism duties. Obama was clear in that "Iraq's future is now its own responsibility." He reminded the American people that the Iraqi six-year war cost more in lives, money, and national stamina than ever envisioned.[93]

This last summing up of the situation in Iraq leaves us with a ray of hope that this devastated country may one day find peace among its people. If true democracy has not yet been established, the regional and international cooperation for enforcing law and order will certainly be of great assistance. Moreover, it is hoped that setting a firm date for withdrawal of U.S. forces from Iraq will give Iraq its true independence, so that reconciliation between factions can be found, and this devastated country can be left to find solutions to its ever-present problems . . . problems that arose because of a war that has been referred to as a "major blunder."

NOTES

CHAPTER 1

1. "A Nation Challenged: President Bush's Address on Terrorism Before a Joint Meeting of Congress," *New York Times*, September 21, 2001, http://www .nytimes.com/2001/09/21/us/nation-challenged-president-bush-s-address -terrorism-before-joint-meeting.html.
2. Carolee Walker, "White House iftar October 16 honors Muslim citizens, military," *America.gov*, October 17, 2006, http://www.america.gov/st/washfile -english/2006/October/20061017122124bcreklaw0.5644037.html.
3. "Joint statement between the United States of America and the Republic of Indonesia," The White House, October 22, 2003, http://georgewbush -whitehouse.archives.gov/news/releases/2003/10/.
4. U.S. Energy Information Administration, "Iraq: Country Analysis Brief," June 2009, http://www.eia.doe.gov/emeu/cabs/Iraq/Background.html.
5. "NBC's 'Meet the Press' Interview with President Bush," *Center for American Progress*, February 8, 2004, http://www.americanprogress.org/issues/kfiles/ b28200.html.
6. Wendell Goler and Liza Porteus, "Bush: No Link Between Iraq, Sept. 11 Attacks," *Fox News*, September 17, 2003, http://www.foxnews.com/ story/0,2933,97527,00.html.
7. "Excerpts: Annan interview," *BBC News*, September 16, 2004, http://news .bbc.co.uk/2/hi/middle_east/3661640.stm.
8. "France's Chirac Says Iraq War Caused U.N. Crisis," *Al Jazeerah*, September 23, 2003, http://www.aljazeerah.info/News.
9. "OIC meeting in Malaysia," *Samirad*, April 21, 2004, http://www.saudinf .com/main/y7079.htm.
10. Fred Barbash, "Bush: Iraq Part of 'Global Democratic Revolution,'" *Washington Post*, November 6, 2003, http://www.washingtonpost.com/wp-dyn/articles/ A7991-2003Nov6.html.
11. Khaled Dawood, "Pushing regional reform," *Al Ahram Weekly Online*, August 21–27, 2003, Issue No. 652, http://weekly.ahram.org.eg/2003/652/re11.htm.
12. Joel Roberts, "Iraq Allies' Deadliest Day," *CBS News*, November 12, 2003, http://www.cbsnews.com/stories/2003/11/13/iraq/main583365.shtml.
13. "UN extends mandate of Iraq troops," *BBC News*, November 8, 2005, http:// news.bbc.co.uk/2/hi/middle_east/4419222.stm.

14. Dafna Linzer, "Poll Shows Growing Arab Rancor at U.S.," *Washington Post*, July 23, 2004, http://www.washingtonpost.com/wp-dyn/articles/A7080-2004 Jul22.html.

15. Statement of Caroline Fredrickson, "American Civil Liberties Union Testimony Before the Subcommittee on National Security, Emerging Threats, and International Relations Regarding Censorship at the Borders," ACLU, March 28, 2006, http://www.aclu.org/national-security/aclu-testimony-subcommittee-national -security-emerging-threats-and-international-r.

16. "Leading Muslim Scholar Tariq Ramadan Denied U.S. Visa to Teach at Notre Dame," *Democracy Now*, September 13, 2004, http://www.democracynow .org/2004/9/13/leading_muslim_scholar_tariq_ramadan_denied.

17. Nicolas Le Quesne, "Trying to bridge a great divide," *Time.com*, December 11, 2000, http://www.time.com/time/innovators/spirituality/profile_ramadan.html.

18. Tom Coyne, "U.S. revokes visa for Muslim scholar," *Campus Watch*, August 24, 2004, http://www.campus-watch.org/article/id/1250.

19. Thom Shanker, "U.S. Fails to Explain Policies To Muslim World, Panel Says," *New York Times*, November 24, 2004, http://www.nytimes.com/2004/11/24/ politics/24info.html.

20. "The civilizing process," *Al Ahram Weekly*, November 29–December 5, 2001, http://weekly.ahram.org.eg/2001/562/op2.htm.

21. Matthew Moore, "'Muslim Massacre' video game condemned for glamorizing slaughter of Arabs," *Telegraph*, September 10, 2008, http://www.telegraph .co.uk/news/uknews/2776951/Muslim-Massacre-video-game-condemned-for -glamorising-slaughter-of-Arabs.html.

22. Donna Leinwand, "Muslims see new opposition to building mosques since 9/11," *USA Today*, March 9, 2004, http://www.usatoday.com/news/religion/ 2004-03-08-mosque-opposition_x.htm.

23. Joseph S. Nye, Jr., "You Can't Get Here from There," *New York Times*, November 29, 2004, http://www.nytimes.com/2004/11/29/opinion/29nye.html.

24. Ibid.

25. "Tubingen University, Germany, 12 December 2003—Secretary-General's lecture on Global Ethics—'Do we still have universal values?'" Secretary General: Office of the Spokesperson, http://www.un.org/apps/sg/sgstats.asp?nid=697.

CHAPTER 2

1. "The Kingdom of Saudi Arabia Public Statements by Senior Officials and Religious Scholars Condemning Extremism and Promoting Moderation, Saudi Embassy Files, November 6–7, 2008," The Royal Embassy of Saudi Arabia, http://www.saudiembassy.net/files/PDF/Reports/Extremism _Report_11-07-08_final.pdf.

2. "Talbani at UN to help Iraq in its fight against terrorists," *Egyptian Gazette*, August 25, 2005.

3. Bureau of International Information Programs, "Six Saudi Clerics Denounce Terrorist Bombings in Saudi Arabia," July 1, 2004, *America.gov*, http://www.america.gov/st/washfile-english/2004/July/20040701120455dmslahrellek0.8 34347.html.

4. "Saudis in Total War on Terror," *CNN.com*, April 22, 2004, http://www.cnn.com/2004/WORLD/meast/04/21/saudi.blast.bandar/index.html.

5. Ibid.

6. Associated Press, "Saudi cleric condemns U.S. consulate attack," December 8, 2004, http://www.msnbc.msn.com/id/6657943/.

7. "Saudis in Total War on Terror," *CNN.com*, April 22, 2004, http://www.cnn.com/2004/WORLD/meast/04/21/saudi.blast.bandar/index.html.

8. Jamal Halaby, "Jordan wages all-out war on militants," *Pittsburgh Post-Gazette*, November 25, 2005, http://news.google.com/newspapers?nid=1129&dat=200 51125&id=d5YNAAAAIBAJ&sjid=7XADAAAAIBAJ&pg=6670,2902233.

9. Alia Shukri Hamzeh, "King asks Bakhit to form gov't," *Jordan Times*, November 25, 2005, http://www.jordanembassyus.org/11252005001.htm.

10. Reuters, "Jordan's King urges war on Islamic militancy," *New York Times*, November 25, 2005, http://www.nytimes.com/2005/11/25/international/middleeast/25jordan.html.

11. Organization of the Islamic Conference in Mecca, December 11, 2005, http://www.saudi-us-relations.org/articles/2005/ioi/051211-oic-wrapup.html.

12. "Arabs need to improve image says Al Chief," *Egyptian Gazette*, December 6, 2005.

13. "Iraq to neighbors: Stop harboring terrorists," *CNN.com*, July 4, 2006, http://www.cnn.com/2006/WORLD/europe/07/03/monday/index.html.

14. Ibid.

15. "Excerpts from the president's address on Iraq," *CNN.com*, June 28, 2005, http://www.cnn.com/2005/POLITICS/06/28/bush.speech/index.html.

16. "A bomber struck the offices of Kurdish party, Ansar al-Sunna claimed responsibility," *Egyptian Gazette*, May 5, 2005.

17. "Iraqi guerrillas shot down Bulgarian plane killing 6 Americans," *Egyptian Gazette*, April 22, 2005.

18. Barbara Starr, "Official 13,000–17,000 Insurgents in Iraq," *CNN.com*, February 9, 2005, http://www.cnn.com/2005/WORLD/meast/02/08/iraq.main/index.html.

19. "110 are killed in 2 days of bomb attacks in Iraq," *Herald Tribune*, October 2, 2005.

20. "Suicide Bombers Kill Scores in 2 Iraqi Cities," *CNN.com*, November 19, 2005, http://www.cnn.com/2005/WORLD/meast/11/18/iraq.main/index.html?section=cnn_topstories.

21. Robert F. Worth, "More Than 950 Iraqis Die in Stampede on Baghdad Bridge," *New York Times*, August 31, 2005, http://www.nytimes.com/2005/08/31/international/middleeast/31cnd-iraq.html.

22. "Iraq 'hostage' to lawlessness," *Egyptian Gazette*, July 26, 2004.

Chapter 3

1. U.S. Senate Intelligence Report on Post War Finding about WMD Programs and Links to Terrorism and How They Comply to Rewar Assessment, September 8, 2006, 105–12.

2. "US Senate: No Saddam, al-Qaeda link," *Aljazeera.net*, September 9, 2006, http://english.aljazeera.net/archive/2006/09/2008410103551590770.html.

3. "President Bush's Address to the United Nations," *CNN.com*, September 12, 2002, http://edition.cnn.com/2002/US/09/12/bush.transcript/.

4. "US Death Toll in Iraq Reaches 2000," *CNN.com*, October 25, 2005, http://edition.cnn.com/2005/WORLD/meast/10/25/iraq.main.1744/index.html.

5. "Bush: I'd Rather Be Right Than Popular," *CNN.com*, July 9, 2006, http://www.cnn.com/2006/POLITICS/07/06/bush.lkl/.

6. "Blix Says Bush, Blair Insincere Salesmen on Iraq," *China Daily*, February 9, 2004, http://www.chinadaily.com.cn/english/doc/2004-02/09/content_3043 99.htm.

7. Wesley Clark, "The Real Battle Winning in Fellujah is just the beginning," *Washington Post*, November 14, 2004, http://www.washingtonpost.com/wp-dyn/articles/A47034-2004Nov12.html.

8. "Iraq, World's Second-Largest Oil Reserves," *Aljazeera.net*, June 16, 2005.

9. Douglas Jehl, "Warned Bush Team About Intelligence Doubts," *New York Times*, November 6, 2005, http://www.nytimes.com/2005/11/06/politics/06intel.ready.html.

10. Bill Nichols, "Iraq Had No WMD After 1994," *USA Today*, March 2, 2004, http://www.usatoday.com/news/world/iraq/2004-03-02-un-wmd_x.htm.

11. Douglas Jehl, "Skeptic may take over Iraq Arms hunt," *New York Times*, January 23, 2004, http://www.nytimes.com/2004/01/23/world/skeptic-may-take-over-iraq-arms-hunt.html.

12. Glenn Frankel and Rajiv Chandrasekaran, "45 Minutes: Behind the Blair Claim," *Washington Post*, February 29, 2004, http://www.washingtonpost.com/ac2/wp-dyn/A15697-2004Feb28.

13. Associated Press, "Powell doubts Iraqi weapons will be found," September 14, 2004, http://www.msnbc.msn.com/id/6000809.

14. "Timeline: Saddam trial," December 29, 2006, http://gulfnews.com/news/region/iraq/timeline-saddam-trial-1.153686.

15. "Bush Defends Stance on WMDs, Report Slams CIA for Iraq Intelligence Failures," July 10, 2004, http://edition.cnn.com/2004/ALLPOLITICS/07/10/senate.intelligence/index.html.

16. David E. Sanger and Jim Rutenberg, "News analysis: Bush and Blair admit mistakes, but defend war in Iraq," *International Herald Tribune*, May 5, 2006, http://www.nytimes.com/2006/05/26/world/americas/26iht-bush.1829645.html.

17. Interview given by M. Jacques Chirac, President of the Republic, to the BBC 2 *Newsnight* program, Broadcast on November 17, 2004, Paris, November 15, 2004, http://www.ambafrance-uk.org/Interview-given-by-M-Jacques,4100.html.

18. "Ex-CIA chief criticizes Iraq war," *Aljazeera.net*, April 28, 2007; George Tenet, *At the Center of the Storm* (New York: HarperCollins, 2007), 495.

19. Ted Barett, "Retiring GOP Congressman Breaks Ranks on Iraq," *CNN.com*, August 19, 2004, http://www.cnn.com/2004/ALLPOLITICS/08/18/congressman.iraq/index.html.

20. "It was a mistake to launch the war (congressman)," *Time*, August 30, 2004, 19.

21. "Iraqi Civilian Death Toll 'up to 20,000,'" *The Times*, January 30, 2004, 22.

22. "Iraq Looms as Top Issue in 1st Bush-Kerry Debate," VOAnews.com, September 30, 2004, http://www1.voanews.com/english/news/a-13-a-2004-09-30-48-1-6899047.html.

23. "Howard Dismisses Former Public Servants' Criticism," ABC News Online, August 9, 2004, http://www.abc.net.au/news/newsitems/200408/s1171439.htm.

24. "Prodi: Iraq War Was 'Grave Error,'" *CNN.com*, May 19, 2006, http://edition.cnn.com/2006/WORLD/europe/05/18/italy.iraq/.

25. "Iraq War 'Lost' Says Top Democrat," *Aljazeera.net*, April 20, 2007, http://english.aljazeera.net/news/middleeast/2007/04/2008525142923542568.html.

26. Return to an address of the Honourable House of Commons, Weapons of Mass Destruction Report of a Committee of Privy Counsellors and chaired by The Rt. Hon, The Lord Butler of Brockwell, July 14, 2004, 124.

27. "Blair defiantly insists war right," *BBC News*, July 14, 2004, http://news.bbc.co.uk/2/hi/uk_news/politics/3893987.stm.

28. Alan Cowell, "Blair vows to stay the course in Iraq," *New York Times*, September 28, 2005, http://www.nytimes.com/2005/09/27/world/europe/27iht-britain.html.

29. Ibid.

30. "British Helicopter Crashed," *Aljazeera.net*, May 7, 2006.

31. "Iraqi insurgents turn against 'out of control' Saudi al-Qaeda fighters," *The Sunday Telegraph*, May 30, 2004, http://www.telegraph.co.uk/news/worldnews/middleeast/iraq/1463223/Iraqi-insurgents-turn-against-out-of-control-Saudi-al-Qaeda-fighters.html.

32. John Burns, "A Conversation on Tiptoes, Wary of Mines," *New York Times*, November 30, 2003, http://www.nytimes.com/2003/11/30/weekinreview/30BURN.html.

33. Leslie Gelb, "The Three State Solution," *New York Times*, November 25, 2003, http://www.cfr.org/publication/6559/threestate_solution.html.

34. Peter W. Galbraith, "The case for dividing Iraq," *Time*, November 13, 2006, 30.

35. "Annan Warns Rule of Law at Risk," *CNN.com*, September 21, 2004, http://www.cnn.com/2004/US/09/21/united.nations/index.html.

36. "Iraq war 'illegal,' UN's Annan says," September 16, 2004, http://www.cbc.ca/world/story/2004/09/16/annan040916.html.

37. Hans Blix, "A War of Utter Folly," *The Guardian*, March 20, 2008, http://www.guardian.co.uk/commentisfree/2008/mar/20/iraq.usa.

38. Mark Mazzetti, "Spy Agencies Say Iraq War Worsens Terrorism Threat," *New York Times*, September 24, 2006, http://query.nytimes.com/gst/fullpage.html.

39. John Leicester and Omar Sinan, "Al-Qaida joins Algerians against France," *Fox News*, September 15, 2006, http://www.foxnews.com/wires/2006Sep15/0,4670,FranceAlQaidaVideo,00.html.

40. "Rumsfeld told suicide bombers pose greatest threat," *USA Today*, February 23, 2004, http://www.usatoday.com/news/world/iraq/2004-02-23-iraq -rumsfeld_x.htm.

41. "Clinton: US cannot isolate itself to fight terror," *Daily Times*, August 10, 2005, http://www.dailytimes.com.pk/default.asp?page=story_10-8-2005_pg4_6.

42. Associated Press, "Global terror attacks surged 25% in 2006," April 30, 2007, http://www.msnbc.msn.com/id/18399660/.

43. "Europe-wide network enlists fighters for Iraq," *Herald Tribune*, December 7, 2003; Damien McElroy, "Mullah named as suspect for Turkey blasts," December 7, 2003, http://www.telegraph.co.uk/news/worldnews/europe/ turkey/1448767/Mullah-named-as-suspect- for-Turkey-blasts.html.

44. Jomana Karadsheh, "Study: War Blamed for 655,000 Iraqi Deaths," *CNN.com*, October 11, 2006, http://www.cnn.com/2006/WORLD/meast/10/11/iraq .deaths/.

45. Ibid.

46. Joel Roberts, "41 Dead in Rampage in Iraq," *CBSNews.com*, July 10, 2006, http://www.cbsnews.com/stories/2006/07/10/iraq/main1786936.shtml.

47. Ann McFeatters, "Kennedy-Rumsfeld showdown illustrates Iraq dilemma," *Desert News*, June 24, 2005, http://www.deseretnews.com/article/ 1,5143,600143934,00.html.

48. "Musharraf: Iraq War Makes World More Dangerous," *CNN.com*, September 26, 2006, http://www.cnn.com/2006/WORLD/asiapcf/09/26/musharraf.terror/ index.html.

49. Zapatero, José. Interview with James Graff: "I Do Not Want to Be a Great Leader," *Time*, September 19, 2004, http://www.time.com/time/magazine/article/ 0,9171,901040927-699350,00.html.

50. Associated Press, "Bush Disappointed by Spanish PM's Decision on Iraq," *Fox News*, April 19, 2004, http://www.foxnews.com/story/0,2933,117506,00.html.

51. "Japanese PM announces troop withdrawal from Iraq," *Fox News*, June 20, 2006, http://www.foxnews.com/story/0,2933,200214,00.html.

52. Masin el-Shawa, "Cost of Iraqi war," *Egyptian Mail*, May 31, 2005.

53. Joe Clein, "Saddam's revenge," *Time*, September 18, 2005, http://www.time .com/time/magazine/article/0,9171,1106307-9,00.html.

54. Deborah Solomon, "Way We Live Now: 4-23-06: Questions for Madeleine Albright; State of the Secretary," *New York Times*, April 23, 2006, http://query.nytimes.com/ gst/fullpage.html?res=9B0CE5DB173FF930A15757C0A9609C8B63.

55. "Annan: Iraq war a disaster for region," *Aljazeera.net*, September 15, 2006; Ewen MacAskill, "Annan Rues Iraq Oil-for-Food Plan," September 6, 2005, http://www.guardian.co.uk/world/2005/sep/06/oil.iraq.

56. Lynn Sweet, "Reacts from Rahm Emanuel, Jesse Jackson Jr., Joe Biden, John Shimkus, Hillary Rodham Clinton, Jan Schakowsky, John Kerry, John Boehner, Roy Blunt, Russ Feingold," *Sun Times Media*, January 10, 2007, http:// blogs.suntimes.com/sweet/2007/01/reacts_from_rahm_emanuel.html.

57. Scott Malone, "France's Villepin Calls for 2008 Iraq Troop Exit," *Reuters.com*, March 17, 2007, http://uk.reuters.com/article/idUKN1625326820070317.

58. Mathew Biggs, "Iraq Worst Disaster for US Foreign Policy-Albright," Alert-Net.org, February 23, 2007, http://www.alertnet.org/thenews/newsdesk/N222 08041.htm.

59. Ted Galen Carpenter, "Iraq 2004, Vietnam 1964," Cato Institute, April 27, 2004, http://www.cato.org/pub_display.php?pub_id=2629.

60. "Iraq Growing More Like Vietnam," *CNN.com*, August 19, 2005, http://www.cnn.com/2005/POLITICS/08/18/hagel.iraq/.

61. Alan Elsner, "Iraq the most expensive war in 60 years, report says," *Sydney Morning Herald*, September 1, 2005, http://www.smh.com.au/news/world/iraq-the-most-expensive-war-in-60-years-report-says/2005/08/31/1125302633906.html.

62. "Iraq War 'Worst Foreign Policy Mistake in U.S. History,'" *CNN.com*, February 19, 2007, http://www.cnn.com/2007/POLITICS/02/18/reid.iraq/index.html.

63. Douglass Daniel, "Bush's Words on Iraq Echo LBJ in 1967," *USA Today*, September 21, 2005, http://www.usatoday.com/news/washington/2005-09-21-bush-vietnam_x.htm.

CHAPTER 4

1. "Saddam Hussein captured," *The Guardian*, December 14, 2003, http://www.guardian.co.uk/world/2003/dec/14/iraq.iraq1.

2. Ibid.

3. "Identity of US informer remains $45 million question," *Sydney Morning Herald*, July 27, 2003, http://www.smh.com.au/articles/2003/07/26/1059084268872.html.

4. "Iraqis Take Legal Custody of Saddam, and 11 Others," *CNN.com*, June 30, 2004, http://edition.cnn.com/2004/WORLD/meast/06/30/iraq.saddam/index.html?iref=allsearch; "Iraqi Guerrillas Threaten to Slay Saddam Lawyers," *Egyptian Mail*, July 10, 2004.

5. "Islamist gunmen threaten to behead Saddam lawyers," *Sydney Morning Herald*, July 9, 2004, http://www.smh.com.au/articles/2004/07/08/1089000296489.html.

6. "A Hopeful Day," *New York Sun*, December 15, 2003, http://www.nysun.com/editorials/a-hopeful-day/78097/.

7. Peter Beaumont, "Judge in Saddam trial axed in neutrality row," *The Guardian*, September 20, 2006, http://www.guardian.co.uk/world/2006/sep/20/iraq.peterbeaumont.

8. Ibid.

9. "Judge throws Saddam out of court," *BBC News*, October 11, 2006, http://news.bbc.co.uk/2/hi/middle_east/6036787.stm.

10. "Saddam 'Confesses' Says Iraq Head," *BBC News*, September 7, 2005, http://news.bbc.co.uk/2/hi/middle_east/4221202.stm.

11. "Baghdad confirms Saddam's trial date," September 8, 2005, http://english.aljazeera.net/archive/2005/09/20084915598241557.html.

12. "Saddam defence lawyer shot dead," *BBC News*, July 21, 2006, http://news.bbc.co.uk/2/hi/5101162.stm.

13. "Saddam defiant in court," October 19, 2005, http://edition.cnn.com/2005/WORLD/meast/10/19/saddam.trial/index.html.

14. "Saddam appeals for a fair trial," October 12, 2006, http://english.aljazeera.net/archive/2006/10/2008410112612212978.html.

15. "Saddam's wife and daughter on most wanted list," July 2, 2006, http://www.msnbc.msn.com/id/13668297/.

16. "Saddam Hussein Sentenced to Hang," November 5, 2006. http://english.aljazeera.net/archive/2006/11/200849155416141647.html.

17. Ibid.

18. "Saddam Hussein sentenced to death," *BBC News*, November 5, 2006, http://news.bbc.co.uk/2/hi/6117910.stm.

19. "Mixed Reaction to Verdict," November 5, 2006, http://english.aljazeera.net/archive/2006/11/20084913437807214.html.

20. "Fighting Erupts in Baghdad After Verdict," November 5, 2006, http://english.aljazeera.net/archive/2006/11/200849144854495186.html.

21. "Saddam Hanged at Dawn," October 27, 2007, http://english.aljazeera.net/news/middleeast/2006/12/2008525115436701440.html.

22. "Baathists: 'Grave Consequences' If Hussein's Hanged," *CNN.com*, December 28, 2006, http://edition.cnn.com/2006/WORLD/meast/12/27/saddam.baath/index.html.

23. William J. Kole, "World Opinion Divided on Saddam Sentence," *Redorbit.com*, November 6, 2006, http://www.redorbit.com/news/general/719681/world_opinion_divided_on_saddam_sentence/index.html.

24. "Execution of Iraqi leader Saddam a crime, says Vatican top justice official," *Catholic Online*, December 29, 2006, http://www.catholic.org/international/international_story.php?id=22526.

25. "Iraqi PM says he refused U.S. Request to Delay Execution," *CNN.com*, January 10, 2007, http://edition.cnn.com/2007/WORLD/meast/01/09/maliki.hussein/index.html.

26. Anita Chang, "Saddam execution Video Draws Criticism," *CNN.com*, January 2, 2007, http://www.redorbit.com/news/general/786418/saddam_execution_video_draws_criticism/index.html.

27. "Bush wishes Hussein Execution 'More Dignified,'" *CNN.com*, January 4, 2007. http://edition.cnn.com/2007/WORLD/meast/01/04/iraq.main/.

28. Ibon Villelabeitia, "Saddam hanging Iraqi Affair, al-Maliki," *CNN.com*, January 6, 2007, http://uk.reuters.com/article/idUKL0673755620070106.

29. "Saddam Hanged at Dawn," December 30, 2007, http://english.aljazeera.net/news/middleeast/2006/12/2008525115436701440.html.

30. "Saddam's former deputy hanged in Iraq," *China Daily*, March 20, 2007, http://www.chinadaily.com.cn/world/2007-03/20/content_832000.htm.

31. "Saddam Judge Flees Iraq," *Aljazeera.net*, March 10, 2007, http://english.aljazeera.net/news/middleeast/2007/03/200852513209132944.html.

CHAPTER 5

1. "Antiwar Voices Address March: Michael Moore, Jesse Jackson, Fernando Suarez, Charles Barron and More," *Democracy Now*, August 30, 2004, http://www .democracynow.org/2004/8/30/antiwar_voices_address_march_michael _moore.

2. "Anti-war rally held in Washington," *BBC News*, September 24, 2005, http:// news.bbc.co.uk/2/hi/americas/4278960.stm.

3. Stephen W. Smith, "Angry Mom Protests President," *CBSNews.com*, August 6, 2005, http://www.cbsnews.com/stories/2005/08/06/national/main763672 .shtml.

4. Ibid.

5. "Bush rebuts critics of Iraq policies," *USA Today*, August 24, 2005, http://www .usatoday.com/news/washington/2005-08-24-bush-iraq_x.htm.

6. Ibid.

7. Eliott C. McLaughlin, "Activist Sheehan Arrested in House Gallery," *CNN.com*, February 1, 2006, http://www.cnn.com/2006/POLITICS/01/31/sheehan.arrest/ index.html.

8. Associated Press, "Thousands around globe call for end of war," *USA Today*, March 20, 2006, http://www.usatoday.com/news/world/2006-03-20-war -protests_x.htm.

9. "World-wide protests mark Iraq war," *Aljazeera.net*, March 20, 2007, http:// english.aljazeera.net/news/middleeast/2007/03/2008525131323845336.html.

10. Associated Press, "Anti-war protests," *Aljazeera.net*, January 12, 2007.

11. "Bush in Europe for international support. Attending the D-day 60 years," *CNN.com*, May 5, 2004.

12. John King and Alessio Vinci, "Bush to leave Italy, head for France," *CNN.com*, June 4, 2004, http://www.cnn.com/2004/WORLD/europe/06/04/bush.italy/ index.html.

13. Al Baker, "Thousands Protest in Rome Against Bush Visit and Iraq War," *New York Times*, April 4, 2004, http://www.nytimes.com/2004/06/04/international/ europe/04CND-ROME.html.

14. Alphonso Van Marsh and Robin Oakley, "Bush, NATO focus on Iraq," *CNN. com*, June 28, 2004, http://edition.cnn.com/2004/WORLD/europe/06/27/ turkey.bush/index.html.

15. "Many detained in Chile protests," *BBC News*, November 17, 2004, http:// news.bbc.co.uk/2/hi/americas/4020801.stm.

16. Nirmala George, "Tens of Thousands Protest Bush India Visit," truthout.org, March 1, 2006, http://www.truthout.org/article/tens-thousands-protest-bush -india-visit.

17. Associated Press, "Bush expresses solidarity with Pakistan," *Fox News*, March 5, 2006, http://www.foxnews.com/story/0,2933,186819,00.html.

CHAPTER 6

1. "'Iraq war illegal,' says Annan," *BBC News*, September 16, 2004, http://news
   .bbc.co.uk/2/hi/3661134.stm.
2. "U.S. says Iraq invasion was legal," *BBC News*, September 16, 2004, http://
   news.bbc.co.uk/2/hi/middle_east/3664234.stm.
3. Jarrett Murphy, "Bush Will Defend Iraq War to U.N.," *CBSNews.com*, September 22, 2003, http://www.cbsnews.com/stories/2003/09/23/iraq/main574
   646.shtml.
4. Ibid.
5. "Draft U.N. resolution on Iraq," *msnbc.com*, May 24, 2004, http://www
   .msnbc.msn.com/id/5052147/.
6. "U.N. resolution on Iraq passes unanimously," *CNN.com*, June 8, 2004, http://
   edition.cnn.com/2004/WORLD/meast/06/08/un.iraq/index.html.
7. Ibid.
8. Press Release SC/8111, "Briefing Security Council, Iraqi Foreign Minister Calls
   for Resolution Endorsing Interim Government, Recognizing continuing Need
   for Multinational Force," UN Security Council, June 3, 2004, http://www
   .un.org/News/Press/docs/2004/sc8111.doc.htm.
9. Rajiv Chandrasekaran, "Iraqi Council Agrees on Terms of Interim Constitution," *Washington Post*, March 1, 2004, http://www.washingtonpost.com/ac2/
   wp-dyn/A17535-2004Feb29.
10. Washington Post, "Council seeks U.N. help," *Trib Total Media*, March 18,
    2004, http://www.pittsburghlive.com/x/pittsburghtrib/s_185049.html.
11. Rajiv Chandrasekaran, "Iraqi Council Agrees to Ask UN for Help," *Washing-
    ton Post*, March 18, 2004, http://www.washingtonpost.com/wp-dyn/articles/
    A2866-2004Mar17.html.
12. Reuters, "Iraq to seek extension of U.S. presence," October 30, 2006, http://
    english.aljazeera.net/archive/2006/10/20084914325296452.html.
13. CNN Late Edition with Wolf Blitzer, December 3, 2006, http://transcripts
    .cnn.com/TRANSCRIPTS/0612/03/le.01.html.
14. Hadjar Wish, "CNN: Dozens killed in triple car bombing near Baghdad market,"
    December 2, 2006, http://www.mail-archive.com/islamkristen@yahoogroups
    .com/msg76655.html.
15. Edward Wong, "U.N. Secretary Says Iraq Is Engulfed in Deadly Civil War,"
    New York Times, December 3, 2006, http://www.nytimes.com/2006/12/03/
    world/middleeast/03cnd-iraq.html.
16. Ibid.
17. "Baghdad blast rattles UN chief," *Aljazeera.net*, March 23, 2007, http://english
    .aljazeera.net/news/middleeast/2007/03/2008525135835807327.html.
18. Nicola Butler, "Deep Divisions over Iraq at NATO's Istanbul Summit," *The
    Acronym Institute for Disarmament Diplomacy*, Issue No. 78, July/August 2004,
    http://www.acronym.org.uk/dd/dd78/78news01.htm.
19. "Karzai: Send NATO troops now," *CNN.com*, June 29, 2004, http://edition
    .cnn.com/2004/WORLD/europe/06/29/turkey.bush/index.html.

CHAPTER 7

1. "U.S. denies widespread abuse at prison in Iraq," *CNN.com*, May 3, 2004, http://edition.cnn.com/2004/US/05/02/iraq.abuse.charges/index.html.
2. Ibid.
3. Rebecca Leung, "Abuse Of Iraqi POWs By GIs Probed," *CBSNews.com*, April 28, 2004, http://www.cbsnews.com/stories/2004/04/27/60II/main614063.shtml?tag=contentMain;contentBody.
4. "Iraq. In: Amnesty International Report 2004," Amnesty International USA, http://www.amnestyusa.org/document.php?id=758A1EBE5BB6C22480256E9E005A99DF&lang=e.
5. "Annan cited prisoner abuse in Iraq," *Egyptian Gazette*, September 22, 2004.
6. "U.S. soldiers abused Iraqis 'for fun,'" *Egyptian Gazette*, August 5, 2004.
7. "Human rights group, Amnesty International saying 14,000 detainees in Iraq without charges," *CNN.com*, March 7, 2006.
8. "GI 'ordered to kill Iraq prisoners,'" *Aljazeera.net*, March 14, 2007, http://english.aljazeera.net/news/americas/2007/03/200852513136305823.html.
9. "Abu Ghraib was 'Animal House' at night," *CNN.com*, August 24, 2004, http://edition.cnn.com/2004/US/08/24/abughraib.report/index.html.
10. "Newspapers Describe more Abuse of Prisoners," *International Herald Tribune*, May 22–23, 2005.
11. "U.S. Soldier Says her Job was to make prison 'Hell,'" *Egyptian Gazette*, May 9, 2004.
12. Reuters, "U.S. dog-handler faces Abu Ghraib trial," *Aljazeera.net*, May 23, 2006.
13. "Confession of an Iraqi Prisoner," *Egyptian Gazette*, May 7, 2004.
14. "The Road to Abu Ghraib," Human Rights Watch Report, June 9, 2004, http://www.hrw.org/en/bios/reed-brody.
15. "Report: U.S. covered up abuse at Abu Ghraib," *CNN.com*, June 9, 2004.
16. "U.S. Frees Abu Ghraib Prisoner," *Egyptian Gazette*, April 15, 2004.
17. "Iraqi Sunnis Reject Slam-dunked Constitution," IslamOnline.net August 24, 2005, http://www.islamonline.net/English/News/2005-08/24/article05.shtml.
18. "Abu Ghraib's shocking photos," *Egyptian Gazette*, September 25, 2004.
19. "Abuse sentence angers many Iraqis," *Herald Tribune*, September 29, 2005, http://www.nytimes.com/2005/09/28/news/28iht-sentence.html.
20. "Iraqis furious at 'lenient' Abu Ghraib abuse sentence," *Timesonline*, September 28, 2005, http://www.timesonline.co.uk/tol/news/world/iraq/article572264.ece.
21. Stone Phillips, "Behind the Abu Ghraib photos—In an exclusive interview, Lynndie England talks about her part in those now infamous pictures," *Dateline NBC*, October 2, 2005.
22. "U.S. denies widespread abuse at prison in Iraq," *CNN.com*, May 3, 2004, http://edition.cnn.com/2004/US/05/02/iraq.abuse.charges/index.html.
23. Julia Preston, "Judge rules on abuse photos at Abu Ghraib," *Herald Tribune*, September 30, 2005.
24. Alvin K. Hellerstein, Federal District Court, U.S. District Court Southern District of New York, "Opinion and Order Granting in Part and Denying in

Part Motions for Partial Summary Judgment," http://www.gwu.edu/~nsarchiv/news/20060313/aOrder092905.pdf.

25. "Bush 'I have never ordered Torture,'" *CNN.com*, June 23, 2004, http://edition.cnn.com/2004/ALLPOLITICS/06/22/rumsfeld.memo/index.html.

26. Agence France-Presse, "U.S. to shut down Abu Ghraib prison," *Aljazeera.net*, March 9, 2006.

27. Joel Roberts, "Abu Ghraib Prison Totally Empty," *CBSNews.com*, August 28, 2006, http://www.cbsnews.com/stories/2006/08/28/iraq/main1940091.shtml.

28. Patrick Tyler, "Blair Offers an Apology for Abuses by Soldiers," *New York Times*, May 10, 2004, http://www.nytimes.com/2004/05/10/international/europe/10BLAI.html.

29. "Beyond Abu Ghraib: Detention and Torture in Iraq," Amnesty International Report, March 18, 2004.

30. Agence France-Presse, "U.S. soldiers charged with Iraq murders," *Aljazeera.net*, June 19, 2006.

31. James M. Klatell, "3 U.S. Soldiers Charged with Murder," *CBSNews.com*, June 19, 2006. http://www.cbsnews.com/stories/2006/06/19/iraq/main1729623.shtml.

32. "GI 'ordered to kill Iraq prisoners,'" *Aljazeera.net*, March 14, 2007, http://english.aljazeera.net/news/americas/2007/03/200852513136305823.html.

33. "Maliki: Haditha a terrible crime," *Aljazeera.net*, June 1, 2006.

34. Thom Shanker, Eric Schmitt, and Richard Oppel, Jr., "Military to report Marines killed Iraqi civilians," *New York Times*, May 26, 2006.

35. Tim McGirk, "Collateral Damage or Civilian Massacre in Haditha?" *Time*, March 19, 2006, http://www.time.com/time/world/article/0,8599,1174649-4,00.html.

36. Associated Press, "Haditha lawyer criticizes U.S," *USA Today*, April 6, 2006, http://www.usatoday.com/news/world/iraq/2006-06-03-iraqi-condemns-probe_x.htm?csp=34

37. Reuters, "U.S. Soldiers Charged in Iraq Rape Case," *Aljazeera.net*, November 3, 2006.

38. Joel Roberts, "5 U.S. Soldiers Charged In Rape-Slay," *CBSNews.com*, July 9, 2006, http://www.cbsnews.com/stories/2006/07/09/iraq/main1786527.shtml.

39. "U.S. soldiers killed 'in rape revenge,'" *Aljazeera.net*, July 11, 2006.

40. "U.S. detains top Iraqi Sunni cleric," *Aljazeera.net*, June 24, 2006.

CHAPTER 8

1. "Transcript: Senate Foreign Relations, Wolfowitz, Armitage Testify before Senate Panel," *Washington Post*, May 18, 2004, http://www.washingtonpost.com/wp-dyn/articles/A37019-2004May18.html.

2. Brian Knowlton, "Legislators Press Bush to Speed Iraqi Vote," *Herald Tribune*, May 19, 2004.

3. "Bush Outlines Iraq Transition," *CNN.com*, May 25, 2004.

4. Ibid.

5. "Iraqi Interim Government," *CNN.com*, April 1, 2004.

6. Dexter Filkins, "U.S. Transfers Power to Iraq 2 Days Early," *New York Times*, June 29, 2004, http://www.nytimes.com/2004/06/29/international/middleeast/29IRAQ.html.

7. Iraq—Interim Constitution, ICL Documents, March 8, 2004, http://www.servat.unibe.ch/law/icl/iz00000_.html.

8. John D. Banusiewicz, American Forces Press Service, "Occupation Ends; Iraqis Take Charge of Country's Fate," Defense.gov, June 28, 2004, http://www.defense.gov/news/newsarticle.aspx?id=26190

9. "Iraqis Hope for Better Security, Real Sovereignty," *CNN.com*, June 28, 2004.

10. Omayma Abdel-Latif, "To Vote or Not to Vote," *Al Ahram Weekly*, December 2–8, 2004, http://weekly.ahram.org.eg/2004/719/re6.htm.

11. "Accelerating Terrorism before Hand-Over Power to Iraqi New End Government," *Egyptian Gazette*, May 14, 2004.

12. "Baghdad Governor Assassinated," *CNN.com*, November 4, 2005.

13. "Al Qaeda Warned Iraqis Not to Vote in Ramadi," *Egyptian Gazette*, December 14, 2005.

14. Luke Harding and Michael Howard, "Blasts Shake Iraq Conference," *The Guardian*, August 16, 2004, http://www.guardian.co.uk/world/2004/aug/16/iraq.lukeharding.

15. Michael Howard, "Iraqi Council Agrees Interim Constitution," *The Guardian*, March 2, 2004, http://www.guardian.co.uk/world/2004/mar/02/iraq.michaelhoward.

16. Rajiv Chandrasekaran, "Iraqi Council Agrees on Terms of Interim Constitution," *Washington Post*, March 1, 2004, http://www.washingtonpost.com/ac2/wp-dyn/A17535-2004Feb29?language=printer.

17. Ibid.

18. "Bush: Iraqis 'Have Their Country Back,'" *CNN.com*, June 28, 2004, http://edition.cnn.com/2004/ALLPOLITICS/06/28/bush.blair/.

19. "Putin Calls for World Cooperation on Iraq," *Egyptian Gazette*, July 4, 2005.

20. "Big Voter Turnout Expected from Iraqis Abroad," *Egyptian Gazette*, January 18, 2005.

21. "Baghdad Fears Rise of 'Iraqi Hitler,'" *CNN.com*, December 13, 2004, http://edition.cnn.com/2004/WORLD/meast/12/13/iraq.president/index.html.

22. Curt Tarnoff, "Iraq: Recent Developments in Reconstruction Assistance," CRS Report for Congress, October 2, 2003.

23. "Conclusion of Madrid Conference on Iraq," The World Bank Group, October 27, 2003, http://web.worldbank.org/WBSITE/EXTERNAL/NEWS/0,,contentMDK:20134476~menuPK:34457~pagePK:34370~piPK:34424~theSitePK:4607,00.html.

24. "Iraq Country Analysis Brief," EIA.com, March 2004, http://usiraq.procon.org/sourcefiles/eiacountryanalysis.pdf.

25. "Iraq Donors Pledge Fresh Resolve," *BBC News*, October 14, 2004, http://news.bbc.co.uk/2/hi/middle_east/3743482.stm.

26. "Meeting of International donors in Tokyo," *CNN.com*, October 15, 2004.

27. "Bush, Iraq Dominate EU Summit," *CNN.com*, November 6, 2004.
28. "Conference for Iraq in Brussels, June 22, 2005," *Egyptian Mail*, June 2, 2005.
29. "Iraqi Construction Funds Go to Security," *Washington Times*, February 9, 2006, http://www.washingtontimes.com/news/2006/feb/09/20060209-124325-7786r/.
30. Ibid.
31. Scott Ritter, "A Base for the Corruption of Democracy," *Aljazeera.net*, June 26, 2005.
32. "Plan for Clinics in Iraq, High Cost Threats Slow Constitution," *USA Today*, February 2, 2006.
33. "U.S. Officers Charged over Iraq Scam," *Aljazeera.net*, February 8, 2007.
34. Associated Press, "Gunmen Kill 47 Iraqi Factory Workers," *Yahoo News*, February 23, 2006.
35. "The New Interim Government," *Egyptian Gazette*, June 2, 2004.
36. "Iraq Forms Election Board, Asks U.S. Troops to Stay," *Egyptian Gazette*, June 5, 2005.
37. "U.S. Returns Sovereignty to Iraq," *CNN.com*, June 28, 2004.
38. Warren Hoge, "UN Renews Mandate for U.S.-Led Iraq Force, Measures Call for Review in 6 Months," *Herald Tribune*, November 9, 2005.
39. Associated Press, "Iraqi Security a Key Topic at Bush Meeting with Iraq Prime Minister," *Yahoo News*, June 24, 2005.
40. "Iraqis Hope for Better Security, Real Sovereignty," *CNN.com*, June 28, 2004.
41. Wiliam Pfaff, "Give Iraqis Complete Sovereignty," *Worldsecuritynetwork.com*, May 22, 2004, http://www.worldsecuritynetwork.com/showArticle3.cfm?article_id=9565
42. Ibid.
43. "NATO Agrees to Train Iraqi Forces," *CNN.com*, June 28, 2004.
44. Patrick Tyler, "Iraq Will Have Veto Power over Military Operations, Blair Said," *International Herald Tribune*, May 26, 2004.
45. "Allawi Repeats Call for U.S.-Led Troops to Stay," *Egyptian Gazette*, June 7, 2004.
46. "Amr Moussa: Iraq Needs Arab Presence," *ArabNews.com*, June 27, 2005, http://www.arabicnews.com/ansub/Daily/Day/050627/2005062727.html.
47. "The Arab Committee on Iraq, Meeting in Jeddah," *Egyptian Gazette*, October 3, 2005.
48. "Arab League Delegation Ambushed in Iraq," *ABC News Online*, October 11, 2005, http://www.abc.net.au/news/newsitems/200510/s1479079.htm.
49. "Iraq Leaders in Cairo Demand Pullout Timetable," *Aljazeera.net*, November 21, 2005.
50. Tom Regan, "Iraqi Leaders Want a Timetable for U.S. Withdrawal," *Christian Science Monitor*, November 22, 2005, http://www.csmonitor.com/2005/1122/dailyUpdate.html.
51. "Security Ring for Baghdad Planned," *Aljazeera.net*, May 27, 2005.

52. "Arab League Chief Begins Iraq Reconciliation between Mission," *Egyptian Gazette*, October 21, 2005.

53. "Arab League Highlights Ties to Iraqi Kurds," *Kurdish Regional Government*, October 23, 2005, http://www.krg.org/articles/detail.asp?rnr=24&lngnr=12& anr=6959&smap=

54. Doug Struck, "New Attacks Threaten Political Truce in Iraq," *Washington Post*, December 4, 2005, http://www.washingtonpost.com/wp-dyn/content/ article/2005/12/03/AR2005120301293.html?nav=rss_world.

55. Salah Nasraw, "Arab League Plans to Open Office in Iraq," *Associated Press*, March 4, 2006.

56. Amin Saikal, "Iraq's Conflict Is Fuelling a Bitter Mideast Split," *Herald Tribune*, October 9, 2005.

57. Samia Nakhoul, "Iraq Revives Sunni-Shia Tensions among Neighbours," Dawn.com, October 5, 2005, http://www.dawn.com/2005/10/05/fea.htm#

58. Ibid.

59. "Technology Road Side Bomb from Iran," *Egyptian Gazette*, November 1, 2005.

60. "Iraq Accuses Iran of Border Violations," *Aljazeera.net*, May 3, 2006.

61. "Iraq FM Slams Arab Stand," *Aljazeera.net*, March 26, 2006.

62. Speech of H. E. the Secretary-General of the organization of the Islamic conference at the meeting of eminent Shiite and Sunna scholars in Iraq, Mecca, Saudi Arabia, October 19–20, 2006.

63. "Saudi King Calls for Unity, Arab League Summit Meeting in Saudi Arabia," *Aljazeera.net*, March 29, 2007.

CHAPTER 9

1. "Blast rips through Baghdad hotel," *BBC News*, March 18, 2004, http://news .bbc.co.uk/2/hi/middle_east/3521200.stm.

2. "Guide: Armed groups in Iraq," *BBC News*, August 15, 2006, http://news.bbc .co.uk/2/hi/middle_east/4268904.stm.

3. Ian Black, "Saudis make up 41% of foreign fighters in Iraq," *The Guardian*, November 23, 2007, http://www.guardian.co.uk/world/2007/nov/23/iraq .saudiarabia.

4. "'No arbitrary date' for withdrawing troops, says Blair," September 25, 2005, http://www.telegraph.co.uk/news/1499172/No-arbitrary-date-for -withdrawing-troops-says-Blair.html.

5. "Iraqi Insurgency Groups," Global Security.org, http://www.globalsecurity.org/ military/ops/iraq_insurgency.htm.

6. "Al-Qaeda in Iraq," Wikipedia, http://en.wikipedia.org/wiki/Al-Qaeda_in_Iraq.

7. Jamaat Ansar al-Sunna. Wikipedia, http://en.wikipedia.org/wiki/Jamaat_Ansar _al-Sunna.

8. "U.S. puts al-Zarqawi's group on terror list," October 16, 2004. http://www .cnn.com/2004/WORLD/meast/10/15/zarqawi.terror/.

9. "Al-Zarqawi: We have Egyptian Envoy," *Aljazeera.net*, July 7, 2005.

10. "Church bombs: Top insurgent blamed," *CNN.com*, August 2, 2004, http://edition.cnn.com/2004/WORLD/meast/08/02/iraq.main/index.html.

11. Michel Chossudovsky, "Who is Abu Musab Al-Zarqawi?", *Centre for Research on Globalisation*, June 11, 2004, http://www.globalresearch.ca/articles/CHO405B.html.

12. Dexter Filkins, "Qaeda Video Vows Iraq Defeat for 'Crusader' U.S," *New York Times*, April 26, 2006, http://www.nytimes.com/2006/04/26/world/middleeast/26zarqawi.html?ex=1303704000&en=a32a19dfa9f75419&ei=5088.

13. "Al-Zarqawi declared war on Iraqi Shia," *Aljazeera.net*, September 14, 2005.

14. "Iraq mosque struck by car bomber," *BBC News*, September 16, 2005, http://news.bbc.co.uk/2/hi/middle_east/4251390.stm.

15. Kirk Semple and Sabrina Tavernise, "U.S. and Iraqi troops continue offensive," *New York Times*, November 8, 2005, http://www.nytimes.com/2005/11/07/world/africa/07iht-iraq.html?scp=1&sq=US%20and%20Iraqi%20troops%20continue%20offensive&st=cse.

16. Khalid al-Ansary and John O'Neil, "U.S. military displays other side of enemy," *New York Times*, May 4, 2006, http://www.nytimes.com/2006/05/04/world/africa/04iht-iraq.html.

17. Mussab Al-Khairella, "Maliki announces reconciliation plan to end Iraq's 'ugly picture,'" *The Independent*, June 26, 2006, http://www.independent.co.uk/news/world/middle-east/maliki-announces-reconciliation-plan-to-end-iraqs-ugly-picture-405525.html.

18. James Hider, "U.S. reporter murdered in Iraq had written his own epitaph," *Times Online*, August 4, 2005, http://www.timesonline.co.uk/tol/news/world/iraq/article551336.ece.

19. "U.S. detains scores in Baghdad sweep," *Aljazeera.net*, August 12, 2006, http://english.*Aljazeera.net*/archive/2006/08/2008410103734418743.html.

20. Sewell Chan, "U.S. Civilians Mutilated in Iraq Attack," *Washington Post*, April 1, 2004.

21. Douglas Jehl, "The Beheading: C.I.A. Says Berg's Killer Was Very Probably Zarqawi," *New York Times*, May 14, 2004, http://www.nytimes.com/2004/05/14/politics/14ZARQ.html.

22. "Militants Behead American Hostage in Iraq," *Fox News*, May 11, 2004, http://www.foxnews.com/story/0,2933,119615,00.html.

23. Associated Press, "Briton abducted in Iraq," *The Independent*, September 16, 2004, http://www.independent.co.uk/news/world/middle-east/briton-abducted-in-iraq-546506.html.

24. Associated Press, "Baghdad Airport Reopens," *Fox News*, September 10, 2005, http://www.foxnews.com/story/0,2933,168997,00.html.

25. "Major attack on Iraq 'rebel town,'" *BBC News*, 10, 2005, http://news.bbc.co.uk/2/hi/middle_east/4232084.stm.

26. "Police: Mosque blast kills at least 25," *CNN.com*, October 5, 2005, http://edition.cnn.com/2005/WORLD/meast/10/05/iraq.main/index.html.

27. Sabrina Tavernise, "Suicide Bomber Kills at Least 29 in Crowded Baghdad Restaurant," *New York Times*, November 10, 2005, http://www.nytimes.com/2005/11/10/international/middleeast/10cnd-iraq.html?fta=y.

28. "Shia pilgrims defy suicide attacks," *Aljazeera.net*, March 9, 2007, http://english.*Aljazeera.net*/news/middleeast/2007/03/200852512658976472.html.

29. "Morgue's toll for April in Baghdad: 1,091 victims," *CNN.com*, May 10, 2006, http://edition.cnn.com/2006/WORLD/meast/05/10/iraq.main/index.html.

30. "Baghdad's security forces to be revamped," *USA Today*, May 11, 2006, http://www.usatoday.com/news/world/iraq/2006-05-11-iraq-security_x.htm.

31. UN Assistance Mission for Iraq, Human Rights Report, March 1–April 30, 2006, http://www.uniraq.org/documents/HR%20Report%20Mar%20Apr%2006%20EN.PDF.

32. "Scores killed in Baghdad university," *Aljazeera.net*, January 17, 2007, http://english.*Aljazeera.net*/news/middleeast/2007/01/200852513128132123.html.

33. Associated Press, "Suicide bomber kills 41 at Baghdad college," *msnbc.com*, February 25, 2007, http://www.msnbc.msn.com/id/17326397/.

34. Sabrina Tavernise, "Gunmen in Iraq add teachers to target list," *New York Times*, September 27, 2005, http://www.nytimes.com/2005/09/26/world/africa/26iht-iraq.html.

35. "U.S.: More than 40 insurgents die in Iraq raids," *CNN.com*, May 15, 2006, http://edition.cnn.com/2006/WORLD/meast/05/15/iraq.main/index.html.

36. "Iraqi violence claims nearly 20 lives, children among dead," *USA Today*, February 15, 2006, http://www.usatoday.com/news/world/iraq/2006-02-15-iraq-bombs_x.htm.

37. "Children die in Iraq wedding bombing," *Aljazeera.net*, November 1, 2006, http://english.*Aljazeera.net*/archive/2006/11/200849163325380626.html.

38. Rory Caroll, "Iraq bombings and shootings leave 150 dead," *The Guardian*, September 15, 2005, http://www.guardian.co.uk/world/2005/sep/15/iraq.rorycarroll.

39. "Woman suicide bomber strikes Iraq," *BBC News*, September 28, 2005, http://news.bbc.co.uk/2/hi/4289168.stm.

40. Robert F. Worth, "Iraqi Civilians Fight Back Against Insurgents," *New York Times*, March 23, 2005, http://www.nytimes.com/2005/03/23/international/worldspecial/23iraq.html.

41. "Bakery workers kidnapped in Baghdad," *Aljazeera.net*, June 18, 2006, http://english.*Aljazeera.net*/archive/2006/06/200849125552772972.html.

42. Associated Press, "14 Iraqi policemen kidnapped, killed," *USA Today*, March 2, 2007, http://www.usatoday.com/news/world/iraq/2007-03-02-kidnapping_x.htm.

43. "Shia pilgrims defy suicide attacks," *Aljazeera.net*, March 9, 2007, http://english.*Aljazeera.net*/news/middleeast/2007/03/200852512658976472.html.

44. Edward Wong, "Bombers Kill at Least 70 Inside Two Shiite Mosques in Iraq," *New York Times*, November 18, 2005, http://www.nytimes.com/2005/11/18/international/middleeast/18cnd-Iraq.html.

45. "Baghdad judge shot dead in ambush," *BBC News*, January 25, 2005, http://news.bbc.co.uk/2/hi/middle_east/4204533.stm.

46. "Dozens of new Iraqi soldiers found dead," *CNN.com*, October 25, 2004, http://edition.cnn.com/2004/WORLD/meast/10/24/iraq.main/index.html.

47. Associated Press, "Head of Iraqi Governing Council Killed in Blast," *Fox News*, May 17, 2004, http://www.foxnews.com/story/0,2933,120090,00.htm.

48. Agence France-Presse, "$45m paid to Iraq kidnappers," *Aljazeera.net*, May 22, 2006, http://english.*Aljazeera.net*/archive/2006/05/200849164548918885.html.

49. "Iraq 'hostage' to lawlessness," *Egyptian Gazette*, July 26, 2004.

50. Jeff Stein, "Can you tell a Sunni from a Shiite?" *New York Times*, October 17, 2006, http://www.nytimes.com/2006/10/17/opinion/17stein.html?scp=1&sq=Can%20you%20tell%20a%20Sunni%20from%20a%20Shiite?%94:%20&st=cse.

51. "Allawi ultimatum to hand over foreign fighters from Fallujah," *Egyptian Gazette*, October 14, 2004.

52. Eric Schmitt, "Marines Battle Insurgents in Streets of Fallujah," *New York Times*, April 9, 2004, http://www.nytimes.com/2004/04/09/international/middleeast/09BATT.html.

53. "Fallujah under Siege," *Egyptian Gazette*, April 9, 2004.

54. Robert F. Worth, Edward Wong, et al., "The Conflict in Iraq: Insurgents, Marines Find Vast Arms Cache in Falluja Leader's Mosque," *New York Times*, November 25, 2004, http://query.nytimes.com/gst/fullpage.html?res=940CE6D9153EF936A15752C1A9629C8B63&sec=&spon=&&scp=1&sq=Huge%20caches%20of%20arms%20discovered%20in%20Falluja&st=cse.

55. "Troops find hostage 'slaughterhouses' in Falluja," *CNN.com*, November 11, 2004, http://edition.cnn.com/2004/WORLD/meast/11/10/iraq.main/index.html.

56. Richard A. Oppel, "Explosion at Big American Base in Mosul Kills 22," *New York Times*, December 22, 2004, http://www.nytimes.com/2004/12/22/international/middleeast/22iraq.html.

57. Jim Miklaszewski, "U.S. to boost Iraq troop strength," *msnbc.com*, November 29, 2004, http://www.msnbc.msn.com/id/6613194/.

58. "Transcript: Bush, Allawi Speak," *Fox News*, September 23, 2004.

59. "Iraqi interim president: Insurgents will be gone in a year," December 9, 2004, http://edition.cnn.com/2004/WORLD/meast/12/08/iraq.interim.president/.

60. "Fast Facts: After Iraq's Elections," *Fox News*, January 28, 2005, http://www.foxnews.com/story/0,2933,145668,00.html.

61. James Gordon Meek, "War May Take Decade.—Iraq must win on its own—Rumsfeld," Nydailynews.com, June 27, 2005, http://www.nydailynews.com/archives/news/2005/06/27/2005-06-27_war_may_take_decade_iraq_mu.html.

62. "Rice in surprise visit to Iraq," *Aljazeera.net*, May 15, 2005, http://english.*Aljazeera.net*/archive/2005/05/200849163659595502.html.

63. "Transcript: Rumsfeld on 'FNS,'" *Fox News*, June 27, 2005, http://www
.foxnews.com/story/0,2933,160716,00.html.
64. Associated Press, "Rumsfeld acknowledges U.S., insurgents met," *msnbc.com*,
June 27, 2005, http://www.msnbc.msn.com/id/8359553/.
65. Associated Press, "Schroeder, Bush Meet at White House," *Fox News*, July 31,
2005, http://www.foxnews.com/story/0,2933,160796,00.html.
66. "Poll: Iraq is top concern," *CNN.com*, December 21, 2004, http://edition
.cnn.com/2004/US/12/21/poll/index.html.
67. "Operation Iron Fist, Operation Kabda Bil Hadid," Globalsecurity.org, October 1, 2005–October 6, 2005, http://www.globalsecurity.org/military/ops/
oif-iron-fist_2005.htm; and "Operation Iron fist against insurgents' sanctuary,"
Egyptian Gazette, October 2, 2005.
68. "Militants down U.S. helicopter in Iraq, killing two," *New York Times*, May 15,
2006, http://www.nytimes.com/2006/05/15/world/africa/15iht-web.0515iraq
.html.
69. "U.S. troops 'seized by insurgents,'" *BBC News*, June 18, 2006, http://news
.bbc.co.uk/2/hi/middle_east/5092072.stm.
70. Kathryn L. Gardner, "Fighting Terrorism the FATF Way," *Encyclopedia Britannica*,
July 2007, http://www.britannica.com/bps/additionalcontent/18/26374870/
Fighting-Terrorism-the-FATF-Way.
71. "Terrorists using Internet," *Egyptian Gazette*, December 14, 2004.
72. "U.S. warns financial firms of al-Qaeda threat," *CNN.com*, November 30,
2006, http://money.cnn.com/2006/11/30/news/economy/al_qaeda/.

CHAPTER 10

1. David E. Sanger, "Bush, Conceding Problems, Defends Iraq War," *New York
Times*, March 14, 2006, http://www.nytimes.com/2006/03/14/politics/14
prexy.html.
2. "U.S., Iraqi officials take sides on civil war debate," *CNN.com*, March 20,
2006, http://edition.cnn.com/2006/WORLD/meast/03/19/iraq.anniversary/
index.html.
3. Robert Worth, "Blast Destroys Shrine in Iraq, Setting Off Sectarian Fury,"
New York Times, February 22, 2006. http://www.nytimes.com/2006/02/22/
international/middleeast/22cnd-iraq.html.
4. "United States Condemns Bombing of Important Shia Mosque in Iraq," U.S.
Embassy in Iraq, February 22, 2006, http://iraq.usembassy.gov/iraq/20060222
_mosque_bombing.html.
5. "Sistani urges end to Iraq 'bloodletting,'" *Aljazeera.net*, July 22, 2006.
6. Reuters, "Suicide Bomber in Iraq's Kufa Leaves 59 Dead," Arabnews.com, July
19, 2006.
7. Agence France-Presse, "Nearly 6,000 civilians killed in Iraq in May, June: UN,"
Chinadaily.com.cn, July 18, 2006.
8. "Shiite fury explodes in Iraq," *Herald Tribune*, February 24, 2006.

9. "Sunni cleric killed in political coercion," *The Washington Times*, February 8, 2006.

10. "Iraqi general killed in ambush," *CNN.com*, March 7, 2006, http://edition.cnn.com/2006/WORLD/meast/03/06/iraq.main/index.html.

11. "Lawyers of Saddam boycott tribunal," *Egyptian Gazette*, October 17, 2005.

12. "Scholars say Iraq meets definition of 'civil war,'" *Herald Tribune*, November 27, 2006.

13. Qassim Abdul-Zahra and Lee Keath, "2,660 Iraqi Civilians Killed in Sept," *Washington Post*, October 11, 2006.

14. "Colin Powell says Iraq in a 'civil war,'" *CNN.com*, November 29, 2006.

15. "144 killed in series of bombings in Baghdad," *Herald Tribune*, November 24, 2006.

16. Sabrina Tavernise, "Baghdad oasis 'falling to terrorists,'" *Herald Tribune*, June 24, 2006.

17. "Iraq devolves into 'civil war'," *CNN.com*, July 21, 2006.

18. Associated Press, "Bush Officials: No Big Move in Iraq Plan," *Yahoo News*, October 24, 2006.

19. Associated Press, "October U.S. Death Toll in Iraq Hits 100," *Yahoo News*, October 30, 2006.

20. "80 Killed or Found Dead in Iraq; 2 U.S. Servicemen Killed," *Fox News*, October 30, 2006, http://www.foxnews.com/story/0,2933,226156,00.html.

21. "Talbani warns of civil war," *Egyptian Gazette*, March 14, 2006.

22. "At least 56 Iraqis dead in new violence," *Yahoo News*, March 23, 2006.

23. "Talabani: Armed groups support talks," *Aljazeera.net*, November 28, 2005.

24. Reuters, "Talabani: U.S. Must Stay for Three Years," *Aljazeera.net*, November 2, 2006.

25. "Abu Musab al-Zarqawi Killed in Bombing Raid," *Fox News*, June 8, 2006. http://www.foxnews.com/story/0,2933,198651,00.html.

26. Associated Press, "Al Zarqawi death prompts attack warning," *Yahoo News*, June 11, 2006.

27. Michael Howard, "Zarqawi group uses website to promise new attacks," *The Guardian*, June 12, 2006, http://www.guardian.co.uk/world/2006/jun/12/alqaida.iraq.

28. Agence France-Presse, "Al Qaeda vows revenge for Zarqawi's death," *ABC News Online*, June 24, 2006.

29. "Explosion Hits Iraqi Parliament, 2 Dead," *AP Online*, April 12, 2007.

30. "Website says new Leader named to replace Zarqawi," *Herald Tribune*, June 13, 2006.

31. Reuters, "Zarqawi successor vows vengeance," *Aljazeera.net*, June 14, 2006.

32. "Zarqawi successor 'in Egypt jail,'" *Aljazeera.net*, July 6, 2006.

33. "Al-Qaeda in Iraq Announces New Leader. Or Do They?," *Your Word Press Blog*, December 29, 2008. www.panteonmemorialtowers.com/2008/12/

34. "Web posting: Al Qaeda in Iraq leader to target Sunni," *CNN.com*, June 14, 2006.

35. "Bin Laden tells Sunnis to fight Shiites in Iraq," *CNN.com*, July 2, 2006.

36. "Will the death of Zarqawi bring a troop down?" *CNN.com*, June 12, 2006.

37. "Al-Zarqawi trained insurgents," *Egyptian Gazette*, June 12, 2006.

38. Associated Press, "Iraqi Authorities: Al Qaeda in Iraq No. 2 Arrested," *Fox News*, September 3, 2006.

39. Zalmay Khalilzad, interview with Dan Bartlett, CNN Late Edition with Wolf Blitzer, January 10, 2006, *CNN.com*, October 1, 2006.

40. Christopher Allbritton, "View from Baghdad: How Zarqawi's Death may change the game," Time.com, June 8, 2006.

CHAPTER 11

1. Samantha L. Quigley, American Forces Press Service, "Coalition buoyed by Iraqi peoples courage, Bush says," Defense.gov, March 16, 2005.

2. Associated Press, "Bush, and Blair acknowledge Iraq 'setbacks,'" *Chinadaily.com .cn*, May 26, 2006.

3. Ibid.

4. CQ Transcriptions Wire, "In the State of the Union, 2006-03-05 war in Iraq," *Washington Post*, January 31, 2006.

5. "Cheney: Iraq will be 'enormous success story,'" *CNN.com*, June 24, 2005, http://edition.cnn.com/2005/POLITICS/06/23/cheney.interview/.

6. "New US envoy nominated for Iraq," *Aljazeera.net*, April 6, 2005, http://english .aljazeera.net/archive/2005/04/20084101627674714.html.

7. Fareed Zakaria, "Elections are not democracy," *Newsweek*, February 7, 2005. p. 13.

8. Ellen Knickmeyer, "Talabani Offers Amnesty to Insurgents," *Washington Post*, April 7, 2005.

9. "Milestone elections begin in Iraq," *CNN.com*, January 30, 2005, http:// edition.cnn.com/2005/WORLD/meast/01/29/iraq.main/index.html.

10. Associated Press/AP Online, "UK Prime Minister make surprise Baghdad visit," *Redorbit.com*, December 21, 2004.

11. "Security measures for election," *Egyptian Mail*, January 29, 2005.

12. "Purported bin Laden tape endorses al-Zarqawi," *CNN.com*, December 27, 2004, http://edition.cnn.com/2004/WORLD/meast/12/27/binladen.tape/index .html.

13. "Zarqawi vows war on Iraq poll," *BBC News*, January 23, 2005, http://news .bbc.co.uk/2/hi/middle_east/4199363.stm.

14. "Polls close in Iraq; Turnout estimated at above 70 percent," CNN Sunday Morning, January 30, 2005, http://edition.cnn.com/TRANSCRIPTS/0501/ 30/sm.02.html.

15. "World leaders praise voter courage," *CNN.com*, January 31, 2005, http:// edition.cnn.com/2005/WORLD/meast/01/30/iraq.internatreax/index.html.

16. "Our pride, by first Iraqis to vote," *CNN.com*, January 31, 2005, http:// edition.cnn.com/2005/WORLD/asiapcf/01/28/iraq.firstvoter/index.html.

17. "Voting a religious duty in Iraq's holy cities," *Egyptian Gazette*, January 28, 2005.

18. "The election transformed once oppressed Shiites and Kurds into the holder of power," *Egyptian Gazette*, May 10, 2005.

19. Lin Noueihed, "Iraqi Sunni clerics: election lacked legitimacy," *Reuters*, February 3, 2005.

20. "Iraq Sunni group meets US official over poll boycott," *Egyptian Gazette*, January 11, 2005.

21. "Sunni Muslim Clerics' Association (MCA) to boycott the Iraqi election," *Al-Ahram Weekly*, December 16–20, 2004.

22. "Iraqi elections 2005," *Al-Ahram Weekly*, January 27, 2005; "Iraqi government formed," *Egyptian Gazette*, April 29, 2005.

23. "Iraq's constitution writers face formidable task," *Egyptian Mail*, March 5, 2005.

24. "Iraqi gov't sworn in amid wave of violence," *Chinadaily.com.cn*, May 4, 2005.

25. "Al-Jaafari unveils Iraqi political agenda," *Aljazeera.net*, May 31, 2005, http://english.aljazeera.net/archive/2005/05/2008410113756267514.html.

26. "Political impasse to have a government in Iraq," *Egyptian Gazette*, April 29, 2005.

27. "Three months political vacuum in forming Iraq government," *Egyptian Gazette*, April 26, 2005.

28. "Iraq cabinet formed," *Aljazeera.net*, April 28, 2005.

29. "Rice in surprise visit to Iraq," *Aljazeera.net*, May 15, 2005.

30. Richard A. Oppel, Jr., "Rice, in Baghdad, Urges Sunni Role in Constitution," *New York Times*, May 16, 2005.

31. "Iraq cabinet structure," *Egyptian Gazette*, April 29, 2005.

32. "American fear regarding el-Jaafari," *Egyptian Mail*, April 16, 2005.

33. "Jaafari (Prime Minister) was never far from Iraq, despite a long exile," *Egyptian Mail*, February 26, 2005.

34. "Allawi party not part of new Iraq cabinet," *Chinadaily.com.cn*, April 25, 2005.

35. "General calling for speeding up political process in Iraq," *Egyptian Gazette*, April 26, 2005.

36. "Rumsfeld urges swift formation of Iraqi government," pbs.org, April 12, 2005.

37. "Condoleezza Rice calls for a new Middle East," *Egyptian Gazette*, April 17, 2005.

38. Hamza Hendawi, "Guns will not solve the problem of Iraq," nysun.com, June 8, 2005.

39. "Ex-PM: Abuse as bad as Saddam era," *CNN.com*, November 27, 2005, http://edition.cnn.com/2005/WORLD/meast/11/27/iraq.allawi/index.html.

40. Associated Press, "Iraq misses deadline for probe on torture allegations," *USA Today*, November 30, 2005.

41. Hamza Hendawi, "Diplomat cites U.S. 'stupidity' in Iraq," Associated Press, October 22, 2006.

42. "Iraqi protesters: 'No, no to America,'" *CNN.com*, April 9, 2005. http://edition.cnn.com/2005/WORLD/meast/04/09/iraq.main/.

43. Terence Hunt, "Bush Unsatisfied with Iraq War Progress," *Fox News*, October 25, 2006.

44. Deb Riechmann, "Bush focusing on Iraqi troop training," *Redorbit.com*, November 29, 2006.

45. "Presidential press conference," *CNN.com*, April 20, 2005.

46. Bush in his State of the Union address in January 2006 regarding Iraqi war.

47. Associated Press, "Bush: No Timetable for Iraq Withdrawal," *Military.com*, June 25, 2005.

48. Associated Press, "Rice: Congress shouldn't micromanage war," *Washingtonpost .com*, February 25, 2007.

49. "US: Iraq doomed if new push fails," *Aljazeera.net*, February 11, 2007.

50. "Group of lawmakers proposed a plan to withdraw US troops from Iraq," *Egyptian Gazette*, June 24, 2005.

51. Agence France-Presse, "US politicians spar over Iraq strategy," *Aljazeera.net*, August 22, 2005.

52. "Iraqi Leader Talks on US Timeline," *Herald Tribune*, October 25, 2006.

53. "Turkey fears 'endless war' in Iraq," *Aljazeera.net*, January 29, 2007.

54. Nicholas D. Kristof, "Iraq: Strategizing the exit," *Herald Tribune*, November 12–14, 2005.

55. "Reduction of South Korean troops," *The Guardian*, November 19, 2005.

56. "Foreign troops to quit Iraq mid 2006," *Aljazeera.net*, May 2, 2005.

57. "Blair announces Iraq troop pullout," *Aljazeera.net*, February 21, 2007.

58. "British troops to be pulled out of Iraq by the middle of 2008," *Egyptian Gazette*, March 8, 2006.

59. Associated Press, "Shiites push for British troops to leave," Washingtonpost .com, October 13, 2006.

60. Associated Press, "Britain may start pulling out of Iraq," Wcbstv.com, November 27, 2006.

61. "US dismisses Iraq withdrawal plan," *Egyptian Gazette*, March 6, 2006.

62. "US-led forces Iraq mandate extended," *Aljazeera.net*, June 1, 2005.

63. "Talabani predicts U.S. exits in two years," *CNN.com*, April 10, 2005.

64. "Talbani: Priority to uproot terrorism," *Al-Ahram Weekly*, April 7, 2005.

65. Ellen Knickmeyer, "Talabani Offers Amnesty to Insurgents," *Washingtonpost .com*, April 7, 2005

66. "Possible Civil War if Allied Forces leave immaturely," *Egyptian Gazette*, May 5, 2004.

67. "Bush: Iraq crucial in war against terror," *CNN.com*, October 7, 2005.

68. "Pulling out now would be 'victory for the terrorists,'" *The Times*, November 22, 2005.

69. "Bush: U.S. to stay in Iraq till war is won," *CNN.com*, December 31, 2005.

70. "Bush says critics are rewriting war history," *Herald Tribune*, November 12–13, 2005.

71. "General: US could start Iraq pullout in Spring," *CNN.com*, July 27, 2005.

72. Reuters, "Talabani: U.S. Must Stay for Three Years," *Aljazeera.net*, November 2, 2006.

73. "US military weighs troop cuts in Iraq," *Aljazeera.net*, November 23, 2005.

74. "Iraq hawk turned dove comes home a puzzle," *Herald Tribune*, November 23, 2005.

75. "Iraqi official expects security transfers," *MWC.com*, November 26, 2005.

76. "US: Iraq troop cuts are an option," *Aljazeera.net*, June 28, 2006.

77. Terence Hunt, "Bush Unsatisfied with Iraq War Progress," *Redorbit.com*, October 25, 2006.

78. "Bush: U.S. shifting tactics in Iraq War," *CNN.com*, October 26, 2006.

79. "US House denounce Bush troop plan," *Aljazeera.net*, February 17, 2007.

80. "Bush to veto Iraq pull out Bill," *Aljazeera.net*, March 24, 2007.

81. "US Senate backs Iraq deadline," *Aljazeera.net*, March 28, 2007

82. Ben Feller, "Bush: Iraq withdrawal would spawn danger," USAToday.com, May 4, 2007.

83. "Demands for setting a timetable for withdrawal of troops in Iraq," *Al-Ahram Weekly*, April 14, 2005.

84. "Talbani met Sunni Arabs concerning withdrawal of troops," *Al-Ahram Weekly*, April 14, 2005.

85. "Iraq calls for US withdrawal," *Egyptian Gazette*, July 23, 2006.

86. "Iraqi Leader Talks on US Timeline," *Herald Tribune*, October 25, 2006.

87. "Saudi Arabia warns to support Iraqi Sunnis," *Egyptian Gazette*, December 14, 2006.

88. "Sadr ministers quit Iraqi cabinet," *BBC News*, April 16, 2007.

89. "40,000 Iraqis to form shield in Baghdad," *Aljazeera.net*, May 27, 2005.

90. "Attacks kill 31 in Iraq. Fear violence deepen sectarian division," *Egyptian Mail*, May 7, 2005.

91. "Iraqi, US forces to rescue Shiite hostages," *Egyptian Gazette*, April 18, 2004.

92. "Shiite politicians accused the Sunni insurgents to kill Shiites," *Newsweek*, May 2, 2005.

93. "Gunmen in Iraq kill top Shiite cleric's aide," *CNN.com*, May 20, 2005.

94. "Poll: 58 percent want Iraq withdrawal by 2008 or sooner," *CNN.com*, March 13, 2007.

95. "Bush's approval rate falls to 28 percent: report," Reuters, May 6, 2007.

96. "Sistani in Najaf decided not to use force against Sunnis," *Newsweek*, May 2, 2005, p. 30.

97. "Shiite follower of Sistani said bewares of Saddamites and their followers," *Newsweek*, May 2, 2005, p. 30.

98. "Shiite Badr Organization killing Sunni cleric," *CNN.com*, May 20, 2005.

99. "Sunni Iraqis announce political coalition," *CNN.com*, May 22, 2005.

100. Thomas Wagner, "Iraqi Leaders Plead for Killing to Halt," *Fox News*, November 26, 2006.

101. Associated Press, "Excerpts from the Iraq Study Group Report," NPR.org, December 6, 2006.

102. "Survey indicated Iraqis in despair," *Aljazeera.net*, December 14, 2006.

103. "Bush calls for new Iraq approach," *Aljazeera.net*, December 8, 2006.

104. Tom Raum, "Bush: U.S. troops will remain in Iraq," *Redorbit.com*, November 30, 2006.
105. "US general favours staying in Iraq," *Aljazeera.net*, November 16, 2006.
106. Ed Johnson, "Gulf States Back U.S. Security Plan for Iraq After Rice Talks," Bloomberg.com, January 17, 2007, http://www.bloomberg.com/apps/news?pid=20601103&sid=aJmm81u7NRok.
107. "Al-Qaeda: Bush gambling in Iraq," *Aljazeera.net*, February 14, 2007.
108. "Kurdish Leader Rejects Iraq Report," AP Online, December 8, 2006.

CHAPTER 12

1. Associated Press/AP Online, "Petraeus: Force will not solve Iraq," *Aljazeera.net*, March 9, 2007.
2. "Iraq delays draft constitution vote," *Aljazeera.net*, August 23, 2005.
3. "Iraq approves final draft of new constitution," *Egyptian Gazette*, September 19, 2005.
4. "How the constitution be defeated," *Egyptian Gazette*, October 18, 2005.
5. "Constitution vote nears," *Egyptian Gazette*, August 25, 2005.
6. Associated Press/AP Online, "Sunni group urges election participation," *Redorbit.com*, July 5, 2005.
7. "Sunnis call to reject federalism," *Aljazeera.net*, August 16, 2005.
8. Associated Press, "Top Sunnis seek changes in constitution," *Chinadaily.com.cn*, August 28, 2005.
9. "Problem of Sunni participation in writing the Iraqi constitution has irritated the government," *Egyptian Gazette*, July 25, 2005.
10. "Iraqi MPs approve federalism," *Aljazeera.net*, October 11, 2006.
11. "Kirkuk Arabs face relocation," *Aljazeera.net*, February 7, 2007.
12. "Establishment of Islamic Iraqi State," *Herald Tribune*, October 16, 2006.
13. "Iraqi Kurd politicians say yes to Unity," *Aljazeera.net*, May 8, 2006.
14. "Iraq PM rebukes Kurds over flag," *Aljazeera.net*, September 3, 2006.
15. "Kirkuk: The potential spark for civil war," *Aljazeera.net*, October 9, 2006.
16. "Kurds 'back' new Draft Iraq oil law," *Aljazeera.net*, February 25, 2007.
17. "Iraq Shia leaders call for federal state," *Aljazeera.net*, August 12, 2005.
18. "Al-Sadr 'rejects' Iraqi constitution," *Aljazeera.net*, February 19, 2006.
19. Associated Press, "U.S., Iraqi forces clash with militia insurgents," *Washingtonpost.com*, October 8, 2006.
20. "Bush describing the delay in the constitution as critical," *Aljazeera.net*, August 16, 2005.
21. "Intense US pressure to finishing drafting the constitution," *Aljazeera.net*, August 16, 2005.
22. "US officials pressed the Sunnis, Shias for ending the draft constitution," *Aljazeera.net*, August 28, 2005.
23. "US envoy seeks talks with Iraq rebels," *Aljazeera.net*, November 29, 2005.
24. Associated Press, "US envoy: Iraq constitution may change," *Fox News*, August 31, 2005.

25. Associated Press, "Top Sunnis seek changes in constitution," *Chinadaily.com .cn*, August 28, 2005; and "Writers of Iraqi constitution to ask for extension," USAToday.com, July 31, 2005.

26. United Press International, "Iraq's Sunnis reject constitution," *BBC News*, August 28, 2005.

27. "Shiites want constitution based on Sharia (Islamic law)," *Egyptian Mail*, April 16, 2005.

28. "Sunni leaders set demands on Iraq Statute Body," Arabnews.com, June 8, 2005.

29. Associated Press/AP Online, "Sunni group urges election participation," *Redorbit.com*, July 5, 2005.

30. "Iraqis ready to vote on new constitution," *Egyptian Gazette*, October 14, 2005.

31. "First Iraq votes cast in poll as Arab League urges turnout," *Egyptian Gazette*, December 13, 2005.

32. "Iraqi referendum ends with little bloodshed," *Egyptian Gazette*, October 16, 2005.

33. Qassim Abul-Zahra, "Iraq unveils security measures for vote," *Redorbit.com*, October 7, 2005.

34. Hamza Hendawi. "Iraqis vote in constitutional referendum," *Redorbit.com*, October 15, 2005.

35. "Final tally of 15 December 2005 election in Iraq," *Washington Times*, February 11, 2006.

36. "Iraq political crises deepens," *Egyptian Gazette*, April 18, 2006.

37. "Rice and Straw in Iraq to brake government deadlock," *Egyptian Gazette*, April 3, 2006.

38. "Jaafari under US pressure to forge a national unity government," *Egyptian Gazette*, February 27, 2006.

39. "Jaafari rejects US sectarian warning," *Egyptian Gazette*, February 22, 2006.

40. "Sunnis and Kurds reject Jaafari," *Aljazeera.net*, April 11, 2006.

41. "Iraq PM rebuffs call to quit," *Egyptian Gazette*, April 2, 2006.

42. "14 killed in five explosions in Baghdad," Yahoo News, February 28, 2006.

43. "New Iraqi leaders are urged to repair oil sector," *Herald Tribune*, April 25, 2006.

44. "New Iraq oil bill," *Aljazeera.net*, March 29, 2007.

45. "Vote on Iraq government," *Egyptian Gazette*, May 18, 2006; and "Iraq's New Parliament sworn in," Yahoo News, March 14, 2006.

46. "New government complete with key security jobs," *Egyptian Gazette*, June 9, 2006.

47. Patrick Quinn, "New Government vows 'Maximum Force' to end attacks," *Washingtonpost.com*, May 22, 2006.

48. "Al-Maliki intends to end sectarian rifts," *Aljazeera.net*, October 4, 2006.

49. "Iraq delays federalism decision," *Aljazeera.net*, September 25, 2006.

50. Reuters/Agence France-Presse, "World leaders hail new Iraqi govt," Abc.net.au, May 21, 2006.

51. César G. Soriano and Bill Nichols, "Bush tells Iraq leader U.S. will back him," USAToday.com, June 13, 2006.
52. Sabrina Tavernise, "Blair declares British will stay in Iraq," *Nytimes.com*, December 17, 2006.
53. "Rice and Rumsfeld stand 'united' in Iraq," *Herald Tribune*, April 27, 2006.
54. "Blair in Iraq: He gives no timetable for withdrawal," *CNN.com*, May 22, 2006.
55. "Government stunned by Army chief's Iraq blast," *Dailymail.com.uk*, October 13, 2006.
56. "Report: British Army chief calls for Iraq pullout," *CNN.com*, October 13, 2006.
57. Associated Press, "Iraqi PM offers olive branch to insurgents," Ctv.ca, June 25, 2006.
58. "Iraq PM moves to ban all militias," *Aljazeera.net*, May 31, 2006.
59. "Al-Maliki plan to end sectarian rifts is unwelcome," *Aljazeera.net*, October 4, 2006.
60. "Iraqi tribal leaders sign pact of honor," *Aljazeera.net*, October 5, 2006.
61. "Al-Maliki in surprise Ramadi visit," *Aljazeera.net*, March 13, 2007.
62. Reuters, "Anti-Qaeda tribes targeted in Iraq attacks," Alertnet.org, March 27, 2007.
63. "Iraqis 'pessimistic' about future," *Aljazeera.net*, March 19, 2007.
64. Steven R. Hurst, "Iraqi militia expressing siege mentality," Sfgate.com, January 18, 2007.
65. "Iraq armed groups set terms for truce," *Aljazeera.net*, June 29, 2006.
66. Reuters, "Iran offers security help to Iraqi premier," Khaleejtimes.com, September 12, 2006.
67. Abdulaziz Sager, "Need for UN resolution to end external intervention in Iraq," commentary, Gulf Research Center, Researchsea.com, September 24, 2006.
68. Alastair Macdonald and Aseel Kami, "Baghdad death squads kill 60, bombs kill 22," Infowars.com, September 13, 2006.
69. "Iran to expand military and economic ties with Iraq," *Egyptian Mail*, January 30, 2007.
70. "Khalilzad: Success in Iraq Still Possible," *Aljazeera.net*, October 24, 2006.
71. "Ahmadinejad wants US out of Iraq," *Aljazeera.net*, December 2, 2006.
72. "Iran denies plans for Iraq summit," *Aljazeera.net*, November 27, 2006.
73. "Assad: No peace without Syria and Iran," *Egyptian Gazette*, December 16, 2006.
74. "Syria and Iran vow unity against USA," *Aljazeera.net*, February 19, 2007.
75. Michael R. Gordon and Dexter Filkins, "Hezbollah Said to Help Shiite Army in Iraq," *Nytimes.com*, November 28, 2006.
76. "Saudi warns 'Interfering' Iran," *Aljazeera.net*, January 27, 2007.
77. "Report: Iran arming groups in Iraq," *Aljazeera.net*, December 18, 2006.
78. William Branigin, "Bush Warns Iran Against Action in Iraq," *Washingtonpost.com*, January 30, 2007.

79. "Saudi's report Shi'ite 'state' inside of Iraq," Washingtontimes.com, December 18, 2006.
80. Lolita C. Baldor, "Gates: Bombs tie the Iran to Iraq extremists," *Washingtonpost.com*, February 9, 2007.
81. "Arrested Iranians 'arming Iraqis,'" *Aljazeera.net*, January 14, 2007.
82. "US hunt foreign networks in Iraq," *Aljazeera.net*, January 16, 2007.
83. "Iran and Saudi pledge friendship," *Aljazeera.net*, March 4, 2007.
84. "Syria promises to stabilize Iraq," *Aljazeera.net*, March 8, 2007.
85. "US Iran talks possible in Regional meeting in Iraq," *Aljazeera.net*, March 1, 2007.
86. Edward Wong and Helene Cooper, "Iraq Premier Moves to Plan Regional Talks," *Nytimes.com*, December 6, 2006.
87. "Security Regional Conference," *Aljazeera.net*, February 1, 2007; "Iraq warns neighbors to stay out (conference)," *Aljazeera.net*, March 11, 2007.
88. Miriam Karouny, "Interview-Iraq will urge U.S., Iran not to use it as pawn," Alertnet.org, March 9, 2007.
89. Miriam Karouny, "Iraq calls on neighbours to help end violence," *Reuters.com*, March 10, 2007.
90. Associated Press, "US, Iran trade accusations at first talks," *Chinadaily.com.cn*, March 11, 2007.
91. "UN urges neighbors to aid Iraqis," *Aljazeera.net*, April 18, 2007.
92. "Iran FM attacks US policy in Iraq," *BBC News*, May 4, 2007.
93. Ben Feller, "Obama sets firm date to end Iraq war he inherited," *Fox News*, February 28, 2009.

FURTHER REFERENCES

Ahmed, Nafeez Mosaddeq. *Behind the War on Terror: Western Secret Strategy and the Struggle for Iraq.* New Society Publishers, 2003.

Allawi, Ali A. *The Occupation of Iraq: Winning the War, Losing the Peace.* Yale University Press, 2008.

Anderson, Liam, and Gareth Stansfield. *The Future of Iraq: Dictatorship, Democracy or Division.* Palgrave Macmillan, 2005.

Baker, James A. *The Iraq Study Group Report.* New York: Random House, 2006.

Bennis, Phyllis. *Ending the Iraq War: A Primer.* Olive Branch Press, 2008.

Bilmes, Linda J., and Joseph E. Stiglitz. *The Three Trillion Dollar War: The True Cost of the Iraq Conflict.* W. W. Norton, 2008.

Bremer, L. Paul, L. Paul Bremer, III, and Malcolm McConnell. *My Year in Iraq.* Simon & Schuster, 2006.

Buzzell, Colby. *My War: Killing Time in Iraq.* Putnam Adult, 2005.

Chandrasekaran, Rajiv. *Imperial Life in the Emerald City: Inside Iraq's Green Zone.* Vintage Books, 2007.

Clarke, Richard A. *Against All Enemies, Inside America's War on Terror.* New York: Free Press, 2004.

Coll, Steve. *Ghost Wars.* New York: Penguin Group, 2004.

Cordesman, Anthony, and Ahmed Hashim. *Iraq: Sanctions and Beyond (CSIS Middle East Dynamic Net Assessment).* Westview Press, 1997.

Dyer, Gwynne. *Ignorant Armies: Sliding into War in Iraq.* McClelland & Stewart, 2003.

El Shibiny, Mohamed. *The Threat of Globalization to Arab Islamic Culture.* Dorrance Publishing, 2005.

Fawn, Rick, and Raymond A. Hinnebusch. *The Iraq War: Causes and Consequences.* Lynne Rienner Publishers, 2006.

Feith, Douglas J. *War and Decision: Inside the Pentagon at the Dawn of the War on Terrorism.* New York: Harper, 2008.

Galbraith, Peter W. *The End of Iraq: How American Incompetence Created a War Without End.* New York: Simon & Schuster, 2006.

Gordon, Michael R., and Bernard E. Trainor. *Cobra II: The Inside Story of the Invasion and Occupation of Iraq.* New York: Pantheon Books, 2006.

Haddad, Yvonne, and Wadi Haddad. *Christian Muslim Encounters.* University Press of Florida, 1995.

Hayden, Tom. *Ending the War in Iraq.* New York: Akashic Books, 2007.

Hiro, Dilip. *Iraq: In the Eye of the Storm.* New York: Thunder's Mouth Press, 2002.

Isenberg, David. *Shadow Force: Private Security Contractors in Iraq*. Praeger Security International, 2008.

Johnson, Chalmers. *Nemesis: The Last Days of the American Republic*. New York: Metropolitan Books, 2006.

Keegan, John. *The Iraq War: The Military Offensive, from Victory in 21 Days to the Insurgent Aftermath*. Vintage, 2005.

Kimball, Charles. *When Religion Becomes Evil*. San Francisco: Harper Collins, 2003.

Kinzer, Stephen. *Overthrow: America's Century of Regime Change from Hawaii to Iraq*. Times Books, 2007.

Kirkpatrick, Jeane J. *Making War to Keep Peace*. Harper Collins, 2007.

Lewis, Bernard. *The Crisis of Islam: Holy War and Unholy Terror*. Random House Trade Paperbacks, 2004.

Nafziger, George, and Mark Walton. *Islam at War; A History*. Praeger Publishers, 2003.

Pollack, Kenneth. *The Threatening Storm: The Case for Invading Iraq*. Random House, 2002.

Rai, Milan, and Noam Chomsky. *War Plan Iraq: Ten Reasons Against War with Iraq*. W. W. Norton, 2002.

Ricks, Thomas E. *Fiasco: The American Military Adventure in Iraq*. Penguin Press, 2006.

Rivers, William, and Scott Ritter. *War on Iraq: What Team Bush Doesn't Want You to Know*. Context Books, 2002.

Schumacher, Gerry, and Steve Gansen. *A Bloody Business: America's War Zone Contractors and the Occupation of Iraq*. Zenith Press, 2006.

Schwartz, Michael. *War Without End: The Iraq War in Context*. Haymarket Books, 2008.

Tripp, Charles. *A History of Iraq*. Cambridge University Press, 2002.

Woodward, Bob. *State of Denial: Bush at War, Part III*. Simon & Schuster, 2007.

BIBLIOGRAPHY

"110 are killed in 2 days of bomb attacks in Iraq." *Herald Tribune*, October 2, 2005.

"14 killed in five explosions in Baghdad." Yahoo News, February 28, 2006.

"144 killed in series of bombings in Baghdad." *Herald Tribune*, November 24, 2006.

"80 Killed or Found Dead in Iraq; 2 U.S. Servicemen Killed." *Fox News*, October 30, 2006. http://www.foxnews.com/story/0,2933,226156,00.html.

Abdel-Latif, Omayma. "To vote or not to vote." *Al Ahram Weekly*, December 2–8, 2004. http://weekly.ahram.org.eg/2004/719/re6.htm.

Abdul-Zahra, Qassim, and Lee Keath. "2,660 Iraqi Civilians Killed in Sept." *Washington Post*, October 11, 2006.

"Abu Ghraib was 'animal House' at night." *CNN.com*, August 24, 2004. http://edition.cnn.com/2004/US/08/24/abughraib.report/index.html.

"Abu Ghraib's Shocking Photos." *Egyptian Gazette*, September 25, 2004.

"Abu Musab al-Zarqawi Killed in Bombing Raid." *Fox News*, June 8, 2006. http://www.foxnews.com/story/0,2933,198651,00.html.

Abul-Zahra, Qassim, Associated Press/AP Online. "Iraq unveils security measures for vote." Redorbit.com, October 7, 2005.

"Abuse sentence angers many Iraqis." *New York Times*, September 29, 2005. http://www.nytimes.com/2005/09/28/news/28iht-sentence.html.

"Accelerating Terrorism before Hand-Over Power to Iraqi New End Government." *Egyptian Gazette*, May 14, 2004.

Agence France-Presse. "$45m paid to Iraq kidnappers." *Aljazeera.net*, May 22, 2006. http://english.aljazeera.net/archive/2006/05/200849164548918885.html.

———. "Al Qaeda vows revenge for Zarqawi's death." *ABC News Online*, June 24, 2006.

———. "Nearly 6,000 civilians killed in Iraq in May, June: UN." *Chinadaily.com.cn*, July 18, 2006.

———. "U.S. soldiers charged with Iraq murders." *Aljazeera.net*, June 19, 2006.

———. "U.S. to shut down Abu Ghraib prison." *Aljazeera.net*, March 9, 2006.

———. "US politicians spar over Iraq strategy." *Aljazeera.net*, August 22, 2005.

———. "40,000 Iraqis to form shield in Baghdad." *Aljazeera.net*, May 27, 2005.

———. "Ahmadinejad wants US out of Iraq." *Aljazeera.net*, December 2, 2006.

———. "Al-Jaafari unveils Iraqi political agenda." *Aljazeera.net*, May 31, 2005. http://english.aljazeera.net/archive/2005/05/2008410113756267514.html.

———. "Allawi party not part of new Iraq cabinet." *Chinadaily.com.cn*, April 25, 2005.

———. "Al-Maliki intends to end sectarian rifts." *Aljazeera.net*, October 4, 2006.

————. "Al-Maliki plan to end sectarian rifts is unwelcome." *Aljazeera.net*, October 4, 2006.

————. "Al-Qaeda: Bush gambling in Iraq." *Aljazeera.net*, February 14, 2007.

————. "Al-Sadr 'rejects' Iraqi constitution." *Aljazeera.net*, February 19, 2006.

————. "Al-Zarqawi Declared War on Iraqi Shia." *Aljazeera.net*, September 14, 2005.

————. "Al-Zarqawi: We have Egyptian Envoy." *Aljazeera.net*, July 7, 2005.

————. "Arrested Iranians 'arming Iraqis.'" *Aljazeera.net*, January 14, 2007.

————. "Bakery workers kidnapped in Baghdad." *Aljazeera.net*, June 18, 2006. http://english.aljazeera.net/archive/2006/06/200849125552772972.html.

————. "Blix says Bush, Blair insincere salesmen on Iraq." *China Daily*, February 9, 2004. http://www.chinadaily.com.cn/english/doc/2004-02/09/content_304399.htm.

————. "British helicopter crashed." *Aljazeera.net*, May 7, 2006.

————. "Bush calls for new Iraq approach." *Aljazeera.net*, December 8, 2006.

————. "Bush Defends Stance on WMDs, Report Slams CIA for Iraq Intelligence Failures." *CNN.com*, July 10, 2004. http://edition.cnn.com/2004/ALLPOLITICS/07/10/senate.intelligence/index.html.

————. "Bush describing the delay in the constitution as critical." *Aljazeera.net*, August 16, 2005.

————. "Bush to veto Iraq pull out Bill." *Aljazeera.net*, March 24, 2007.

————. "Children die in Iraq wedding bombing." *Aljazeera.net*, November 1, 2006. http://english.aljazeera.net/archive/2006/11/200849163325380626.html.

————. "GI 'ordered to kill Iraq prisoners.'" *Aljazeera.net*, March 14, 2007. http://english.aljazeera.net/news/americas/2007/03/200852513136305823.html.

————. "Intense US pressure to finishing drafting the constitution." *Aljazeera.net*, August 16, 2005.

————. "Iran and Saudi pledge friendship." *Aljazeera.net*, March 4, 2007.

————. "Iran denies plans for Iraq summit." *Aljazeera.net*, November 27, 2006.

————. "Iraq armed groups set terms for truce." *Aljazeera.net*, June 29, 2006.

————. "Iraq delays federalism decision." *Aljazeera.net*, September 25, 2006.

————. "Iraq FM Slams Arab Stand." *Aljazeera.net*, March 26, 2006.

————. "Iraq Leaders in Cairo Demand Pullout Timetable." *Aljazeera.net*, November 21, 2005.

————. "Iraq PM moves to ban all militias." *Aljazeera.net*, May 31, 2006.

————. "Iraq PM rebukes Kurds over flag." *Aljazeera.net*, September 3, 2006.

————. "Iraq Shia leaders call for federal state." *Aljazeera.net*, August 12, 2005.

————. "Iraq war 'lost' says top democrat." *Aljazeera.net*, April 20, 2007. http://english.aljazeera.net/news/middleeast/2007/04/200852514292354268.html.

————. "Iraqi gov't sworn in amid wave of violence." *Chinadaily.com.cn*, May 4, 2005.

————. "Iraqi Kurd politicians say yes to Unity." *Aljazeera.net*, May 8, 2006.

————. "Iraqi MPs approve federalism." *Aljazeera.net*, October 11, 2006.

————. "Iraqi official expects security transfers." MWC.com, November 26, 2005.

————. "Iraqi tribal leaders sign pact of honor." *Aljazeera.net*, October 5, 2006.

————. "Iraqis 'pessimistic' about future." *Aljazeera.net*, March 19, 2007.

————. "Khalilzad: Success in Iraq Still Possible." *Aljazeera.net*, October 24, 2006.

————. "Kirkuk Arabs face relocation." *Aljazeera.net*, February 7, 2007.

————. "Kirkuk: The potential spark for civil war." *Aljazeera.net*, October 9, 2006.

————. "Kurds 'back' new Draft Iraq oil law." *Aljazeera.net*, February 25, 2007.

————. "Maliki: Haditha a terrible crime." *Aljazeera.net*, June 1, 2006.

————. "New Iraq oil bill." *Aljazeera.net*, March 29, 2007.

————. *"New US Envoy Nominated for Iraq."* *Aljazeera.net*, April 6, 2005. http:// english.aljazeera.net/archive/2005/04/20084101627674714.html.

————. "Report: Iran arming groups in Iraq." *Aljazeera.net*, December 18, 2006.

————. "Rice in surprise visit to Iraq." *Aljazeera.net*, May 15, 2005. http://english .aljazeera.net/archive/2005/05/200849163659595502.html.

————. "Saddam hanged at dawn." *Aljazeera.net*, October 27, 2007. http://english .aljazeera.net/news/middleeast/2006/12/2008525115436701440.html.

————. "Saddam Hussein Sentenced to Hang." *Aljazeera.net*, November 5, 2006. http://english.aljazeera.net/archive/2006/11/200849155416141647.html.

————. *"Saudi King Calls for Unity, Arab League Summit Meeting in Saudi Arabia."* *Aljazeera.net*, March 29, 2007.

————. "Saudi warns 'Interfering' Iran." *Aljazeera.net*, January 27, 2007.

————. "Security Regional Conference." *Aljazeera.net*, February 1, 2007.

————. "Shia pilgrims defy suicide attacks." *Aljazeera.net*, March 9, 2007. http:// english.aljazeera.net/news/middleeast/2007/03/2008525126589/64/2.html.

————. "Sistani urges end to Iraq 'bloodletting.'" *Aljazeera.net*, July 22, 2006.

————. "Sunni leaders set demands on Iraq Statute Body." *Arabnews.com*, June 8, 2005.

————. "Sunnis call to reject federalism." *Aljazeera.net*, August 16, 2005.

————. "Syria and Iran vow unity against USA." *Aljazeera.net*, February 19, 2007.

————. "Syria promises to stabilize Iraq." *Aljazeera.net*, March 8, 2007.

————. "Talabani: Armed groups support talks." *Aljazeera.net*, November 28, 2005.

————. "Timeline: Saddam trial." *Gulfnews.com*, December 29, 2006. http:// gulfnews.com/news/region/iraq/timeline-saddam-trial-1.153686.

————. "Turkey fears 'endless war' in Iraq." *Aljazeera.net*, January 29, 2007.

————. "U.S. detains scores in Baghdad sweep." *Aljazeera.net*, August 12, 2006. http://english.aljazeera.net/archive/2006/08/2008410103734418743.html.

————. "U.S. Officers Charged over Iraq Scam." *Aljazeera.net*, February 8, 2007.

————. "U.S. soldiers killed 'in rape revenge.'" *Aljazeera.net*, July 11, 2006.

————. "UN urges neighbors to aid Iraqis." *Aljazeera.net*, April 18, 2007.

————. "US envoy seeks talks with Iraq rebels." *Aljazeera.net*, November 29, 2005.

————. "US hunt foreign networks in Iraq." *Aljazeera.net*, January 16, 2007.

————. "US Iran talks possible in Regional meeting in Iraq." *Aljazeera.net*, March 1, 2007.

————. "US military weighs troop cuts in Iraq." *Aljazeera.net*, November 23, 2005.

————. "US officials pressed the Sunnis, Shias for ending the draft constitution." *Aljazeera.net*, August 28, 2005.

————. "US Senate backs Iraq deadline." *Aljazeera.net*, March 28, 2007.

―――. "US Senate: No Saddam, al-Qaeda link." *Aljazeera.net*, September 9, 2006. http://english.aljazeera.net/archive/2006/09/2008410103551590770.html.

―――. "US: Iraq troop cuts are an option." *Aljazeera.net*, June 28, 2006.

―――. "US-led forces Iraq mandate extended." *Aljazeera.net*, June 1, 2005.

―――." Iraq, world's second-largest oil reserves." *Aljazeera.net*, June 16, 2005.

―――. "Ex-CIA chief criticizes Iraq war." *Aljazeera.net*, April 28, 2007.

"Al Qaeda Warned Iraqis Not to Vote in Ramadi." *Egyptian Gazette*, December 14, 2005.

Al-Ansary, Khalid, and John O'Neil. "U.S. military displays other side of enemy." *New York Times*, May 4, 2006. http://www.nytimes.com/2006/05/04/world/africa/04iht-iraq.html.

Al Jazeera and Agencies. "Baghdad blast rattles UN chief." *Aljazeera.net*, March 23, 2007. http://english.aljazeera.net/news/middleeast/2007/03/2008525135835807327 .html.

―――. "Blair announces Iraq troop pullout." *Aljazeera.net*, February 21, 2007.

―――. "Foreign troops to quit Iraq mid 2006." *Aljazeera.net*, May 2, 2005.

―――. "Iraq Accuses Iran of Border Violations." *Aljazeera.net*, May 3, 2006.

―――. "Iraq Cabinet Formed." *Aljazeera.net*, April 28, 2005.

―――. "Iraq delays draft constitution vote." *Aljazeera.net*, August 23, 2005.

―――. "Scores killed in Baghdad university." *Aljazeera.net*, January 17, 2007. http:// english.aljazeera.net/news/middleeast/2007/01/200852513128132123.html.

―――. "Security Ring for Baghdad Planned." *Aljazeera.net*, May 27, 2005.

―――. "Survey indicated Iraqis in despair." *Aljazeera.net*, December 14, 2006.

―――. "U.S. Detains Top Iraqi Sunni Cleric." *Aljazeera.net*, June 24, 2006.

―――. "US general favours staying in Iraq." *Aljazeera.net*, November 16, 2006.

―――. "US House denounce Bush troop plan." *Aljazeera.net*, February 17, 2007.

―――. "US: Iraq doomed if new push fails." *Aljazeera.net*, February 11, 2007.

―――. "Zarqawi successor 'in Egypt jail.'" *Aljazeera.net*, July 6, 2006.

Al-Khairella, Mussab. "Maliki announces reconciliation plan to end Iraq's 'ugly picture.'" *The Independent*, June 26, 2006. http://www.independent.co.uk/news/ world/middle-east/maliki-announces-reconciliation-plan-to-end-iraqs-ugly -picture-405525.html.

"Allawi Repeats Call for U.S.-Led Troops to Stay." *Egyptian Gazette*, June 7, 2004.

"Allawi ultimatum to hand over foreign fighters from Fallujah." *Egyptian Gazette*, October 14, 2004.

Allbritton, Christopher. "View from Baghdad: How Zarqawi's Death may change the game." *Time.com*, June 8, 2006.

"Al-Maliki in surprise Ramadi visit." *Aljazeera.net*, March 13, 2007.

Al-Qaeda in Iraq. Wikipedia, http://en.wikipedia.org/wiki/Al-Qaeda_in_Iraq.

"Al-Qaeda in Iraq Announces New Leader. Or Do They?" *Your Word Press Blog*, December 29, 2008. http://www.panteonmemorialtowers.com/2008/12/.

"Al-Zarqawi trained insurgents." *Egyptian Gazette*, June 12, 2006.

"American fear regarding el-Jaafari." *Egyptian Mail*, April 16, 2005.

"Amr Moussa: Iraq Needs Arab Presence." *ArabNews.com*, June 27, 2005, http://www .arabicnews.com/ansub/Daily/Day/050627/2005062727.html.

"Annan Cited Prisoner Abuse in Iraq." *Egyptian Gazette*, September 22, 2004.

"Annan warns rule of law at risk." *CNN.com*, September 21, 2004. http://www.cnn.com/2004/US/09/21/united.nations/index.html.

"Annan: Iraq war a disaster for region." *Aljazeera.net*, September 15, 2006.

"Anti-war rally held in Washington." *BBC News*, September 24, 2005. http://news.bbc.co.uk/2/hi/americas/4278960.stm.

"Antiwar Voices Address March: Michael Moore, Jesse Jackson, Fernando Suarez, Charles Barron and More." *Democracy Now*, August 30, 2004. http://www.democracynow.org/2004/8/30/antiwar_voices_address_march_michael_moore.

"The Arab Committee on Iraq, Meeting in Jeddah." *Egyptian Gazette*, October 3, 2005.

"Arab League Chief Begins Iraq Reconciliation between Mission." *Egyptian Gazette*, October 21, 2005.

"Arab League Delegation Ambushed in Iraq." *ABC News Online*, October 11, 2005, http://www.abc.net.au/news/newsitems/200510/s1479079.htm.

"Arabs need to improve image says Al Chief." *Egyptian Gazette*, December 6, 2005.

"Assad: No peace without Syria and Iran." *Egyptian Gazette*, December 16, 2006.

Associated Press. "14 Iraqi policemen kidnapped, killed." *USA Today*, March 2, 2007. http://www.usatoday.com/news/world/iraq/2007-03-02-kidnapping_x.htm.

———. "Anti-War Protests." *Aljazeera.net*, January 12, 2007.

———. "Al Zarqawi death prompts attack warning." *Yahoo News*, June 11, 2006.

———. "Baghdad Airport Reopens." *Fox News*, September 10, 2005. http://www.foxnews.com/story/0,2933,168997,00.html.

———. "Britain may start pulling out of Iraq." Wcbstv.com, November 27, 2006.

———. "Briton abducted in Iraq." *The Independent*, September 16, 2004. http://www.independent.co.uk/news/world/middle-east/briton-abducted-in-iraq-546506.html.

———. "Bush, and Blair Acknowledge Iraq 'Setbacks.'" *Chinadaily.com.cn*, May 26, 2006.

———. "Bush Disappointed by Spanish PM's Decision on Iraq." *Fox News*, April 19, 2004. http://www.foxnews.com/story/0,2933,117506,00.html.

———. "Bush Expresses Solidarity with Pakistan." *Fox News*, March 5, 2006. http://www.foxnews.com/story/0,2933,186819,00.html.

———. "Bush: No Timetable for Iraq Withdrawal." Military.com, June 25, 2005.

———. "Bush Officials: No Big Move in Iraq Plan." *Yahoo News*, October 24, 2006.

———. "Excerpts from the Iraq Study Group Report." *NPR.org*, December 6, 2006, http://www.npr.org/templates/story/story.php?storyId=6586404.

———. "Global Terror Attacks Surged 25% in 2006." *Msnbc.com*, April 30, 2007. http://www.msnbc.msn.com/id/18399660/.

———. "Gunmen Kill 47 Iraqi Factory Workers." *Yahoo News*, February 23, 2006.

———. "Haditha lawyer criticizes U.S." *USA Today*, April 6, 2006. http://www.usatoday.com/news/world/iraq/2006-06-03-iraqi-condemns-probe_x.htm?csp=34.

———. "Head of Iraqi Governing Council Killed in Blast." *Fox News*, May 17, 2004. http://www.foxnews.com/story/0,2933,120090,00.htm.

———. "Iraqi Authorities: Al Qaeda in Iraq No. 2 Arrested." *Fox News*, September 3, 2006.

———. "Iraqi PM offers olive branch to insurgents." Ctv.ca, June 25, 2006.

———. "Iraqi Security a Key Topic at Bush Meeting with Iraq Prime Minister." *Yahoo News*, June 24, 2005.

———. "October U.S. Death Toll in Iraq Hits 100." *Yahoo News*, October 30, 2006.

———. "Powell doubts Iraqi weapons will be found." *msnbc.com*, September 14, 2004. http://www.msnbc.msn.com/id/6000809.

———. "Rice: Congress shouldn't micromanage war." *Washingtonpost.com*, February 25, 2007.

———. "Rumsfeld acknowledges U.S., insurgents met." *msnbc.com*, June 27, 2005. http://www.msnbc.msn.com/id/8359553/.

———. "Saudi cleric condemns U.S. consulate attack." *msnbc.com*, December 8, 2004. http://www.msnbc.msn.com/id/6657943/.

———. "Schroeder, Bush Meet at White House." *Fox News*, July 31, 2005. http://www.foxnews.com/story/0,2933,160796,00.html.

———. "Shiites push for British troops to leave." *Washingtonpost.com*, October 13, 2006.

———. "Suicide bomber kills 41 at Baghdad college." *msnbc.com*, February 25, 2007. http://www.msnbc.msn.com/id/17326397/.

———. "Thousands around globe call for end of war." *USAtoday.com*, March 20, 2006, http://www.usatoday.com/news/world/2006-03-20-war-protests_x.htm.

———. "Top Sunnis seek changes in constitution." *Chinadaily.com.cn*, August 28, 2005.

———. "U.S., Iraqi forces clash with militia insurgents." *Washingtonpost.com*, October 8, 2006.

———. "US envoy: Iraq constitution may change." *Fox News*, August 31, 2005. http://www.foxnews.com/story/0,2933,167652,00.html.

———. "US, Iran trade accusations at first talks." *Chinadaily.com.cn*, March 11, 2007.

———. "Iraq misses deadline for probe on torture allegations." *USA Today*, November 30, 2005.

Associated Press/AP Online. "Petraeus: Force will not solve Iraq." *Aljazeera.net*, March 9, 2007.

———. "Sunni group urges election participation." Redorbit.com, July 5, 2005.

———. "UK Prime Minister make surprise Baghdad visit." Redorbit.com, December 21, 2004.

"At least 56 Iraqis dead in new violence." *Yahoo News*, March 23, 2006.

"Attacks kill 31 in Iraq. Fear violence deepen sectarian division." *Egyptian Mail*, May 7, 2005.

"Baathists: 'Grave consequences' if Hussein's hanged." *CNN.com*, December 28, 2006. http://edition.cnn.com/2006/WORLD/meast/12/27/saddam.baath/index.html.

"Baghdad confirms Saddam's trial date." *Aljazeera.net*, September 8, 2005. http://english.aljazeera.net/archive/2005/09/20084915598241557.html.

"Baghdad Fears Rise of 'Iraqi Hitler.'" *CNN.com*, December 13, 2004. http://edition.cnn.com/2004/WORLD/meast/12/13/iraq.president/index.html.

"*Baghdad Governor Assassinated*." *CNN.com*, November 4, 2005.

"Baghdad judge shot dead in ambush." *BBC News*, January 25, 2005. http://news.bbc.co.uk/2/hi/middle_east/4204533.stm.

"Baghdad's security forces to be revamped." *USA Today*, May 11, 2006. http://www.usatoday.com/news/world/iraq/2006-05-11-iraq-security_x.htm.

Baker, Al. "Thousands Protest in Rome Against Bush Visit and Iraq War." *New York Times*, April 4, 2004. http://www.nytimes.com/2004/06/04/international/europe/04CND-ROME.html.

Baldor, Lolita C. "Gates: Bombs tie the Iran to Iraq extremists." *Washingtonpost.com*, February 9, 2007.

Banusiewicz, John D., American Forces Press Service. "Occupation Ends; Iraqis Take Charge of Country's Fate." Defense.gov, June 28, 2004, http://www.defense.gov/news/newsarticle.aspx?id=26190.

Barbash, Fred. "Bush: Iraq Part of 'Global Democratic Revolution.'" *Washington Post*, November 6, 2003. http://www.washingtonpost.com/wp-dyn/articles/A7991-2003Nov6.html.

Barett, Ted. "Retiring GOP congressman breaks ranks on Iraq." *CNN.com*, August 19, 2004. http://www.cnn.com/2004/ALLPOLITICS/08/18/congressman.iraq/index.html.

BBC. "Iran FM attacks US policy in Iraq." *BBC News*, May 4, 2007.

Beaumont, Peter. "Judge in Saddam trial axed in neutrality row." *The Guardian*, September 20, 2006. http://www.guardian.co.uk/world/2006/sep/20/iraq.peterbeaumont.

"Beyond Abu Ghraib: Detention and Torture in Iraq." Amnesty International Report, March 18, 2004.

"Big Voter Turnout Expected from Iraqis Abroad." *Egyptian Gazette*, January 18, 2005.

Biggs, Mathew. "Iraq worst disaster for US foreign policy-Albright." Reuters Alert-Net, February 23, 2007. http://www.alertnet.org/thenews/newsdesk/N22208041.htm.

"Bin Laden tells Sunnis to fight Shiites in Iraq." *CNN.com*, July 2, 2006.

Black, Ian. "Saudis make up 41% of foreign fighters in Iraq." *The Guardian*, November 23, 2007. http://www.guardian.co.uk/world/2007/nov/23/iraq.saudiarabia.

"Blair defiantly insists war right." *BBC News*, July 14, 2004. http://news.bbc.co.uk/2/hi/uk_news/politics/3893987.stm.

"Blast rips through Baghdad hotel." *BBC News*, March 18, 2004. http://news.bbc.co.uk/2/hi/middle_east/3521200.stm.

Blix, Hans. "A War of Utter Folly." *The Guardian*, March 20, 2008. http://www
.guardian.co.uk/commentisfree/2008/mar/20/iraq.usa.

"A bomber struck the offices of Kurdish party, Ansar al-Sunna claimed responsibility."
Egyptian Gazette, May 5, 2005.

Branigin, William. "Bush Warns Iran Against Action in Iraq." *Washingtonpost.com*,
January 30, 2007.

"British troops to be pulled out of Iraq by the middle of 2008." *Egyptian Gazette*,
March 8, 2006.

Bureau of International Information Programs. "Six Saudi Clerics Denounce Terrorist
Bombings in Saudi Arabia." *America.gov*, July 1, 2004. http://www.america.gov/
st/washfile-english/2004/July/20040701120455dmslahrellek0.834347.html.

Burns, John. "A Conversation on Tiptoes, Wary of Mines." *New York Times*, November
30, 2003. http://www.nytimes.com/2003/11/30/weekinreview/30BURN.html.

"Bush 'I have never ordered Torture.'" *CNN.com*, June 23, 2004. http://edition.cnn
.com/2004/ALLPOLITICS/06/22/rumsfeld.memo/index.html.

"Bush: I'd rather be right than popular." *CNN.com*, July 9, 2006. http://www.cnn
.com/2006/POLITICS/07/06/bush.lkl/.

"Bush in Europe for international support. Attending the D-day 60 years." *CNN.com*,
May 5, 2004.

"Bush, Iraq Dominate EU Summit." *CNN.com*, November 6, 2004.

"Bush: Iraqis 'Have Their Country Back.'" *CNN.com*, June 28, 2004. http://edition
.cnn.com/2004/ALLPOLITICS/06/28/bush.blair/.

"Bush Outlines Iraq Transition." *CNN.com*, May 25, 2004.

"Bush rebuts critics of Iraq policies." *USA Today*, August 24, 2005. http://www
.usatoday.com/news/washington/2005-08-24-bush-iraq_x.htm.

"Bush says critics are rewriting war history." *Herald Tribune*, November 12–13,
2005.

"Bush wishes Hussein execution 'more dignified.'" January 4, 2007. *CNN.com*, http://
edition.cnn.com/2007/WORLD/meast/01/04/iraq.main/.

"Bush's approval rate falls to 28 percent: report." Reuters, May 6, 2007.

Butler, Nicola. "Deep Divisions over Iraq at NATO's Istanbul Summit." *The Acronym
Institute for Disarmament Diplomacy*. Issue No. 78, July/August 2004. http://www
.acronym.org.uk/dd/dd78/78news01.htm.

Caroll, Rory. "Iraq bombings and shootings leave 150 dead." *The Guardian*, September 15, 2005. http://www.guardian.co.uk/world/2005/sep/15/iraq.rorycarroll.

Carpenter, Ted Galen. "Iraq 2004, Vietnam 1964." Cato Institute, April 27, 2004.
http://www.cato.org/pub_display.php?pub_id=2629.

Chan, Sewell. "U.S. Civilians Mutilated in Iraq Attack." *Washington Post*, April 1,
2004.

Chandrasekaran, Rajiv. "Iraqi Council Agrees on Terms of Interim Constitution."
Washington Post, March 1, 2004. http://www.washingtonpost.com/ac2/wp-dyn/
A17535-2004Feb29.

Chandrasekaran, Rajiv. "Iraqi Council Agrees to Ask UN for Help." *Washington
Post*, March 18, 2004. http://www.washingtonpost.com/wp-dyn/articles/A2866
-2004Mar17.html.

Chang, Anita. "Saddam execution video draws criticism." Redorbit.com, January 2, 2007. http://www.redorbit.com/news/general/786418/saddam_execution_video _draws_criticism/index.html.

Chirac, Jacques. Interview. *BBC 2 Newsnight,* November 17, 2004.

Chossudovsky, Michel. "Who is Abu Musab Al-Zarqawi?" *Centre for Research on Globalisation,* June 11, 2004. http://www.globalresearch.ca/articles/CHO405B.html.

"Church bombs: Top insurgent blamed." *CNN.com,* August 2, 2004. http://edition .cnn.com/2004/WORLD/meast/08/02/iraq.main/index.html.

"The civilizing process." *Al Ahram Weekly,* November 29–December 5, 2001. http:// weekly.ahram.org.eg/2001/562/op2.htm.

Clark, Wesley. "The Real Battle Winning in Fellujah is just the beginning." *Washington Post,* November 14, 2004. http://www.washingtonpost.com/wp-dyn/articles/ A47034-2004Nov12.html.

Clein, Joe. "Sadam's revenge." *Time,* September 18, 2005. http://www.time.com/ time/magazine/article/0,9171,1106307-9,00.html.

"Clinton: US cannot isolate itself to fight terror." *Daily Times,* August 10, 2005. http://www.dailytimes.com.pk/default.asp?page=story_10-8-2005_pg4_6.

CNN Late Edition with Wolf Blitzer. *CNN.com,* December 3, 2006. http:// transcripts.cnn.com/TRANSCRIPTS/0612/03/le.01.html.

CNN Sunday Morning. "Polls close in Iraq; Turnout estimated at above 70 percent." *CNN.com,* January 30, 2005. http://edition.cnn.com/TRANSCRIPTS/0501/30/ sm.02.html.

———. "Blair in Iraq: He gives no timetable for withdrawal." *CNN.com,* May 22, 2006.

———. "Bush: Iraq crucial in war against terror." *CNN.com,* October 7, 2005.

CNN. "Bush: U.S. shifting tactics in Iraq War." *CNN.com,* October 26, 2006.

———. "Bush: U.S. to stay in Iraq till war is won." *CNN.com,* December 31, 2005.

———. "Cheney: Iraq will be 'enormous success story.'" *CNN.com,* June 24, 2005. http://edition.cnn.com/2005/POLITICS/06/23/cheney.interview/.

———. "General: US could start Iraq pullout in Spring." *CNN.com,* July 27, 2005.

———. "Gunmen in Iraq kill top Shiite cleric's aid." *CNN.com,* May 20, 2005.

———. "Milestone elections begin in Iraq." *CNN.com,* January 30, 2005. http:// edition.cnn.com/2005/WORLD/meast/01/29/iraq.main/index.html.

———. "Our pride, by first Iraqis to vote." *CNN.com,* January 31, 2005. http:// edition.cnn.com/2005/WORLD/asiapcf/01/28/iraq.firstvoter/index.html.

———. "Poll: 58 percent want Iraq withdrawal by 2008 or sooner." *CNN.com,* March 13, 2007.

———. "Purported bin Laden tape endorses al-Zarqawi." *CNN.com,* December 27, 2004. http://edition.cnn.com/2004/WORLD/meast/12/27/binladen.tape/index. html.

———. "Report: British Army chief calls for Iraq pullout." *CNN.com,* October 13, 2006.

———. "Sunni Iraqis announce political coalition." *CNN.com,* May 22, 2005.

———. "Talabani predicts U.S. exits in two years." *CNN.com,* April 10, 2005.

————. "World leaders praise voter courage." *CNN.com*, January 31, 2005. http:// edition.cnn.com/2005/WORLD/meast/01/30/iraq.internatreax/index.html.

"Colin Powell says Iraq in a 'civil war.'" *CNN.com*, November 29, 2006.

"Conclusion of Madrid Conference on Iraq." The World Bank Group, October 27, 2003, http://web.worldbank.org/WBSITE/EXTERNAL/NEWS/0,,contentMD K:20134476~menuPK:34457~pagePK:34370~piPK:34424~theSitePK:4607,00 .html.

"Condoleezza Rice calls for a new Middle East." *Egyptian Gazette*, April 17, 2005.

"Conference for Iraq in Brussels, June 22, 2005." *Egyptian Mail*, June 2, 2005.

"Confession of an Iraqi Prisoner." *Egyptian Gazette*, May 7, 2004.

"Constitution vote nears." *Egyptian Gazette*, August 25, 2005.

Cowell, Alan. "Blair vows to stay the course in Iraq." *New York Times*, September 28, 2005. http://www.nytimes.com/2005/09/27/world/europe/27iht-britain.html.

Coyne, Tom. "U.S. revokes visa for Muslim scholar." Campus Watch, August 24, 2004. http://www.campus-watch.org/article/id/1250.

CQ Transcriptions Wire. "In the State of the Union, 2006-03-05 war in Iraq." *Washington Post*, January 31, 2006.

Daily Mail. "Government stunned by Army chief's Iraq blast." Dailymail.com.uk, October 13, 2006.

Daniel, Douglass. "Bush's Words on Iraq Echo LBJ in 1967." *USA Today*, September 21, 2005. http://www.usatoday.com/news/washington/2005-09-21-bush-vietnam _x.htm.

Dawood, Khaled. "Pushing regional reform." *Al Ahram Weekly Online*, August 21–27, 2003, Issue No. 652. http://weekly.ahram.org.eg/2003/652/re11.htm.

"Demands for setting a timetable for withdrawal of troops in Iraq." *Al-Ahram Weekly*, April 14, 2005.

"Dozens of new Iraqi soldiers found dead." *CNN.com*, October 25, 2004. http:// edition.cnn.com/2004/WORLD/meast/10/24/iraq.main/index.html.

"Draft U.N. resolution on Iraq." *msnbc.com*, May 24, 2004. http://www.msnbc.msn .com/id/5052147/.

"The election transformed once oppressed Shiites and Kurds into the holder of power." *Egyptian Gazette*, May 10, 2005.

El-Shawa, Masin. "Cost of Iraqi war." *Egyptian Mail*, May 31, 2005.

Elsner, Alan. "Iraq the most expensive war in 60 years, report says." *Sydney Morning Herald*, September 1, 2005. http://www.smh.com.au/news/world/iraq-the-most -expensive-war-in-60-years-report-says/2005/08/31/1125302633906.html.

"Establishment of Islamic Iraqi State." *Herald Tribune*, October 16, 2006.

"Europe-wide network enlists fighters for Iraq." *Herald Tribune*, December 7, 2003.

"Excerpts from the president's address on Iraq." *CNN.com*, June 28, 2005. www.cnn .com/2005/POLITICS/06/28/bush.speech/index.html.

"Excerpts: Annan interview." *BBC News*, September 16, 2004. http://news.bbc .co.uk/2/hi/middle_east/3661640.stm.

"Execution of Iraqi leader Saddam a crime, says Vatican top justice official." *Catholic Online*, December 29, 2006. http://www.catholic.org/international/ international_story.php?id=22526.

"Explosion Hits Iraqi Parliament, 2 Dead." *AP Online*, April 12, 2007.

"Ex-PM: Abuse as bad as Saddam era." *CNN.com*, November 27, 2005. http://edition.cnn.com/2005/WORLD/meast/11/27/iraq.allawi/index.html.

"Fallujah under Siege." *Egyptian Gazette*, April 9, 2004.

"Fast Facts: After Iraq's Elections." *Fox News*, January 28, 2005. http://www.foxnews.com/story/0,2933,145668,00.html.

Feller, Ben. "Obama sets firm date to end Iraq war he inherited." *Fox News*, February 28, 2009.

———. "Bush: Iraq Withdrawal Would Spawn Danger." *USAToday.com*, May 4, 2007.

"Fighting Erupts in Baghdad After Verdict." *Aljazeera.net*, November 5, 2006. http://english.aljazeera.net/archive/2006/11/200849144854495186.html.

Filkins, Dexter. "Qaeda Video Vows Iraq Defeat for 'Crusader' U.S." *New York Times*, April 26, 2006. http://www.nytimes.com/2006/04/26/world/middleeast/26zarqawi.html?ex=1303704000&en=a32a19dfa9f75419&ei=5088.

———. "U.S. Transfers Power to Iraq 2 Days Early." *New York Times*, June 29, 2004. http://www.nytimes.com/2004/06/29/international/middleeast/29IRAQ.html.

"Final tally of 15 December 2005 election in Iraq." *Washington Times*, February 11, 2006.

"First Iraq votes cast in poll as Arab League urges turnout." *Egyptian Gazette*, December 13, 2005.

"France's Chirac Says Iraq War Caused U.N. Crisis." *Al Jazeerah*, September 23, 2003. http://www.aljazeerah.info/News.

Frankel, Glenn, and Rajiv Chandrasekaran. "45 Minutes: Behind the Blair Claim." *Washington Post*, February 29, 2004. http://www.washingtonpost.com/ac2/wp-dyn/A15697-2004Feb28.

Galbraith, Peter W. "The case for dividing Iraq." *Time*, November 13, 2006.

Gardner, Kathryn L. "Fighting Terrorism the FATF Way." *Encyclopedia Britannica*, July 2007. http://www.britannica.com/bps/additionalcontent/18/26374870/Fighting-Terrorism-the-FATF-Way.

Gelb, Leslie. "The Three State Solution." *New York Times*, November 25, 2003. http://www.cfr.org/publication/6559/threestate_solution.html.

"General calling for speeding up political process in Iraq." *Egyptian Gazette*, April 26, 2005.

George, Nirmala. "Tens of Thousands Protest Bush India Visit." Truthout, March 1, 2006. http://www.truthout.org/article/tens-thousands-protest-bush-india-visit.

Goler, Wendell, and Liza Porteus. "Bush: No Link between Iraq, Sept. 11 Attacks." *Fox News*, September 17, 2003. http://www.foxnews.com/story/0,2933,97527,00.html.

Gordon, Michael R., and Dexter Filkins. "Hezbollah Said to Help Shiite Army in Iraq." *New York Times*, November 28, 2006.

Graff, James. Interview with PM Zaptero. "I do not want to be a great leader." *Time*, September 19, 2004. http://www.time.com/time/magazine/article/0,9171,901040927-699350,00.html.

"Group of lawmakers proposed a plan to withdraw US troops from Iraq." *Egyptian Gazette*, June 24, 2005.

"Guide: Armed groups in Iraq." *BBC News*, August 15, 2006. http://news.bbc .co.uk/2/hi/middle_east/4268904.stm.

Halaby, Jamal. "Jordan wages all-out war on militants." *Pittsburgh Post-Gazette*, November 25, 2005. http://news.google.com/newspapers?nid=1129&dat=20051 125&id=d5YNAAAAIBAJ&sjid=7XADAAAAIBAJ&pg=6670,2902233.

Hamzeh, Alia Shukri. "King asks Bakhit to form gov't." *Jordan Times*, November 25, 2005. http://www.jordanembassyus.org/11252005001.htm.

Harding, Luke, and Michael Howard. "Blasts Shake Iraq Conference." *The Guardian*, August 16, 2004, http://www.guardian.co.uk/world/2004/aug/16/iraq .lukeharding.

Hellerstein, Alvin K. Federal District Court, U.S. District Court Southern District of New York. "Opinion and Order Granting in Part and Denying in Part Motions for Partial Summary Judgment." The National Security Archive, http://www.gwu .edu/~nsarchiv/news/20060313/aOrder092905.pdf.

Hendawi, Hamza. "Guns will not solve the problem of Iraq." *nysun.com*, June 8, 2005.

———. "Iraqis vote in constitutional referendum." Redorbit.com, October 15, 2005.

———. "Diplomat Cites U.S. 'Stupidity' in Iraq." Associated Press, October 22, 2006.

Hider, James. "U.S. reporter murdered in Iraq had written his own epitaph." *Times Online*, August 4, 2005. http://www.timesonline.co.uk/tol/news/world/iraq/ article551336.ece.

Hoge, Warren. "UN Renews Mandate for U.S.-Led Iraq Force, Measures Call for Review in 6 Months." *Herald Tribune*, November 9, 2005.

"A Hopeful Day." *New York Sun*, December 15, 2003. http://www.nysun.com/ editorials/a-hopeful-day/78097/.

"How the constitution be defeated." *Egyptian Gazette*, October 18, 2005.

Howard, Michael. "Iraqi Council Agrees Interim Constitution." *The Guardian*, March 2, 2004, http://www.guardian.co.uk/world/2004/mar/02/iraq.michaelhoward.

———. "Zarqawi group uses website to promise new attacks." *The Guardian*, June 12, 2006. http://www.guardian.co.uk/world/2006/jun/12/alqaida.iraq.

"Howard dismisses former public servants' criticism." *ABC News Online*, August 9, 2004. http://www.abc.net.au/news/newsitems/200408/s1171439.htm.

"Human rights group, Amnesty International saying 14,000 detainees in Iraq without charges." *CNN.com*, March 7, 2006.

Hunt, Terence. "Bush Unsatisfied with Iraq War Progress." Redorbit.com, October 25, 2006.

———. "Bush Unsatisfied with Iraq War Progress." *Fox News*, October 25, 2006.

Hurst, Steven R. "Iraqi militia expressing siege mentality." *Sfgate.com*, January 18, 2007.

"Identity of US informer remains $45 million question." *The Sydney Morning Herald*, July 27, 2003, http://www.smh.com.au/articles/2003/07/26/1059084268872 .html.

"Iran to expand military and economic ties with Iraq." *Egyptian Mail*, January 30, 2007.

Iraq—Interim Constitution. ICL Documents, March 8, 2004. http://www.servat .unibe.ch/law/icl/iz00000_.html.

"Iraq 'Hostage' to Lawlessness." *Egyptian Gazette*, July 26, 2004.

"Iraq approves final draft of new constitution." *Egyptian Gazette*, September 19, 2005.

"Iraq Cabinet Structure." *Egyptian Gazette*, April 29, 2005.

"Iraq Calls for US Withdrawal." *Egyptian Gazette*, July 23, 2006.

"Iraq Country Analysis Brief." EIA.com, March 2004, http://usiraq.procon.org/ sourcefiles/eiacountryanalysis.pdf.

"Iraq devolves into 'civil war.'" *CNN.com*, July 21, 2006.

"Iraq Donors Pledge Fresh Resolve." *BBC News*, October 14, 2004, http://news.bbc .co.uk/2/hi/middle_east/3743482.stm.

"Iraq Forms Election Board, Asks U.S. Troops to Stay." *Egyptian Gazette*, June 5, 2005.

"Iraq growing more like Vietnam." *CNN.com*, August 19, 2005. http://www.cnn .com/2005/POLITICS/08/18/hagel.iraq/.

"Iraq hawk turned dove comes home a puzzle." *Herald Tribune*, November 23, 2005.

"Iraq Looms as Top Issue in 1st Bush-Kerry Debate." VOANews.com, September 30, 2004. http://www1.voanews.com/english/news/a-13-a-2004-09-30-48 -1-6899047.html.

"Iraq mosque struck by car bomber." *BBC News*, September 16, 2005. http://news .bbc.co.uk/2/hi/middle_east/4251390.stm.

"Iraq PM rebuffs call to quit." *Egyptian Gazette*, April 2, 2006.

"Iraq political crises deepens." *Egyptian Gazette*, April 18, 2006.

"Iraq Sunni group meets US official over poll boycott." *Egyptian Gazette*, January 11, 2005.

"Iraq to neighbors: Stop harboring terrorists." *CNN.com*, July 4, 2006. http://www .cnn.com/2006/WORLD/europe/07/03/monday/index.html.

"Iraq war 'illegal,' UN's Annan says." September 16, 2004. CBC, http://www.cbc.ca/ world/story/2004/09/16/annan040916.html.

"Iraq war 'worst foreign policy mistake in U.S. history.'" *CNN.com*, February 19, 2007. http://www.cnn.com/2007/POLITICS/02/18/reid.iraq/index.html.

"'Iraq war illegal,' says Annan." *BBC News*, September 16, 2004. http://news.bbc .co.uk/2/hi/3661134.stm.

"Iraq Warns Neighbors to Stay Out" (Conference). *Aljazeera.net*, March 11, 2007.

"Iraq. In: Amnesty International Report 2004." Amnesty International USA. http:// www.amnestyusa.org/document.php?id=758A1EBE5BB6C22480256E9E005A9 9DF&lang=e.

"Iraq's constitution writers face formidable task." *Egyptian Mail*, March 5, 2005.

"Iraq's New Parliament sworn in." *Yahoo News*, March 14, 2006.

"Iraqi Civilian Death Toll 'up to 20,000.'" *The Times*, January 30, 2004.

"Iraqi Construction Funds Go to Security." *Washington Times*, February 9, 2006, http://www.washingtontimes.com/news/2006/feb/09/20060209-124325 -7786r/.

"Iraqi Elections 2005." *Al-Ahram Weekly*, January 27, 2005.

"Iraqi general killed in ambush." *CNN.com*, March 7, 2006. http://edition.cnn .com/2006/WORLD/meast/03/06/iraq.main/index.html.

"Iraqi Government Formed." *Egyptian Gazette*, April 29, 2005.

"Iraqi guerrillas shot down Bulgarian plane killing 6 Americans." *Egyptian Gazette*, April 22, 2005.

"Iraqi Guerrillas Threaten to Slay Saddam Lawyers." *The Egyptian Mail*, July 10, 2004.

Iraqi Insurgency Groups. Global Security.org. http://www.globalsecurity.org/military/ ops/iraq_insurgency.htm.

"Iraqi insurgents turn against 'out of control' Saudi al-Qaeda fighters." *Sunday Telegraph*, May 30, 2004. http://www.telegraph.co.uk/news/worldnews/middleeast/ iraq/1463223/Iraqi-insurgents-turn-against-out-of-control-Saudi-al-Qaeda -fighters.html.

"Iraqi Interim Government." *CNN.com*, April 1, 2004.

"Iraqi Interim President: Insurgents Will Be Gone in a Year." *CNN.com*, December 9, 2004. http://edition.cnn.com/2004/WORLD/meast/12/08/iraq.interim.president/.

"Iraqi Leader Talks on US Timeline." *Herald Tribune*, October 25, 2006.

"Iraqi PM says he refused U.S. request to delay execution." January 10, 2007. *CNN .com*, http://edition.cnn.com/2007/WORLD/meast/01/09/maliki.hussein/index .html.

"Iraqi protesters: 'No, no to America.'" *CNN.com*, April 9, 2005. http://edition.cnn .com/2005/WORLD/meast/04/09/iraq.main/.

"Iraqi referendum ends with little bloodshed." *Egyptian Gazette*, October 16, 2005.

"Iraqi violence claims nearly 20 lives, children among dead." *USA Today*, February 15, 2006. http://www.usatoday.com/news/world/iraq/2006-02-15-iraq-bombs_x .htm.

"Iraqi, US forces to rescue Shiite hostages." *Egyptian Gazette*, April 18, 2004.

"Iraqis furious at 'lenient' Abu Ghraib abuse sentence." *The Times*, September 28, 2005. http://www.timesonline.co.uk/tol/news/world/iraq/article572264.ece.

"Iraqis Hope for Better Security, Real Sovereignty." *CNN.com*, June 28, 2004.

"Iraqis Ready to Vote on New Constitution." *Egyptian Gazette*, October 14,2005.

"Iraqis Take Legal Custody of Saddam, and 11 Others." *CNN.com*, June 30, 2004. http://edition.cnn.com/2004/WORLD/meast/06/30/iraq.saddam/index .html?iref=allsearch.

"Islamist gunmen threaten to behead Saddam lawyers." *The Sydney Morning Herald*, July 9, 2004. http://www.smh.com.au/articles/2004/07/08/1089000296489 .html.

IslamOnline.net and News Agencies. "Iraqi Sunnis Reject Slam-dunked Constitution." *IslamOnline.net*, August 24, 2005. http://www.islamonline.net/English/News/2005-08/24/article05.shtml.

"It was a mistake to launch the war (congressman)." *Time*, August 30, 2004.

"Jaafari (Prime Minister) was never far from Iraq, despite a long exile." *Egyptian Mail*, February 26, 2005.

"Jaafari rejects US sectarian warning." *Egyptian Gazette*, February 22, 2006.

"Jaafari under US pressure to forge a national unity government." *Egyptian Gazette*. February 27, 2006.

Jamaat Ansar al-Sunna. Wikipedia, http://en.wikipedia.org/wiki/Jamaat_Ansar _al-Sunna.

"Japanese PM announces troop withdrawal from Iraq." *Fox News*, June 20, 2006. http://www.foxnews.com/story/0,2933,200214,00.html.

Jehl, Douglas. "Skeptic may take over Iraq Arms hunt." *New York Times*, January 23, 2004. http://www.nytimes.com/2004/01/23/world/skeptic-may-take-over-iraq-arms-hunt.html.

———. "The Beheading: C.I.A. Says Berg's Killer Was Very Probably Zarqawi." *New York Times*, May 14, 2004. http://www.nytimes.com/2004/05/14/politics/14ZARQ.html.

———. "Warned Bush Team About Intelligence Doubts." *New York Times*, November 6, 2005. http://www.nytimes.com/2005/11/06/politics/06intel.ready.html.

Johnson, Ed. "Gulf States Back U.S. Security Plan for Iraq After Rice Talks." Bloomberg.com, January 17, 2007. http://www.bloomberg.com/apps/news?pid =20601103&sid=aJmm81u7NRok.

"Joint statement between the United States of America and the Republic of Indonesia." The White House, October 22, 2003. http://georgewbush-whitehouse .archives.gov/news/releases/2003/10/.

"Judge throws Saddam out of court." *BBC News*, October 11, 2006. http://news.bbc .co.uk/2/hi/middle_east/6036787.stm.

Karadsheh, Jomana. "Study: War blamed for 655,000 Iraqi deaths." *CNN.com*, October 11, 2006. http://www.cnn.com/2006/WORLD/meast/10/11/iraq.deaths/.

Karouny, Miriam. "Iraq calls on neighbours to help end violence." Reuters.com, March 10, 2007.

———. "Interview-Iraq Will Urge U.S., Iran Not to Use It as Pawn." Alertnet.org, March 9, 2007.

"Karzai: Send NATO troops now." *CNN.com*, June 29, 2004. http://edition.cnn .com/2004/WORLD/europe/06/29/turkey.bush/index.html.

Khalilzad, Zalmay. Interview with Dan Bartlett. CNN Late Edition with Wolf Blitzer, October 1, 2006.

King, John, and Alessio Vinci. "Bush to leave Italy, head for France." *CNN.com*, June 4, 2004. http://www.cnn.com/2004/WORLD/europe/06/04/bush.italy/index .html.

"The Kingdom of Saudi Arabia Public Statements by Senior Officials and Religious Scholars Condemning Extremism and Promoting Moderation." Saudi Embassy

Files, November 6–7, 2008. The Royal Embassy of Saudi Arabia. http://www
.saudiembassy.net/files/PDF/Reports/Extremism_Report_11-07-08_final.pdf.

Klatell, James M. "3 U.S. Soldiers Charged With Murder." *CBS News*, June 19, 2006.
http://www.cbsnews.com/stories/2006/06/19/iraq/main1729623.shtml.

Knickmeyer, Ellen. "Talabani Offers Amnesty to Insurgents." *Washington Post*, April
7, 2005.

Knowlton, Brian. "Legislators Press Bush to Speed Iraqi Vote." *Herald Tribune*, May
19, 2004.

Kole, William J. "World Opinion Divided on Saddam Sentence." Redorbit.com,
November 6, 2006. http://www.redorbit.com/news/general/719681/world
_opinion_divided_on_saddam_sentence/index.html.

Kristof, Nicholas D. "Iraq: Strategizing the Exit." *Herald Tribune*, November 12–14,
2005.

"Kurdish Leader Rejects Iraq Report." AP Online, December 8, 2006.

"Lawyers of Saddam boycott tribunal." *Egyptian Gazette*, October 17, 2005.

Le Quesne, Nicolas. "Trying to bridge a great divide." *Time*, December 11, 2000.
http://www.time.com/time/innovators/spirituality/profile_ramadan.html.

"Leading Muslim Scholar Tariq Ramadan Denied U.S. Visa to Teach at Notre Dame."
Democracy Now, September 13, 2004. http://www.democracynow.org/2004/9/13/
leading_muslim_scholar_tariq_ramadan_denied.

Leicester, John, and Omar Sinan. "Al-Qaida joins Algerians against France." *Fox
News*, September 15, 2006. http://www.foxnews.com/wires/2006Sep15/0,4670,
FranceAlQaidaVideo,00.html.

Leinwand, Donna. "Muslims see new opposition to building mosques since 9/11."
USA Today, March 9, 2004. http://www.usatoday.com/news/religion/2004-03
-08-mosque-opposition_x.htm.

Leung, Rebecca. "Abuse Of Iraqi POWs By GIs Probed." *CBS News*, April 28,
2004. http://www.cbsnews.com/stories/2004/04/27/60II/main614063.shtml?tag
=contentMain;contentBody.

Linzer, Dafna. "Poll Shows Growing Arab Rancor at U.S." *Washington Post*, July 23,
2004. http://www.washingtonpost.com/wp-dyn/articles/A7080-2004Jul22.html.

MacAskill, Ewen. "Annan rues Iraq oil-for-food plan." *The Guardian*, September 6,
2005. http://www.guardian.co.uk/world/2005/sep/06/oil.iraq.

Macdonald, Alastair, and Aseel Kami. "Baghdad death squads kill 60, bombs kill 22."
Infowars.com, September 13, 2006.

"Major attack on Iraq 'rebel town.'" *BBC News*, September 10, 2005. http://news
.bbc.co.uk/2/hi/middle_east/4232084.stm.

Malone, Scott. "France's Villepin calls for 2008 Iraq troop exit." Reuters.com, March
17, 2007. http://uk.reuters.com/article/idUKN1625326820070317.

"Many detained in Chile protests." *BBC News*, November 17, 2004. http://news.bbc
.co.uk/2/hi/americas/4020801.stm.

Marsh, Alphonso Van, and Robin Oakley. "Bush, NATO focus on Iraq." *CNN.com*,
June 28, 2004. http://edition.cnn.com/2004/WORLD/europe/06/27/turkey
.bush/index.html.

Mazzetti, Mark. "Spy Agencies Say Iraq War Worsens Terrorism Threat." *New York Times*, September 24, 2006. http://query.nytimes.com/gst/fullpage.html.

McElroy, Damien. "Mullah named as suspect for Turkey blasts." *Telegraph*, December 7, 2003. http://www.telegraph.co.uk/news/worldnews/europe/turkey/1448767/Mullah-named-as-suspect- for-Turkey-blasts.html.

McFeatters, Ann. "Kennedy-Rumsfeld showdown illustrates Iraq dilemma." *Desert News*, June 24, 2005. http://www.deseretnews.com/article/1,5143,600143934,00.html.

McGirk, Tim. "Collateral Damage or Civilian Massacre in Haditha?" *Time*, March 19, 2006. http://www.time.com/time/world/article/0,8599,1174649-4,00.html.

McLaughlin, Eliott C. "Activist Sheehan arrested in House gallery." *CNN.com*, February 1, 2006. http://www.cnn.com/2006/POLITICS/01/31/sheehan.arrest/index.html.

Meek, James Gordon. "War May Take Decade.—Iraq Must Win on Its Own—Rumsfeld." *Nydailynews.com*, June 27, 2005. http://www.nydailynews.com/archives/news/2005/06/27/2005-06-27_war_may_take_decade__iraq_mu.html.

"Meeting of International Donors in Tokyo." *CNN.com*, October 15, 2004.

Miklaszewski, Jim. "U.S. to boost Iraq troop strength." *msnbc.com*, November 29, 2004. http://www.msnbc.msn.com/id/6613194/.

"Militants Behead American Hostage in Iraq." *Fox News*, May 11, 2004. http://www.foxnews.com/story/0,2933,119615,00.html.

"Militants down U.S. helicopter in Iraq, killing two." *New York Times*, May 15, 2006. http://www.nytimes.com/2006/05/15/world/africa/15iht-web.0515iraq.html.

"Mixed Reaction to Verdict." *Aljazeera.net*, November 5, 2006. http://english.aljazeera.net/archive/2006/11/20084913437807214.html.

Moore, Matthew. "'Muslim Massacre' video game condemned for glamorizing slaughter of Arabs." *Telegraph*, September 10, 2008. http://www.telegraph.co.uk/news/uknews/2776951/Muslim-Massacre-video-game-condemned-for-glamorising-slaughter-of-Arabs.html.

"Morgue's toll for April in Baghdad: 1,091 victims." *CNN.com*, May 10, 2006. http://edition.cnn.com/2006/WORLD/meast/05/10/iraq.main/index.html.

Murphy, Jarrett. "Bush Will Defend Iraq War to U.N." *CBS News*, September 22, 2003. http://www.cbsnews.com/stories/2003/09/23/iraq/main574646.shtml.

"Musharraf: Iraq war makes world more dangerous." *CNN.com*, September 26, 2006. http://www.cnn.com/2006/WORLD/asiapcf/09/26/musharraf.terror/index.html.

Nakhoul, Samia. "Iraq Revives Sunni-Shia Tensions among Neighbours." *Dawn.com*, October 5, 2005, http://www.dawn.com/2005/10/05/fea.htm#.

Nasraw, Salah. "Arab League Plans to Open Office in Iraq." *Associated Press*, March 4, 2006.

"A Nation Challenged: President Bush's Address on Terrorism before a Joint Meeting of Congress." *New York Times*, September 21, 2001. http://www.nytimes.com/2001/09/21/us/nation-challenged-president-bush-s-address-terrorism-before-joint-meeting.html.

"NATO Agrees to Train Iraqi Forces." *CNN.com*, June 28, 2004.

"NBC's 'Meet the Press' Interview with President Bush." Center for American Progress, February 8, 2004, http://www.americanprogress.org/issues/kfiles/b28200.html.

"New government complete with key security jobs." *Egyptian Gazette*, June 9, 2006.

"The New Interim Government." *Egyptian Gazette*, June 2, 2004.

"New Iraqi leaders are urged to repair oil sector." *Herald Tribune*, April 25, 2006.

News Agencies. "Arab League highlights ties to Iraqi." Kurdish Regional Government, October 23, 2005, http://www.krg.org/articles/detail.asp?rnr=24&lngnr=12&anr=6959&smap=.

"Newspapers Describe More Abuse of Prisoners." *International Herald Tribune*, May 22–23, 2005.

Nichols, Bill. "Iraq Had No WMD After 1994." *USA Today*, March 2, 2004. http://www.usatoday.com/news/world/iraq/2004-03-02-un-wmd_x.htm.

"'No arbitrary date' for withdrawing troops, says Blair." *Telegraph*, September 25, 2005. http://www.telegraph.co.uk/news/1499172/No-arbitrary-date-for-withdrawing-troops-says-Blair.html.

Noueihed, Lin. "Iraqi Sunni clerics: election lacked legitimacy." Reuters, February 3, 2005.

Nye, Joseph S., Jr. "You Can't Get Here from There." *New York Times*, November 29, 2004. http://www.nytimes.com/2004/11/29/opinion/29nye.html.

"OIC Meeting in Malaysia." *Samirad*, April 21, 2004. http://www.saudinf.com/main/y7079.htm.

"Operation Iron fist against insurgents' sanctuary." *Egyptian Gazette*, October 2, 2005.

"Operation Iron Fist, Operation Kabda Bil Hadid." GlobalSecurity.org, October 1, 2005–October 6, 2005. http://www.globalsecurity.org/military/ops/oif-iron-fist_2005.htm.

Oppel, Richard A. "Rice, in Baghdad, Urges Sunni Role in Constitution." *New York Times*, May 16, 2005.

———. "Explosion at Big American Base in Mosul Kills 22." *New York Times*, December 22, 2004. http://www.nytimes.com/2004/12/22/international/middleeast/22iraq.html.

"Organization of the Islamic Conference Summit Wrap-up." Saudi-US Relations Information Service, December 11, 2005. http://www.saudi-us-relations.org/articles/2005/ioi/051211-oic-wrapup.html.

Pfaff, William. "Give Iraqis Complete Sovereignty." *Worldsecuritynetwork.com*, May 22, 2004, http://www.worldsecuritynetwork.com/showArticle3.cfm?article_id=9565.

Philips, Stone. "Behind the Abu Ghraib photos—In an exclusive interview, Lynndie England talks about her part in those now infamous pictures." *Dateline NBC*, October 2, 2005.

"Plan for Clinics in Iraq, High Cost Threats Slow Constitution." *USA Today*, February 2, 2006.

"Police: Mosque blast kills at least 25." *CNN.com*, October 5, 2005. http://edition.cnn.com/2005/WORLD/meast/10/05/iraq.main/index.html.

"Political impasse to have a government in Iraq." *Egyptian Gazette*, April 29, 2005.

"Poll: Iraq is top concern." *CNN.com*, December 21, 2004. http://edition.cnn .com/2004/US/12/21/poll/index.html.

"Possible Civil War if Allied Forces leave immaturely." *Egyptian Gazette*, May 5, 2004.

"President Bush's address to the United Nations." *CNN.com*, September 12, 2002. http://edition.cnn.com/2002/US/09/12/bush.transcript/.

"Presidential press conference." *CNN.com*, April 20, 2005.

Preston, Julia. "Judge rules on abuse photos at Abu Ghraib." *Herald Tribune*, September 30, 2005.

"Problem of Sunni participation in writing the Iraqi constitution has irritated the government." *Egyptian Gazette*, July 25, 2005.

"Prodi: Iraq war was 'grave error.'" *CNN.com*, May 19, 2006. http://edition.cnn .com/2006/WORLD/europe/05/18/italy.iraq/.

"Pulling out now would be 'victory for the terrorists.'" *The Times*, November 22, 2005.

"Putin Calls for World Cooperation on Iraq." *Egyptian Gazette*, July 4, 2005.

Quigley, Samantha L., American Forces Press Service. "Coalition buoyed by Iraqi peoples courage, Bush says." Defense.gov, March 16, 2005.

Quinn, Patrick. "New Government vows 'Maximum Force' to end attacks." *Washingtonpost.com*, May 22, 2006.

Raum, Tom. "Bush: U.S. troops will remain in Iraq." Redorbit.com, November 30, 2006.

"Reduction of South Korean troops." *The Guardian*, November 19, 2005.

Regan, Tom. "Iraqi Leaders Want a Timetable for U.S. Withdrawal." *Christian Science Monitor*, November 22, 2005. http://www.csmonitor.com/2005/1122/ dailyUpdate.html.

"Report: U.S. covered up abuse at Abu Ghraib." *CNN.com*, June 9, 2004.

Return to an address of the Honourable House of Commons. Weapons of Mass Destruction Report of a Committee of Privy Counsellors and chaired by The Rt Hon The Lord Butler of Brockwell, July 14, 2004.

Reuters. "Iraq to seek extension of U.S. presence." October 30, 2006. http://english .aljazeera.net/archive/2006/10/20084914325296452.html.

———. "Anti-Qaeda tribes targeted in Iraq attacks." Alertnet.org, March 27, 2007.

———. "Iran offers security help to Iraqi premier." *Khaleejtimes.com*, September 12, 2006.

———. "Jordan's King urges war on Islamic militancy." *New York Times*, November 25, 2005. http://www.nytimes.com/2005/11/25/international/middleeast/25jordan .html.

———. "Suicide Bomber in Iraq's Kufa Leaves 59 Dead." *Arabnews.com*, July 19, 2006.

———. "Talabani: U.S. Must Stay for Three Years." *Aljazeera.net*, November 2, 2006.

———. "U.S. dog-handler faces Abu Ghraib trial." *Aljazeera.net*, May 23, 2006.

———. "U.S. Soldiers Charged in Iraq Rape Case." *Aljazeera.net*, November 3, 2006.

———. "Zarqawi successor vows vengeance." *Aljazeera.net*, June 14, 2006.

Reuters/Agence France-Presse. "World leaders hail new Iraqi govt." Abc.net.au, May 21, 2006.

"Rice and Rumsfeld stand 'united' in Iraq." *Herald Tribune*, April 27, 2006.

"Rice and Straw in Iraq to brake government deadlock." *Egyptian Gazette*, April 3, 2006.

Riechmann, Deb. "Bush focusing on Iraqi troop training." Redorbit.com, November 29, 2006.

Ritter, Scott. "A Base for the Corruption of Democracy." *Aljazeera.net*, June 26, 2005.

"The Road to Abu Ghraib." Human Rights Watch Report, June 9, 2004. http://www .hrw.org/en/bios/reed-brody.

Roberts, Joel. "41 Dead In Rampage In Iraq." *CBS News*, July 10, 2006. http://www .cbsnews.com/stories/2006/07/10/iraq/main1786936.shtml.

————. "5 U.S. Soldiers Charged in Rape-Slay." *CBS News*, July 9, 2006. http:// www.cbsnews.com/stories/2006/07/09/iraq/main1786527.shtml.

————. "Abu Ghraib Prison Totally Empty." *CBS News*, August 28, 2006. http:// www.cbsnews.com/stories/2006/08/28/iraq/main1940091.shtml.

————. "Iraq Allies' Deadliest Day." *CBS News*, November 12, 2003. http://www .cbsnews.com/stories/2003/11/13/iraq/main583365.shtml.

"Rumsfeld told suicide bombers pose greatest threat." *USA Today*, February 23, 2004. http://www.usatoday.com/news/world/iraq/2004-02-23-iraq-rumsfeld_x.htm.

"Rumsfeld urges swift formation of Iraqi government." pbs.org, April 12, 2005.

"Saddam appeals for a fair trial." *Aljazeera.net*, October 12, 2006. http://english .aljazeera.net/archive/2006/10/2008410112612212978.html.

"Saddam 'confesses' says Iraq head." *BBC News*, September 7, 2005. http://news.bbc .co.uk/2/hi/middle_east/4221202.stm.

"Saddam defence lawyer shot dead." *BBC News*, July 21, 2006. http://news.bbc .co.uk/2/hi/5101162.stm.

"Saddam defiant in court." *CNN.com*, October 19, 2005. http://edition.cnn .com/2005/WORLD/meast/10/19/saddam.trial/index.html.

"Saddam hanged at dawn." *Aljazeera.net*, October 27, 2007, http://english.aljazeera .net/news/middleeast/2006/12/2008525115436701440.html.

"Saddam Hussein captured." *The Guardian*, December 14, 2003. http://www.guardian .co.uk/world/2003/dec/14/iraq.iraq1.

"Saddam Hussein sentenced to death." *BBC News*, November 5, 2006. http://news .bbc.co.uk/2/hi/6117910.stm.

"Saddam Judge flees Iraq." *Aljazeera.net*, March 10, 2007. http://english.aljazeera .net/news/middleeast/2007/03/200852513209132944.html.

"Saddam's former deputy hanged in Iraq." *China Daily*, March 20, 2007. http://www .chinadaily.com.cn/world/2007-03/20/content_832000.htm.

"Saddam's wife and daughter on most wanted list." *msnbc.com*, July 2, 2006. http:// www.msnbc.msn.com/id/13668297/.

"Sadr ministers quit Iraqi cabinet." *BBC News*, April 16, 2007.

Sager, Abdulaziz. "Commentary by Gulf Research Center, Need for UN resolution to end external intervention in Iraq." Researchsea.com, September 24, 2006.

Saikal, Amin. "Iraq's Conflict Is Fuelling a Bitter Mideast Split." *Herald Tribune*, October 9, 2005.

Sanger, David E. "Bush, Conceding Problems, Defends Iraq War." *New York Times*, March 14, 2006. http://www.nytimes.com/2006/03/14/politics/14prexy.html.

Sanger, David E., and Jim Rutenberg. "News analysis: Bush and Blair admit mistakes, but defend war in Iraq." *International Herald Tribune*, May 5, 2006. http://www.nytimes.com/2006/05/26/world/americas/26iht-bush.1829645.html.

"Saudi Arabia warns to support Iraqi Sunnis." *Egyptian Gazette*, December 14, 2006.

"Saudi's report Shi'ite 'state' inside of Iraq." *Washingtontimes.com*, December 18, 2006.

"Saudis in Total War on Terror." *CNN.com*, April 22, 2004. http://www.cnn.com/2004/WORLD/meast/04/21/saudi.blast.bandar/index.html.

Schmitt, Eric. "Marines Battle Insurgents in Streets of Fallujah." *New York Times*, April 9, 2004. http://www.nytimes.com/2004/04/09/international/middleeast/09BATT.html.

"Scholars say Iraq meets definition of 'civil war.'" *Herald Tribune*, November 27, 2006.

"Security measures for election." *Egyptian Mail*, January 29, 2005.

Semple, Kirk and Sabrina Tavernise. "U.S. and Iraqi troops continue offensive." *New York Times*, November 8, 2005. http://www.nytimes.com/2005/11/07/world/africa/07iht-iraq.html?scp=1&sq=US%20and%20Iraqi%20troops%20continue%20offensive&st=cse.

Shanker, Thom. "U.S. Fails to Explain Policies To Muslim World, Panel Says." *New York Times*, November 24, 2004. http://www.nytimes.com/2004/11/24/politics/24info.html.

Shanker, Thom, Eric Schmitt, and Richard Oppel, Jr. "Military to report Marines killed Iraqi civilians." *New York Times*, May 26, 2006.

"Shiite Badr Organization killing Sunni cleric." *CNN.com*, May 20, 2005.

"Shiite follower of Sistani said bewares of Saddamites and their followers." *Newsweek*, May 2, 2005.

"Shiite fury explodes in Iraq." *Herald Tribune*, February 24, 2006.

"Shiite politicians accused the Sunni insurgents to kill Shiites." *Newsweek*, May 2, 2005.

"Shiites want constitution based on Sharia (Islamic law)." *Egyptian Mail*, April 16, 2005.

"Sistani in Najaf decided not to use force against Sunnis." *Newsweek*, May 2, 2005.

Smith, Stephen W. "Angry Mom Protests President." *CBS News*, August 6, 2005. http://www.cbsnews.com/stories/2005/08/06/national/main763672.shtml.

Solomon, Deborah. "Way We Live Now: 4-23-06: Questions for Madeleine Albright; State of the Secretary." *New York Times*, April 23, 2006. http://query.nytimes.com/gst/fullpage.html?res=9B0CE5DB173FF930A15757C0A9609C8B63.

Soriano, César G., and Bill Nichols. "Bush tells Iraq leader U.S. will back him." *USAToday.com*, June 13, 2006.

Speech of H. E. the Secretary-General of the organization of the Islamic conference at the meeting of eminent Shiite and Sunna scholars in Iraq, Mecca, Saudi Arabia (October 19–20, 2006).

Starr, Barbara. "Official 13,000–17,000 insurgents in Iraq." *CNN.com*, February 9, 2005. http://www.cnn.com/2005/WORLD/meast/02/08/iraq.main/index.html.

Fredrickson, Caroline. Statement. American Civil Liberties Union Testimony Before the Subcommittee on National Security, Emerging Threats, and International Relations Regarding Censorship at the Borders. ACLU, March 28, 2006. http://www.aclu.org/national-security/aclu-testimony-subcommittee-national-security-emerging-threats-and-international-r.

Stein, Jeff. *"Can You Tell a Sunni from a Shiite?"* *New York Times*, October 17, 2006. http://www.nytimes.com/2006/10/17/opinion/17stein.html?scp=1&sq=Can%20you%20tell%20a%20Sunni%20from%20a%20Shiite?%94:%20&st=cse.

Struck, Doug. "New Attacks Threaten Political Truce in Iraq." *Washington Post*, December 4, 2005, http://www.washingtonpost.com/wp-dyn/content/article/2005/12/03/AR2005120301293.html?nav=rss_world.

"Study: War blamed for 655,000 Iraqi deaths." *CNN.com*, October 11, 2006. http://www.cnn.com/2006/WORLD/meast/10/11/iraq.deaths/.

"Suicide bombers kill scores in 2 Iraqi cities." *CNN.com*, November 19, 2005. http://www.cnn.com/2005/WORLD/meast/11/18/iraq.main/index.html?section=cnn_topstories.

"Sunni cleric killed in political coercion." *The Washington Times*, February 8, 2006.

"Sunni Muslim Clerics' Association (MCA) to boycott the Iraqi election." *Al-Ahram Weekly*, December 16–20, 2004.

"Sunnis and Kurds reject Jaafari." *Aljazeera.net*, April 11, 2006.

Sweet, Lynn. "Reacts from Rahm Emanuel, Jesse Jackson Jr., Joe Biden, John Shimkus, Hillary Rodham Clinton, Jan Schakowsky, John Kerry, John Boehner, Roy Blunt, Russ Feingold." *Sun Times Media*, January 10, 2007. http://blogs.suntimes.com/sweet/2007/01/reacts_from_rahm_emanuel.html.

"Talbani at UN to help Iraq in its fight against terrorists." *Egyptian Gazette*, August 25, 2005.

"Talbani met Sunni Arabs concerning withdrawal of troops." *Al-Ahram Weekly*, April 14, 2005.

"Talbani: Priority to uproot terrorism." *Al-Ahram Weekly*, April 7, 2005.

"Talbani warns of civil war." *Egyptian Gazette*, March 14, 2006.

Tarnoff, Curt. "Iraq: Recent Developments in Reconstruction Assistance." CRS Report for Congress, October 2, 2003.

Tavernise, Sabrina. "Baghdad oasis 'falling to terrorists.'" *Herald Tribune*, June 24, 2006.

———. "Blair declares British will stay in Iraq." Nytimes.com, December 17, 2006.

———. "Gunmen in Iraq add teachers to target list." *New York Times*, September 27, 2005. http://www.nytimes.com/2005/09/26/world/africa/26iht-iraq.html.

———. "Suicide Bomber Kills at Least 29 in Crowded Baghdad Restaurant." *New York Times*, November 10, 2005. http://www.nytimes.com/2005/11/10/international/middleeast/10cnd-iraq.html?fta=y.

"Technology Road Side Bomb from Iran." *Egyptian Gazette*, November 1, 2005.

Tenet, George. *At the Center of the Storm*. New York: HarperCollins, 2007.

"Terrorists using Internet." *Egyptian Gazette*, December 14, 2004.

"Three months political vacuum in forming Iraq government." *Egyptian Gazette*, April 26, 2005.

"Transcript: Bush, Allawi Speak." *Fox News*, September 23, 2004.

"Transcript: Rumsfeld on 'FNS.'" *Fox News*, June 27, 2005. http://www.foxnews.com/story/0,2933,160716,00.html.

"Transcript: Senate Foreign Relations, Wolfowitz, Armitage Testify before Senate Panel." *Washington Post*, May 18, 2004. http://www.washingtonpost.com/wp-dyn/articles/A37019-2004May18.html.

"Troops find hostage 'slaughterhouses' in Falluja." *CNN.com*, November 11, 2004. http://edition.cnn.com/2004/WORLD/meast/11/10/iraq.main/index.html.

"Tubingen University, Germany, 12 December 2003—Secretary-General's lecture on Global Ethics—'Do we still have universal values?'" Secretary General: Office of the Spokesperson, http://www.un.org/apps/sg/sgstats.asp?nid=697.

Tyler, Patrick. "Blair Offers an Apology for Abuses by Soldiers." *New York Times*, May 10, 2004. http://www.nytimes.com/2004/05/10/international/europe/10BLAI.html.

———. "Iraq Will Have Veto Power over Military Operations, Blair Said." *International Herald Tribune*, May 26, 2004.

United Nations Assistance Mission for Iraq. Human Rights Report. 1 March–30 April 2006. http://www.uniraq.org/documents/HR%20Report%20Mar%20Apr%2006%20EN.PDF.

"United Nations extends mandate of Iraq troops." *BBC News*, November 8, 2005. http://news.bbc.co.uk/2/hi/middle_east/4419222.stm.

United Nations Security Council. Press Release SC/8111. "Briefing Security Council, Iraqi Foreign Minister Calls for Resolution Endorsing Interim Government, Recognizing continuing Need for Multinational Force." June 3, 2004. http://www.un.org/News/Press/docs/2004/sc8111.doc.htm.

United Press International. "Iraq's Sunnis reject constitution." *BBC News*, August 28, 2005.

"United States Condemns Bombing of Important Shia Mosque in Iraq." U.S. Embassy in Iraq, February 22, 2006. http://iraq.usembassy.gov/iraq/20060222_mosque_bombing.html.

"U.N. resolution on Iraq passes unanimously." *CNN.com*, June 8, 2004. http://edition.cnn.com/2004/WORLD/meast/06/08/un.iraq/index.html.

"U.S. denies widespread abuse at prison in Iraq." *CNN.com*, May 3, 2004. http://edition.cnn.com/2004/US/05/02/iraq.abuse.charges/index.html.

"U.S. Soldiers Abused Iraqis 'for Fun.'" *Egyptian Gazette*, April 15, 2004.

"U.S. puts al-Zarqawi's group on terror list." *CNN.com*, October 16, 2004. http://www.cnn.com/2004/WORLD/meast/10/15/zarqawi.terror/.

"U.S. Returns Sovereignty to Iraq." *CNN.com*, June 28, 2004.

"U.S. says Iraq invasion was legal." *BBC News*, September 16, 2004. http://news.bbc.co.uk/2/hi/middle_east/3664234.stm.

"U.S. Soldier Says her Job was to make prison 'Hell.'" *Egyptian Gazette*, May 9, 2004.

"U.S. Soldiers Abused Iraqis 'for Fun.'" *Egyptian Gazette*, August 5, 2004.

"U.S. troops 'seized by insurgents.'" *BBC News*, June 18, 2006. http://news.bbc.co.uk/2/hi/middle_east/5092072.stm.

"U.S. Warns Financial Firms of Al-Qaeda Threat." *CNN.com*, November 30, 2006. http://money.cnn.com/2006/11/30/news/economy/al_qaeda/.

"U.S., Iraqi officials take sides on civil war debate." *CNN.com*, March 20, 2006. http://edition.cnn.com/2006/WORLD/meast/03/19/iraq.anniversary/index.html.

"U.S.: More than 40 insurgents die in Iraq raids." *CNN.com*, May 15, 2006. http://edition.cnn.com/2006/WORLD/meast/05/15/iraq.main/index.html.

"US death toll in Iraq reaches 2000." *CNN.com*, October 25, 2005. http://edition.cnn.com/2005/WORLD/meast/10/25/iraq.main.1744/index.html.

"US Dismisses Iraq Withdrawal Plan." *Egyptian Gazette*, March 6, 2006.

U.S. Energy Information Administration. Iraq: Country Analysis Brief, June 2009, http://www.eia.doe.gov/emeu/cabs/Iraq/Background.html.

U.S. Senate Intelligence Report on Post War Finding about WMD Programs and Links to Terrorism and How They Comply to Rewar Assessment, September 8, 2006. 105–112.

Villelabeitia, Ibon. "Saddam Hanging Iraqi Affair, al-Maliki." Reuters.com, January 6, 2007. http://uk.reuters.com/article/idUKL0673755620070106.

"Vote on Iraq government." *Egyptian Gazette*, May 18, 2006.

"Voting a religious duty in Iraq's holy cities." *Egyptian Gazette*, January 28, 2005.

Wagner, Thomas. "Iraqi Leaders Plead for Killing to Halt." *Fox News*, November 26, 2006.

Walker, Carolee "White House iftar October 16 honors Muslim citizens, military". *America.gov*, October 17, 2006, http://www.america.gov/st/washfile-english/2006/October/20061017122124bcreklaw0.5644037.html.

Washington Post. "Council seeks U.N. help." *Trib Total Media*, March 18, 2004. http://www.pittsburghlive.com/x/pittsburghtrib/s_185049.html.

"Web posting: Al Qaeda in Iraq leader to target Sunni." *CNN.com*, June 14, 2006.

"Website says new Leader named to replace Zarqawi." *Herald Tribune*, June 13, 2006.

"Will the death of Zarqawi bring a troop down?" *CNN.com*, June 12, 2006.

Wish, Hadjar. "CNN: Dozens killed in triple car bombing near Baghdad market." December 2, 2006. http://www.mail-archive.com/islamkristen@yahoogroups.com/msg76655.html.

"Woman suicide bomber strikes Iraq." *BBC News*, September 28, 2005. http://news.bbc.co.uk/2/hi/4289168.stm.

Wong, Edward. "Bombers Kill at Least 70 Inside Two Shiite Mosques in Iraq." *New York Times*, November 18, 2005. http://www.nytimes.com/2005/11/18/international/middleeast/18cnd-Iraq.html.

———. "U.N. Secretary Says Iraq Is Engulfed in Deadly Civil War." *New York Times*, December 3, 2006. http://www.nytimes.com/2006/12/03/world/middleeast/03cnd-iraq.html.

Wong, Edward, and Helene Cooper. "Iraq Premier Moves to Plan Regional Talks." *New York Times*, December 6, 2006.

"World-Wide Protests Mark Iraq War." Aljazeera.net, March 20, 2007. http://english
.aljazeera.net/news/middleeast/2007/03/2008525131323845336.html.

Worth, Robert F. "Iraqi Civilians Fight Back Against Insurgents." *New York
Times*, March 23, 2005. http://www.nytimes.com/2005/03/23/international/
worldspecial/23iraq.html.

———. "More Than 950 Iraqis Die in Stampede on Baghdad Bridge." *New York
Times*, August 31, 2005. http://www.nytimes.com/2005/08/31/international/
middleeast/31cnd-iraq.html.

———. "Blast Destroys Shrine in Iraq, Setting Off Sectarian Fury." *New York
Times*. February 22, 2006. http://www.nytimes.com/2006/02/22/international/
middleeast/22cnd-iraq.html.

Worth, Robert F., Edward Wong, et al. "The Conflict in Iraq: Insurgents, Marines
Find Vast Arms Cache in Falluja Leader's Mosque." *New York Times*, November
25, 2004. http://query.nytimes.com/gst/fullpage.html?res=940CE6D9153EF9
36A15752C1A9629C8B63&sec=&spon=&&scp=1&sq=Huge%20caches%20
of%20arms%20discovered%20in%20Falluja&st=cse.

"Writers of Iraqi constitution to ask for extension." USAToday.com, July 31, 2005.

Zakaria, Fareed. "Elections Are Not democracy." *Newsweek*. February 7, 2005.

"Zarqawi vows war on Iraq poll." *BBC News*, January 23, 2005. http://news.bbc
.co.uk/2/hi/middle_east/4199363.stm.

INDEX

9/11 attacks, 1–15

abductions/kidnappings, 10, 11, 24–34,
    38, 41, 78, 82, 86, 104, 106, 110,
    112–14, 115, 161, 162, 165, 169
Abdullah bin Abdul Aziz, King of Saudi
    Arabia, 19, 20, 96, 60, 194, 195
Abizaid, John, 166
Abu Ghraib prison (Baghdad), 13, 37,
    66–71, 73, 74, 80–81, 105, 136,
    148, 189
Abu Qudama (Tunisian terrorist),
    123–24
Ahmadinejad, Mahmoud, 191–92, 193,
    195
Albright, Madeleine, 42–43
Algeria/Algerians, 2, 38, 100, 101, 104
AlJazeera.net (Web site), 68, 78, 100,
    113, 119, 161, 190
Allawi, Ayad, 46, 47, 48, 81, 83, 87,
    92, 116, 119, 123, 139, 140, 144,
    146, 147, 148, 182
Allbritton, Christopher, 134
American Civil Liberties Union, 12, 74
Amin, Bakhtiar, 105
Amnesty International, 67, 68, 198
Anbar province (Iraq), 76, 128, 151,
    152, 159, 170, 190
Andy Warhol Museum (Pittsburgh),
    71–72
Anfal campaign (Operation Anfal), 47
Annan, Kofi, 6, 15, 37, 43, 46, 61, 63,
    64, 67, 85
antiwar sentiment, 54, 55–59, 156
Arab League, 14, 20, 92–97, 170, 178

"Arab nation" designation, 174, 176,
    179
Arbil, 174, 175, 195
Askariya, Al (Golden Mosque),123–24,
    125
Association of Muslim Scholars (AMS),
    78, 94, 111–12, 141, 159, 163,
    164, 179
Assyrians, 81, 94
Australia, 31, 61, 83

Ba'ath Party/Ba'athists, 6, 22–23, 26,
    35, 36, 45, 48, 51–52, 53, 99,
    100, 105, 124, 141, 147, 169,
    171, 172, 179, 186, 189
Badr Brigade, 152, 163, 164, 189
Baghdad, 34, 36–37, 50, 61, 92, 105,
    125, 151, 161, 186, 191; Green
    Zone, 65, 83, 113, 130, 131, 132
Baker, James, vii, 149, 164, 165, 194
Baquba, 113, 116, 129
Barzani, Massoud, 51, 167, 173–74,
    175
Basra, 33, 104, 153, 187, 191
beheadings, 116, 129, 139
Berlusconi, Silvio, 58
bin Laden, Osama, 6, 20, 31, 34, 35,
    38, 41, 59, 100, 102, 131, 139
biological and chemical weapons, 26, 28
Blair, Tony, 26–27, 29, 32–33, 57, 67,
    74, 85, 91, 96, 100, 117, 129,
    136, 139–40, 149, 153, 166
Blix, Hans, 27, 37–38
Brahimi, Lakhdar, 62, 63, 64
Bremer, Paul, 45, 63, 84

Britain/British, 14–15, 32–33, 57–58, 61, 83, 85, 114, 152–53, 187–88
Brown, Gordon, 153
Burns, John (journalist), 35
Bush, George W., 2, 3–4, 5–6, 8, 27, 41, 46, 47, 53, 55–59, 63, 65, 73, 75, 85, 90, 120, 123, 124, 135, 136, 140, 148, 150, 154, 155, 162, 186–87; on occupying Iraq, 21–22, 27, 29, 40, 44, 80–81, 133, 149

Carpenter, Ted Galen, 43–44
Casey, George, 155, 156, 193, 195
casualties, American, 11, 27, 79, 120, 121, 133, 145
chemical and biological weapons, 26, 28
Cheney, Dick, 136–37, 144, 154–55, 160
Cheney, Liz, 9–10
Chirac, Jacques, 7, 30, 65, 85
Christians, 102, 110, 145, 175
civilians, attacks on, 75–76, 99, 107–8, 111, 124
civil war, 64, 93, 94, 96, 97, 109, 110, 122, 123–34, 137, 152, 155, 161, 164, 169, 182
Clark, Wesley, 27
Clarke, Michael, 28
clerics, 83, 88, 111, 146, 162, 163, 180
Clinton, Bill and Hillary, 39, 43
Coalition Provisional Authority, 45, 84
courts, Sharia, 148

Dabaan, Jamal Abd al-Karim al- (sheik), 78
Danish troop withdrawal, 153
Daawa Party, 146, 170, 183
death sentence, 47, 48–50
death squads, 127, 149, 163
democracy/democratization, vi, vii, 9, 42–43, 134, 137, 148; promotion of by George W. Bush and the United States, 2, 8–9, 44, 136

Department of Homeland Security, U.S., 12, 122
detainees, 67–71, 74, 188
detention camps, 70, 188, 189
diplomats, attacks on, 101, 104, 113
Diyala (province), 50, 129, 174
Dujail, killings in, 48, 49–50, 53, 54
Durbin, Dick, 154

education and social reforms, 7, 20
Egypt/Egyptians, 104, 111, 113, 137, 144, 150, 166
election(s), vi–vii, 2, 64, 83, 137, 139–40, 141, 180
ethnic groups/factions, v–vi, 94, 95, 142, 161
European Union, 65–66, 87, 88
extremism, Islamic, 4, 20, 115

Fahd, king of Saudi Arabia, 17
Faisal , Saud al- (prince), 195
Fallujah, 21, 37, 205, 114, 115–17, 125
fanaticism, 115, 137
federalism, 142, 170, 171, 172, 173, 174, 176, 178, 179, 186
Fernandez, Alberto, 149
foreign fighters in Iraq, 93, 100, 154
Foundation of Holy War in Mesopotamia group, 101
Fredrickson, Caroline, 12
freedom of speech, assembly and religion, 84
fundamentalists/fundamentalism, 4, 23, 34, 104, 111

Gelb, Leslie, 36
General Conference for Sunnis in Iraq, 180
Geneva Convention, 70, 71, 75
Graham, Lindsey, 127
Green, Steven, 77–78
Guantanamo Bay, 13, 28
guerrillas, Iraqi, 22, 83, 120, 161
Gül, Abdullah, 152
Gulf countries, 95, 144, 166

Haditha, civilian killings in, 75–76, 162
Hagel, Chuck, 44
Hakim, Abdul Aziz al-, 64, 170, 176
Hashmi, Tarek al-, 185, 195
Hassan, Nashe, 113
Hatim, Mubdar, 125
Hesba, Al (Web site), 130
Hezbollah, 96, 193–94
hostages, 11, 19, 38, 105, 115, 117
Houghton, Nick, 152–53
Howard, John, 31
Human Rights Report (UN), 112
human rights violations, 14–15, 67–78, 142, 148
Human Rights Watch (HRW), 70–71, 197
Husayba (Iraq), 107
Hussein, Imam, 107
Hussein, Raghad Saddam, 50
Hussein, Saddam, v, vi, 5–6, 8, 13, 22, 25, 26, 29, 30, 32, 35, 37, 42, 45–53, 148, 186

Ibn al-Nima mosque (Hilla), 107
Ibrahim, Busho, 74
Immigration and Nationality Act, U.S., 12
Indonesia/Indonesians, 4, 111
infrastructure reconstruction, 24, 80, 86–89, 144
insurgents and militants, 17, 21, 23, 26, 39–40, 61, 77, 79, 82, 89, 93, 94, 97, 99–122, 134, 136, 137, 140, 147, 150, 154, 177, 189; al-Qaeda insurgency, 145, 147, 169, 178
intellectuals, 5–6, 8, 130, 148, 150
intelligence information, 28, 29, 30, 32, 56, 129
International Center of Photography (New York City), 71–72
International Conference for Security and Reconstruction of Iraq (Sharm El-Sheikh, Egypt, 2007), 197
Iran, vi, 39, 52, 110, 156, 160, 165, 166, 191, 194

Iranian Revolutionary Guard group, 195
Iraq/Iraqi, vi, 5, 8, 27; armed forces, 93, 118, 156, 186; civil war in, 123–34; constitution, 23, 62, 63, 82, 84–85, 109, 118, 135, 136, 139, 142, 143, 169, 170–73, 177–84; defense and interior ministries, 86, 149, 185; democratization of, 134, 135–67; election(s) in, vi–vii, 9, 62, 82, 85, 138, 140; financial debt, 88, 96; flag of, 175; government, democratic, 184–89; insurgents/terrorists in, 9, 19, 20–24, 34, 132, 133; interim Governing Council, 7, 10, 21, 22, 46, 62, 63, 64, 78, 80, 81–82, 113; lawlessness in, 24, 82–83; national assembly, 118, 134, 135, 136, 139, 142–43, 169, 179; occupation of, v, 2, 10, 21, 82, 111; parliament/parliament building, 128, 130, 170, 184; power transfer, U.S. administration to Iraqis, 79–97; reconstruction of, 37, 61–65, 78, 86–89, 147, 184; security in, 143, 147; security forces, 66, 85, 88, 89, 91, 95, 138, 165, 186; sovereignty in, 62, 80, 82, 89–91; "three-state" solution, 36–37
Iraqi Accord Front (Sunni), 181
Iraqi Front for National Dialogue (Sunni), 181
Iraqi Islamic Party, 172
Iraqi National Conference (2004), 83–84
Iraqi National Guard, 113, 117
Iraqi Resistance Movement, 113
Iraqi Special Tribunal, 46, 125
Iraq Study Group, vii, 160, 164–67
Iraq war, 25–44
Islam/Islamic, vii, 2, 4, 19, 20, 33, 179; militants/militias, 17, 18, 19, 61, 100; role in government, 63, 84, 169, 176

Islamic Jihad, 46
Islamic State of Iraq (Sunni group), 111
Islamic Unification and Jihad, 113
Islamist(s), vi, vii, 4, 9, 23, 111, 181
Islamization, 180
Islamophobia, 3, 15
Israel, 12, 102
Italy, 32, 57, 114, 152, 153

Jaafari, Ibrahim al-, 87, 90, 107, 142,
    143, 144, 145, 146–47, 182, 183
Jaish Ansar al-Sunna, 11, 22, 100, 113,
    117, 119, 144
Janabi, Mohamed al- (sheik), 111
Janabi, Saadoun, 48
Japan, 41–42, 88
jihad (holy war), 10, 13, 130
jihadist(s), 2, 102, 122, 130, 131, 178
"Jihad Luaibi," 140
John Paul II, Pope, 58, 102
Johnson, Lyndon, 44
Jordan, 2, 19, 83, 100, 137, 144, 150,
    152, 166
Jordon, Darren, 193
Juburi, Halima Ahmed Hussein al-, 34

Kaczynski, Lech, 153
Kadhimya/Kazimiyah/Khadamiya
    (Baghdad district), 106, 110, 125,
    163
Karbala, 49, 103, 111, 141
Kay, David, 28
Kazemi, Hassan, 192
Khadawi, Lamia Abid, 144
Khairallah, Sajidah, 50
Khalil, Bushra al-, 51
Khalilzad, Zalmay, 50, 108, 124, 130,
    134, 137, 146, 156187, 183,
    192–93, 195, 197
Khamenei, Ali, 192
Khanaqin, mosques in, 112
Khomeini, Ruhollah (ayatollah), 180
Ki-moon, Ban, 65, 197
Kirkuk, 152, 173, 174, 175
Koizumi, Junichiro, 41

Koran, desecration of, 13, 70
Kristof, Nicholas, 152
Kroc Institute for International Peace
    Studies, 12
Kufa, 124, 148
Kurdistan Democratic Party (KDP),
    174
Kurdistan Islamic Union, 181
Kurdistan Workers Party (PKK), 96
Kurds/Kurdistan, 22, 29, 36, 47–49,
    63, 81, 94, 100, 106, 126, 135,
    137, 140, 141, 142, 143, 145,
    152, 170, 173–76, 179
Kuwait, 5, 26, 185

Langley, Dustin, 59
law/legal system, 146, 171, 176
lawyers, 46, 48–49, 125
legislation, 84, 176
Levin, Carl, 151, 158
Libi, Ibn al-Shaykh al-, 28
Lugar, Richard, 80
Lynch, Rick, 103

Madrid, bomb attacks in, 41
Mahdi, Adel, 143
Mahdi, Muhammad al- (twelfth imam),
    124
Mahdi Shiite Militia Army, 33, 36, 127,
    133, 152, 176–77, 189, 191, 194
Mahmudiya, 78, 124
Maliki, Nouri al-, 50, 53, 65, 75, 76,
    105, 108, 124, 130, 149–50, 151,
    160, 161, 164, 165, 166, 176,
    185–86, 187, 189, 191, 192,
    195–96
Mashhadani, Mahmoud, 160, 164
Mecca and Medina, 17, 18, 20
Medico Legal Institute (Baghdad), 108
military priorities, 165, 169
militias, vi, 21, 33–35, 36, 85, 137,
    147, 155, 169, 189–91
Ministerial Arab Committee on Iraq, 92
Moallem, Walid, 193
Morocco, 2, 100

Moslem Association of Britain, 57
Moslem Council for Britain, 14–15
mosques, 14, 21, 37, 101, 107, 112, 123–25, 162
Mosul, 21, 101, 111, 116, 117, 172
Mottaki, Manouchehr, 197
Moussa, Amr, 14, 20, 92, 94, 181
Mubarak, Hosni, 52
Muhajir, Abu Hamza al-, 50, 130–32
Muhammad Army, 191
Mujahedeen, 167
Mujahedeen Shura Council, 104, 191
multinational force, 7, 61, 62, 74, 90
Murtha, John, 155–56
Musharraf, Pervez, 59, 97
Muslims, 3–4, 6, 14–15
Mustansiriya University, al- (Baghdad), 108
Myers, Richard, 147, 154

Najaf (holy city), 13, 5083, 101, 140, 141, 163, 176, 179
Nasiriyah episode (2003), 10
National Conciliation Plan, 190
National Concord Front, 160
National Dialogue Front, 130
National Endowment for Democracy, 8
NATO countries, 65–66, 91
Nineveh province, 36, 170, 174
Nogaidan, Mansour, 95

Obama, Barack, 198
oil/pipelines/resources/revenue, 2, 5, 25, 27–28, 35, 77, 84, 152, 165, 169, 170–71, 175–76, 184
Operation "Iron Fist," 120
Organization of the Islamic Conference (OIC), 7, 20, 37

Pakistan/Pakistanis, 59, 111, 137
Patriotic Union for Kurdistan (PUK), 138, 143, 174
Pelosi, Nancy, 157, 158
Persian Gulf War, 49
Peshmerga militia, 174, 189

Petraeus, David, 158, 169
"phantom enemy," 77
photography, influence on public view of war, 72–73
pilgrims, attacks on, 18, 107, 111
Poland, 153
police/police stations, 37, 99, 100, 110, 111, 117, 128, 140, 147, 148, 156, 161
Political Council for National Security, 164
political reform, vi, 2, 20, 147, 180
politicians, Iraqi, 143, 150
polling stations, 135, 138, 139, 140, 181
Powell, Colin, 8, 29, 126
Prescott, John, 53
prisons and prisoners, 7–13, 14, 67–73, 80, 93, 111, 112, 148–49
Prodi, Romano, 32, 153
Prudential Financial, 122
Putin, Vladimir, 85

Qadir, Abd al- (general), 185
Qaeda, al-,1, 24, 28, 35, 38, 39–40, 41, 50, 59, 101, 114, 121, 132; in Iraq, 9, 19, 21, 23, 34, 35–36, 50, 78, 124, 127, 129, 130, 133, 139, 185, 189, 191; in Saudi Arabia, 18, 19

Rafsanjani (Iranian cleric), 193
Ramadan, Taha Yassin, 53
Ramadan, Tariq, 12–13
Ramadi, 79, 83, 190
reconciliation, 92, 94, 95, 165, 169, 186, 188, 189–91
referendum, on Constitution, 179, 180–84
refugees, Iraqi, 193, 197
Regional Conference (Baghdad, 2007), 196–97
Reid, Harry, 32, 44, 127
religion and state, 1, 85, 147
resistance, 24, 93

revenge, vi, 125, 126
Rice, Condoleezza, 119, 144, 145, 147, 150, 166, 182–83, 187, 193
Rumsfeld, Donald, 11, 38, 40, 69, 71, 119, 135, 147, 151, 187
Russia/Russian, 2, 85, 104
Rutherford, Paul, 55

Sabah, Mohammad al-Salem al-, 166
Saddam loyalists/Saddamists, 118, 178
Sadr, Muqtada al-, 10, 107, 110, 111, 127, 130, 148, 159, 161, 164, 170, 176–77, 179, 189, 190, 191
Sadra militias, al-, 21, 127, 150, 159
Sadr City district, 49, 50, 51, 127, 128
Sadrist Shiite movement, 111
Saeedi, Hamad Jumaa Farid al-, 133
Salafist (Algerian insurgent group), 38
Salahaddin province, 36, 50, 170
Salim, Izzedin, 80, 113
Samarra, 37, 108, 118–24
Sanchez, Ricardo, 116
Sarkozy, Nicolas, 38
Saudi Arabia/Saudis, 15, 17–19, 35, 99, 100, 111, 137, 150, 152, 160
school(s), 9–10, 108–9
Schroeder, Gerhard, 85
Scruggs, Kenneth, 35
sectarian division/tensions/violence, v, 22, 23, 30, 34–35, 64, 95, 111, 112, 115, 122, 123–34, 141, 151, 155, 161, 186–93
sectarianism, 176, 195
security/security services, 169, 186, 187
sexual abuse, 69, 78
Shameri, Qais (judge), 112
Sharia: courts, 148; in legal system, 146, 176, 179
Shawa, Nasim el-, 42
Shays, Christopher, 69
Sheehan, Cindy, 55–56
Sheikh, Abdul Aziz bin Abdullah al- (Grand Mufti of Saudi Arabia), 18
Shiite Alliance, 183

Shiite(s), 23, 49, 63, 82, 95, 122, 123–24, 141, 145, 170, 176–77, 183, 194; militias/insurgent groups, vi, 9, 34–35, 39, 90, 110, 125, 127, 149, 151, 160, 176, 177, 186
Sistani, Ali (Aytollah), 63, 82, 91, 94, 101, 124, 135, 139, 140, 141, 146, 162–63, 164, 179–80
South Korean troops in Iraq, 152
Spanish troops in Iraq, 41
stalemate, political, 143–44
Straw, Jack, 182
Subeih mosque, Al (Baghdad),162
suicide bombings, vi, 10, 18, 19, 21, 23, 34, 37, 82, 83, 90, 94, 103, 138, 169, 184
Sulaimaniya (province), 174
Sunni Arab Coalition, 163
Sunni Muslim Clerics Association (SMCA), 93, 141
Sunni National Dialogue Council, 172
Sunnis, 35, 71, 82, 94, 125, 132, 135, 142, 144, 145, 149, 150, 159, 161, 170, 171–73, 180; extremists/insurgents/militants/militias, vi, 21, 22, 34–35, 90, 103–4, 110, 180, 185
Supreme Council for the Islamic Revolution in Iraq (SCIRI), 156, 163, 164
Syria, 83, 85, 165, 166

Takfiri (Islamic extremists), 164
Talabani, Jalal, 17, 48, 64, 108, 128–29, 139, 143, 154, 155, 164, 165, 175, 176, 180, 182, 193
Tal Afar, 103, 106–7, 108
Tavernise, Sabrina, 127
Tenet, George, 30
terrorism and terrorists, vi, 1, 2, 3, 4, 7, 8, 11, 17–24, 82, 85, 93, 101–3, 120, 121–22, 123–24, 129, 137, 154, 183
Tikrit, 37, 45, 50, 76, 83, 138, 144–45, 172

Tikriti, Barzan Ibrahim al-, 53, 54
torture, 41, 69, 149
"Triangle of Death," 77, 121, 161
tribal leaders, 186, 190
Turkey/Turks, 6, 56–59, 83, 100, 111, 152
Turkomans, 81, 94, 135, 175
Tuz Khurmatu (Great Prophet mosque), 103
"twelve imams," 124

Um al-Aura mosque (Baghdad), 116
Unification and Jihad (insurgent group), 100, 101, 139
United Iraq Alliance (Shiite), 135, 140, 141, 142, 143, 181
United Nations, 5, 6, 7–8, 10, 43, 47, 48, 61–65, 91, 178, 198; Security Council, 25, 26, 90, 153
United States, 4, 21–22, 79, 156; invasion and occupation of Iraq, 21–22, 79; troop withdrawal from Iraq, vi, 90, 91, 134, 135, 150, 152, 155, 156, 158, 159, 164, 165, 166, 179, 198
Ureybi, Mohamed al-, 47, 54
U.S. Congress, 25, 29, 42, 80, 150–51, 157–58
U.S. National Security Council, 25
U.S. State Department, 39, 101

Vatican, 52, 58
Vincent, Steven, 104
voters/voting, 138, 140–41, 181

Wahhabi Muslims, 34, 115
"war against terror," 15, 17, 21, 31
war photography, 71–72
Wasit (province), 174
weapons inspectors/weapons of mass destruction, v, 5, 25, 26, 27, 28–29, 30
Web sites, Islamist, 100, 105, 122, 130, 132, 181
Wolfensohn, James, 86
women, 34, 66, 76, 130, 144, 145, 161, 169
World Bank, 86

Yawar, Ghazi al-, 82, 84, 85, 89, 118, 138, 142, 143
Youssifiyah (town), 103, 121

Zakaria, Fareed, 137
Zapatero, Jose, 41
Zarkawi, Abu Musab al-, 78, 87, 100, 101–3, 105, 106, 109, 113, 114, 116, 122, 129–30, 139
Zawahiri, Ayman al-, 38, 39, 40, 42, 167
Zebari, Hoshyar, 63, 64, 96, 171, 197
Zubeidi, Adel al-, 48